CAMBRIDGE GEOGRAPHICAL STUDIES

Editorial Board: B.H.FARMER,A.T.GROVE,B.T.ROBSON,E.A.WRIGLEY

5 · THE AGRICULTURAL SYSTEMS OF THE WORLD:
AN EVOLUTIONARY APPROACH

CAMBRIDGE GEOGRAPHICAL STUDIES

Cambridge Geographical Studies presents new methods of geographical analysis, publishes the results of new research work in all branches of the subject, and explores topics which unite disciplines that were formerly separate. In this way it helps to redefine the extent and concerns of geography. The series is of interdisciplinary interest to a wide range of natural and social scientists, as well as to planners.

THE AGRICULTURAL SYSTEMS OF THE WORLD
An Evolutionary Approach

D. B. Grigg

CAMBRIDGE
UNIVERSITY PRESS

Published by the Press Syndicate of the University of Cambridge
The Pitt Building, Trumpington Street, Cambridge CB2 1RP
40 West 20th Street, New York, NY 10011-4211 USA
10 Stamford Road, Oakleigh, Melbourne 3166, Australia

Library of Congress catalogue card number 75-82451

First published 1974
Reprinted 1976, 1977, 1978, 1980, 1982, 1984, 1987, 1988, 1990, 1992, 1996

ISN 0-521 09843 2 paperback

Transferred to digital printing 2002

For Jill, Susan, Catherine and
Stephen, with much love

'I will make you brooches and toys for your delight
Of bird-song at morning and star-shine at night.
I will make a palace fit for you and me
Of green days in forests and blue days at sea.'

R. L. Stevenson

CONTENTS

ACKNOWLEDGEMENTS

I am grateful to many people who have helped me in the preparation of this book. The editors of Cambridge Geographical Studies have been remarkably tolerant of the elephantine gestation process, and have made many useful suggestions on earlier drafts of the work. Sir Joseph Hutchinson read an earlier version of Chapter 3 and made many helpful comments on it, as did Mr John Harriss on Chapter 2.

Officials of a number of libraries have been of great assistance, particularly those of the Geographical Association in Sheffield, the University Library in Sheffield and the library of the Department of Agriculture in Cambridge. I am most grateful to the Master and Fellows of St John's College, Cambridge, for hospitality on a number of visits to Cambridge. The Research Fund of the University of Sheffield has supported some of my travels with a generous grant. Early versions of this work were typed by Mrs Bernie Bicknell, Miss Delia Bough and Mrs Joan Dunn; most of the final version was typed by Mrs Penny Shamma and Mrs Sheila Naylor, to whom I am particularly grateful. The maps were drawn by Mr Jack Hall, Miss Sheila Ottewell and Mr Christopher Jones, to whom my thanks are due. Lastly, I suppose I should be grateful to my colleagues in the Department of Geography, University of Sheffield, whose more or less good natured derision has spurred me on; certainly I am grateful to my friends in the Senior Common Rooms of Earnshaw Hall and Stephenson Hall, which though not, perhaps, the best clubs in Sheffield, nonetheless provide some of the pleasantest company.

D. B. GRIGG

Endcliffe Crescent, Sheffield
Michaelmas 1972

CHAPTER 1

INTRODUCTION

The aim of this book is to describe the chief characteristics of the major agricultural regions of the world and to attempt some explanation of how they came into being. Although there is some description of contemporary features, the emphasis is upon the historical geography of the major farming systems; first, because the author believes that a proper understanding of present geographies cannot be reached without some knowledge of past development; and second, because whilst there is no shortage of contemporary descriptions of the world's major agricultural regions, there have been few attempts to describe their evolution.[1]

But how is the distribution of the major types of agriculture to be explained? There have been many approaches to this problem; some have argued that the distribution is largely a response to variations in the physical environment; others have seen the growth of population and the consequent intensification of farming methods as a major factor differentiating one part of the world from the other, whilst yet others have laid great stress upon the distance that farmers are from their markets. Those who believe that farmers respond readily to changes in prices for products and inputs prefer to see the growth of regional specialisation in starkly economic terms. Nor does this exhaust the list of explanations. But – with a few exceptions – most analyses of the distribution of types of agriculture have been couched largely in contemporary terms, with little reference to the past.

Yet there have been farmers on earth for ten, perhaps twelve thousand years. And farmers as a whole have been – until the last half century – remarkably slow to respond to technical and economic change. The imprint of the past is still clearly to be seen in the world pattern of agriculture. To understand the present, it is essential to know something of the evolution of the modern types of agriculture.

Typologies of agriculture

The origins of some of the modern systems of agriculture can be traced back at least 10 000 years. Further, until a century ago some four-fifths of the world's population were living outside towns and thus directly or indirectly dependent upon agriculture. Even today, after a century of industrialisation and urbanisation, half the world's working population are still employed in agriculture. Clearly the factual evidence available is enormous. Thus some classification of

1

modern agriculture must be attempted in order to provide a framework for discussion.

It would seem at first sight self-evident that although farms are different from each other, yet many show a fair family-likeness and can thus be grouped together as a 'type of agriculture', or an 'agricultural system'. Furthermore in much of the world similar types predominate in one area, and that area can then be described as an agricultural region. Unfortunately there are many practical and methodological difficulties in establishing a world typology of agriculture, just as there are, for that matter, in devising typologies of soils, vegetation, climate, race, economies or terrain.[2] Although this book does not purport to make any original contribution to the methodology of agricultural typology, some of the problems which arise in constructing a world typology must be noted.

The first of these is simply the lack of information. Most agricultural geographers would agree that the best way to construct an agricultural typology, be it for the world or simply for a part of a country, is to try to group the fundamental units of agricultural production – that is, farms – on the basis of similarity; that these similarities should be inherent properties of the farm, rather than external forces which influence the type of farming. Thus there should be used as criteria of similarity elements such as the crops grown, the animals reared, the implements used and the size of the farm, rather than the type of climate or soil or the distance from the market. Further, these criteria should be measurable, but this is rarely possible.

Agricultural statistics are collected annually in many countries of the western world, and cover most of the criteria which are thought suitable for use in classifying farms. But they are rarely publicly available for individual farms; more commonly the published data for individual farms are aggregated into parishes, communes or counties. Clearly a county or a *département* may include within it many different types of farms whose characteristics are lost in the aggregation of the data. But at least such data allow some attempt at the establishment of agricultural regions, and have been used for such a purpose in many parts of the western world. When dealing with relatively small areas the investigator can use the sample questionnaire method; farmers are asked to complete forms giving information on crops, livestock and income; the great advantage of this approach is that data are available for the *farm* rather than for the aggregation of farms. But it is only practicable for small areas.[3]

But for much of Latin America and Afro-Asia no such data are available either for the farm or for any administrative level below that of the state, and for a variety of reasons the accuracy of the information is far less reliable than in western countries.

Thus at a severely practical level, the construction of a world agricultural typology is well-nigh impossible. Even where data are available, there are considerable problems. What criteria should be used to assign farms to a given 'type of agriculture'? Derwent Whittlesey, in his classic discussion of the problems of agricultural typology, believed that there were five criteria by which characteristic types of agriculture could be recognised.[4]

1. The crop and livestock association
2. The methods used to grow the crops and produce the stock
3. The intensity of application to the land of labour, capital and organisation, and the out-turn of product which results
4. The disposal of the products for consumption (i.e. whether used for subsistence on the farm or sold off for cash or other goods)
5. The *ensemble* of structures used to house and facilitate the farming operations

There would be general agreement amongst geographers that these 'elements' – as Whittlesey called them – are critical, with the exception of the fifth. But there would be equal agreement that there are important omissions, not the least being the type of land tenure and the size and layout of the farm.

Since Whittlesey's essay was published in 1936 there has been much discussion of the problems of agricultural typology and the allied problems of regionalisation. In 1964 the International Geographical Union set up a Commission on Agricultural Typology, which has tried to establish uniform criteria by which farms should be classified, and to persuade individual geographers to use these criteria in their work on different parts of the world.[5] Thus in the long-run such work could be collated, and a hierarchy of agricultural types established for the world as a whole. This is an entirely praiseworthy aim; but one is constantly reminded of Lord Keynes' definition of the long-run.

A different approach has been pursued by many writers of textbooks on economic geography. They have taken Whittlesey's original classification and modified it in the light of changes in agricultural practice since the 1930s.[6] A number of writers have also criticised the individual 'types' that Whittlesey suggested: the plantation system and shifting agriculture have received particular attention.[7]

We are left, however, without an entirely satisfactory solution to our problem. Pragmatism must – sadly – take precedence over principle, and the basis of the discussion in this book is Whittlesey's map of the agricultural regions of the world, as modified by subsequent writers (Fig. 1). The major types of farming which are considered are:

1. Shifting agriculture
2. Wet-rice cultivation in Asia
3. Pastoral nomadism
4. Mediterranean agriculture
5. Mixed farming in western Europe and North America
6. Dairying
7. The plantation system
8. Ranching
9. Large-scale grain production

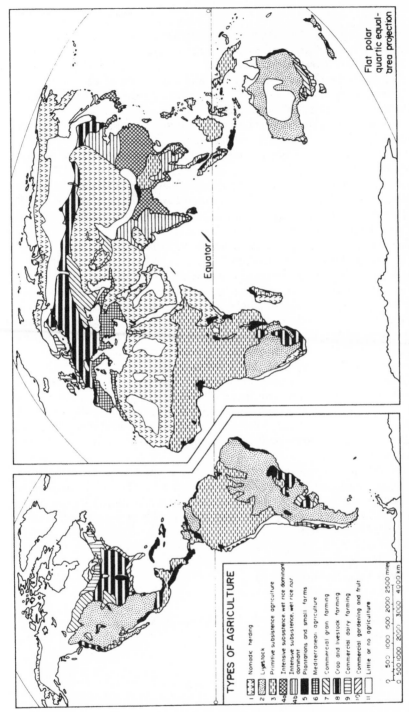

TYPES OF AGRICULTURE

1 Nomadic herding
2 Livestock
3 Primitive subsistence agriculture
4a Intensive subsistence wet rice dominant
4b Intensive subsistence wet rice not dominant
5 Plantations and small farms
6 Mediterranean agriculture
7 Commercial grain farming
8 Crop and livestock farming
9 Commercial dairy farming
10 Commercial gardening and fruit
11 Little or no agriculture

0 500 1000 1500 2000 2500 miles
0 500 1000 2000 3000 4000 km

Equator

Flat polar quartic equal-brea projection

Fig. 1. The agricultural regions of the world, after D. Whittlesey.
[Source: Finch et al., 1957, Plate 8]

This is not a comprehensive typology of world agriculture. But these types occupy much of the earth's agricultural area and employ most of the world's agricultural population. Their discussion should be sufficient to demonstrate the historical approach to agricultural geography which is advocated in this book.

Processes and periods

Before dealing with each of the major types of agriculture, it may be useful to consider some of the major processes which have influenced their development.

The growth of world population, and in particular the regional differences in growth, have been of paramount importance in determining the characteristic features of modern agriculture. Until recently most writers assumed that pre-industrial populations were dependent upon food supply; thus population numbers were a function of the nature and efficiency of the type of agriculture. A number of writers have inverted this thesis, and have suggested that the growth of population has caused the intensification of agriculture, and thus led to changes in the type of farming in a particular area.[8] This argument begs a number of questions; no satisfactory explanation of the change in population has yet been offered that excludes the role of food supply. There are, however, other aspects of population growth of great importance, in particular, migration. At the end of the Pleistocene man already had a very wide distribution.[9] But the establishment of relatively dense populations dates only from the rise of village farming communities in the seventh and sixth millennia B.C. From that time there have been repeated migrations of farmers into unoccupied or sparsely occupied land. The 'frontier concept' is one associated primarily with the European occupation of North America, Russia and Australia.[10] It is worth remembering, however, that there have been equally important expansions of the agricultural frontier from much earlier times. Thus the Bantu occupation of Africa south of the tropical forest took most of the first millennium A.D., as did the Chinese settlement of the lands south of the Yangtse, whilst the same period saw the agricultural colonisation of much of Europe north of the Alps.

The growth of the world population has accelerated since the last century. From about 250 000 000 in the early Christian period, it had only grown to about 430 000 000 at the time of Columbus' arrival in the Americas and somewhat less than 1 000 000 000 at the beginning of the nineteenth century.[11]

Since then, not only has the population continued to increase, but the *rate* of increase has risen (Table 1). The area under cultivation has increased as population has grown. But in the last hundred years there has been relatively little increase in the cultivated areas of the old agricultural civilisations of Europe, the Indian sub-continent and East Asia. Instead, most of the expansion has been in the recently settled areas of Russia, Australia, North America and Latin America (Table 1).

In spite of the great migrations which have been going on for some 10 000 years, remarkably little of the earth's land surface is cultivated. About 11 per cent is used for crops and another fifth used for grazing. Further, in spite of the continuing pressure to expand the *ecumene,* the world's population is still remarkably concentrated. In 1960 about four-fifths of the world's population lived on only 16 per cent of the earth's land surface, whilst only 15 per cent of the land surface had densities above 20 per km^2.[12]

TABLE 1   *Regional increases in population, A.D. 14–1970 (millions)*

Region	14	600	1000	1340	1500	1700	1800	1900	1920	1950	1970
North Africa	11	4	4	5	6	2	5	27	46	51	87
Rest of Africa	12	33	46	65	79	97	95	106	94	166	257
North America	3	7	13	29	1	1	6	82	117	166	228
Latin America					40	12	19	74	91	162	283
East Asia[a]	80	65	80	89	131	201	391	586	597	830	1217
South Asia	70	75	70	75	79	200	190	297	326	481	762
South West Asia	34	26	22	22	15	13	13	43	44	44	77
Europe[b]	39	24	44	90	82	112	179	430	486	572	705
Oceania	1	1	1	2	2	2	2	6	8	12	19
World	256	237	280	378	427	641	890	1651	1810	2486	3632

[a] Including South East Asia   [b] Including Soviet Union
Sources: Clark C., 1967, 64; U.N. *Demographic yearbook*, 1958, and 1970, 104–5

There are many reasons for this continuing concentration of population, but one of considerable significance is the physical environment. Although geographers have recently been apt to discount the importance of environment, as a reaction to the period when geographical determinism was used as a basis of all explanations, the great importance of the physical environment in explaining the development of types of agriculture can hardly be gainsaid, and will be apparent throughout this book.

A third important process has been the diffusion of crops, livestock and farming techniques. The wild plants from which crop plants have been domesticated were found in relatively few parts of the world, but the crop plants are now widely distributed. Similarly, farming techniques have been carried from their areas of origin and practised in new environments.

Fourth is the complex series of changes which have accompanied economic development in the last 200 years: industrialisation, urbanisation, commercialisation and transport improvements, combined with radical changes in agricultural technology, have revolutionised farming since 1850.

Although agriculture has a history of at least 10000 years, technical change was remarkably slow until the middle of the nineteenth century. Most of the major crop plants and livestock were domesticated by the second millennium B.C., if not before; and by the middle of the first millennium B.C. the techniques and implements which prevailed in the major agricultural civilisations until the nineteenth century had already been devised, if not widely adopted. Thus the ox-drawn plough, the hoe, the digging stick, the sickle, harrow, axe and machete were used; fallowing, the use of cattle manure, the growth of legumes to maintain soil fertility, irrigation, water-lifting techniques and a variety of other fundamental techniques were all known to farmers.

The early history of agriculture is so important in understanding the present distribution of peasant farming systems that it is given special attention in Chapter 2, whilst the diffusions of crops and livestock, particularly those that took place after the discovery of the New World, are treated in Chapter 3. In Chapter 4 an outline of the major economic changes of the last 100 years is given, and the change in the pace of agricultural innovation is discussed. This completes the systematic discussion of factors influencing the evolution of agricultural systems. Part Two is devoted to a discussion of the evolution of individual types of agriculture.

PART ONE

CHAPTER 2

THE EARLY HISTORY OF AGRICULTURE

There are few subjects in which there have been such great changes in recent years as the prehistory of agriculture; and probably few in which there will be greater changes in the near future. Fortunately our only purpose here is to describe those features of the early history of agriculture which are relevant to an understanding of the development of modern types of agriculture.

Agriculture is generally understood to mean both the cultivation of crops and the rearing of livestock, and thus the beginnings of agriculture go back to the first domestication of plants and animals. It is helpful to make a distinction between 'seed' agriculture and 'vegeculture'. The latter refers to plants reproduced by vegetative propagation, mainly tropical roots such as taro, manioc, yams, sweet potatoes and arrowroot. In tropical vegeculture rhizomes have to be cut from the growing plant and individually planted. There is less need to completely clear the natural vegetation; if a mixture of roots is grown, crops may be harvested, by digging up each root individually, over a long period, rather than at one specific time; there is thus less need for storage. Most tuber-growing communities also collected the fruits of trees such as bananas or coconuts, and little more than protection, rather than domestication, was necessary to provide a food supply.[1]

In seed agriculture, which includes of course the cereals which are now the staple food crops in all but a few parts of the world, more initial clearance of vegetation is necessary, seed is sown *en masse* and harvested in one short period. The crops are predominantly annuals, and have a marked growing season, necessitating some form of storage during the winter or dry season. Seed agriculture has formed the basis of the major agricultural civilisations and was associated early on with the plough and draught animals. The importance of vegeculture in early agricultural history has been neglected. It now seems likely however that primitive vegeculture developed in the tropics, on the boundary between forest and grassland, in the Americas, Africa and South East Asia. The area in which these systems predominated has been reduced by the expansion of seed agriculture.

The best-known tropical vegeculture is that of South East Asia which may be taken to include not only the mainland and the Malaysian archipelago, but also Assam and South China. A number of important root and tree crops are indigenous to this region, including taro, the greater yam, the breadfruit, the sago palm, the bamboo, coconuts and bananas. Poultry and pigs were also independently domesticated in this region. Little is known of the methods of farming, but it is likely to have been primitive, relying upon stone axes, fire and the digging stick. The earliest archaeological evidence of vegeculture is in Thailand where legumes – possibly domesticated – have been dated at about 9000 B.C.;[2] plant domestication was certainly achieved on the mainland of South East Asia by 7000 B.C. This farming system was found above the valley bottoms and deltas, and expanded into – or developed independently in – eastern India, southern China, Taiwan and possibly Japan.[3] It also spread eastwards from western Malaysia into Melanesia and the Polynesian islands. The chronology of this movement is in doubt; but the earliest evidence of migrants in the Marianas was about 1500 B.C., in New Caledonia 847 B.C., the Marquesas 120 B.C., Fiji 46 B.C., Hawaii A.D. 124 and New Zealand in the tenth century A.D.[4] What is significant is that rice, presumably domesticated in the mainland after the domestication of the tuber and tree crops, was not taken to Melanesia or Polynesia, although it later penetrated the western part of the Malaysian archipelago.[5] Thus when Europeans first arrived in Polynesia the crops and methods in use were still those of the original vegeculture of the mainland.

In South East Asia vegeculture almost certainly preceded seed agriculture. This is less sure in Africa or South America. But it is possible that a vegeculture developed in West Africa on the margins of the tropical forest and savanna, based upon the yam indigenous to West Africa (*Dioscorea cayenensis*), and the oil-palm tree.[6] West Africa remains one of the few areas where root crops form a major part of the agricultural economy, although the indigenous crops have been supplemented by roots from America and South East Asia.

There was a third centre of tropical vegeculture in South America, where the major root crops were manioc (*Manihot utilissima*), the sweet potato (*Xanthosoma*) and arrowroot. These crops, together with the peanut, were probably domesticated in the tropical lowlands east of the Andes at some time between 7000 B.C. and 3000 B.C. in an area stretching both north and south of the Amazon. By 3000 B.C. the crops had been combined into a system, which was subsequently taken into the islands of the Caribbean, and the southern part of Central America.[7]

A quite different selection of root crops characterised the plateau areas of the Andes around Lake Titicaca. Most important was the potato, but oca (*Oxalis tuberosa*), ulluco (*Ullucus tuberosus*) and anu (*Tropaeolum tubersom*) were probably domesticated there together with the grain crop, quinoa (*Chenopodium quinoa*). This highland tuber culture was possibly a derivative of the tropical lowland root culture.[8]

Little is known of the methods of farming practised by these early groups. They probably used the digging stick, stone axes and fire to clear the vegetation, and practised shifting cultivation, whilst continuing to rely upon hunting, gathering and fishing for much of their food supply. Domesticated animals were unimportant, and quite absent in South America. Pigs and poultry, both scavengers, were early domesticates in South East Asia, and were taken to the Polynesian islands.

Vegeculture based on roots was essentially tropical in location, and has contracted as the farming systems based upon cereals have expanded from their heartlands. There were three major centres of cereal domestication in the Old World: South West Asia, North China and South East Asia, and possibly two in the New World, southern Mexico and Peru.

South West Asia and the eastern Mediterranean

The first archaeological evidence for the domestication of cereals, and some of the earliest evidence for the domestication of animals, comes from a broad region stretching from Greece and Crete in the west to the foothills of the Hindu Kush south of the Caspian in the east.[9] Here are found the wild plants from which wheat and barley were domesticated[10] (Fig. 2), whilst it is only in this zone that the wild progenitors of sheep, goats, cattle and pigs were found together, for the latter two had a much broader distribution than wild sheep and goats (Fig. 3). By the tenth millennium B.C. peoples who relied upon hunting and gathering were reaping wild barley and wild wheat with knives, grinding the grain and using storage pits.[11] By the sixth millennium there is evidence of village communities growing wheat and barley, and keeping sheep and goats, in Greece and Crete in the west, in southern Turkey, the Galilean uplands of the eastern littoral of the Mediterranean, in the Zagros mountains of Iran and Iraq, the interior plateaux of Iran, and in the foothills south east of the Caspian.[12] Subsequently the number of domesticated plants grown was increased, including flax, for its oil rather than for fibre, peas, lentils and vetch. By the fourth millennium the olive, vine and fig, the crops which give traditional Mediterranean agriculture much of its distinctiveness, had been domesticated in the eastern Mediterranean.[13] Cattle and pigs are thought to have been domesticated after sheep and goats. Cattle were used as draught animals, and for meat; not until the late fourth millennium is there evidence of milking in South West Asia.[14]

In the sixth and fifth millennia there was a significant change in the location of farming communities; they appear for the first time on the flood plains of the Tigris and Euphrates.[15] In Egypt, agriculture was derived from South West Asia; the first farming communities appear in the fifth millennium B.C., but above the flood plains of the river. It was not until the middle of the fourth millennium that farmers occupied the Nile flood plains and began to use the annual floods to irrigate crops.[16] By the late fifth millennium B.C. the farms and villages of the Ubaid culture were widely scattered in southern Mesopotamia, whilst Dynastic Egypt had emerged by the late fourth millennium. The rise of these literate urban civilisations was the result of a long period of development of food production methods, and the changes which took place on the flood plains may have been a critical prerequisite for urban growth.

Farming methods in South West Asia and the eastern Mediterranean

The earliest farmers had reaping knives, sickles and simple methods of grinding

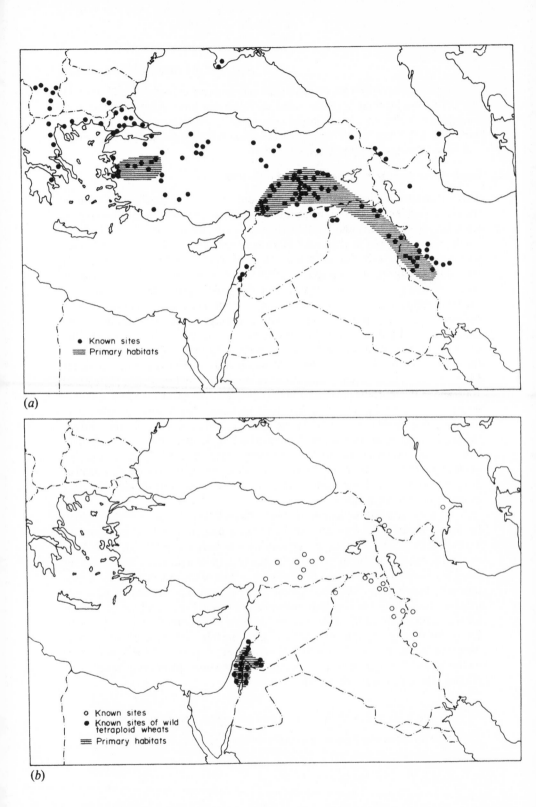

(a)

● Known sites
≡ Primary habitats

(b)

○ Known sites
● Known sites of wild
  tetraploid wheats
≡ Primary habitats

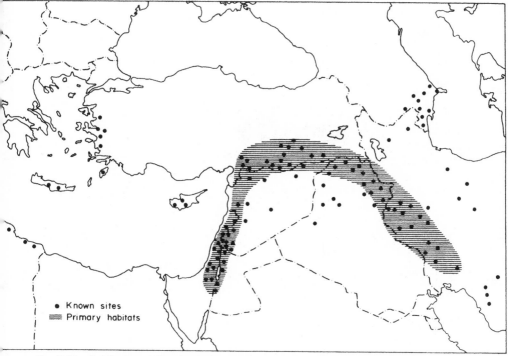

Fig. 2. The distribution of (*a*) wild einkorn, *Triticum boeticum*, (*b*) wild emmer, *Triticum dicoc-
coides*, and (*c*) wild barley, *Hordeum spontaneum*. [Source: Zohary, 1969, 50, 51, 54]

grain. They probably had weighted digging sticks, and later primitive hoes, made
at first from wood, and later from stone.[17] Except in the higher upland areas,
rainfall throughout most of the region was low, erratic and seasonally concentrated, so that crop yields must have been, as they still are, low and unreliable.
There is no evidence to suggest that rainfall was higher between 10000 B.C. and
4000 B.C. than it is at present; but woodland probably covered a smaller, and
steppe conditions a greater, area than at present.[18] It is likely that the early
cultivators practised some form of shifting cultivation, although the continuous
occupation of many excavated sites suggests that the occupants had discovered
the value of allowing livestock to graze the arable stubble, and possibly the value
of fallowing to conserve moisture. At nearly all the early sites in the region crops
were grown and livestock kept; from the beginning a primitive form of mixed farming was practised.

The lowlands of the Tigris and Euphrates and the Nile have insufficient rainfall
for even dry farming, and there is no reason to suppose that the rainfall was
greater when the urban civilisations of Sumer and Egypt began. In Egypt flood
control and basin irrigation had appeared by the end of the fourth millennium
B.C. The annual deposition of silt must have been a major factor in maintaining

13

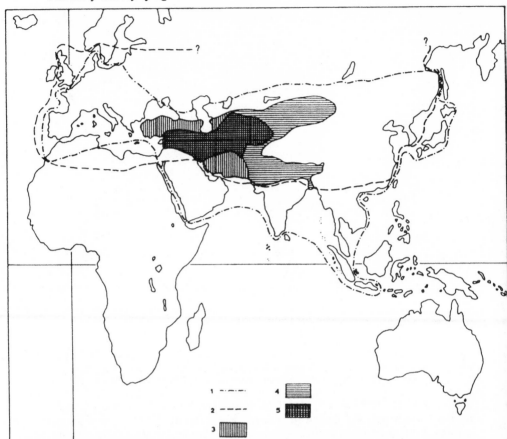

Fig. 3. Distribution of the wild ancestors of pigs, cattle, goats and sheep. [Source: Isaac, 1970, 78]
1. Pigs. 2. Cattle. 3. Goats. 4. Sheep. 5. Area of overlap of pigs, cattle, goats and sheep

soil fertility, whilst the relative reliability of the Nile floods probably gave higher yields than were possible in the dry-farmed areas. The receding floods also washed away any salt accumulation in the basins.[19]

The development of irrigation in Mesopotamia was more difficult, for the floods came in late spring and early summer, when the snow melted in the Turkish mountains, which was convenient neither for spring nor for autumn sown crops. Thus embankments to control the floods, canals, and some form of storage would have been necessary. Indeed it was not until after Sumer had been politically unified in the second millennium B.C. that large-scale irrigation works were established. Problems of salinity, which still hinder farming in this area, may have been responsible for the shift in political power northwards to Babylon at that time. New varieties of wheat and barley and new crops were added in the flood plains, and indeed their settlement may not have been possible until this was achieved.[20] Six-row barley replaced two-row, and breadwheat joined emmer and einkorn, the latter becoming dominant in Mesopotamia because of the unsuitability of emmer for saline soils. The date palm and a number of vegetables were also grown in Sumerian times.[21]

But perhaps the most important change was the slow adoption of the ox-drawn plough. The earliest ploughs in South West Asia were primitive wooden *ards* which did little more than scratch the surface. They were known in both Mesopotamia and Egypt at the end of the fourth millennium B.C. It is believed by some writers that cross-ploughing was practised on the flood plains. Certainly this technique would have been useful in the dry-farmed areas, where it would have aided the conservation of soil moisture.

By about 3000 B.C. two distinctive types of agriculture had emerged in South West Asia and the eastern Mediterranean. One was dry-farming, possibly based upon shifting cultivation, with wheat and barley as the main crops; sheep, goats, cattle and pigs were kept. The plough was later adopted and then oxen added their manure to that of livestock grazing on the arable stubbles. Reaping knives and sickles were used in harvesting.

The second type did not differ fundamentally in crops, stock or implements, but was found in the flood plains of the Nile and the Tigris–Euphrates, where the very low rainfall necessitated a dependence upon irrigation. Irrigation of an elementary form had doubtless been practised in a primitive manner on a small scale and at a much earlier date in various parts of South West Asia, but it was in Egypt and Mesopotamia that the construction of embankments to control the floods of large rivers, and canals to deliver water to more distant fields, was begun. Here also were found water-lifting devices such as the shaduf; by the end of the first millennium B.C. the water-wheel and the cerd were also in use.[22] A third agricultural community based upon irrigation grew up in Turkestan east of the Caspian between the fifth and second millennia B.C., on rivers which flow north from the Kopet Dagh and Hindu Kush, based on the same combination of crops and livestock which characterised Mesopotamia.[23]

Westward Expansion

Whilst the development of agriculture described above was proceeding in South West Asia and the eastern Mediterranean, farming and herding were spreading westward into Europe and North Africa. Domestication in Greece, Crete and Cyprus may have been as early as that in South West Asia;[24] from there farming was taken north into the Danube basin and thence north-westwards towards the Baltic and the North Sea, following the loess soils which lie to the north of the Hercynian mountains of central Europe; an offshoot of the Danubian culture penetrated the Ukrainian steppes.[25] By 4000 B.C. agriculture had reached the shores of the North Sea and the Baltic, and possibly the British Isles, whilst by 2500 B.C. at the latest it had reached the southern edge of the coniferous forest in

Scandinavia and Russia. Farming also spread through the countries to the north of the Mediterranean Sea, and had reached Spain and southern France by about 4000 B.C.[26] It also spread along the southern shores of the Sea. In Egypt the first evidence of agriculture is on the edge of the delta where wheat and flax were grown about 4900 B.C. The South West Asian complex appears to have diffused westwards along the North African coast, reaching the Maghreb in the fourth millennium B.C. Wheat, barley, sheep and goats were all indigenous to South West Asia, but *Bos primigenius* was also found in North Africa, and cattle may have been independently domesticated there.[27]

In Europe north of the Alps the basic agricultural complex was acquired from South West Asia; however, whilst the wild progenitors of goats and sheep were not found in Europe, the wild pig and the auroch were, and domestication of these may have occurred independently. Wheat, barley, lentils, flax, vetch and peas were all taken north, but millet (*Panicum miliaceum*) appears to have been domesticated in the Balkans.[28] Oats and rye are both indigenous to South West Asia, but were carried into Europe as weeds and domesticated there, possibly as early as the fourth millennium, but they did not assume any great importance until the first millennium.[29] As agriculture pushed northwards barley became more important than wheat and, more significant, cattle assumed a greater role than sheep or goats, a marked contrast with the Mediterranean basin and South West Asia. This may reflect an adjustment to cooler and moister conditions, but it may also be that whilst the early farmers could domesticate local aurochs and pigs, they were some distance from fresh stocks of sheep and goats.[30]

As in South West Asia, the exact methods used by farmers must be a matter of speculation. It is likely that the farmers who carried farming northwards into Europe used slash-and-burn methods, with digging sticks and hoes. The earliest evidence of ploughs – or more precisely, *ards* – in northern Europe is in the third millennium B.C. The spread of the ox-drawn plough may have been instrumental in creating permanent agriculture. By the first millennium B.C. the clearance of woodland had allowed an increase in the importance of sheep, which could not feed in woodland areas; it has also been suggested that sheep were being folded with hurdles, and cattle kept in stalls at quite early dates.[31]

Eastward expansion

Indian agriculture has long had a great variety of crops, yet relatively few were first domesticated there, for the Indian sub-continent lies at the junction of two major centres of domestication, South West Asia and South East Asia.[32] As yet the earliest evidence for agriculture in India lies in the north west, in the hills of Baluchistan, and somewhat later, in the plains of the Indus. About 3500 B.C. there were farming communities in the hills overlooking the Indus plains from the Zhob valley in the north to the Makran coast in the south; they grew club wheat, kept sheep, goats and cattle and possibly dammed seasonal streams with stone walls, called *gabarands,* to irrigate their crops. By about 3000 B.C. farmers had settled the plains of the lower Indus and were using the summer floods to grow wheat and barley.[33]

From these settlements grew the Harappa civilisation, which bears comparison with those of Sumer or Egypt. It covered a great area, from the Himalayan foothills in the north, east to the Jamuna River, south east to the Narmada River and south west to the Makran coast; but most of the sites are on the Indus or its tributaries and former courses. The largest known are those of Mohenjodaro on the lower Indus, and Harappa, 400 miles to the north on the Ravi. The crops and livestock were mainly derived from South West Asia; wheat, barley, dates and peas were grown, and cattle, sheep and goats kept. But there were important additions. Cotton was domesticated here, probably at the end of the third millennium B.C., *Sesame indicum* was grown, and also rice. Further, the cattle had the distinctive hump of the modern zebu. Little is known of the methods used. The plough is not thought to have reached India until after the Aryan invasion, which *inter alia* led to the abrupt eclipse of the Harappa civilisation between 1700 and 1500 B.C.[34]

Farming had spread outside the Indus plains well before the fall of the Harappa civilisation. In the first half of the second millennium B.C. there is evidence of communities keeping sheep and goats in the Aravalli hills, whilst farther south farmers at Navdatoli kept sheep, goats and cattle, grew South West Asian crops such as wheat, flax and lentils and also cotton and rice. Even further south, in the upper reaches of the Krishna, were people who kept domesticated cattle in the third millennium, and by 1500 B.C. were growing the distinctively Indian millets, *ragi* and *bajra*. Both these crops, it should be noted, are probably indigenous to Africa, as is *Sesame indicum* which was grown by the Harappa farmers.[35]

The spread of cereal cultivation into the Ganges valley seems to have been much slower than the penetration southwards into the peninsula; the earliest occupation of the upper Ganges dates only from about 1100 B.C., whilst the effective settlement of the middle Ganges does not seem to have begun until the eighth and ninth centuries B.C. By then settlers were probably equipped with ploughs and iron axes. It may have been the dense forest cover which delayed settlement. The first evidence of rice being grown on the margins of the Ganges delta dates only from 700 B.C., and effective occupation was even later. Thus most archaeological evidence suggests that agriculture in India was a result of diffusion from South West Asia, together with the local domestication of rice and cotton, and some unexplained imports of African crops.[36]

Early 'seed' agriculture in East and South East Asia was once thought to be a result of diffusion from South West Asia via both India and what later became the Old Silk Road. It is now thought that northern China and South East Asia may have been centres of independent domestication.

The first known farmers in northern China lived in the loess uplands of the middle Hwang Ho, the Fen Ho and the Wei Ho, in the sixth and fifth millennia B.C. (Fig. 4). They grew foxtail millet, kept pigs, and probably practised shifting cultivation. These farmers, whose culture is called the Yangshao, later expanded eastwards into the marshy plains of the lower Hwang Ho where the first villages were on mounds to avoid the floods. Here developed the Luganshoid culture, which took agriculture north into Manchuria and south of the Yangtse; but for long Chinese civilisation remained predominantly northern. Wheat, barley,

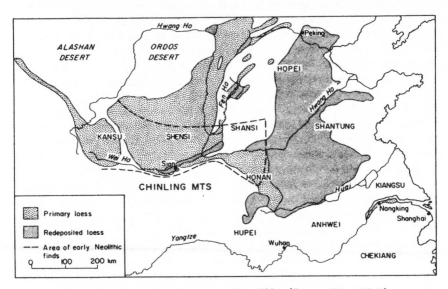

Fig. 4. The origins of agriculture in northern China. [Source: Ho, 1969, 5]

sheep, goats and cattle were acquired from South West Asia, whilst soy beans and the mulberry tree were domesticated locally. Until the middle of the first millennium B.C., when ox-drawn ploughs became more common, the chief implements were digging sticks, hoes and spades. It has been argued that the Chinese independently developed a plough, although there is little archaeological evidence to support this view and the plough was probably acquired from South West Asia.

Early agriculture in East and South East Asia

Contrary to common belief, irrigation was unimportant in northern China until well into the first millennium B.C., except for the use of wells in the loess uplands, and the early Chinese agronomies were more concerned with moisture conservation than with irrigation.[37] Nor did wet-rice cultivation begin in northern China. The first archaeological evidence of domesticated rice in Asia is in Gujarat in 1800 B.C., in central China *c.* 2300 B.C. (although recent finds in the same area have been dated *c.* 3000 B.C.) and in Thailand *c.* 3500 B.C. The origins of the domestication of rice and the development of wet-rice techniques have been a matter of great controversy and remain a major unsolved problem.[38]

Cultivated rice (*Oryza sativa*) is commonly held to be derived from two wild varieties, *O. perennis* and *O. spontanea*, which were found in marshy sites throughout the Indian sub-continent, South East Asia, and the Philippines, but not apparently – though this is disputed – in southern China.[39] It could thus have been first domesticated anywhere within this region, or carried outside, as a weed associated with the taro, and domesticated. It could also have been domesticated independently in several places within the region. A distinction must be made between upland rice and wet-rice. The former is grown like any other cereal and relies upon rainfall. Wet-rice, however, has to be partially submerged for much of its growing period. It has been argued that upland rice was domesticated first, and that the development of the elaborate techniques associated with wet-rice cultivation were developed much later. Thus upland rice would have expanded from its first centre of domestication, but subsequently would have been displaced by the more intensive wet-rice. However, it should be noted that wet-rice can be cultivated without elaborate techniques, and indeed is so grown at present in parts of Malaya and the Philippines.[40] Flat pieces of ground which were seasonally flooded by rivers or heavy rainfall could be sown easily to rice by broadcasting and a harvest of sorts obtained. Transplanting, terracing, the levelling of fields, the construction of bunds, water control and irrigation would all increase and maintain yields. But wet-rice cultivation would have been quite possible without such elaborate methods.

Recent archaeological work in South East Asia suggests that the area was not the cultural cul-de-sac that it was long thought to be. It is now believed by some prehistorians that rice was first domesticated on the mainland and that in the fourth millennium B.C. farmers, who had hitherto been confined to the upland, colonised the river valleys. Rice-growing spread from there into southern China and eastern India and southwards into the Malaysian archipelago: it was not however carried eastwards into Melanesia or Polynesia. The development of wet-rice techniques came much later.[41]

Early agriculture in Africa

The origins of agriculture in Africa south of the Sahara are still a matter of dispute. Vegeculture was probably practised on the northern margins of the tropical forest in West Africa as early as the fifth millennium B.C., but the beginnings of cereal cultivation are less clear. It has been claimed that there were two centres of independent plant domestication in Africa south of the Sahara, one in the western Sudan zone, and one in the east in Ethiopia. G. P. Murdock has argued that the Mande-speaking peoples of the middle Niger domesticated a number of indigenous plants, including several millets, whilst Vavilov thought Ethiopia to be a centre of plant domestication.[42] Other writers believe, however, that agriculture only reached Africa south of the Sahara by diffusion from Egypt and the Maghreb. Between 6500 B.C. and 2500 B.C. the Sahara was moister than at present and was occupied by pastoral nomads who may have practised some incipient agriculture. Wheat and barley would have proved unsuitable in the summer rainfall areas of the Sudan zone, and thus local plants such as pearl millet, finger millet (*Eleusine coracana*) and sorghum (*Sorghum vulgare*) were domesticated. Certainly agriculture was being practised in the savannas north of the tropical rain forest by the third and second millennia B.C.; whilst in eastern Africa pastoral peoples from Arabia moved southwards with sheep, goats and cattle, and may also have grown grain crops. But by the end of the first millennium B.C. there had been little penetration of the rain forest, and agriculture had made little progress into southern Africa. The plough, which had by then diffused over nearly all the Old World, did not reach Africa until the nineteenth century.[43]

The Americas

Man reached the Americas across the Bering Straits before plant and animal domestication had appeared in the Old World, and so agriculture in the Americas is an independent development.[44] Whilst there were certainly contacts between the Americas and the Old World before Columbus, they did not significantly affect agriculture, and American farming showed a number of major differences from Old World agriculture until the arrival of Europeans.

First, the crops indigenous to the Americas were quite different from those domesticated in the Old World. Maize, squash, beans, manioc, the potato and groundnuts were the major food crops. Wild cotton seems to have occurred in both India and the Americas, and was domesticated independently in each region. Second, the only animals domesticated in the Americas were the llama, alpaca and turkey. There were no herding animals until after Columbus. Third, the plough was not invented in the Americas, whilst the *coa* was more akin to the digging stick than the hoe. Metals were rarely used for agricultural implements. Thus the agricultural civilisations of the Americas were quite different from those in the Old World, although there were common techniques. Slash-and-burn, irrigation, terracing, and the use of llama dung for manure were all practised.[45]

It has been noted that South America was the scene of early vegeculture. There were also two areas where cereal domestication took place and significant civilisations appeared – Meso-America and coastal Peru.[46] Meso-America embraces southern Mexico, Guatemala and Honduras. Maize appears to have been domesticated in southern Mexico in the sixth millennium and by 3000 B.C. beans, squash, avocados, gourds, zapotes, pumpkins and chillies were also grown, as well as cotton. For two or three millennia hunting and gathering remained a more important source of food than domesticated plants, and it was not until the third millennium B.C. that farming villages mainly dependent upon agriculture appeared in Meso-America. Crops were grown by slash-and-burn techniques; maize, squash and beans were the major food crops, grown together on the same plot, in a symbiotic relationship. By the first millennium B.C., if not earlier, crops first domesticated in South America were being cultivated in Meso-America – tomatoes, manioc, peanuts and lima beans. In the drier upland areas permanent

20

agriculture based upon irrigation developed, although in the lowlands slash-and-burn remained the usual method.[47]

The second major centre of agriculture in the Americas was the coast of northern Peru, where there is evidence of plants domesticated in the fifth millennium B.C.: the early farmers relied upon fishing, but grew squash, beans, chilli pepper, and used cotton for textiles. Maize is not known until about 2000 B.C., and may have been acquired from Meso-America. By the second millennium B.C. there were farming villages based upon irrigation, with quite considerable monumental buildings; there must have been contacts with areas to the east, for potatoes, manioc and groundnuts were all grown by the first millennium.[48]

Summary

By the middle of the first millennium B.C. there were already very marked differences in the types of agriculture to be found in the world. They can be categorised as follows.

A. *South West Asian and its derivatives*

The basic crops in this complex were wheat, barley, flax, lentils, peas, beans and vetch. Sheep, cattle, pigs and goats were kept by most sedentary farmers, and the plough was drawn by oxen. This system had a number of important sub-types:

(i) The irrigated farming communities of the Nile Valley, the Tigris and Euphrates, Turkestan and the Indus. In all these regions farming was impossible without irrigation, and embankments to control floods, large canals, and a variety of lifting devices had been developed. There were of course differences between these four areas. Thus for example, farmers in Turkestan and the lower Indus had added cotton and rice to the basic crops of South West Asia.

(ii) Dry-farming: this was the basic South West Asian complex, and it seems likely that methods of moisture conservation such as fallowing and cross-ploughing had been developed by the first millennium B.C.

(iii) Mediterranean agriculture: this was a combination of the dry-farming of cereals combined with the more intensive cultivation of the tree-crops, figs, olives and grapes. These crops did not play a major role in South West Asia proper, nor were they important in the eastward diffusion of the South West Asian complex into Turkestan and the Indus valley.

(iv) Northern Europe: north of the Alps oats and rye were added to the South West Asian crops, whilst cattle and pigs were of greater importance than south of the Alps.

By about 500 B.C. most farmers in the area influencd by the South West Asian complex were permanent cultivators; the ox-drawn *ard* was found in most of the region, and simple methods of maintaining soil fertility such as fallowing and the use of manure were practised. Farming implements included most of those used in the seventeenth and eighteenth centuries A.D. There were no major innovations, but continuous improvement of ploughs, harrows, sickles and drills went on for the next 2000 years.

B. *The South East Asian complex and its derivatives*

Two agricultural complexes had their origins in the mainland of South East Asia.

(i) Tropical vegeculture: taro, the greater yam, bananas and coconuts were the major crops. Shifting agriculture was practised, and the digging stick and the axe were the major implements. Pigs and poultry were the only livestock kept.

(ii) Wet-rice cultivation: vegeculture was largely displaced by the expansion of wet-rice cultivation. Tropical vegeculture survived in the remoter areas and in mixed gardens, but dry-rice was often adopted and grown as well as the root crops. In eastern Melanesia and Polynesia the original system remained intact until Europeans arrived in the eighteenth and nineteenth centuries A.D. Wet-rice cultivation, together with zebu cattle and the plough, expanded from South East Asia into eastern India, southern China and Indonesia.

C. *Northern China*

The farming of northern China was based upon local domesticates such as pigs, foxtail millet, soy beans, and mulberry, and imports from South West Asia of wheat, barley, sheep, goats and cattle. By 500 B.C. the plough was in use and there were a number of practices for maintaining soil fertility. Although rice was grown, it was not the major crop, and in most of the region moisture conservation rather than irrigation was the main aim of the farmer.

D. *Africa*

In Africa there were two farming systems, one tropical vegeculture, based upon local yams, and secondly the cultivation of various millets and *Sorghum vulgare*. The plough had not been adopted, shifting cultivation was practised, and both the tropical forest and much of southern Africa were unoccupied by farmers. Livestock were kept, but they were not integrated with crop production.

E. *The Americas*

The two systems here were the cultivation of roots, mainly by shifting cultivation, and the maize–squash–beans complex, again grown by slash-and-burn, although in parts of Peru and Mexico irrigation was practised. By about 500 A.D. maize, squash and beans had spread as far north as the Great Lakes and south to the Rio Plata. Neither system had livestock or the plough.

This typology is obviously speculative; nor is it complete. In northern India farming was a mixture of crops and methods derived from South West Asia and

22

South East Asia. The subsequent history of farming systems saw the decline of isolation, and a greater interchange of crops, livestock and methods. Two periods are of particular importance: the age of the Great Discoveries, and the subsequent exchange of crops; and the modern period. We turn first to the exchange of crops.

CHAPTER 3

THE DIFFUSION OF CROPS AND LIVESTOCK

The distribution of crops and livestock is obviously an important part of any study of agricultural geography; particularly significant are the combinations of crops that characterise different types of agriculture. Explanations of such distributions are usually couched in terms of climatic requirements, the suitability of soil, variations of demand and the availability of labour. But in the longer perspective there is a different problem. Most crops are, within their climatic limits, very widely grown. Wheat, for example, is found near the Arctic Circle and in upland areas near the Equator, whilst it is grown in the east of the Old World in Japan and in Ireland in the west. The great range of modern crops has led one authority to write 'at the present time almost everything is almost everywhere'.[1]

In contrast, the wild varieties from which crops have been bred were confined to a very small part of the earth's surface – about 10 per cent according to Vavilov – and most of the earth has produced no significant plants for man (Fig. 5). Most of the crops now grown had been domesticated by 2000 B.C. or before, but many were confined until quite recently to the region in which they were first domesticated. (See Appendix.) Until the fifteenth century, the diffusion of crops was slow – and there had been no exchange of plants between the Old and the New World. But by the late seventeenth century botanical gardens were established with the express intention of speeding the exchange of crop and decorative plants.[2] In the nineteenth century the rise of modern industry greatly increased the demand for raw materials which in turn led to the greater dispersal of industrial crops, whilst the prosperity of European populations influenced the dispersal of food crops, as had the emigration of the European peoples themselves at an earlier date.

Fig. 5 shows the major areas in which plant domestication took place and Table 2 the principal crops domesticated in these areas. More recent opinion among archaeologists and botanists suggests that the North East of India and the South of China are part of the South East Asian realm, and that rice, taro and jute should be assigned to this region. This has been allowed for in Table 2. From this it can be seen that South West Asia is the home of crops which occupy a third of present-day world cropland, Latin America a little over a fifth, and Africa south of the Sahara rather less than a fifth. No other region has made a *major* contribution. The same table shows the origin of the crops in each major region. South West and South East Asia rely most upon indigenous crops, owing

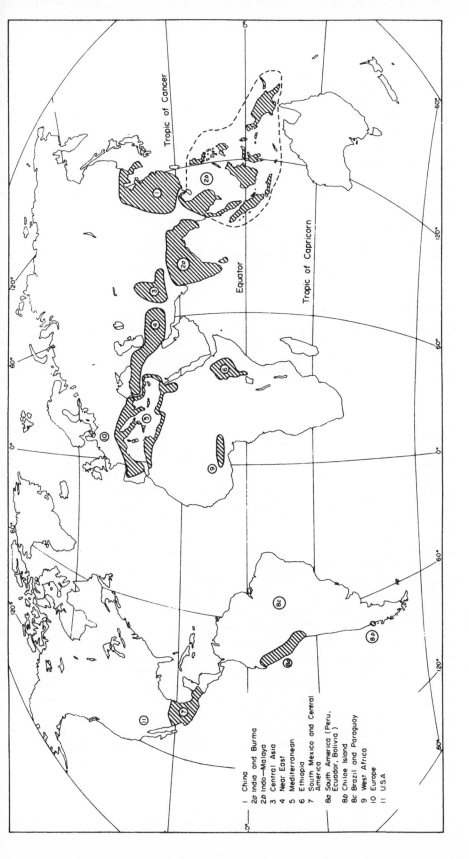

Fig. 5. Major areas of plant domestication after Vavilov and others. (Source: Darlington, 1963, 138–9)

1 China
2a India and Burma
2b Indo-Malaya
3 Central Asia
4 Near East
5 Mediterranean
6 Ethiopia
7 South Mexico and Central America
8a South America (Peru, Ecuador, Bolivia)
8b Chiloe Island
8c Brazil and Paraguay
9 West Africa
10 Europe
11 U.S.A.

to the predominance of wheat and barley in the former and rice in the latter. Latin America and Africa, in contrast, although the home of major grains, have been profoundly influenced by later plant exchanges, whilst North America, northern Europe and Australasia, the most advanced of modern agricultural regions, rely largely upon crops which were domesticated elsewhere. The low figure for India is partly explained by the assignment of rice, taro and jute to South East Asia. It also indicates how India has stood at the meeting place of three major centres of domestication: South West Asia, South East Asia and Africa. The table also gives a measure of the impact of the discovery of the Americas upon the crops of different regions. Africa has been most influenced, particularly by the introduction of maize and manioc. American crops have had least influence in Australia, South West Asia, China and India.

Early dispersal of crop plants

The early diffusion of plants has been dealt with in Chapter 2. By early Christian times there had been a considerable interchange of plants between South West Asia, Europe, North Africa, Turkestan and North West India. The South East Asian complex of roots and rice had expanded into India, China and Malaysia, whilst there had been diffusion between northern China, Turkestan and South West Asia.

After the Fall of Rome, the diffusion of plants was slowed as the great civilisations became relatively isolated from each other. For a long period the Arabs were the most important agents of plant migration. By the eighth century A.D. the Islamic empire stretched from Spain and Morocco in the west, to the Indus and the Jaxartes in the east, and thus effectively cut Europe's land routes to India, China and Africa. However, the Arabs were instrumental in spreading citrus and other crops into the western Mediterranean. The sweet orange, the sour orange, the lime, the lemon and the citron were all indigenous to southern China and South East Asia. The time of their arrival in the Mediterranean is a matter of dispute. The citron was used by the Jews in a religious festival, and was carried westwards in the *diaspora* of the early centuries A.D. They may have taken other citrus fruits as well, but this is more commonly attributed to the Arabs.[3] The sour, or Seville, orange was introduced into Spain in the tenth century, the lemon in the twelfth century and the lime in the thirteenth century. The sweet orange was not known in the Mediterranean until the fifteenth century, when it was popularised by the Portuguese. The Crusades, and the revival of northern European connections with the Levant in the thirteenth century A.D., slowly made citrus fruit known north of the Alps and from the fourteenth century 'orangeries' were established.[4] Thus when European expansion began in the fifteenth century, citrus fruits, although of Asian origin, became closely associated with the spread of Europeans.

Rice, cotton and possibly sugar-cane were grown in Mesopotamia in the first millennium B.C., and may have been grown in the Levant by Roman times, but

TABLE 2 *Source areas of major crops and the current importance of these crops within specified areas*

	South West Asia	South East Asia	Latin America	Africa	Northern Europe	China	India	Mediter-ranean	North America	Australia
South West Asia	79.5	3.2	8.1	1.9	4.1	–	–	0.2	–	–
South East Asia	0.4	69.9	22.3	2.6	–	1.7	–	–	–	–
Latin America	14.4	14.4	48.0	9.1	1.7	0.9	0.1	0.4	1.6	–
Africa	3.7	7.0	39.7	41.8	0.2	–	3.8	0.2	–	–
Northern Europe	47.9	0.1	21.4	0.1	24.2	0.1	–	3.8	0.2	–
China	29.1	22.2	12.0	12.5	1.4	16.9	–	2.0	–	–
India	21.7	28.8	14.6	26.2	–	–	1.2	–	–	–
Mediterranean	67.6	0.6	16.8	–	7.5	–	–	1.6	–	–
North America	40.9	1.4	26.1	5.7	9.2	14.3	0.1	0.4	0.1	–
Australia	84.3	0.4	1.7	0.3	10.6	–	–	–	–	–
World	34.9	15.1	21.4	18.3	6.2	3.4	0.6	0.6	0.8	–

Source: F.A.O. *Production yearbook*, vol. 23, 1969

All the major crops having been assigned to their source area (see Appendix) the currently cultivated area under these major crops has been calculated for each specified region. The table may be read in two ways. Horizontally it shows the proportion of all cropland in the specified area derived from crops indigenous to the source areas indicated at the head of the columns, e.g. in South East Asia 0.4 per cent of the total cropland is sown to crops indigenous to South West Asia, 22.3 per cent to Latin America. Reading vertically down the columns in the table indicates the importance of the crops indigenous to a particular area to the other areas at the present time, e.g. Latin American crops make up 8.1 per cent of South West Asia's recorded cropland, 22.3 per cent of South East Asia's, 39.7 per cent of Africa's, and so on.

they did not become important until the Muslim defeat of the Persians in the late seventh century and the consequent Arab control of Mesopotamia. All these crops were brought westwards to North Africa, Spain and Sicily. Rice was introduced to Valencia and later Lombardy, whilst Sicily became a thriving centre of sugar-cane production. Again these Arab introductions were of direct importance to the Mediterranean, but of greater significance for the Americas, which were settled by people familiar with these South East Asian crops.[5] Many of these Asian crops were indigenous to areas with a summer rainfall maximum, and were thus difficult to grow in the Mediterranean without irrigation. Again the Arabs were instrumental in introducing, into the Maghreb and the western Mediterranean, irrigation techniques which had long been known in South West Asia.[6]

Even before Mohammed's time Arab traders had been sailing both east to India and south to East Africa. From the eighth century they settled on the African coast, and introduced rice, citrus fruits, coconut palms, cucumbers and mango, all plants indigenous to South and South East Asia but long grown in Mesopotamia and Iran.[7] Africa may also have acquired South East Asian plants by a quite different route. In early Christian times – and possibly earlier – Indonesian traders crossed the Indian Ocean to Madagascar, whence they brought the greater yam, the banana and Asian rice (*Oryza sativa*). There is little historical or archaeological evidence of this migration, but many writers believe that these crops reached the African coast from Madagascar, and were carried northwards. The first historical reference to the banana is not however until A.D. 1300, at Mombasa.[8]

In South and East Asia the early diffusion of plants was mainly out of the South East Asian hearth into India, China and Malaysia, a point which has already been touched upon. But northern China had by Han times acquired wheat, barley, linseed and peas from South West Asia, the millet (*Panicum italicum*) and hemp (*Cannabis indica*) from Turkestan, whilst the traveller Chang Chien brought the grape vine and lucerne from Turkestan to China.[9] Southern China had received bananas, rice, the greater yam, sugar-cane and tea from South East Asia.[10] Sugar-cane however was never grown in any significant quantities in China. Cotton was unknown in Han China, and as late as the seventh century A.D. was only grown as an ornamental shrub; not until the twelfth century A.D. was it grown as a fibre. About the same time *Sorghum vulgare* was introduced into the North by the Mongols.[11]

Plant dispersal since the fifteenth century A.D.

Since the fifteenth century the dispersal of crops has been greatly accelerated. Of most importance was the discovery of the Americas by Columbus in 1492; until then there had been no exchange of crops between Old and New World with the exception of the sweet potato, which was known in parts of Polynesia before Europeans arrived in the eighteenth century; the crop is undoubtedly American in origin, and was probably taken to Tahiti from the Americas at some time before A.D. 1000.[12]

Prior to Columbus' voyage the Portuguese had opened up the sea route to the East. In the first half of the fifteenth century they explored the African coast and settled the offshore islands, taking with them a number of crops grown in the Mediterranean, including sugar-cane, bananas and the grape vine. In 1497 Vasco da Gama rounded the Cape of Good Hope and reached Calicut in India. Two years later Cabral made the voyage to India via Brazil. In a period of quite remarkable expansion the Portuguese seized Malacca in 1511, reached the spice islands of the Moluccas in 1513, and Canton in the same year. Thus a regular sailing route linked Europe, Brazil, South Africa, India, the East Indies and China.

The Spanish conquest of the Americas began with Columbus' first voyage to Cuba and Hispaniola. In 1509 the mainland was first settled at Darien in the isthmus of Panama, by 1521 the Aztecs had been overthrown by Cortez and by 1535 Pizarro had conquered the Incas of Peru. The first shipment of African slaves to the West Indies took place in 1505, and to Brazil in 1525. There was thus a regular movement of ships – and hence of plants – between Europe, Africa and the New World. In 1564 the Spanish crossed the Pacific from Mexico to the Philippines; until 1815 galleons regularly plied this route, and American crops reached Asia this way as well as via Europe.

By the beginning of the seventeenth century only the southern Pacific remained isolated. Although Tasman circumnavigated Australia in 1642 and sighted New Zealand in the same year, it was not until the eighteenth and nineteenth centuries that Australasia and Polynesia became drawn into the world's affairs.

The exchange of plants now became much more rapid than before the fifteenth century. European colonists took their crops with them, to the Americas, to South Africa and to Australasia. They also took crops which would sell at home – sugar-cane being the best example. The slave ships led to an exchange of plants between America and Africa. By the nineteenth century different forces were at work. Hitherto little-used plants proved to have an economic value in industry, such as rubber and the oil-palm, whilst higher incomes in Europe prompted the spread of fruits and other semi-luxury crops, such as coffee and cocoa. This remarkable expansion radically changed the number of crops which farmers had available to choose from. We shall examine the major regions individually.

Europe

In 1500 the crops grown in Europe were either derived from South West or South East Asia, and the latter were for climatic reasons confined largely to the Mediterranean. There were two major developments after 1500. First, potatoes and maize from America were adopted. Second, grasses and root crops were bred from indigenous plants.

Maize and potatoes both gave much higher yields than the grain crops grown in Europe in 1500, and may have been instrumental in sustaining the great increase in population that had its beginnings in the seventeenth century. The potato was first seen by Europeans in Peru in 1537 and was first grown in Europe in Spain in about 1570; from there it spread to Italy in 1587 and had reached England and Germany by 1588; it was not, however, introduced into Scandinavia until the eighteenth century. The early crops were not particularly successful. The Andean species are short-day plants and the crop was thus not widely grown in Europe until a long-day plant had been selected. Nor was it accepted as a food crop until the nineteenth century, previously being grown mainly for fodder. Only in Ireland did it become a staple food before the nineteenth century.[13]

Maize was brought back to Europe after Columbus' first voyage, and spread rapidly through the Mediterranean countries, although its cultivation was restricted by the need for irrigation. In the sixteenth century the Turks took the crop into the Levant and Egypt, and in the eighteenth century into the Balkans, where the climate is more suited to its cultivation; it is now a major crop in South East Europe, and Europe *in toto* has a tenth of the world's acreage. Potatoes and maize were thus complementary, for potatoes are mainly a northern European crop whilst maize is confined to the Balkans and the Mediterranean. Of other American crops, only tobacco and tomatoes have been of any great importance. Tobacco was used in Spain for snuff and for medicinal purposes in the early sixteenth century, although smoking tobacco seems to have been introduced into Europe by the English.[14] The tomato is indigenous to South America, but was grown in Mexico at an early date and was brought from there to Iberia between 1535 and 1554. It remained however little more than a curiosity until the nineteenth century, when cross pollination was developed and the modern form was bred. Europe now produces 40 per cent of the world's tomato output, mainly in the Mediterranean, whilst Latin America, the home of the crop, produces less than a fifth of this amount.[15]

By the seventeenth century Europe had most of the plants now grown. Two important exceptions, the cultivated grasses and legumes, and root crops, were bred from indigenous plants. Farmers in Classical times were aware that some wild plants gave better grazing than others, and lucerne was brought to Europe from Persia. Its value seems to have been forgotten, and it did not reappear as a cultivated crop until the sixteenth century in Spain, and from there it spread to Italy, France and Germany. In the sixteenth and seventeenth century cultivated grasses began to be grown in Italy, the Low Countries, and later in England. Timothy has a curious history, for the seed of cat's tail was taken from England to New England, and selected there for cultivation about 1700. Later it was popularised by Timothy Hanson, under whose name it eventually returned to England.[16]

Nearly all the cultivated grasses – some fifty out of 10 000 wild species – are indigenous to the Mediterranean and northern Eurasia (Fig. 6). Thus the development of cultivated grasses was important not only for Europe itself but also for European farming in the Americas, South Africa, Australia and New Zealand, which lacked suitable grasses and have had to import European seed. New Zealand is the example *par excellence*; perennial rye grass was introduced there from England in the 1880s and 1890s.[17]

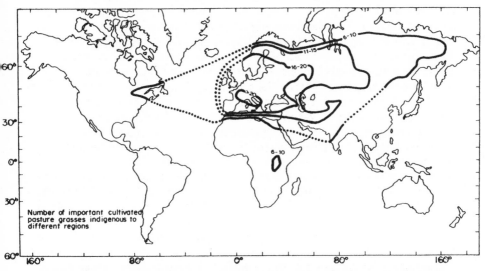

Fig. 6. Areas of origin of the major cultivated grasses. The numbers indicate the important cultivated pasture grasses indigenous to different regions. [Source: Hartley and Williams, 1956]

Beets were grown in the Mediterranean at least as early as the fifth century B.C., but the development of forage crops from *Beta vulgaris* and also from the brassica family, such as the turnip, mangel-wurzel and swede, did not come until the sixteenth century. The most important development from *Beta vulgaris* was the sugar-beet. Silesian forage beets with a sugar content of only 6–7 per cent were bred by Pierre Philippe de Vilmorin to a content of 20 per cent in the eighteenth century.[18]

Africa

Africa south of the Sahara had a limited range of crops when Europeans first arrived in the fifteenth century. The most important were *Sorghum vulgare* and a number of millets. In parts of West Africa the indigenous yams and African rice were grown. Bananas, the greater yam and Asiatic rice were also found. But after the discovery of the Americas two new food crops, manioc and maize, were introduced. Maize arrived in Africa by two routes. Introduced into Spain, it spread rapidly eastwards, and was taken by the Turks to Egypt in 1517, spreading from

31

there into the West African savanna. Maize was also taken from Brazil to the West African coast by the Portuguese. Both varieties arrived in West Africa between 1525 and 1535. By the late sixteenth century the crop was being grown in East Africa, and by the middle of the nineteenth century was grown throughout most of the continent.[19]

The sweet potato was introduced into West Africa in the sixteenth century, but it and the indigenous African yam lost ground to the greater yam. Although some authorities believe the Asian greater yam had arrived with the Indonesian migrants to Madagascar, and been carried north so that it was grown in West Africa before the arrival of Europeans, this is not certain. It is possible that the greater yam was brought to West Africa from the East Indies by the Portuguese, who valued its keeping qualities on long voyages. However it arrived, the greater yam is still a major crop but has been overtaken by manioc. Manioc was the principal food crop in Brazil when the Portuguese arrived in the sixteenth century and it probably reached Africa on slave ships. It was grown on the island of São Tomé in the late sixteenth century, and was known on the mainland by the early seventeenth century. But it spread slowly, partly because it was poisonous unless properly prepared. It is possible that freed Brazilian slaves brought South American methods of preparation to West Africa in the late eighteenth century. The crop reached its present range about 1850. It gives yields comparable to those of yams, but less has to be used in the propagation of the next crop, it needs less careful management, and will tolerate poorer soils and a lower rainfall than yams.[20]

The indigenous African rice (*Oryza glaberrima*) was grown in Africa west of the Ivory Coast from a very early date, both as swamp and upland rice. *Oryza sativa,* the Asian rice, was introduced by the Portuguese in the sixteenth century, but it was grown mainly as a dry crop and did not penetrate the interior. Not until the late nineteenth century were wet-rice methods of cultivation adopted in Sierra Leone.[21]

Food crops were on the whole adopted more rapidly in Africa than other crops. Groundnuts were brought from Brazil to West Africa in the sixteenth century, but it was not until the nineteenth-century demand for vegetable oils that it was widely grown; exports began in the 1840s. Cacao had long been grown in Mexico, and was used to make a bitter-tasting porridge. It was taken by the Portuguese to São Tomé in the seventeenth century, and was grown there and on Fernando Po in the nineteenth century, but it was not introduced to the Gold Coast until 1879.[22] Rubber was introduced to West Africa in the 1880s at much the same time as it was being introduced into South East Asia, but was not developed on any scale, although briefly important on the Gold Coast; it is still comparatively unimportant in Africa.

The late nineteenth and early twentieth centuries saw a number of plant introductions made by colonial governments to encourage the growing of cash crops amongst the indigenous population. Sisal was taken to Tanganyika in 1893, pyrethrum to Kenya in 1928, and the tung tree to Nyasaland in 1930.[23]

But perhaps the most interesting developments have been in coffee and cotton growing.

All three coffees are indigenous to Africa: *Coffea arabica* to Ethiopia, although it was first domesticated in the Yemen; *Coffea canephora* or *robusta* to the Congo basin, and *Coffea liberica* to the West African coast. There is little evidence that the shrubs were ever cultivated in Africa. The habit of coffee drinking spread through the Near East and Europe in the sixteenth and seventeenth centuries and *Coffea arabica* became an important cash crop in the European colonies in the West and East Indies. Although coffee trees were taken from Martinique to West Africa in the late eighteenth century, little came of this. The important re-introductions of *Coffea arabica* came in the late nineteenth century when it was introduced to Nyasaland in 1878, Kenya in 1895 and Uganda in 1900. *Coffea canephora* was not identified until the 1890s, when it was taken to Belgium and from there to Asia; it has subsequently been re-introduced into Africa where it is now the principal species grown.[24]

The history of cotton domestication remains remarkably complex. Cotton was being grown for lint in Egypt and the Sudan in early Christian times, but whether these cottons were of Indian or African origin is unclear. However American cottons were introduced into West Africa in the seventeenth century; most African cottons, with the exception of Egyptian cotton, which is derived from *Gossypium barbadense,* are derived from Upland cotton. The introduction of cotton into East Africa is comparatively recent; thus although Egyptian cotton was taken to Uganda in 1872, the modern industry dates from the introduction of Upland cotton in 1904.[25]

Asia

Asia provides an interesting contrast to Africa, where American food plants were rapidly and widely adopted, but where cash crops were tardily taken up. In contrast there have been few changes in the major food crops in Asia since 1500, whilst plantation crops have transformed much of South East Asia. American crops were brought to Asia by two routes; first via Europe and around the Cape; second, from Mexico to the Philippines. Within Asia there was interchange between India and China via Burma and Yunnan. The Indian sub-continent has been surprisingly little influenced by American plants, for although India has few indigenous crops, most of them being acquired from Africa, South West Asia or South East Asia, they were well established by 1500. Maize, chillies, tomatoes and sweet potatoes were brought by the Portuguese in the early sixteenth century, groundnuts in the late seventeenth century, potatoes and manioc in the late eighteenth century. None have become of significance except groundnuts, which since 1918 have become the major oil-bearing plant.

Coffee was first brought to India about 1600 and planted in the hills of Mysore, but never became important, although in Ceylon it became a major crop after its introduction by the Dutch in the late seventeenth century. Tobacco however was more rapidly adopted; it reached India in 1607 and Ceylon in 1610 and India now has a tenth of the world's area. Tea was probably indigenous to the mainland of South East Asia, but its cultivation was confined to China and Japan until the nineteenth century. It was introduced into Assam after the abolition of the East India Company's monopoly of the China tea trade in 1833, and into Ceylon in 1845. Tea of course has become a major crop in the subcontinent.

Ironically, although it was the Indian government that sponsored the attempt to acquire seeds of rubber (*Hevea brasiliensis*) from Brazil, those obtained by H. A. Wickham in 1876 were sent from Kew, not to India, but to Ceylon. From there seeds were sent to Singapore's botanical gardens, and were the basis of the great rubber industries of Malaya and the Dutch East Indies. India, in contrast, produces no more than 3 per cent of the world's natural rubber.[26]

Cotton was first domesticated in the Indus valley, but until the seventeenth century cottons were all perennial shrubs. However in the eighteenth century *Gossypium herbaceum persicum* spread from Iran into north-western India and from this were selected the first annuals. Upland cottons (*G. hirsutum latifolium*) are grown in southern India, having arrived from Mexico via the Philippines and Cambodia.[27]

China has been even less affected by the introduction of crops from outside. The importance of tea in Chinese life perhaps accounts for the negligible significance of coffee and cocoa, whilst rubber has never been grown in the country. Other American crops have been of significance however, particularly in southern China. Groundnuts were being grown south of the Yangtse by the 1530s, maize in Honan by the 1550s, and sweet potatoes were known in the 1560s. These crops proved particularly important in bringing into cultivation the southern hilly areas, above the lands suitable for wet-rice, in the seventeenth and eighteenth centuries. These crops arrived by two routes; overland from India, where they had been brought by the Portuguese, and from the Philippines and the Indies, where they had been brought both by the Portuguese from the West and the Spanish from the East. These food crops have become important supplementary foods, without however challenging the dominance of wheat and rice. Tobacco was introduced in 1608 and rapidly became an important cash crop; China now has the largest area in the world.[28]

South East Asia has been economically transformed by crops introduced from other areas, yet 70 per cent of the crop area is planted with crops indigenous to the region. This paradox is explained by the overwhelming importance of rice as a food crop throughout the region. However American crops, introduced by the Spanish and Portuguese in the sixteenth century, have been adopted as supplementary foods, particularly maize, although sweet potatoes, manioc and groundnuts are also grown.[29]

But it is the introduced plantation crops which have so changed South East Asia. Tobacco was the first commercial crop to be grown. It was brought to the Philippines by the Spanish in 1600, and was grown in Java in 1601. It spread to the mainland during the seventeenth century, and was the first plantation crop to be grown in Sumatra in the 1860s, and still remains important. Cocoa, in contrast, has never become significant. It was brought to the Philippines by the Spanish in the 1670s and by the Dutch to Ceylon and Java, and to Malaya in the eighteenth century, but American, or later African, supremacy was never challenged. It is now of negligible importance, as is coffee output, though coffee has played an important role in the past in South East Asia. *Coffea arabica* was taken by the Dutch from the Yemen to Java in 1654; cuttings made in Bogor were taken back to Amsterdam, and from there, via Paris, provided the first shrubs in the West Indies. Until the nineteenth century it was an important crop in Ceylon and Malaya, but in the 1870s the fungus *Hemileia vastatrix* destroyed much of the crop. There were two responses. Planters experimented with alternative crops, such as tea and rubber; but they also introduced different coffees. *Liberica* was imported into Java in 1876 and *robusta* in 1900, and the latter makes up the bulk of the still substantial Indonesian output. Tea has never assumed any great importance as an export crop, although Chinese tea plants were taken to Java by the Dutch in 1690, long before it was introduced into India or Ceylon. Nor did the re-introduction of Chinese types from Japan in 1824 or Assam types in 1878 lead to any substantial output.[30]

The most celebrated introductions into South East Asia have been of rubber and oil palm from America and Africa respectively. Rubber seeds were taken from Ceylon to Singapore in 1877, but they were not grown by planters until 1895. In Indonesia rubber was tapped in the 1860s, but from *Ficus elastica*, an Asian species; *Hevea brasiliensis* was not introduced into Sumatra until 1906. Seedlings from the botanical gardens reached Vietnam in 1897, Thailand in 1908 and the Philippines in 1928. The oil palm was introduced into Indonesia before rubber, but developed later. Seedlings were taken from Amsterdam to Bogor in 1848 and grown as decorative plants, but they were not grown in Sumatra for oil until 1911. Similarly the tree was introduced into Malaya as a decorative plant in 1875, but was not planted commercially until 1917.[31]

The Americas

The arrival of Europeans in the Americas in 1492, and the subsequent colonisation, not only led to the introduction of Old World plants, but to the dispersal of American crops, hitherto confined to limited regions, to other parts of the continent. Wheat was taken by Columbus to Hispaniola, but it had little success until the drier uplands of Mexico and Peru were reached. The other northern European grains, rye, oats and barley, were little grown except in the colder Andean areas. Asian rice, which was grown in Spain in the fifteenth century, was introduced into the Indies in 1512, but was not important until the late nineteenth century, when Indian emigrants to the sugar plantations established wet-rice cultivation in British Guiana. In Brazil, where most of Latin America's rice is produced, it is grown as a dry-land crop, generally by slash and burn methods.[32]

The slave trade led to the early exchange of crops between Brazil, the Indies and West Africa, for not only were crops such as yams used to feed the slaves in transit, but they were allowed scraps of land on the plantations to provide for themselves. In this way the greater yam, *Sorghum vulgare*, pearl millet, cowpeas and colocasia reached Brazil and the Indies, but none has become of major significance.[33]

Both the Spanish and the Portuguese took the characteristic Mediterranean crops with them – the grape vine, figs, olives and citrus fruits. The olive however never became well-established in the Americas and current output is small outside Chile and Argentina. Viticulture also had a chequered history. Early efforts to produce wine in the Indies, Mexico and Peru were largely a failure. By the 1560s only Peru produced a surplus. The Spanish government saw this as a threat to home production and tried to discourage it. The result was that wine production was confined to areas remote from official eyes, such as in northern Mexico. Important wine industries have developed only in California, Chile and Argentina, in the last two areas largely as a result of heavy immigration from Mediterranean countries in the last 100 years. Viticulture was introduced into California by missionaries whilst it was still part of Mexico; the earliest references date from 1769, but the modern industry really dates from the introduction of European cuttings in 1857.[34]

By the fifteenth century citrus fruit were well established in the Mediterranean: these, and particularly the orange, were more easily established in the West Indies and the mainland than was viticulture. Citrus fruit were introduced into Mexico in 1518 and Brazil in 1540. To the imported citrus fruit were later added the pineapple, a native of Brazil, and the grapefruit, a crossbreed of the pummelo and the orange, which first appeared in Jamaica in the late eighteenth century. Although the Bahia navel was first selected in Brazil, and in the nineteenth century spread to most citrus-growing areas, it was the Spanish who played the major role in spreading citrus fruit in the Americas. Missionaries established the first orange grove in California in 1798. Oranges were taken to Florida and the Carolinas in the sixteenth century, whilst the grapefruit was brought to Florida from Cuba in 1809.[35]

The Portuguese grew sugar-cane, bananas and rice in their island possessions off the African coast, and had used Negro slaves both there and at home. Not surprisingly both these crops and also slavery were soon introduced into the Americas. Columbus is reputed to have taken sugar-cane from the Canaries on his second voyage, and although these first cuttings were not successful, sugar was being manufactured on Hispaniola in 1509 and the first American sugar reached Spain in 1512. The crop was later taken to Cuba, Puerto Rico, Mexico and Peru. Peru was exporting sugar to Europe by the late sixteenth century. Sugar-cane spread rapidly, for not only was it planted by Spaniards but it was also adopted by the Indians. Sugar-cane was introduced into Brazil in 1532 and here the plantation system matured, spreading in the seventeenth century to the English settlements on the West Indian islands. The first canes grown in America, called 'Creole', came from the Canaries and were thin and low-yielding. In 1768 the French explorer Bougainville discovered 'Noble' canes in Tahiti and took them to Réunion, from where they were taken to the French West Indies in 1792. A year later Captain Bligh brought Noble canes to Jamaica, and this higher-yielding species soon displaced Creole throughout the Indies.[36]

It has been argued that bananas were grown in the Americas before Columbus, but it seems more likely that they were taken from the Canaries to Hispaniola in 1516, and later introduced into Brazil from São Tomé. In Brazil and some other countries they became an important subsistence food, although largely confined to humid lowland areas, but it was not until the 1850s that bananas were exported, from Jamaica to Boston.[37]

The early settlers in Brazil, the West Indies and the British colonies in North America relied heavily upon tobacco and sugar as exports. But the crop which was to become of such importance in Central and South America did not arrive until 1718. In 1706 coffee plants from Indonesia were taken to Amsterdam, and later presented to Louis XIV. Progeny of these trees then found their way to French and Dutch possessions all over the world. It was introduced into Surinam in 1718, Martinique in 1720, French Guinea in 1722, Jamaica in 1730 and Cuba in 1748. By the 1780s it was being grown in Central America in Guatemala and El Salvador, and had spread to Venezuela, Bolivia, Panama and Columbia by 1790. Coffee growing spread from Surinam into northern Brazil in 1727, Rio de Janeiro in 1775, São Paulo in 1782 and Bahia in 1787.[38]

The arrival of Europeans in the Americas led not only to the introduction of Old World crops, but to the wider dispersal of some indigenous crops within the continent. Cocoa, for example, although indigenous to the Andean slopes of the Amazon basin, was only grown in Mexico at the time of the Conquest. The Spanish however introduced it into Trinidad in the early sixteenth century, and the Dutch brought it to Surinam in the later seventeenth century, whilst in the eighteenth century it began to be grown in Venezuela, Brazil and Ecuador.[39]

Cotton was grown for textiles in Mexico and Peru at a very early date, its domestication being independent of that in India. Two American cottons proved to be of particular importance in the eighteenth century. *Gossypium hirsutum latifolium* was found in Chiapis in Mexico, but in the eighteenth century was taken into the southern United States, and from this was bred Upland cotton. *G. barbadense* was introduced into the Sea Islands off South Carolina in about 1786 from Jamaica. This high-quality cotton formed the basis for modern Egyptian cotton.[40]

Rubber, although indigenous to the Americas, has played a very small role in the agricultural history of the continent. The Aztecs obtained rubber from *Castilla*, not *Hevea brasiliensis*, and it was only the destruction of the former that turned attention to *Hevea*, which was native to South America. The growth of the motor car industry gave rise to a boom in the tapping of wild trees in Brazil in the 1890s, but the industry did not spread to other countries in Latin America nor could Brazil compete with the plantations of South East Asia.[41]

North America

North America has no important indigenous crops and thus all those grown there now are introductions. Maize, squash and beans were grown as far north as the Great Lakes when Europeans first arrived to settle the eastern seaboard, and maize was soon adopted by them and remains a major crop.[42] Other crops came from two directions; either brought by settlers from north-western Europe, or from the West Indies and Central America to the South East and the South West.

The Spanish settled California and the South West in the eighteenth century, and were responsible for the introduction of wheat, viticulture and citrus, whilst they also took citrus fruit to Florida. The southern English colonies also acquired crops from the Caribbean, many brought by slaves who came from the West Indies to Virginia, the Carolinas and Georgia. Groundnuts and manioc were both introduced into the South East in the early seventeenth century. Perhaps the most important early introduction was that of tobacco. *Nicotania rustica* was grown and smoked by the Indians of the east coast, but it was *N. tabacum* which was the basis of the early Virginian industry. Seeds of this were brought to Virginia from Trinidad, via England. Potatoes were another American crop which reached North America via Britain, for the first potatoes planted in South Carolina in 1674 came from Ireland. Asian rice was introduced into the Carolinas from Madagascar in 1694 and Egypt in 1712. American cottons, as was noted earlier, were all acquired from Mexico and the West Indies in the eighteenth century.[43] Thus the early debt of American agriculture to Central America and the West Indies was considerable. But more important have been the crops which have been brought from north-western Europe. A generation after the arrival of the Pilgrim Fathers virtually all the common crops of England were grown in New England. The first wheats did not thrive in New England, and the settlers turned to maize. But a variety of wheats were available by the nineteenth century, for the Spanish had introduced wheat to California, whilst in 1863 Russian immigrants brought durum wheat to North Dakota and later Russian immigrants took hard red winter wheats to Central Kansas in 1873.[44]

When the first settlers arrived in New England, the value of roots and temporary grasses was little understood in north-western Europe, and root crops, except for the sugar-beet, have never been of much importance in American agriculture. Seeds from hay used to feed cattle on the early crossings grew in the new environment and spread so rapidly that by the end of the seventeenth century many of these grasses were thought to be indigenous. Lucerne, now of such importance in America, had a chequered history. In the sixteenth century Spain was one of the few countries where it was grown, and it was established by the Spanish in Peru, and found its way to California in the eighteenth century. In 1736 it had been introduced to Georgia from the West Indies. But neither of these varieties would tolerate the cold winters of the interior, and it was not until a German immigrant brought cold-resistant varieties to Minnesota in 1857 that it could be grown there.[45] One recent crop introduction should be noted. The soy bean was brought to the United States from China in 1804, but was not commercially exploited on any scale until the 1920s; but within two decades the United States had replaced China as the leading producer.[46]

Australia, New Zealand and the Pacific Islands

Australia and New Zealand, like North America, had no indigenous plants of any value, and their modern crops are all introductions. The first settlers arrived in 1788 via Tenerife, Rio de Janeiro and Cape Town and carried with them not only crops grown in England but a wide variety of tropical plants.[47] Few of these early introductions flourished in their new environment. Bananas, grapes, sugarcane, cotton, rice and citrus fruits were all grown in the first thirty years of settlement, but few survived. Thus the first grape vines were planted in 1789, but the modern wine industry only got under way when cuttings from South Africa and Spain were introduced in the 1840s. English wheats were not satisfactory and the wheat industry awaited the introduction of Mediterranean varieties.[48]

New Zealand, like Australia, had no indigenous crop plants, although the Maori brought with them taro and sweet potatoes. Between Cook's arrival in 1769 and the first formal settlement in 1840 there were numerous visitors who grew crops, the seed of some being used by the Maori. By the 1840s most common English crops were grown. But the most important introduction, cultivated grasses, came later.[49]

The Pacific islands of Polynesia, Micronesia and Melanesia remained isolated until the sixteenth century, and the crops grown there, with the exception of sweet potatoes, remained those of the South East Asian roots complex. Rice did not spread into the islands, with the interesting exceptions of Guam and the Marianas.[50] The first European contacts were made by the Spanish who introduced American crops into Guam and the Marquesas, which lay on the galleon route between Acapulco and Manila,[51] but contacts with the other island groups were delayed until the explorations of Cook and Bougainville in the eighteenth century. Subsequently maize and manioc were widely adopted, without however displacing the indigenous crops. More successful was the introduction of tropical crops for export, particularly after the annexation of many of the islands in the later nineteenth century. But although sugar-cane, bananas, coffee, cocoa, rubber and citrus fruits have all been tried with varying degrees of success, the most important cash crop remains coconuts, which were brought from the Malaysian archipelago by the first migrants.[52]

The dispersal of livestock

It is even more difficult to define the 'domestication' of animals than the domestication of plants. Many prehistorians now believe that man lived in a symbiotic relationship with herding animals in the Pleistocene, and also that the transition to 'domestication' took place in several parts of the Old World, not simply in South West Asia.[53]

All modern cattle are descendants of *Bos primigenius*, the wild auroch, which in the early Neolithic was found in most of Europe, North Africa and South West Asia. The first archaeological evidence of domesticated cattle is from Greece and is dated at 8500 B.C. or 6500 B.C.[54] By the fifth and fourth millennia B.C. most of the excavated sites in the East Mediterranean and South West Asia have evidence of cattle, and cattle had diffused, or been domesticated independently, in North Africa and Europe. A second type of domesticated cattle appears in the archaeological record in the third millennium B.C., *Bos brachyceros*, with a different-shaped head and shorter horns. *Bos brachyceros*, once believed to be a sub-species of *Bos primigenius*, is now thought to be a result of selection amongst domesticated *Bos primigenius* in isolation from stocks of wild aurochs.[55] Thus the distinction between longhorns and shorthorns is of considerable antiquity.

The first cattle to enter Egypt, about 5000 B.C., and migrate westwards along the North African coast, were longhorns. They entered Spain and were also brought to coastal areas of western Europe. Among modern descendants of this type are the Highland cattle of Scotland, whilst longhorned cattle were taken by the Spanish and Portuguese to the Americas in the sixteenth century. Until the nineteenth century most cattle in the Americas – including the Texas Longhorn – were descendants of these animals. This early diffusion of longhorns from South West Asia also reached the savannas of West Africa. However in the third millennium shorthorns or *Bos brachyceros* followed the same routes.

In western Europe the Jersey and Guernsey cattle are descendants of these cattle. In North Africa and West Africa they largely displaced the earlier longhorns. In West Africa the N'dama, or West African Shorthorn, is a descendant of this migration.[56]

Cattle entered Europe through the Balkans, but it is increasingly thought that there were independent domestications in Europe. Both *Bos primigenius* and *Bos brachyceros* are found in Iron Age sites in Europe, and some modern breeds may be traced back to this early division. Thus, for example, modern Shorthorns, Red Danish and Brown Swiss are descendants of *Bos brachyceros*, and the Homagira breed of Italy of *Bos primigenius*.[57]

Although all cattle are thought to be descendants of *Bos primigenius*, a distinction is usually made between European cattle, *Bos taurus*, and the Zebu cattle of the tropics, *Bos indicus*. The latter are humped, and as there is no evidence of a wild species with a hump, it is thought to be a post-domestication feature. Zebu first appeared in India in the fourth millennium B.C. From there they spread into South West Asia and Africa, and east into South East and East Asia, so that most modern cattle in the tropics are of zebu origin (Fig. 7). Zebu were found in South West Asia in the fourth millennium. Three waves of zebu now made their way into Africa. The first, from Syria, reached only into Egypt and no further; thus North African cattle remain humpless, being largely descended from *brachyceros*. A second wave reached North East Africa from India via southern Arabia. Here they bred with *Bos primigenius* to give the modern zebu, which has a neck hump, and with *brachyceros*, to give the sanga, with a chest or neck hump. Zebu continued to be brought into North East Africa, especially by the Arabs after the seventh century A.D. The sanga and the zebu were carried south, and modern Afrikander cattle are descendants of these cattle. By the fifteenth century A.D. they had reached the West African savannas, but not North Africa. Most cattle in Africa south of the Sahara are zebu crosses, but not those in Egypt or North Africa.[58]

Cattle, sheep and goats from South West Asia spread to northern China early in the Chinese Neolithic and the cattle of northern China are still of South West Asian origin, whereas cattle in southern China are a cross between *brachyceros* and zebu, which came from India at an early but unknown date. Similar crosses predominate in the Philippines and eastern Indo-China, but in contrast the cattle of Burma, Malaya and Indonesia are largely zebu in origin. This latter area corresponds very closely to the parts of South East Asia where milking is practised, which were influenced by Hindu civilisation in the early modern period, in contrast to Vietnam, where Chinese civilisation has been preponderant, and milking is not practised. When Europeans first arrived in Polynesia the only livestock kept were pigs and poultry. Cattle have been introduced only subsequently.[59]

The Americas had no important domesticated animals before the arrival of Europeans, but cattle, sheep and goats were brought to the Indies by Columbus on his second voyage, and multiplied rapidly. Cattle were soon introduced into Mexico, and by the end of the sixteenth century the ranching industry had been established in the North. The cattle were longhorns from Spain, and they were taken into New Mexico and Texas in the early seventeenth century and California in the eighteenth century. In the North the seventeenth-century settlers brought cattle from North West Europe, but the modern cattle of the United States are for the most part not descendants of either of these types, but of improved breeds, subsequently imported from North West Europe in the nineteenth century. Herefords were first brought in 1817, but only late in the century did they replace the Texas Longhorns. Brown Swiss were brought to the United States in 1869, Friesians between 1875 and 1885 and the Aberdeen Angus in 1873. In Latin America cattle were mainly longhorns from Spain and Portugal, and they have not been replaced by improved North European breeds, except in Uruguay and Argentina, where Herefords, Shorthorns and Aberdeen Angus were introduced in the late nineteenth century. In Brazil however Indian zebu were imported between 1870 and 1920, and there is now a large element of zebu in the cattle of southern and central Brazil, whilst in the southern United States there are crosses between zebu and shorthorns.[60]

In most of the tropics cattle act as draught animals, but the water buffalo is an important auxiliary in South, East and South East Asia. It was domesticated in India about 3000 B.C., and was known in Mesopotamia by 2500 B.C.; its further progress westwards was slow for it was first known in the Jordan valley only by the eighth century A.D., in the Balkans by A.D. 1200 and in Egypt at about the same time. Its progress eastwards from India was far more rapid, and the water buffalo is an important draught animal in southern China, Thailand, the Philippines, Indonesia, India and Pakistan. In areas of Indian influence it is often milked, indeed in India water buffalo provide more milk than cattle. As a draught animal it is particularly useful in rice-growing areas. Outside Asia it is of little importance except in parts of the Balkans and the Near East.[61]

Sheep and goats were domesticated before cattle and pigs and the earliest village sites in South West Asia all have bones of these two animals. Four species of wild sheep were found in Eurasia in the tenth millennium B.C. The most likely progenitor of modern sheep is the ural, which suggests that domestication may have taken place in the steppes of Central Asia, near the Aral and Caspian seas, but it now seems certain that the domestication of sheep took place independently in several places in south-eastern Europe, south-western and central Asia.[62] Wild goats were also widely distributed throughout Europe, North Africa and western Asia, but the most likely ancestor of the modern goat is the beozar, which was confined to South West Asia. Some wild goats in northern India may, however, have contributed to South Asian breeds.[63] Sheep and goats were taken by the early agriculturalists east into China, west into Europe and Africa, and south east into India. They were widely distributed in the Old World by early Christian times, but were not, of course, found in the Americas.

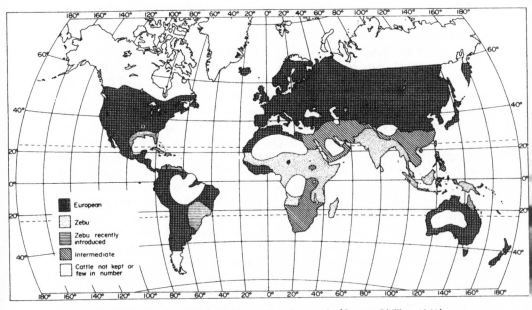

Fig. 7. Distribution of the major types of modern cattle. [Source: Phillips, 1961]

Sheep bones are found in the earliest sites in Egypt, and sheep diffused westwards into the Maghreb and also southwards into West Africa. Two important sub-types evolved in these areas. The merino has its origins in North Africa, but its wool-bearing capacity was developed in Spain. The date of its introduction into Spain is uncertain; it is possible that it was brought to Spain from Carthage just before the birth of Christ, but it may not have been introduced until the Arabs arrived in Spain in the seventh century A.D. The merino was confined to Spain until the sixteenth century, when it was taken to Latin America, where the unimproved merino is the dominant breed except in the West Indies, Columbia and Brazil.

The sheep which had spread southwards into the West African savannas at an early date evolved into a number of distinct breeds. One of these, the long-legged guinea sheep, was hairy rather than woolly, and it was this animal which was taken by the Portuguese to Brazil and by the Spanish to the West Indies in the sixteenth century.[64]

It was not until the eighteenth century that the merino was established in Europe outside Spain. Two important introductions were made at the end of the century. In 1791 a merino flock was established at George III's farm at Windsor. It did not flourish and was discontinued in 1810, but not before members of the flock had been taken to Cape Colony; it was from there that John McArthur obtained merinos for his farm in New South Wales. Merino flocks were also established in France under royal patronage in 1786 and 1799, from which was developed the Rambouillet breed later widely introduced into European-settled areas overseas in the nineteenth century.[65]

Merinos continue to account for a high proportion of all the world's sheep, and it was not until the later nineteenth century that English breeds began to play a role in overseas development. The merino was largely a wool producer and

TABLE 3   *The regional distribution of livestock (per cent of world total in each region)*

	Cattle	Pigs	Sheep	Goats	Buffaloes
Northern Europe	10	19.2	9.6	0.1	0.07
Mediterranean Europe	2.5	3.5	8.2	5.2	0.2
South West Asia	3.3	0.2	14.1	14.4	1.5
Africa	12.6	1.1	10.9	25.1	1.4[a]
India	22.5	0.9	6.2	21.4	54.6
South East Asia	2.4	4.9	0.3	3.5	16.4
China	6.2	39.7	8.2	15.4	25.2
Polynesia	0.3	0.5	0.01	–	–
North America	12.6	11.2	2.89	1.1	–
Latin America	24.9	18.8	15.8	12.3	0.8[b]
Australasia	2.6	0.5	24.7	–	–

[a] Egypt only   [b] Brazil and Trinidad
Source: F.A.O. *Production yearbook*, vol. 23, 1969

adapted to warm, dry conditions. When sheep that would give mutton and wool were needed, and also where cool and moist climates prevailed, English varieties, notably the Lincoln, Southdown and Leicester, were crossbred with merinos, particularly in Argentina and New Zealand.[66]

The wild boar, *Sus scrofa*, was found throughout much of Eurasia and was independently domesticated in Europe, Russia and China. By origin a forest animal, it did not penetrate into the drier regions of Africa or the Mediterranean in any numbers, and later religious taboos kept it unimportant in South West Asia. Indeed it has only remained of major importance in the areas of its original domestication. Nine-tenths of the world's pigs are to be found in China, northern Europe and the Americas (Table 3).

CHAPTER 4

TECHNICAL AND ECONOMIC CHANGES IN AGRICULTURE

Although certain types of agriculture have an ancestry which can be traced back to the Neolithic, others are a product of the profound economic, technical and demographic changes which have taken place since the late eighteenth century. Thus although dairying, ranching and large-scale grain production can be traced well back into agricultural history, their modern forms date only from the last hundred years.

Of greatest significance has been the growth of world population (Table 1). Until the seventeenth century world population had increased very slowly, but from then onwards it accelerated in nearly every part of the world. Until 1920 the rate of increase was highest in Europe and the areas of European settlement overseas; since 1920 mortality rates have declined in Africa, Asia and Latin America, and the rate of increase in these regions now not only exceeds that in the European-settled areas, but exceeds the rate at which they increased in the nineteenth century. One consequence has been a great increase in the cultivated area since the middle of the nineteenth century (Table 4), not only in the established agricultural civilisations of Europe, India and East Asia but in the hitherto sparsely settled areas of Russia, North America, Argentina, Australia, New Zealand, South Africa and Manchuria. Except in the latter area the colonisation of these areas was undertaken by people who migrated from Europe. The flow of European migrants abroad – mainly to the Americas and South Africa – was small until the nineteenth century. But between 1850 and 1960 over 60 000 000 left Europe (Table 5). The only comparable migrations

TABLE 4   *The arable area in selected regions, 1870–1960*
       (million hectares)

	1870	1910	1960
Europe	141.4	147.4	151.5
China	81.6	91.7	113.1
India and Pakistan	68.6	85.8	151.5
North America	80.8	154.3	183.4
Argentina and Uruguay	0.4	28.2	24.2
Australia	0.4	4.4	11.7
	373 2	512.8	635.4

Sources: Robertson, 1956; and see Tables 11, 14, 29, 31, 43, 46, 48

Table 5 *Migration to recently settled areas, 1851–1960 (millions)*

	1851–60	1861–70	1871–80	1881–90	1891–1900	1901–10	1911–20	1921–30	1931–40	1941–50	1951–60
U.S.A.	2.5	2.1	2.4	4.8	3.6	8.6	4.7	2.7	0.4	0.8	1.6
Canada	–	0.29	0.22	0.35	0.23	0.94	1.15	0.98	0.82	0.41	1.46
Argentina	0.02	0.16	0.26	0.84	0.64	1.76	1.20	1.39	0.31	0.46	0.53
Brazil	0.12	0.09	0.21	0.52	1.12	0.67	0.79	0.84	0.23	0.13	0.59
Australia	–	0.16	0.19	0.38	0.02	0.04	0.20	0.31	0.03	0.36	0.81
New Zealand	0.03	0.06	0.14	0.06	0.03	0.08	0.09	0.11	0.03	0.05	0.22
South Africa	n.a.	n.a.	n.a.	n.a.	n.a.	n.a.	0.07	0.10	0.05	0.09	0.11
Asiatic Russia	0.19	0.25	0.24	0.41	1.20	2.2	0.91	0.50	–	–	9.2
Uruguay	n.a.	0.08	0.11	0.14	0.09	0.02	0.05	0.02	0.05	–	0.05

Source: Woodruff, 1966, 108; all figures gross except for Australia

were, first, of the Chinese north into Manchuria and south into South East Asia in the late nineteenth and early twentieth centuries; and, second, of Africans to the Americas. Between the sixteenth century and the mid-nineteenth century approximately 10 000 000 slaves were taken to the Americas.[1]

These migrations had many consequences; they directly led to the great expansion of new cropland in the interior of the Americas and Russia, and provided labour for the industrialisation of the United States and later other overseas areas. Industrialisation got under way in Britain in the late eighteenth century and spread first to western Europe and later to the European areas overseas. By the late nineteenth century a substantial proportion of the population of western Europe was employed in industry and living in towns. In 1800 no more than 2.5 per cent of the world's population lived in towns of 20 000 or more, but by 1900 there were 10 per cent, most of whom were in western Europe and the eastern United States, forming a 'world metropolis'. For the first time a large proportion of the world's population did not provide their own food, and this accelerated the commercialisation of agriculture in many parts of the world.[2]

One consequence was a great increase in trade in food-stuffs; in the 1850s world exports of foodstuffs were less than 4 000 000 metric tons, but this had quadrupled by the 1880s and by the eve of the First World War the figure was nearly 40 000 000 metric tons (Table 6).

TABLE 6   *Volume of exports of food products, 1854–8 to 1962–6 (million metric tons)*

	1854–8	1884–8	1901–13	1924–8	1934–8	1952–6	1962–6
Wheat	2.5	9.5	19.6	23.8	17.3	27.1	54.4
Rye	0.3	2.0	2.3	1.9	0.9	1.3	4.5
Barley	0.3	1.9	5.5	3.4	2.6	5.9	6.8
Oats	0.2	1.4	3.0	1.6	0.8	1.5	1.3
Maize	0.5	2.5	6.8	8.4	10.0	5.3	22.3
Beef and veal	0.03	0.1	0.6	1.2	0.9	0.9	1.4
Pork, bacon and ham	0.04	0.3	0.4	0.6	0.5	0.5	0.8
Mutton and lamb	–	0.02	0.2	0.2	0.3	0.4	0.5
Butter	0.03	0.1	0.3	0.4	0.6	0.4	0.6
	3.9	17.82	38.7	41.5	33.9	43.3	92.6

Sources: R. M. Stern, *Kyklos*, **13**, 1960, 58–61; F.A.O. *Trade yearbook*, vol. 22, 1968

Most of the trade was between western Europe – particularly Britain – and the European-settled areas overseas, particularly the United States. The trade in food products was[3] partly a result of Britain's inability to feed her growing urban population; but it was also a result of greater prosperity. Real income per caput grew steadily in western Europe and the European areas overseas in the second half of the nineteenth century, and this led to a growing demand for meat, milk, fruit and vegetables, as well as products such as coffee, cocoa and tea which had hitherto been luxuries. Annual British consumption of tea for example was 0.8 kg per head in 1850 but 2.9 kg in 1900.[4]

Nor did economic growth affect food products alone, for early industrialisation was based upon textiles, and this prompted not only the expansion of cotton growing in the United States – and during the American Civil War in many other parts of the world – but also wool production in Australia and Argentina, and jute in India. Later other agricultural products entered international trade. Vegetable oils for soap, candles, lubricants and margarine began to be important in the later nineteenth century, prompting the increased cultivation of groundnuts, oil-palms and coconuts, and towards the end of the century demand from the motor-car and electrical industries led to the spectacular growth of rubber plantations in South East Asia.[5]

The commercialisation of agriculture in the nineteenth century and the growth of new agricultural regions would have been impossible without substantial improvements in transport and the consequent reduction of freight rates. Until the middle of the nineteenth century the most common form of land transport was by ox or horse-drawn cart, and the cost of moving agricultural produce limited trade to high-value products such as silk, wool, spices, wines, tobacco and sugar unless water transport was available. Thus, for example, in the 1830s the cost of moving one ton of goods from Salta to Buenos Aires – about 1600 km – was thirteen times the cost of shipping one ton from Buenos Aires to Liverpool. In the first half of the century there was little reduction in land freights, but oceanic freight rates moved downwards, and fell again in the later nineteenth century when steam began to replace sail, steel was substituted for wood and the size of ships increased (Fig. 8). In the later part of the century the decline in oceanic freight rates was greatest on long hauls; whereas the freight on a bushel of wheat from New York to Liverpool was 21 cents in 1873, it had fallen to 3 cents by 1901, and over the same period freights on wool from Australia to England were halved.[6]

The fall in land freight rates was even more spectacular as the railway spread in the second half of the century. The railway was faster and cheaper than the cart; rail freights fell throughout the century. In 1873 it cost 34 cents to send a bushel of wheat from Chicago to New York, but by 1905 only 8 cents. In the later nineteenth century the spread of the railway promoted the expansion of farming in North America, southern Brazil, Argentina, Australia and Siberia.[7]

The development of trade in animal products other than wool was slower, for it awaited advances in refrigeration and canning. Cattle could of course be marketed on the hoof, although they lost value on the journey. A trade in live cattle existed between Britain, Argentina and the United States, but the numbers involved were not great. The introduction of refrigeration and canning altered this. In the 1860s ice-boxes were used on American railways to transport meat, and refrigerated cars were common by the 1880s, so that dressed meat rather than live cattle could be moved. The meat canning industry was established in the

Mid-West in the early 1870s, and again reduced the weight to be moved. Refrigeration was subsequently introduced into ships, and the first chilled beef reached England from New York in 1875, and Le Havre from Buenos Aires in 1877. Frozen meat, kept at −10°C as against −1°C for chilled meat, reached London from Australia in 1879 and from New Zealand in 1882. The application of refrigeration to dairy products came a little later, but by the 1890s New Zealand butter was reaching London. In 1901 the first refrigerated banana boat left Jamaica for England.[8]

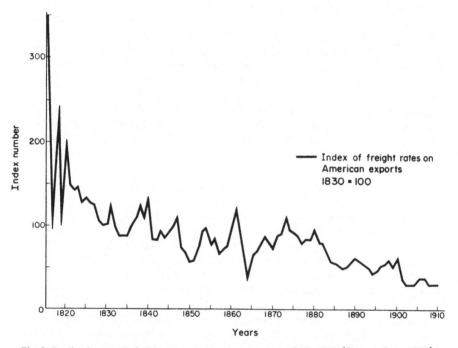

Fig. 8. Decline in oceanic freight rates on American exports, 1815–1910. [Source: Peet, 1969]

The remarkable growth of the world economy in the nineteenth century was the result of British and later western European industrialisation, and its diffusion to European areas overseas. European immigrants provided much of the labour for economic growth overseas, and Europe also provided most of the foreign investment. Until 1870 Britain, by far the most important source of capital, was mainly concerned with investment in Europe, and particularly in railways. After 1870 there was a significant shift in new investment which went to the temperate, European-settled areas in North America, Chile, Argentina, Uruguay, southern Brazil, South Africa, Australia and New Zealand. Very little went into tropical

49

territories, in spite of the British, French and German imperial acquisitions in the later nineteenth century. Direct investment in agriculture was small, for most of the capital went into railways and other forms of infra-structure. Such direct investment as there was in agriculture went into plantations in the colonies and pastoral companies in the United States, Australia and Argentina.[9]

From the middle of the nineteenth century agriculture became increasingly 'industrialised'; farmers began to buy more and more inputs from industry, not only farm machinery, which had once been made by local craftsmen, but fertilisers, coal for steam-driven threshers, and oil-cake to feed cattle. Agricultural products were increasingly processed in factories rather than on the farm or in local small-scale plants. This was especially true of the dairy industry. Between 1860 and 1910 cheese – and to a lesser extent butter – production was transferred from the farm to the factory, whilst the fluid milk industry was transformed by the introduction of the railway, cooling apparatus, pasteurisation, the milk bottle and the rise of large wholesale milk companies.[10] Some agricultural products were only profitable after mechanical advances in the processing industries had been made. Thus cotton lint could not be economically separated from the seed until Eli Whitney's gin was adopted. The grindstone was replaced by rollers in flour mills in Hungary in 1840; this method reached the United States in the 1870s and allowed the cultivation of hard wheats, which could not be milled by the old methods.[11]

The remarkable changes in economic conditions in the nineteenth century were not matched by advances in agricultural technology except in the United States, Canada, parts of north-western Europe and Australia. Indeed the pace of technological change in farming has always been remarkably slow. This is partly because most of the basic implements and methods of farming were known at a very early date and subsequent agricultural progress has been a matter of the wider adoption of techniques known to a minority of farmers, and the slow improvement of implements such as the plough. Radical changes were few until recently.

The earliest farmers in South West Asia and China, and probably South East Asia, relied upon hoes and digging sticks to till and plant, and had reaping knives and sickles with which to gather the crop. The same implements were known in Africa at an early date, but not in the Americas, where the hoe was unknown until the arrival of Europeans, or in Polynesia where the digging stick was the major implement. Axes were used by all farmers to clear vegetation, and fire was a universal method of clearing undergrowth. The introduction of the plough was thus a fundamental advance. It appeared in Mesopotamia in the fourth millennium B.C. and by the later part of the first millennium B.C. was in use in the major agricultural civilisations, with three exceptions: Africa, south of the Sahara, where it still remains uncommon and the hoe is the major implement; the Americas, where it was unknown until the arrival of the Europeans; and Polynesia (Fig 9).

The earliest ploughs – generally described as *ards* – were very simple. They were made of wood and had a beam, stilt and sole. In the late part of the first millennium B.C. iron shares became common in the Mediterranean and in China. The *ard* was drawn by two yoked oxen; it did little more than scratch the soil, and to ensure the preparation of an adequate seed bed, cross-ploughing was practised, a technique which also helped to conserve soil moisture. Many different varieties of the *ard* evolved, but it has remained the basic implement in southern Europe, North Africa, South West Asia, South East Asia, India and East Asia.[12]

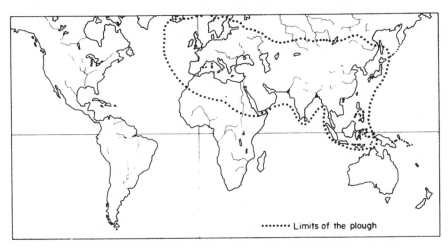

•••••••• Limits of the plough

Fig. 9. Distribution of the plough in pre-modern times. [Source: Isaac, 1970, 41]

By classical times farmers had a variety of other implements to help them. A primitive seed drill was attached to some early ploughs in Mesopotamia, and was found in China in Han times, but never seems to have developed, although it spread from South West Asia into India. Broadcasting remained the dominant method of sowing in China, India and Europe until the nineteenth century, when the seed drill was widely adopted in Europe, although in parts of Asia rice was transplanted. In the Americas maize was planted in hills with the help of a digging stick and the *coa*, a digging stick with a wide blade. In Latin America the wooden *ard* was introduced from Andalusia by the Spanish, and the hoe and *machete* were adopted by the Indians. In North America the plough remained less important than the hoe until the nineteenth century.[13]

Farmers in the Mediterranean region, India and China all had primitive harrows, although thorn bushes often sufficed, hoes for weeding, rakes, forks and spades. The hoe and the spade were particularly important in northern China and Japan, and were never completely replaced by the *ard*, whilst in parts of north-western Europe the spade has a long history.[14]

Other farming techniques were known to Old World farmers in classical times. The value of green manuring was known if not understood. Animal manure was spread on the fields, and the folding of sheep on stubble and the stall feeding of cattle were practised by some farmers. In East Asia human as well as cattle dung was used, as it was by the Incas; intensive practices such as double cropping and intertillage were known. Indeed double cropping was also practised in South West Asia, but only in the irrigated river valleys of the Nile and Mesopotamia. Much of the early farming took place in semi-arid areas and the value of an alternating fallow to conserve soil moisture was well known. Marl and lime were used as fertilisers in parts of Europe. Terracing of steep slopes was found not only in the Old World, but also in Mexico and Peru, whilst irrigation was also a widely practised technique. The *shaduf*, the *noria* and the *saqiya* were known in northern China, northern India and South West Asia in the early centuries of the Christian period. In short, many implements and techniques of farming were known in the classical period if not before, although it is not clear how widely they were practised.[15]

By the early centuries of the Christian period the great agricultural civilisations of northern China, northern India, southern Europe and South West Asia were on a par technically.[16] Between classical times and the Age of Discovery the greatest innovations came in northern Europe. The first ploughs used in northern Europe were *ards*, which were not very successful on the cold heavy clays. The major advance in the first millennium A.D. was the development of the heavy plough, which had a coulter to cut the turf and a mouldboard to turn it. Later wheels were attached to the plough. The origin of the heavy plough is still a matter of dispute. Coulters and mouldboards seem to have existed in Roman times, although it was not until the end of the millennium that the heavy plough was widely adopted in northern Europe, drawn by four or more oxen. The plough allowed the cultivation of heavy soils, and by forming ridges made drainage easier. The last half of the first millennium A.D. saw the appearance of the three-field system. In the Mediterranean one winter crop was sown in alternation with a bare fallow; a summer crop was impossible because of the lack of rainfall. In northern Europe summer rain was sufficient to allow a spring sown crop, and gradually a rotation of winter corn, fallow and spring corn replaced the two-field system. In the eighth and ninth centuries the invention of the horse collar and shoe allowed ploughs to be pulled by horses. They were faster than oxen, although more expensive to feed; they replaced oxen only very slowly in northern Europe, where oxen still outnumbered horses in the eighteenth century; they made even less progress in southern Europe. By the sixteenth century horse-drawn harrows and rollers were in use in parts of northern Europe, and the forerunner of the modern seed drill was constructed in Italy in 1602. But the drill was only slowly adopted, even after Jethro Tull's advocacy in eighteenth-century England. Most crops in the U.S.A. were still broadcast in the 1840s.[17]

Most of the technical advances in farming in northern Europe were concerned with expanding the cultivated area and improving the preparation of the seed bed. Methods of harvesting changed more slowly. The scythe had been introduced into northern Europe by the Romans, but had not begun to replace the sickle or the reaping hook until the labour shortages of the fourteenth century. Even at the end of the eighteenth century the sickle was still the most common implement, although towards the middle of the nineteenth century labour shortages speeded the adoption of the scythe in harvesting grain.[18]

In A.D. 1500 northern Europe was significantly in advance of southern Europe in farming methods. But there was as yet no great gap in agricultural productivity between Europe, India and East Asia. In East Asia crop yields were probably higher than in Europe, although output per man was lower. There is no reason to suppose that Indian agriculture lagged significantly behind Europe. The major difference was in the use of the heavy plough, which did not spread outside Europe until the mid-nineteenth century, when it was greatly improved in North America. On the other hand there were major differences between the plough civilisations, with their rudimentary mixed farming, and Africa, the Americas and Polynesia, where the plough had still yet to penetrate.

The great divide in the history of agricultural technology came in the middle of the nineteenth century. It was this period which created the great gulf in productivity between the present agricultures of Asia, Africa and much of Latin America, and western Europe, North America and Australasia. The agricultural revolution in England in the eighteenth and early nineteenth centuries involved little more than the final destruction of medieval institutions and the more general adoption of techniques and crops which had been known for a long time. In the nineteenth century, more fundamental changes got under way.

First was the application of power to agricultural production. Steampower was first applied to threshing machines and drainage pumps in the early part of the nineteenth century and to ploughing in the 1850s. The steam plough, although able to plough ten times the area that horses could plough in a day, was cumbersome and costly, and had only a limited impact on farming in either Europe or the United States.[19] Thus the horse remained the main source of power until the early twentieth century, and oxen in most of the world. The first gasolene-powered tractor was built in 1892, and the first tractor factory opened in the United States in 1907. But it was not until the inter-war period that the tractor replaced the horse in North America and Australia, and in Europe it was since the end of the Second World War. Over much of the rest of the world the tractor remains of little significance.[20]

The introduction of new implements has proceeded more rapidly than the changes in power. Between the seventeenth and early nineteenth centuries there were slow but effective increases in crop yields in parts of western Europe as a result of better preparation of the seed bed, the wider use of rotations and greater application of cattle manure. The result was that harvesting became a greater problem at the very time when rural populations were stagnant, or even declining. In the United States and Canada there was abundant land, but few labourers. Thus it was labour shortage which prompted the search for reaping machinery. Although there were many attempts to produce such a machine,

Technical and economic changes in agriculture

McCormack's reaper was the one to succeed and was widely adopted in the United States in the second half of the nineteenth century. In Europe it was much less widely adopted. Indeed only in England did it replace the scythe and the sickle. By 1874 about half the cereal acreage in Britain was harvested with a horse-drawn reaper; but in the 1890s only about one-tenth of the French and German harvests was so mechanised. Indeed the main change in Europe was the replacement of the sickle by the scythe, a substitution which did not occur in south-eastern Europe until the 1930s. The combine-harvester was first widely used in California, but hardly found east of the Rockies until after the First World War, whilst elsewhere – except in Australia – its adoption has come only since 1945.[21] All these advances greatly reduced the labour needed to sow and harvest one hectare of wheat. In the United States the number of man-hours per hectare fell from 148 in 1830 to 37 in the 1890s, whilst in California, where the first combine-harvesters were in use by the end of the century, to only 6.25 hours. Conversely it greatly increased the area which one man could farm, and allowed the increases in farm size which took place at this time. But it was not only harvesting that was improving after 1850. The first all-iron plough, the Rotherham plough, was built in the 1770s and began to replace local ploughs in the nineteenth century. In the United States John Deere's steel plough made the ploughing of the prairies easier, and by the later part of the century multi-share ploughs were becoming common. The modern seed drill, the horse-drawn harrow and a variety of other implements improved and quickened the preparation of the seed bed.[22]

Farmers had been aware of methods of maintaining soil fertility from the very earliest times – the use of manure, fallowing and green manuring all have a long history. By the fifteenth and sixteenth centuries the idea of rotations was known to agricultural writers and slowly spread through north-western Europe. In the nineteenth century farmers for the first time began to buy in fertilisers on a large scale. Guano and superphosphate were in use in the 1840s in England, and later basic slag. The use of chemical fertilisers had been made possible by the work of Liebig in Germany and Lawes in England in the mid-nineteenth century. But the general use of such fertilisers and the compound fertilisers produced by the chemical industries in the twentieth century was for long confined to a minority of farmers, and substantial application of fertilisers in western Europe and the eastern United States has only taken place since 1945. Other applications of the chemical industry such as herbicides and pesticides were not widely available until after the Second World War, although Bordeaux mixture was produced in France in the late nineteenth century.[23]

For millennia farmers had empirically selected higher-yielding seed, and in the nineteenth century the introduction of new varieties began to play an important role in agriculture. The introduction of Red Fife into the Canadian Prairies and the north-western United States was an early instance, whilst at the beginning of the twentieth century the breeding of Marquis, a wheat which needed a shorter growing season, allowed the northward extension of wheat growing in Canada and Scandinavia. In Australia the breeding of the drought-resistant wheat variety Federation assisted the expansion of wheat cultivation into the semi-arid lands. But plant breeding as a science did not really get under way until the rediscovery of Mendel's theory at the beginning of the century. Amongst the more conspicuous successes have been the breeding of hybrid corn and its adoption in the United States, and more recently of new varieties of rice.[24]

The antecedents of modern scientific agriculture can be traced back into the nineteenth century; but, with the exception of the mechanisation of the harvest, the general adoption of the techniques by farmers dates really only from the 1930s, and indeed many writers have seen the last thirty years as a period of agricultural revolution, for not only have yields risen considerably but output per man-hour also increased.[25] But the adoption of new methods of farming has made little progress outside western Europe, North America, and Australasia, as can be seen from Table 7.

TABLE 7   *Selected indices of scientific agriculture, 1970* ⟵

	Nitrogen fertiliser (metric tons per 100 hectares arable land)	Tractors (per 1000 hectares arable land)	Combine-harvesters (per 1000 hectares arable land)
Europe	6.5	41	4.1
North America	3.4	24.1	4.6
Australia and New Zealand	0.3	9.5	1.8
U.S.S.R.	1.9	8.4	2.2
South and Central America	1.17	5.5	0.4
China	0.27	1.5	0.06
Africa	0.4	1.7	0.1
Rest of Asia	1.25	1.7	0.1

Source: F.A.O. *Production yearbook*, vol. 25, 1971

Thus until the mid-nineteenth century not only was the pace of agricultural change slow, but no great gulf in agricultural productivity was created between the major agricultural civilisation of Europe, India and China, although it is possible that northern Europe, by its adoption of the heavy plough and the partial adoption of the scythe, had a higher output per man. It is difficult to compare these societies with the less complex farming communities in Africa south of the Sahara, where the plough remained largely unknown until the twentieth century. In the Americas the arrival of Europeans transformed much of the continent, and North America and temperate South America largely followed European practices. The Indian communities of the uplands of Mexico and the Andes acquired the hoe, the *machete* and the metal axe, but few adopted the plough. The plough remained relatively unimportant in the southern United States until the middle of the nineteenth century, the hoe being the dominant implement.[26]

Technical and economic changes in agriculture

The great differences in agricultural productivity which have appeared between Europe, North America and Australasia, on the one hand, and Africa, Latin America and Asia, on the other hand, seem closely related to the progress of industrialisation. In nineteenth-century Europe reduced mortality initially increased the rural population and exerted considerable pressure on the land which was partly relieved by migration, and by the adoption of more intensive farming practices. But by the second half of the nineteenth century rural populations stagnated or declined, as growing industries attracted agricultural workers to the towns, and labour shortages enforced the adoption of labour-saving devices. In contrast there was no significant industrialisation in Africa, Asia or much of Latin America, although populations slowly, and then after 1920 rapidly, increased. One consequence was intensification by the wider adoption of established farming practices; but there was no fundamental break with the past.

PART TWO

CHAPTER 5

SHIFTING AGRICULTURE

In most agricultural systems the same piece of land is cropped continuously, with occasional fallows. Frequently the fields are bounded by hedges, fences or ditches, and the agricultural landscape is ordered and permanent. In shifting agriculture this is not so. The farmer chooses a patch of forest, secondary or primary, cuts down some of the trees with an axe, leaving only the larger and economically useful, clears the undergrowth with a knife or cutlass, and burns the debris. Crops are sown on the clearing – or swidden – with a minimum of preparation, and receive only cursory attention during growth. After the first harvest crops are sown again for a further year or two, and then the land is left uncropped and colonisation by the natural vegetation is allowed whilst another patch of land is cleared for cultivation. Ideally the first clearing will not be used for crops again until it has been under a natural fallow for some years and soil fertility restored. Thus, the essential features of shifting cultivation are, first, the rotation of fields rather than crops, with short periods of cropping alternating with long periods of natural fallow; second, the use of slash-and-burn methods to clear the vegetation, and third, the maintenance of fertility by allowing the vegetation to regenerate.[1]

Such a method of clearing land and maintaining soil fertility, although so different from the methods found in most of Europe, China and India, would hardly justify describing shifting agriculture as a farming system were it not that these features are invariably associated with other characteristics.

Foremost among these is the absence of the plough. In Africa the primary implements are the axe, cutlass and hoe, occasionally supplemented with the digging stick. The plough was introduced into Africa in the nineteenth century, but has not been widely adopted, except where shifting cultivation has given way to rotational bush fallow. Nor is this surprising, for the plough cannot easily be used where tree stumps are left in the swiddens, as is common in shifting cultivation; further, cultivation and furrow turning encourage both soil erosion and evaporation.[2] In both the Americas and Asia the digging stick was for long the main implement in shifting cultivation, and often, with axes and cutlasses, remains so. The hoe was introduced into the Americas only after 1492 and has been adopted by some Indian communities. In South East Asia the digging stick was the prime implement in the root complex which spread outwards from the mainland of South East Asia, and it was only when cereals were added to the shifting cultivators' crops that the hoe became important. In Polynesia the

57

digging stick still predominates. Harvesting methods vary; some shifting cultivators pick cereal heads by hand, others reap with sickles, whilst root crops are dug up with sticks and hoes, and in South America coas and foot-ploughs.[3]

Few shifting cultivators keep livestock. The most common are pigs and poultry, particularly in the Americas and Asia, and they survive by scavenging. In Africa sheep, goats and cattle are kept, but receive little attention, and cattle are hardly kept at all in the tropical forest regions and those parts of the savannas where the tsetse fly is found. But many shifting cultivators still hunt and fish and are not so lacking in protein supplies as might be thought.[4]

Methods of cultivation are, at first sight, primitive. The axe, cutlass and fire are used to clear the garden or swidden. Latosols are friable and this property is further increased by burning so that seed is usually broadcast without cultivation, although in some places dibbling sticks are used, whilst in parts of Africa soil is heaped into ridges or mounds with a hoe. Intertillage or mixed cropping is common. A number of different crops are sown in the same patch; roots, cereals and shrubs sown together simulate the original forest cover and protect the soil from erosion. Both sowing and harvesting are often staggered. But intertillage is by no means universal, and often only one crop is grown in the swidden.[5]

Once the crops are sown little cultivation is done during growth. No animal manure is used, and generally the only fertiliser the crops receive is the ash from the initial burning which provides potash. Nor is much attempt made to control the exuberant weed growth, except possibly in the second and third years of cropping. In savanna areas grass roots have to be hoed away before the second and third crops. Indeed it is the rapidity of weed growth as much as the decline in soil fertility which prompts the abandonment of a swidden.[6]

Amongst many shifting cultivators land tenure is still communal and there are frequently co-operative elements in working the land, particularly in clearing the vegetation. Shifting cultivation was once characteristic of areas with low population density and thus an abundance of land. This, combined with the need to move to new swiddens or gardens at regular intervals, means there is relatively little incentive to have private ownership of individual plots. On the other hand trees planted – or merely protected – in individual swiddens often belong to the individual who planted them, even after the plot has been abandoned.

The land tenure systems of shifting cultivators are extremely diverse. But most of them include the following concepts: land belongs to the tribe rather than to individuals; boundaries with neighbouring groups are well-defined physical features; the allocation of the communal land is undertaken by the tribal chief, but every member has a right to land.

Each individual has the right to the products of his swidden – usufruct – as long as it is being cropped. When the swidden is left to fallow, rights to it lapse, except for the fruit of perennial trees. The idea of the alienation of land has been, until recently, completely unknown. Wherever shifting cultivation has been practised the unit of ownership has been the village or tribe, and not the family. The exception to this is found in Latin America, where farmers of European origin have resorted to shifting cultivation. However the system of land tenure among shifting cultivators in every part of the world has changed in this century, under the influence of, first, increasing population and, second, the introduction of cash crops.[7]

The size and layout of the 'farms' of shifting cultivators vary. Each family may have a number of plots in crops at any one time, widely scattered around the village and often at a considerable distance away. The size and number of plots vary according to the fertility of the soil, the density of population, the length of the fallow, and the degree of commercialisation. Thus for example in fertile parts of Samoa three or four plots of 0.04 hectare are sufficient; but on the same island up to 20 hectares in three plots have been known. In Africa the area in crops under shifting cultivation averages about 0.44 hectare per head. Generally the area under crops is small, but if the area under fallow is included then 'farms' are much larger. Thus for example in eastern Guatemala each family needs between 40 and 80 hectares in crops and fallow.[8]

There are still shifting cultivators who are outside a monetary system and whose exchange of goods is limited to bartering or exchange by gifts to chieftains or kin-groups. But since the late nineteenth century many shifting cultivators have grown crops specifically for sale, often to get money for tax purposes; many however still respond to price changes in quite a different way from western commercialised farmers, and may be regarded as transitional between subsistence and commercial.[9]

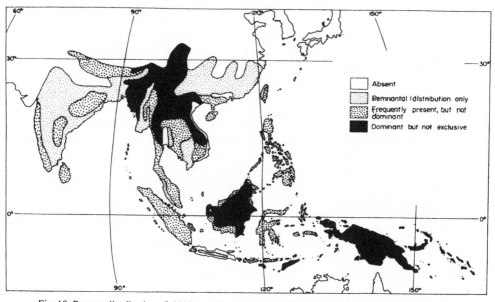

Fig. 10. Present distribution of shifting cultivation in South East Asia. [Source: Spencer, 1966, 12]

59

Shifting agriculture

Agriculture with most of the above characteristics is found in parts of the Americas, Asia and Africa (Figs. 1, 10, 11), and for the most part is confined to the tropical areas within these continents. In 1957 it was estimated that 200 000 000 people depended upon shifting cultivation and that they occupied – including cropland and fallow – 33 000 000 km², an area more than twice the world's total cropland.[10] Clearly not all these farmers conform in every way to the stereotype of the shifting cultivator outlined above. It is, for example, often combined with other types of agriculture. Thus in the Dry Zone of Ceylon farmers who cultivate irrigated rice may also practise *chena* – the local term for shifting cultivation – on the unirrigated land; the Boro people of the western Amazon basin combine shifting cultivation with hunting and gathering, whilst the Munda people of Bengal are pastoralists who also practise some shifting cultivation of rice and millet.[11]

But a more important distinction is related to the length of the fallow, which in turn is often linked to population density and the rate of increase. Where twenty or thirty years of fallow are allowed for the restoration of crop fertility, the land available for new swiddens becomes increasingly scarce, and the farmers have to travel long distances to clear new swiddens. There comes a point where it is more convenient to move the village rather than travel the long distances. This, *true shifting cultivation*, is rare. The movement of the village is clearly limited by the territories of neighbouring communities, and with any significant increase in population the group is compelled to reduce the period under fallow and clear the secondary vegetation before the restoration of soil fertility by the natural fallow is complete. Villages then become fixed, and this type of farming, of far more importance than true shifting cultivation, was described by Whittlesey as Rudimental Sedentary tillage (see Fig. 1). Thus many writers regard the term shifting cultivation, with its implication of village movement, as inappropriate, and prefer the term rotational bush fallowing or land rotation. Further increases in population require further adjustments in the method, and in Africa a sequence of stages, at least partly related to population increase and density, may be distinguished. Shifting cultivation, with long fallows, is confined to central, eastern and southern Africa. In most of West Africa rotational bush fallow predominates (Fig. 11). Fields become permanent and fallows are progressively reduced, so that woodland is never fully re-established. Yet a further stage is reached where fallows are planted, and finally fallows give way to continuous cropping, with the use of animal manure to maintain crop yields. Unfortunately, it is equally common for the fallow to be reduced without any efforts to maintain soil fertility being made, so that soil fertility is reduced and crop yields decline.[12]

Shifting cultivation is now largely confined to the tropics, and there is no doubt, given a long enough fallow, that is an efficient method of maintaining soil fertility in the *humid* tropics. No satisfactory alternative, except the plantation, which also simulates the primary forest, or wet-rice cultivation, which is confined to deltas and river valleys, has yet been devised. Not unnaturally some writers have argued that the distribution of shifting cultivation may be explained in terms

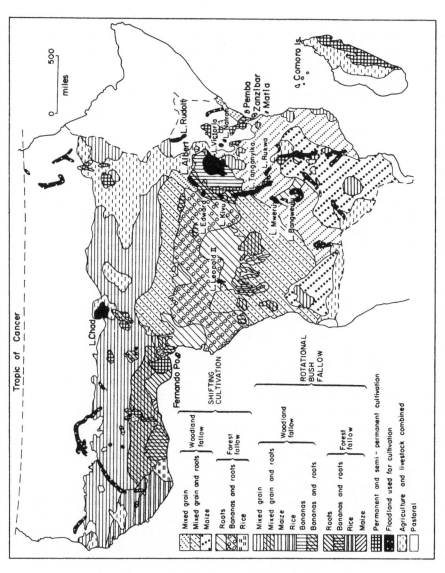

Fig. 11. Shifting cultivation in Africa. [Source: Morgan, 1969, 252–3]

61

of adjustment to the environment. However shifting cultivation is still found in temperate upland areas such as Japan and Korea and in the past was much more widely distributed. Thus an alternative explanation is that it has been replaced by the expansion of more intensive systems. Every year between 400 000 and 800 000 hectares of land used for shifting cultivation in South East Asia are converted to permanent agriculture. Shifting cultivation may then be regarded as a residual feature remaining only in those regions as yet unpenetrated by the plough and where population densities are low enough to allow an adequate fallow. There is much evidence to support this view, but some problems remain.[13]

The early distribution of shifting cultivation

The people of the earliest farming villages in South West Asia, northern China and South East Asia had digging sticks and hoes, grew cereals and kept livestock. But the latter were only loosely integrated in the farming system, feeding for the most part upon rough grazing. There was no alternative means of maintaining soil fertility, and it has consequently been assumed that the earliest farmers had to practise shifting cultivation. Indeed it has been argued that the movement of agriculture out of South West Asia into Europe and from the loess highlands of northern China into the lower Hwang Ho valley was enforced by a shortage of land resulting from soil exhaustion. Only in river valleys where the annual deposition of silt replenished soil fertility was permanent agriculture possible.[14] The early farmers of Europe seem to have been shifting cultivators; farmers of the Danubian culture of central Europe practised slash-and-burn, occupying and reoccupying the same village site several times over in a few hundred years.[15] Farming became permanent as a result of a number of pressures. The growth of population would have limited the movement of the village, whilst the replacement of woodland by grass after prolonged slash-and-burn and grazing, would have limited the area available for forest fallow. The increase in the number of livestock, and the provision of more manure upon the arable stubbles, would have helped to maintain fertility, as would the folding of sheep and stall-feeding of cattle. The spread of the *ard*, drawn by two oxen, would have provided more manure and further encouraged permanent agriculture.[16] Shifting agriculture however disappeared only slowly; it was still a fairly common method of farming in western Europe in the later part of the first millennium A.D. and survived as a supplementary technique until the eighteenth and nineteenth centuries. Poorer land around the permanent village lands was occasionally cleared of scrub and grass with axe and fire, and one or two crops were taken, before the land was left to regenerate. The infield-outfield system of western Britain is a good example of the use of slash-and-burn to supplement permanent agriculture; it also survived into the eighteenth century in parts of eastern England.[17] In Europe shifting agriculture survived as a supplementary technique, particularly in mountainous and infertile areas; it remained an independent farming system longest in the forests of Scandinavia and Russia, which are not only those parts of Europe remotest from South West Asia, but where extensive forests have survived longest. It was still widely practised in Finland and Russia in the sixteenth century and survived in Sweden until the nineteenth century. Descriptions of nineteenth-century slash-and-burn in Russia, Sweden and Finland are remarkably similar to those of shifting agriculture in the tropics in the twentieth century.[18]

Europeans who migrated overseas often reverted to techniques of slash-and-burn when they found themselves in areas of more abundant land. In the southern United States farming exhibited many characteristics of shifting cultivation until the nineteenth century, not least in the westward expansion of the cotton frontier, where planters cleared the woodland by ring-barking with the axe and by burning, took crops of cotton and corn, and then let the land revert to scrub. The plough and the drill were only belatedly adopted in the South, and the clearing of woodland for cotton lasted well into the twentieth century.[19] In Brazil the coffee planters in the late nineteenth century practised slash-and-burn, although, like the cotton planters of the southern United States, they had few other characteristics in common with the modern shifting cultivator. Recent European settlers in the more temperate parts of southern Brazil have also practised slash-and-burn in the early stages of colonisation.[20]

Shifting cultivation in Asia

In India, South East Asia and southern China (Fig. 10) about 50 000 000 people depend upon shifting cultivation. They grow crops each year on between 10 000 000 and 18 000 000 hectares out of a total area of from 100 000 000 to 110 000 000 hectares of crops and fallow. In contrast, in the same area some 675 000 000 live by permanent agriculture, using between 220 000 000 and 230 000 000 hectares of cropland.[21] Shifting cultivation is characteristically found in upland areas, whilst the dominant farming system in the lowlands is wet-rice cultivation. But there is no reason to suppose that shifting cultivation is an adaptation to upland areas and steep slopes. On the contrary, it was probably more widely distributed formerly and has been pushed into the uplands by more intensive systems, particularly wet-rice cultivation.

The first type of agriculture in South East Asia was tropical vegeculture, based upon taro and yams, and trees such as the coconut and banana. Vegetative propagation and shifting cultivation went hand in hand, and expanded south into Malaysia, where breadfruit and the sago palm were added, and were carried eastwards to Melanesia and Polynesia; the tuber complex was also found in southern China and north-eastern India. Seed agriculture in the region dates from at least as early as the fourth millennium B.C. when rice was domesticated. Millet was also an early seed crop. The earliest tools used were the digging stick combined with axes and knives. The domestication of rice did not have the profound effect upon farming in the region that might be expected. Although it allowed farmers to settle the flooded lowlands, the methods of farming were not comparable to those of modern wet-rice cultivation. Wet-rice can be grown by very simple techniques. Little more is necessary then to clear the vegetation from a flat piece of ground, leaving the tree stumps, dibble in rice seed and then divert water from a nearby stream or rely upon natural flooding. Dry-rice can be of course grown on steeper slopes and without irrigation. The adoption of rice growing then did not need any great advance in agricultural technology, and it is likely that rice production in South East Asia remained primitive until the later part of the first millennium B.C.[22]

The original tuber complex of South East Asia seems to have been first displaced in the northern part of mainland South East Asia, South China and northeastern India. When the first European descriptions of Asian agriculture became available in the fifteenth and sixteenth centuries, Indian shifting cultivators were growing millets, grains and pulses, with root crops such as taro of minor importance. In southern China and northern South East Asia tubers had become a residual feature by the time of early European contact, and millets and rice were the main crops of the shifting cultivator. Further south, in Malaysia, Melanesia and Polynesia, the old tuber complex had not given way before the advance of seed agriculture. In Malaysia yams, taros and the sago palm were being challenged by rice and millets; shifting cultivators grew both seed and root crops. Further east, in Melanesia and Polynesia, the old tuber complex remained unchallenged, and indeed has done so to this day. It thus seems likely that the proto-Malays who settled Polynesia from western Malaysia did so before rice had arrived – or become established – from the north.[23]

Since the sixteenth century shifting cultivation in South East Asia has been profoundly influenced by the arrival of Europeans. American crops have been incorporated in the system, and it is noticeable that maize has been most rapidly adopted in the west, where a tradition of seed agriculture was well established, and root crops such as manioc and sweet potatoes in the east, particularly in Melanesia and Polynesia. Equally significant has been the decline of shifting cultivation before the advance of wet-rice cultivation, particularly in lowland areas. In some cases, such as in the deltas of southern Indo-China, the shifting cultivation of rice has been replaced by more intensive methods of wet-rice cultivation comparatively recently.[24] Shifting cultivation in the uplands of southern China has largely disappeared since the mid-nineteenth century, whilst in India shifting cultivation in the uplands of central India, still important in the mid-nineteenth century, has largely been replaced by sedentary farming. In Java, shifting cultivation was still practised in the mountainous regions in the nineteenth century, but is now found only in the west of the island although it is still important in Sumatra and Borneo. But even in the Outer Islands shifting cultivation has been displaced by the growth of rubber by smallholders. The decline of shifting cultivation has often been accelerated by the attempts of colonial governments, inspired by the need to conserve forests, to make it illegal.[25]

Shifting cultivation is clearly a residual feature in much of Asia, having given way to more intensive systems. Only in Polynesia does the original root complex survive, although even there the introduction of plantation crops and the recent increase of population have greatly modified the old system. It appears as a residual form in Asia largely because it presents such great contrasts to the other major forms of agriculture in the area, wet-rice cultivation and the plantation. In the former areas population densities often exceed 400 per km², whilst in shifting cultivation they are more commonly below 40 per km², with the occasional exception such as the areas of New Guinea where sweet potatoes are grown.

Shifting cultivation in Africa

Although Africa is frequently described as an area dominated by shifting cultivation, the term is inappropriate. It is true that many African farmers use the hoe, cultivate only a small acreage and use slash-and-burn techniques combined with a natural fallow; that communal tenure survives in many areas and that population densities are generally low. But the exceptions are so numerous that qualifications must be made. Morgan has distinguished a number of types of agriculture in tropical Africa.[26] *True shifting cultivation*, where the settlement itself is moved, is rare, being found only in parts of the Ivory Coast and the Cameroons. Shifting cultivation where there are no permanent fields, where clearings are allowed to regenerate naturally and there are short periods of cropping alternating with long fallows, characterises much of central, eastern and southern Africa (Fig. 11). A variety of crops are grown by these farmers. In the Congo basin bananas, cassava, maize and yams are the major staples; to the south and north of the forest grains and roots are grown – manioc, maize, sorghum, pearl millet are staples. South and south east of the Congo basin in the drier savannas the tuber crops are of little importance, and maize, sorghum, pearl millet and finger millet are the main crops. Of the root crops only manioc, which is tolerant of drought, is grown away from the tropical forest and its fringes.[27] Over much of this area population densities are low.

Morgan distinguishes between shifting cultivation, which predominates in much of central, eastern and southern Africa, and rotational bush fallowing, which is typical of most of West Africa. The essential differences are that in the latter system fields are often permanent, fallows are created rather than allowed to regenerate, and mature trees are never allowed to re-establish themselves. In some parts of West Africa – such as Iboland – fallows are planted. Continuous cropping is practised in parts of northern Ghana and northern Nigeria, and cattle manure rather than natural fallow is used to maintain soil fertility. These are clearly not cases of shifting cultivation. In West Africa crop combinations vary; as a rough generalisation it may be said that sorghum, pearl millet and maize are the main food crops of the savannas, whilst in the forest and the savanna woodlands manioc, yams and maize predominate. In the south west rice is the staple.[28]

Shifting agriculture

At the end of the first millennium B.C. agriculture was confined to the savannas of West Africa and the northern edges of the tropical forest. In the former region shifting cultivation was practised with stone hoes and digging sticks; *Sorghum vulgare*, fonio, pearl millet and, further east, finger millet were grown. In the forest shifting cultivators grew the African yams and the Kaffir potato. Further east in northern Ethiopia there was more contact with the South West Asian complex, and not only African crops but also wheat and barley were grown, as well as teff (*Poa abyssinica*), a local domesticate which has never spread out of Ethiopia. But most of the tropical forest was unoccupied save by Pygmies, who relied upon hunting and gathering, whilst the savannas from the Horn of Africa to the Cape of Good Hope were occupied by Bushmanoid peoples who were also without agriculture. The next thousand years of African history are dominated by the expansion of the Bantu-speaking people, who settled in central, eastern and southern Africa and brought with them crops and livestock. The direction and chronology of the Bantu migrations is still a matter of dispute. Until recently the only evidence has been linguistic,[29] but some archaeological evidence is now available. It has been argued that the Bantu originated on the borders of Nigeria and the Cameroons, passed south through the forests of the Congo basin and, in the first half of the first millennium A.D., built up to great numbers in the Katanga; from there, armed with the iron spear, they moved south east toward Mozambique:[30] there they divided, some to turn north into Tanzania and Kenya, and others to move south into southern Africa. In the first century A.D. they had reached just north of the Zambesi, and were in Rhodesia by the second century. They had reached the Transvaal by the eleventh century and the Transkei by at least the sixteenth century, and possibly long before.[31] The Hottentot, or Khoikhoi-speaking peoples, who were nomadic pastoralists, had thus been driven into the South West of the continent by the time the Portuguese and Dutch arrived.[32] The Bantu speakers in southern Africa were both herders and cultivators, keeping sanga cattle, in contrast to the Khoikhoi who had longhorned cattle; they grew two varieties of *Sorghum vulgare*, beans, melons and cocoyam. Until the nineteenth century they still used *wooden* digging sticks and hoes and practised shifting cultivation.[33]

The Bantu who moved north into what is now Uganda, Kenya and Tanzania came into contact with different peoples, although the precise nature of this contact is controversial. One argument is that the Bantu drove the indigenous hunters and gatherers into the mountains, and by A.D. 1300 the area was entirely settled by Bantu agriculturalists who thereafter were in conflict with pastoral peoples who came in a series of invasions from the North.[34] Others believe that this area was already occupied by agriculturalists, the Cushites, who were of Caucasoid origin and had brought farming southwards in about 1000 B.C. from Ethiopia. They had intensive farming practices, including the use of terraces, animal manure and irrigation. This culture was absorbed by the Bantu, who reached the region between the sixth and ninth centuries.[35]

Equally in doubt is the timing of the occupation of the tropical forests. Most prehistorians believe that a form of tropical vegeculture, using the indigenous yams and the oil-palm tree, is of a very early date in West Africa. On the other hand many anthropologists have argued that the forest could not be effectively settled until South East Asian plants – the banana, taro and yam – arrived in Africa. These were most probably brought by the Malaysians who crossed the Indian Ocean to Madagascar at some time in the late first millennium B.C. or in the early Christian period. From there the crops were taken to the African coast, northward to the Lakes region, and then westward along the northern Sudanic zone into West Africa.[36] The date at which these crops became established in Uganda, the Congo and West Africa, where they were staples at the time of European contact, is unknown; some argue that the South East Asian plants did not arrive in West Africa until after A.D. 1000.

However it should be noted that 95 per cent of the yams grown in West Africa today belong to the three sub-species *Dioscorea rotundata, D. cayennensis* and *D. alata* L. The latter is Asian in origin, but the former two are African. It may be that it is unnecessary to date the occupation of the African tropical forest from the date of introduction of Asian plants,[37] for the settlement of the forests could have been undertaken with the indigenous yams.

Although there had been contacts between Europe and Africa across the Sahara for a long period, it was not until the fifteenth century that the Portuguese began to trade along the West African coast, and thereafter Europeans were an important influence upon African agriculture. Of major significance was the introduction of American food crops, which has already been touched upon in Chapter 3. Maize was the most rapidly adopted of the new crops, for in areas of adequate rainfall it was possible to get two crops a year, whilst the method of planting in hills was not dissimilar to the method of growing yams on the West African coast.[38]

Maize was a major crop in the sub-Guinean zone and in the Congo basin by the seventeenth century, and spread rapidly in the Gold Coast in the eighteenth century. Its adoption in eastern and southern Africa, however, came much later, and dates mainly from the nineteenth century.[39] In southern Africa the millets and sorghum were the staple crops until late in the nineteenth century, since when, however, these areas have become the major producers on the continent. Indeed maize is now the dominant crop in the areas in which it was most tardily adopted, although it is the most widely distributed crop in tropical Africa.[40]

The sweet potato seems to have been adopted quite rapidly in West Africa and the Congo basin, not surprisingly considering the suitability of the climate and the similarity of its cultivation to that of the yam. Manioc was not widely adopted until the late nineteenth and twentieth centuries, for reasons already discussed (see above, Chapter 3, p. 32). Thus, although it had reached its present range by about 1850, it was not of major importance. However the reduction of fallows and declining soil fertility in the twentieth century led Africans to grow it instead of yams, whilst colonial governments have encouraged its growth as a famine crop. Manioc or cassava, as it is called in Africa, is cheaper than yams, and the growth of an impoverished urban population in this century has increased demand for it.[41]

Contacts with Europeans had little effect upon the agricultural technology of the African farmer. The plough had reached northern Ethiopia at an early date, but penetrated no further south. Nor did the diffusion of iron greatly affect agriculture in the late first millennium B.C. Implements were still made mainly of wood and stone in some parts of Africa until the late nineteenth century. However in parts of West Africa axes were made of local iron; their replacement by European steel axes made the clearing of forest easier, whilst iron hoes improved cultivation. The hoe was the dominant implement throughout Africa long before the arrival of Europeans.[42]

The most important effects of Europe upon African agriculture – if we exclude the development of cash crops for export – have been indirect. The elimination of tribal warfare, the improvement of transport and thus the reduction of famines, combined with the slow spread of modern medicine, have reduced the death rate in Africa and led to substantial population increases, particularly after the 1920s (Table 8).

TABLE 8 *Population of West Africa, 1500–1970 (millions)*

1500	20	1910	36
1700	25	1940	48
1800	25	1965	88
		1970	100

Sources: Fage, 1969, 86; U.N. *Demographic yearbook*, 1971

West African population in the eighteenth and early nineteenth centuries stagnated; the slave trade took off the natural increase[43], but population rose by a third between 1910 and 1940 and has doubled since 1940. This has put a considerable strain upon the agricultural systems of West Africa. A first reaction has been to reduce the length of the fallow, and in some cases to increase the periods under crops. Where there has been no alternative means of maintaining soil fertility, soil erosion and declining crop yields have set in. A number of writers however believe that increasing population has compelled the shifting cultivator to turn first to rotational bush fallow, then to planted fallows, and finally to continuous cropping with the use of animal manure and fertilisers.[44] However, whilst the recent population increase may be a major cause of the breakdown of shifting cultivation in Africa and its replacement by quite different farming systems, it should be noticed that shifting agriculture had disappeared in some areas before the very high rates of population growth which are now current. Thus in the Gold Coast in the early eighteenth century true shifting cultivation was found only in the north, whilst rotational bush fallowing was the practice in the south.[45] In Nigeria the northern edge of the forest zone already had bush fallowing rather than shifting cultivation in the sixteenth century. Conversely bush fallowing rather than shifting cultivation does occur in areas of low population density, particularly near small towns and markets.[46] Thus the earlier development of trade and states in West Africa than in East and southern Africa may have been a factor in the early introduction of bush fallowing. Not all permanent agriculture can be attributed simply to the elimination of shifting agriculture in response to population growth. Thus for example the Ganda had permanent groves of plantains, cultivated by the hoe in the eighteenth century, when population densities were not high, whilst in other parts of Africa permanent agriculture has also a long history on some of the better soils, particularly in East Africa.[47]

The growth of urban population has also undermined some features of shifting cultivation. The need to provide food for the towns has helped, combined with the spread of cash crops for export, to break down subsistence economies. It has also undermined the systems of communal tenure which once prevailed, so that the individual ownership of land has become increasingly common, as has the sale of land and the creation of a class of tenant farmers. There have also been efforts by colonial governments to replace shifting cultivation with permanent agriculture, most noticeably in southern Rhodesia, Kenya and northern Nigeria.[48]

Shifting cultivation in Latin America

Latin America has the most complex of agricultural heritages, for not only is there the agricultural tradition of the Indians, but also the influence of Europeans, who brought the farming practices of medieval Iberia, and also established stock-raising and the plantation system, the latter based initially on introduced crops.

Shifting cultivation is still an important method of farming, particularly in the areas where Indian communities remain relatively isolated from European influence (Fig. 1). Thus in Mexico about a fifth of the cropland is still farmed by slash-and-burn methods. Two types may be recognised. On the Caribbean coast shifting cultivation, locally called *roça*, with a long fallow, is practised; the forest is cleared with *machete* and fire, and allowed to regenerate after three years under crops. In the uplands of the Mesa Central, and particularly on the steeper slopes, is found the *barbecho* system. There is some preparation of the soil after burning, and the fallow period rarely exceeds the period under crops so that the natural vegetation is not allowed to regenerate. This more intensive system is clearly akin to the bush fallowing of West Africa. The main crops in both *barbecho* and *roça* are maize, beans and squash, generally grown together in the same clearing. The *roça* farmers still rely upon the *coa* and the *machete*, but the *barbecho* farmers have adopted the *azada*, the European hoe, and in some cases the plough or, more accurately, the *ard*.[49]

Shifting cultivation is widespread in Central America, both in the Indian communities of the uplands, as in Guatemala for example, and in the lowland areas, particularly on the Caribbean coast. South of Nicaragua maize and beans are supplemented by root crops such as arrowroot, manioc and sweet potatoes.

In South America forms of shifting cultivation are found in both the tropical lowlands and the Andean uplands. On the Pacific coast of Columbia farmers in the tropical rain-forest, which has an exceptionally high rainfall and no dry season, cut the undergrowth *after* seeds have been broadcast; the vegetation is allowed to rot rather than being burned.[50] East of the Andes Indian communities in the Amazon basin practise a shifting cultivation where roots are of greater importance than maize, where hunting and fishing are an important source of food, and where the settlements themselves are still moved, although only once in a generation.[51]

In the Andean *altiplano* a farming system similar to the *barbecho* of Mexico is practised among some Indian communities. Land is tilled for three years or more, under potatoes, quinoa or barley, and then left fallow for up to ten years. The natural short-grass that regenerates is grazed by sheep and llama; the foot-plough is still used in many of these communities, and the communal holding of land prevailed until recently.[52]

Although shifting cultivation is most closely associated with Indian farmers, and also found in the least favourable environments, variants of shifting cultivation are found in eastern Brazil. In the North East *caatinga* pastoralism is still the dominant form of land use away from the coast. The absence of natural grasses has prompted landlords to rent land to tenants who burn the scrub, sow seed in the ash-covered ground, often without clearing the tree stumps, and take a mixture of food crops – manioc, maize, rice and beans – for three years. As yields decline the tenant sows grass and moves on to another holding. Similar practices are found in southern Brazil, an area of recent European immigration. Here German immigrants have reverted to *roça*, growing beans, manioc, sweet potatoes and maize, and using only the dibble stick and hoe. With time these farmers gradually adopt more intensive methods, and particularly where population has increased. The horse-drawn plough replaces the hoe, the fallow is shortened, and eventually a form of mixed farming is pursued.[53]

Shifting cultivation is of considerable antiquity in Latin America; archaeological investigations suggest that at the beginning of the Christian era it was the predominant method of land use over most of lowland Central and South America, and *barbecho* was practised in many of the upland areas. More intensive and permanent farming systems did exist; in Peru the coastal oases relied upon irrigation, which was also locally found in the Valley of Mexico; later the Incas built irrigation canals and aqueducts, whilst a number of other intensive farming methods such as the *chinampas*, reclaimed lakeland and drained fields, suggesting the draining of marshy land, were found in southern Mexico, and equally intensive farming methods were found in the Central Andean uplands by the time of the Incas.[54] Two types of shifting cultivation can be distinguished at least as early as the first millennium B.C. In Mexico and as far south as western Nicaragua, the dominant crops were maize, beans and squash. They were grown in clearings called *milpa,* and along with a variety of minor crops provided some protection for the soil from high temperatures and heavy rainfall. Beans could climb on the stalks of the maize, and squash, a creeper, provided some protection.

In southern Central America and in the tropical lowlands shifting cultivation was based largely on tubers – manioc, sweet potatoes and arrowroot, a system described as *conuco,* a form of vegeculture; in contrast *milpa* was based on seed agriculture. The maize complex spread from Mexico to southern Canada and as far south as the Rio Plata by about A.D. 500, but there is still a marked tendency for root crops to dominate shifting cultivation in the tropical lowlands south of Nicaragua and east of the Andes.[55]

By the time of European arrival in the Americas there had been no *radical* change in American farming systems, and population densities, except in the Valley of Mexico and parts of the Andes, were still remarkably low.[56] The Indian farmers adopted few European introductions. The *coa* was supplemented by the metal hoe, and the steel *machete* made the clearance of *milpas* easier. Pigs and poultry were adopted, and are now kept by most farmers. Cattle were shunned except where the wooden *ard* was adopted. Sheep, on the other hand, more amenable than the half-wild longhorns brought by the Spanish, were integrated into the Andean upland farming systems, whilst wheat and barley were also grown in the Peruvian *altiplano.*

The initial impact of Europeans led to a disastrous decline in the American population, and it was not until the eighteenth century that Indian populations began to increase again. In the last twenty years Central America has had the highest growth rate in the world. This has had familiar consequences; fallows have been shortened and soil erosion has become common. In many parts of Latin America shifting cultivation is characteristically found on the steeper slopes overlooking level basin floors, which have been pre-empted for ranching or wheat cultivation: soil erosion has thus been more disastrous in its effects.

In eastern Brazil the prevalence of slash-and-burn methods cannot be attributed to the persistence of the Indian population. It is rather a function of a long history of abundant land, or at least a belief in the presence of abundant land, that has led to its destructive use. Only in the last thirty years have there been attempts to intensify and stabilise farming in eastern Brazil, the result again of soil erosion and poor yields.

Summary

We may now turn to the problem posed earlier. May the distribution of shifting cultivation be explained as an adjustment to environment? Or is it a residual type of farming which once had a wider distribution but is now confined only to those areas where it has not been replaced by more intensive forms of farming?

Under certain circumstances shifting cultivation is a remarkable adjustment to the environment. In the humid tropics, where primary or secondary rain-forest still survives, the fallow period – provided it is of sufficient length – is fully capable of restoring plant nutrients to the soil, and thus plays the role that manures, fertilisers, legumes and rotations play in other farming systems.[57] Further, the apparent disorder of the system has some positive advantages. Burning the debris not only clears the undergrowth but makes it more friable, and thus allows seeding to be undertaken with the minimum of effort. Although burning destroys organic matter, it does provide other nutrients. The intermixture of crops on the same small plot of land provides a cover of plants not unlike the layered structure of the rain-forest; it protects the soil from leaching and erosion, and this halts the decline in soil fertility. Shifting cultivation can be carried on with a minimum of implements – in the extreme case only the axe and fire are necessary.[58] Furthermore, although the data on inputs and outputs in shifting cultivation are of necessity difficult to come by, it appears to give a higher output per man-hour than most other peasant agricultural systems. The most laborious period of work is clearing the forest. Yields are low, and decline after a year or two's cultivation, but they are not low compared with those in other forms of peasant agriculture. The staggered sowing of crops, and the great variety grown, ensure a regular supply of food over a long period, rather than a concentration of harvesting in one short period of the year.[59]

It is as well to consider here the alternative methods of farming to be found within the rain-forest and its peripheries. Any farming system which involves the clearance of the forest and the use of the plough runs the risk of exposing the soil to very high rates of leaching and also to the impact of rain-drops and the risk of soil erosion. Wet-rice cultivation avoids the problems of soil erosion but it can only be carried out successfully in a limited number of environments. Plantation crops – generally trees or bushes – to some extent simulate the rain-forest but are not a satisfactory basis for family farming. Any alternative systems require considerable outlays on fertilisers, or the cultivation of legumes, which rarely fix nitrogen in the tropics as efficiently as they do in temperate areas; or the keeping of livestock, which is difficult for both environmental and social reasons in the humid tropics.

Outside the rain-forest the natural fallow is a far less efficient method of restoring fertility, and shifting cultivation is thus a less satisfactory method of farming. Grasses, whether in the savanna or in the tropical uplands, not only restore plant nutrients more slowly than the forest, but require more cultivation, for grass roots cannot be removed simply by slashing with a *machete* and burning; the hoe is a necessary implement.[60]

It will be clear that in an area of forest or woodland where shifting cultivation is carried on for long periods, the cleared and burnt areas will, in the long-run, experience a degradation of the vegetation; forest areas will be invaded by scrub and grass, that will fail to fully restore soil fertility. Furthermore, outside the tropics, in temperate areas, the ability of forest to restore plant nutrients is far below that of the tropical rain-forest. Thus one may argue that the incentive to replace shifting cultivation with another form of cultivation would have been greater in temperate and sub-tropical areas than in the humid tropics and the wooded savannas, the latter themselves possibly a result of repeated clearing and burning.

For all this, slash-and-burn is a method of farming which has been adopted in a variety of environments when land has been abundant, for it gives a reasonable return for a limited input of labour, and negligible inputs of capital. Thus it has frequently been adopted by pioneer farmers in forest lands at a variety of times and in a variety of places. The Bantu farmers who occupied southern Africa in the second half of the first millennium, the Europeans in the eastern United States and the Portuguese in Brazil have all adopted varieties of shifting cultivation.

A number of writers have argued that shifting cultivation was once a universal system of farming, that was replaced by more intensive forms of farming as population grew.[61] Thus Ester Boserup has discounted the significance of environment in causing differences in types of farming and has seen the growth of permanent and intensive systems as a response to the need for greater outputs per acre to feed an increasing population. She thus has classified types of land use into *forest-fallow*, with a fallow of 20–25 years, *bush-fallow*, with a fallow of 6–10 years, *short-fallow*, with only a year or two of grass fallow, *annual cropping*, and finally *multi-cropping* where the same plot of land bears two or three crops in the same year.[62] The mechanism of change is population growth. As the fallow is reduced the farmer is compelled to adopt methods of farming which maintain yields, which involves more weeding, more preparation of the soil before seeding, and some method of maintaining soil fertility, such as keeping livestock for their manure, growing complementary crops in rotation, or planting legumes and grasses in leys. This of course involves more work, so that although yields per acre may be higher than in shifting cultivation, output per man-hour declines.

This is a very appealing way of explaining the distribution of shifting cultivation. As has been shown earlier, some form of shifting cultivation appears to have been practised in most parts of the world when they were first occupied, but has subsequently been displaced by more intensive systems. In South East Asia, for example, shifting cultivation has been displaced in the valleys and deltas by wet-rice cultivation, a system of farming which gives higher yields per acre, and can thus support greater densities, but often has a lower output per man-hour than shifting cultivation. Assuming that most societies would prefer to avoid the arduous work of wet-rice cultivation, one can only conclude that increases in population enforced intensification. To substantiate this argument, which has also been put forward to explain the evolution of agricultural systems in West Africa,[63] one would require more data on the rate of population change in a given area, and its correlation with the adoption of intensive methods. Such evidence is not to hand, and indeed, in the nature of things, is hardly likely to be. Even more significant, we have to explain how and why populations did increase if we are to discount the increase in the food supply as a factor.

Nonetheless there are parts of the world where contemporary studies suggest that the intensity of farming is related to the density of population and its rate of growth. Amongst the Indian communities of Mexico the lowest densities of population are associated with *roça*; with population growth the fallow is reduced, and *barbecho* replaces shifting cultivation. The next stage is *secano-intensivo*, permanent dry land farming, the last *humedad-y-riego*, irrigation farming. The stages in West Africa have been noted above, whilst in New Guinea variations in farming practice are closely related to differences in population density.[64] What is very clear from any detailed study of modern practices by shifting cultivators is the great variety of methods adopted, and the difficulty of distinguishing between shifting and sedentary cultivation.

The roles of environment and population growth in accounting for changes in shifting cultivation in time and space are clearly important. Attention should also be drawn to the spread of commercialisation and changes in land tenure. Shifting cultivators have generally had some form of communal tenure, a system that avoids many of the iniquities of landlord–tenant relationships. Whilst such societies remain subsistence cultivators and whilst population densities are low, this is an acceptable form of tenure; but the introduction of cash crops frequently prompts the individualisation of tenure, and this in turn leads to the intensification of production. Such a sequence of events can be seen in parts of West Africa.

CHAPTER 6

WET-RICE CULTIVATION IN ASIA

Wet-rice cultivation is perhaps the most distinctive of the types of agriculture discussed in this book, and certainly one of the most important, for it supports a majority of the rural population of the Far East. It is the dominant mode of farming in China as far north as the Hsin Ho; in South Korea; in most of Japan; in Taiwan; in the Tonkin delta and the Annamite coastlands in North Vietnam; in the Mekong delta and around the Tonlé Sap; in the Central Plain of Thailand; the Irrawaddy delta; the Ganges–Brahmaputra delta, the lower Ganges plain, the deltas of the eastern coast of India, and in Kerala; in Sri Lanka (Ceylon) it is important in both the Dry and Wet Zones. In the islands of South East Asia wet-rice cultivation is less widespread than on the mainland, but it is found in Java and the central plain of Luzon (Fig. 12).

Although wet-rice cultivation supports much of the rural population of the Far East, it occupies but a small part of the total area. Rice is tolerant of a wide range of soils. It requires high temperatures in the growing season, with mean monthly temperatures of at least 20 °C for three or four months, but this does not greatly restrict its range, and it is grown as far north as Korea and Hokkaido. Nor are the minimum moisture requirements excessive, although ideally it requires at least 1778 mm during the growing season, which is, throughout the area under discussion, the period of the summer monsoon.[1]

None of these requirements greatly limits the distribution of wet-rice; it is tolerant of a wide range of environmental conditions, and there are a multitude of varieties adapted for many different macro- and micro-environments. Perhaps the most striking of these are the 'floating rices' of southern Indo-China. However, unlike upland rice, which is grown in much the same way as other cereals, it has to be submerged beneath slowly moving water to an average height of 100–150 mm for three-quarters of its growing period. This restricts wet-rice cultivation to flat lands near to rivers. Ideally the water in the fields should be the same height upon the stalks, and so wet-rice is normally grown in small, levelled fields, surrounded by low earthen bunds which keep the water in, and which can be easily breached to drain the field. Most wet-rice cultivation is thus found in deltas or the lower reaches of rivers. In these areas little cost is involved in levelling the fields – the elaborate terracing of valley slopes is not typical of most rice-growing areas – and a water supply is nearby. Water for the *sawahs*, as the small fields are called in Java, can come simply from the rainfall of the monsoon, as it does, for example, in the Malayan rice areas, but more commonly this is supplemented by river floods. Sometimes inundation canals are built to carry flood waters to more distant fields; the water is then lifted from the canal into the maze of small ditches that bring water to each field.

From early times wet-rice farmers have attempted, first to protect their farms from floods by embanking the major rivers, and second to ensure their water supply by using irrigation. Irrigation of wet-rice should be distinguished from the water control methods which direct river floods and from the ditches which drain the water away before harvest, and, indeed, from the embanking of rivers. This distinction is not always made in contemporary literature, although it must be admitted that it is one that is difficult to make. But irrigation implies some form of storage of water, even if it be only in ponds; canals that carry water from rivers; weirs or barrages that divert river waters, and methods of lifting water from one level to another.

The ease of levelling land for *sawahs,* and the nearness of a water supply, whether it be irrigation from canals or wells, clearly make river plains favourable

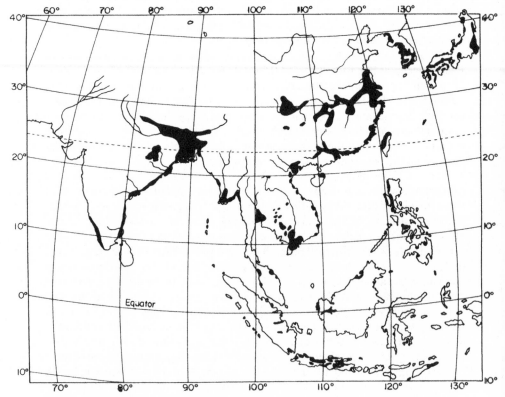

Fig. 12. The distribution of wet-rice cultivation in Asia. [Source: Ginsburg, 1958, 88, 136, 174, 326, 340, 380, 399, 411, 446, 512, 514]

sites for wet-rice. Furthermore wet-rice requires an impermeable sub-soil, else the water in the *sawahs* will soon drain away. Rice also yields best on heavy soils. As rivers deposit mainly fine-grained material in their lower reaches, heavy soils predominate.[2]

The micro-environment of the *sawah* also helps to explain the ability of the wet-rice cultivator to produce constant crop yields from the same field for year after year, often without the use of manures or rotations, in contrast to the up-land farming of the Far East, where shifting cultivation is practised. This phenomenon has not been satisfactorily explained, but a partial explanation can be offered. First, the water-covered *sawah* is protected from high temperatures, the direct impact of tropical raindrops, and high winds; soil erosion is thus reduced to a minimum. Second, the high water table reduces the vertical move-ment of water and thus limits the leaching of plant nutrients. Third, both floods and irrigation water bring silt in suspension and other plant nutrients in solution, renewing soil fertility each year. Fourth, the water in the *sawahs* contains blue-green algae which promote the fixation of nitrogen. Nonetheless in the last thirty or forty years rice yields have shown signs of decline in parts of the Far East, par-ticularly where double-cropping has been introduced.

Until the 1960s changes in traditional wet-rice agriculture had been few: in-creases in output were obtained by expanding the area under cultivation and by greater labour inputs. Only in a few areas had modern engineering allowed the creation of dams, reservoirs and canals. Yet since the mid 1960s there have been the beginnings of radical change. The central feature of the so-called Green Revolution in Asia has been the adoption of hybrid varieties of rice bred initially at research stations in the Philippines. These varieties give a much higher yield than traditional varieties and have a shorter growing season, thus making double-cropping easier. But they only yield well if there is an abundant supply of irrigation water and liberal supplies of fertiliser. In the late 1960s it was thought that these new varieties would revolutionise wet-rice cultivation and solve Asia's food problems. Yet comparatively few farmers have adopted the new varieties, and it is difficult to assess how great the changes have been in the last decade. Hence the description of current practices in wet-rice cultivation which follows refers mainly to the 1950s – before the Green Revolution.[3]

General characteristics of wet-rice cultivation

There are great variations in the way in which rice cultivation is carried on. Indeed one writer has identified thirty-six different sub-types in Malaysia alone.[4] Nonetheless some generalisations are possible.

First, farms are small, and fields invariably small and widely scattered. The typical rice farmer has only one or two hectares (Table 9). Only in the more recently settled areas of the lower Irrawaddy, Menam and Mekong are farms larger, averaging 4–6 hectares. Most wet-rice farms consist of a number of scattered fields; in Japan the average rice farm consists of fifteen separate fields,

TABLE 9 *Characteristics of wet-rice farming in Asia*

	Yield (tons/ hectare)	% of cultivated area in rice	% of rice irrigated	% of rice transplanted	% of land double cropped	% of land double cropped with rice	Average size of farm (hectares)	Chemical fertilisers; tons/ 1000 hectares of arable
Japan	5.1	54	96	95	35	0.3	1.0	392
South China	4.5	68	62	–	66	13–15	1.12	–
Taiwan	3.2	62	79	–	93	42	1.4	322
South Korea	3.3	60	58	100	28	–	1.2	200
Tonkin Delta	2.5	90	46	–	–	50	0.4	–
Mekong Delta	2.1	90	20	80	low	10	8.9	40
Thailand	1.5	79	24	80	low	–	4.8	9
Cambodia	1.2	80	–	–	–	–	–	2
Lower Burma	1.6	90	11	90	low	–	–	4
Malaya	2.4	17	11	94	low	6	0.8	30
Java	1.7	45	49	79	25	15–20	0.5	17
Philippines	1.2	42	30	80	–	16	3.0	25
Bangla Desh	1.7	71	12	74	24	–	1.4	13
Sri Lanka	1.7	28	60	6	–	32	–	56
India	1.5	23	20	–	13	–	–	10

Sources: Based on a wide variety of sources, mainly dating from about 1950. This table therefore represents conditions before the Green Revolution

and in southern China, six. Again the more recently settled rice areas have less fragmentation. The average Thai farm, for example, consists of only 2.7 plots. Rapid population growth combined with inheritance laws that require the equal division of property are the main causes of fragmentation.[5]

Most wet-rice farms are operated by family labour alone. In pre-war China, for example, 85 per cent of all farm work was carried out without hired labour; it is equally rare in modern Japan.[6] The very rapid growth of population in rural Asia in this century has, however, created a class of landless labourers who are sometimes hired in the critical periods of harvesting and sowing. The exception to this is in Japan, where industrialisation has syphoned off the surplus rural labour, and where consequently the rural population has been stagnant since 1886. India has a rather longer history of landless labourers, for lower castes were not allowed to own land, and often supplemented their living by working on farms.[7]

Wet-rice farmers are usually described as subsistence farmers; and indeed about one-half of the world's rice is consumed on the farms where it is produced.[8] In the 1930s only about one-tenth of the rice produced in the Tonkin delta was marketed. Before the Second World War about three-quarters of all the rice farmers in South East Asia were primarily subsistence producers. Even now two-thirds of the farmers in the Mekong delta, an area more commercialised than most, can still be described as subsistence producers.[9]

Most wet-rice areas support very high population densities; parts of the Ganges and Tonkin deltas, together with a few areas in Java, have densities of more than 1500 per km^2 although these are admittedly exceptional; nonetheless very high densities are sustained over large areas. The average density in the delta lands of Bangla Desh exceeds 390 per km^2 and few parts of the lower Ganges plain in Bihar have less than this. The state of Kerala has an average density of 428 per km^2.[10] Densities are higher of course when total population is related to the cultivated area, that is, the nutritional density.[11]

The principal exceptions to the high densities of wet-rice areas are the deltas of the Irrawaddy, Menam and Mekong, where average densities are much lower than in East Asia, India or Java.[12] But even in these areas densities are much higher than in most agricultural areas. Thus, for example, the densities of these deltas in the 1930s were some six or seven times those in eastern England. Indeed the only densities in the rest of Asia comparable with those of the wet-rice regions are in the upper Ganges and in northern China, where rice is grown but is not the major crop.[13]

Rice is the dominant crop in the wet-rice farming system, a fact not always clearly shown when figures are only available for countries. It is virtually a monoculture in Kwantung, the Tonkin delta, the lower Mekong, the lower Menam, the lower Irrawaddy, the delta of the Ganges–Brahmaputra and the coastlands of Orissa. Away from these rice bowls it occupies less of the cultivated area but is still the major crop, occupying about two-thirds of the crop-land in Korea, the rest of southern China, south-western Japan and

Taiwan. In the rest of India and in Sri Lanka, Malaya, Java and the Philippines a greater variety of crops are grown. Nonetheless, even in these regions, rice is almost a monoculture in some areas, such as the north east and north west coasts of Malaya, the central plain of Luzon and in north west Java.[14]

One of the most distinctive features of wet-rice farming is the intensive use of land and the high inputs of labour. A distinction can be made between East Asia, the area influenced by China, on the one hand, and the Indian sub-continent and South East Asia, on the other.

1. *Irrigation*

The difficulty of distinguishing between the natural supply of water for the *sawahs*, by flooding and rainfall, and the artificial supply, irrigation, has already been touched upon. Thus the figures in Table 9 should perhaps be treated with some scepticism. However a clear distinction is apparent between East Asia, where at least half the wet-rice acreage is irrigated, and South East Asia and the Indian sub-continent, where the irrigation of rice is less common. Most of the rice in the lower Mekong and the lower Menam is grown with flood water, together with monsoon rainfall. In the Irrawaddy delta the monsoon is reliable enough for most of the supply to come from rainfall alone, and the major problem of the Burmese is to prevent the Irrawaddy floods damaging the rice fields. The Ganges–Brahmaputra delta and the Orissa coast rely upon the heavy monsoon rainfall together with natural inundation. Indeed outside East Asia only Sri Lanka and Java have much irrigated rice land.[15]

2. *Multiple cropping*

A distinction must be made between double-cropping, where a rice crop is grown in the summer and a dry crop taken in the winter on the drained *sawah*, and the growth of two rice crops in the year on the same *sawah*. The latter is unusual, and is important only in Kwantung, the Tonkin delta and Taiwan, although the introduction of hybrid rices with shorter growing periods has made this more common. In Japan the shortness of the growing season confines the growth of two rice crops a year to the extreme south west, although the recent development of early maturing – but not hybrid – varieties may extend the range.[16] Elsewhere in Asia a shortage of water is the principal limiting factor, although shortage of labour may also be important in some places. Double-cropping of rice and a winter crop is much more widespread, particularly in East Asia (Table 9), where wheat and barley are grown on the *sawahs* in winter. Again temperature is a limiting factor in Korea, China and Japan, but equally important is the difficulty of draining the *sawahs* quickly enough for the winter crop. Traditionally double-cropping was rare in the mainland of South East Asia, but of some significance in the wet-rice areas of the Indian sub-continent, particularly in the lower Ganges (Table 10).[17]

TABLE 10   *Land-use characteristics in Indian wet-rice regions, 1951*

Region	% of gross sown area in rice	% of gross sown area irrigated	% of net sown area cropped twice	Total population per km² of cultivated land
West Bengal	76.5	15.9	12.5	504
Lower Ganges plain	37.5	23.8	32.1	420
Upper Ganges plain	12.4	24.6	25.2	384
North East Frontier	65.5	17.2	14.0	356
Bombay–Konkan coast	52.3	2.4	3.9	400
Malabar coast	41.8	15.4	13.9	579
Tamilnad	32.3	33.5	16.7	409
Andrha–Orissa coast	50.0	34.0	22.9	359
North East Peninsular uplands	54.9	12.4	19.3	259
All India	22.9	15.7	13.4	269

Source: Ginsburg, 1958, 568–9, 598–9

Few farmers have only wet-rice land. Indeed throughout the southern parts of the wet-rice region, a common combination is of irrigated rice land, dry upland – called *tegalan* in Java – and a garden plot around the farmstead, where fruits, vegetables and root crops are grown. In Java these 'mixed gardens' occupy 15 per cent of the cultivated land.[18]

3. *Terracing*

Terracing is commonly associated with wet-rice cultivation: but it is the exception rather than the rule. In broad level plains terracing is unnecessary and should be distinguished from the rudimentary levelling of *sawahs* and the construction of bunds. However in some areas wet-rice cultivation has been pushed up the steeper slopes of valley sides, and here the construction of terraces is essential. It is particularly noteworthy in southern China, where about a quarter of the cultivated land is terraced, and in Japan. Terracing is also practised in Sri Lanka, Java, Bali and parts of the Philippines, but it is rare in the Indian subcontinent and mainland South East Asia. Nor is terracing undertaken solely for wet-rice. It is as common in northern China, where little rice is grown, as in the south, whilst in Japan dry upland terraces are as frequent as wet-rice terraces, as they are also in Java.[19]

4. *Other farm practices*

Compared with most farming systems wet-rice cultivation is labour-intensive. At the beginning of the agricultural year dykes, bunds and canals have to be repaired. Attention is then turned to the preparation of the *sawahs;* the soil has to be reduced to a muddy consistency before the seed is sown. This is done with the assistance of a plough drawn by water buffalo or zebu oxen, although in some areas a water buffalo is simply driven around the field.[20] Draught animals are less numerous in East Asia than in the Indian sub-continent, or indeed in South East Asia. In Tonkin in the 1930s there was only one draught animal to every 2.7 farms whilst in Japan only half the farms had draught animals.[21] Thus in East Asia there is more resort to hand labour and the seed bed may be prepared with a hoe or, as in Japan, a spade.[22] In nearly all of the Far East draught animals are either water buffalo, ideally suited to the muddy *sawahs,* or zebu. Japan is an exception, for the water buffalo is unknown, and horses are also used as well as oxen, whilst more recently the hand cultivator has been of growing importance.[23]

Rice seed is not usually drilled, and is thus either broadcast or transplanted. Transplanting is by far the most common method in East and South East Asia (Table 9). Indeed it is only in India, Bangla Desh and Sri Lanka that broadcasting is of significance.[24] About one-tenth of the farmers' *sawah* is set aside for the nurseries, which are very carefully cultivated and manured. After four to five weeks the seedlings are pulled, and transplanted in the *sawahs,* a task usually undertaken by women. In East Asia, and also in Java, although less commonly elsewhere, the seedlings are planted in rows to make weeding easier. Water is withdrawn from the *sawahs* some weeks before the harvest, much of which is gathered ear by ear with a knife or alternatively with a sickle.

The use of rotations is rare among rice cultivators, although in parts of East Asia green manuring is practised, Chinese milk vetch (*Astragalus chinensis*) being ploughed in.[25] In the same areas remarkable efforts are made to fertilise the soil with canal mud, compost, rice stalks and night-soil.[26] Elsewhere the *sawahs* receive little manure other than the droppings of draught animals.[27] The use of chemical fertilisers is, of course, a recent phenomenon, being first used on any scale in Japan in the 1920s. Japanese agriculture now uses more chemical fertilisers per hectare than any country in the world. Taiwan and Korea, both occupied by the Japanese in this century, are the only other countries with comparable use of chemical fertilisers (Table 9).

There is clearly a very marked contrast between the wet-rice cultivation of East Asia and the rest of Asia. This is reflected in rice yields (Table 9), which are only matched elsewhere in Malaya. This is partly due to the greater use of fertiliser, both artificial and natural, and partly to the greater use of irrigation. It may also reflect differences in latitude, for rice yields are favoured by the length of day and hours of sunshine, both of which are greater in high than low latitudes.[28] Although rice yields are high in East Asia, output per man is not, in comparison with the mechanised rice farming of the United States. Indeed output per man-hour has been compared unfavourably not only with the *ray* system of shifting cultivation in South Vietnam but also with bush fallowing in Africa.[29]

A last characteristic of wet-rice farming is the unimportance of livestock in the farm economy. The animals kept are used primarily for draught purposes; thus three-quarters of all the livestock in China are so used.[30] Meat and milk form a negligible part of the diet. In China pigs and poultry, which can exist on scraps and residues, are the main providers of meat.[31] Thus livestock and crop production are not combined in the wet-rice system as they are in most European farming systems. Even where farmers have access to uncultivated uplands, they have generally failed to develop any system of upland grazing.[32]

The reasons for the neglect of livestock are numerous. The extreme pressure on the cultivated land means that few farmers can spare the land to grow fodder crops. The hot, humid climate gives natural grasses that have a poor feed content, whilst animal diseases are common. High temperatures make the preservation of milk and butter difficult and also retard the growth and fertility of cattle. In parts of the Far East religious inhibitions preclude the slaughter of cattle and consumption of meat. Further, it should be noted that there has been a marked difference between Indian and Chinese attitudes to cattle. Although Hindu society has not favoured the slaughter of cows, there have been no prohibitions on the use of milk. Chinese peasants in contrast have rarely practised milking, even before the development of acute population pressure. There is thus a difference in the role of livestock between Indian-influenced societies and Chinese-influenced societies.[33]

Neither the general characteristics of wet-rice farming nor the regional variations in practice can be properly understood solely in terms of present conditions, and so the second part of this chapter is devoted to the history of wet-rice farming.

The origins of wet-rice cultivation

It is often stated that the present areas of wet-rice cultivation were all occupied – and densely populated – 2000 years ago; and that the methods of cultivation now in use have remained unchanged since early Christian times. Both these statements require considerable qualification.

Two major wet-rice areas can be distinguished in Asia. First, those where wet-rice farming, in some form, was already established in early Christian times, and which were slowly colonised in the following thousand years. By the time that Europeans arrived in Asia these regions already had high population densities; in the case of Japan and China, the total population per km² of cultivated land had reached 500 by the sixteenth century. Comparable densities were attained in Korea and northern Vietnam by the nineteenth century, if not before. The Indian sub-continent also falls into this category of 'old' settlement, although *nutritional* densities were lower than in East Asia. Java can also be regarded as an 'old' area of wet-rice cultivation, for although it experienced very marked expansion of population and rice acreage in the nineteenth century, there was a well-established wet-rice system in central Java in the early nineteenth century, and nutritional densities were already high.

Wet-rice cultivation in Asia

Second were those areas where rice had been grown since at least the beginning of the Christian period, but no significant wet-rice civilisations had developed; this included all of South East Asia except Java. The total population and the densities were low, and rice was grown either as a part of a system of shifting cultivation, as in Malaya, or with *extensive* wet-rice methods, as in the lower Mekong delta and the Tonlé Sap. However population growth in South East Asia in the nineteenth century was more rapid than that in the older settled areas (Table 17).[34] Furthermore these areas came under European influence, and became part of the international economy. Between 1850 and 1930 the former sparsely populated deltas of the Irrawaddy, Menam and Mekong were occupied and turned into areas of rice cultivation primarily for export, both to Europe and the rest of Asia.

It is thus possible to interpret the regional variations in wet-rice farming outlined earlier in this chapter in terms of the date of settlement and the density of population; areas of long-established settlement had to adopt intensive practices at an early date, whilst the more recently settled areas have still to adopt the elaborate labour-intensive methods of East Asia.

The settlement of the 'old' rice areas; China

In the first century A.D. – the time of the Han Dynasty in China and of the Guptas in India – the rice regions were sparsely populated (Fig. 13). The most densely populated part of China was the lower Hwang Ho valley, in India the middle Ganges, and in neither area was rice the dominant crop. In A.D. 2 there were 58 000 000 people in the Han Empire, and of these 43 000 000 lived north of the Yangtse delta, 35 000 000 on the alluvial plains of the Hwang Ho, and its tributaries the Wei Ho and Fen Ho.[35] South of the Yangtse there were few Han Chinese; most of the area was occupied by Thai-speaking peoples, who practised shifting cultivation in the uplands and a primitive form of wet-rice cultivation in the river valleys, and kept zebu cattle and water buffaloes. Further south rice was grown in the Tonkin delta, but when the Chinese occupied the area in 111 B.C. they did not find a very advanced farming technology. Nor had the Chinese themselves particularly sophisticated methods of cultivating rice. In the Yangtse valley, then a frontier region, the vegetation was cleared with fire, and natural inundations were the only source of water.[36]

Although rice was certainly grown in the Hwang Ho valley in Han times, it was probably not the leading crop, nor are there many references in the contemporary literature to small bunded fields and the associated methods of water control. There are no references to irrigation works before the sixth century B.C. and it was not until the first century B.C. that there were large-scale schemes. Canals were built from the Hwang Ho and its tributaries; but these may have been for flood control or navigation rather than irrigation. However the canals built by Li Ping in the Ch'engtu plains of Szechwan in the first century B.C. were undoubtedly for irrigation.

This is not to say that farming in northern China was backward, rather that a mature system of wet-rice cultivation was absent. However there is every evidence that the Han Chinese were familiar with intensive farming practices. Contemporary writers advocated the use of rotations, intertillage and the application of manure and night-soil, although how far these principles were practised is unknown. Hand cultivation with the hoe and the spade still predominated, although the use of the ox-drawn plough, with a metal share, was

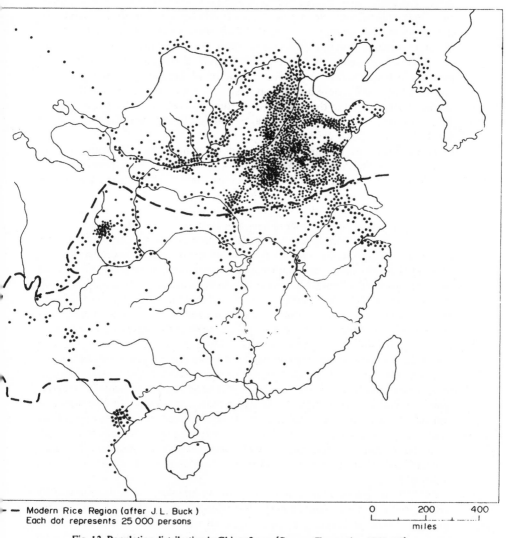

— — Modern Rice Region (after J L. Buck)
Each dot represents 25 000 persons

0   200   400
miles

Fig. 13. Population distribution in China, 2 A.D. [Source: Trewartha, 1969, 16]

becoming increasingly important. Although irrigation was by no means as common as is sometimes believed, the Chinese already had several methods of lifting water, including the *shaduf* and the square-pallet chain pump.[37]

Thus the characteristic features of Chinese wet-rice cultivation emerged later, when the Han Chinese migrated south of the Yangtse; they combined wet-rice, the zebu, the water buffalo and the poultry of the Thai-speaking peoples, bringing with them pigs and the intensive practices of the North, but abandoning their sheep. The Han had of course been migrating into southern China for centuries, but it was only after the fourth century A.D. that this movement involved substantial numbers, prompted by civil disturbances in the North and later by Mongol invasions. The migrants moved southwards from the Yangtse, following the valleys of the great rivers, particularly the middle Han, the Hsiang Chan, and the Chiang Kan. So rapidly did Han migration proceed that by the eighth century A.D. half the Chinese population lived in the Yangtse valley and the areas further south; indeed in the fourteenth century A.D. when the Mongols pillaged the North, over four-fifths of the total population lived in the Yangtse and the South.[38]

By the fourteenth century the major rice-growing areas of the present were already well-established – the Yangtse delta, the Hsiang valley, Szechwan and the lowlands of Kwantung; of the modern areas only Chekiang and Fukien were still sparsely populated.[39] Indeed by this time many of the characteristic modern Chinese methods had emerged. Irrigation became progressively more important. In the eighth century the number of new water control projects constructed in the South exceeded those in the North for the first time; these projects became more numerous after the tenth century. By the fourteenth century there were about 8 500 000 hectares of irrigated land in all China, and between a third and a half of the rice grown in the South was irrigated.[40] In the fourth century some farmers in the Yangtse valley grew a rice crop in the summer, and wheat or barley in the winter on the drained *sawahs;* but this was rare, for the rice varieties then grown in China took so long to mature. However in the eighth century early-maturing varieties were introduced from Champa, an Indian state in Indo-China. This had a number of consequences; the cultivation of two crops in a year – rice and wheat – became more common in the Yangtse valley, particularly after the tenth century, whilst further south two rice crops in a year became possible. The early-maturing varieties also needed less water than the superseded late-maturing varieties. It thus became possible to grow rice on terraces on the slopes of the southern uplands, using water from springs or relying upon rainfall alone; much of southern China was terraced by the fourteenth century. The new crops were well fertilised; by the fourteenth century the use of night-soil and silt was well established.[41]

By the fourteenth century most of the present intensive methods practised by wet-rice cultivators were known in the Rice Region of southern China. The population of China, however, was not then greatly above what it had been in Han times. What had changed was the distribution, for in 1395 45 000 000 of the total population of 70 000 000 lived in the Rice Region – the Yangtse valley and the areas further south. Thereafter there were prodigious increases in population. It was 160 000 000 in 1600, and after a period of stagnation in the seventeenth century due to civil war, there was a rapid increase in the eighteenth century, so that by 1813 the population of China was 347 000 000;[42] the rate of increase in the Rice Region was as rapid as in the country as a whole (Table 11).

How was this great increase fed, for there were no radical changes in farming technology?[43] In the first place the area under crops was extended, partly by increasing the rice acreage, but also by utilising the uplands in the south, which hitherto had been little used because of their unsuitability for wet-rice cultivation. The introduction of tropical American crops – maize, groundnuts and sweet potatoes – allowed their use. But whilst population quadrupled between 1400 and 1770, the cultivated area only doubled; arable land per caput thus declined markedly (Table 11). Yet the eighteenth century was regarded as a golden age and it was not until the 1820s that problems of congestion, underemployment and hunger became apparent in the south. Thus until the nineteenth century increases in rice yields kept pace with population growth.

This was not achieved by the adoption of any new farming methods – although new varieties of rice were selected and used – but by the wider adoption of established techniques. Thus double-cropping was practised in the seventeenth century, but not widely so, for there was still cultivable but uncultivated land remaining; but double-cropping of wheat and rice steadily increased in the eighteenth century, whilst double-cropping of rice became more common in the far south. The irrigated area also increased; it probably doubled in the Rice Region between 1400 and 1900. Equally important, there were progressive increases in labour inputs; more cultivation, more careful transplanting, more weeding, more application of manure, and thus gradual increases in crop yields.[44]

The early nineteenth century, however, proved an age of crisis. By then most of the cultivable land in the Rice Region was under rice; and there has been little increase since. For the first time the signs of acute population pressure became apparent; farms were sub-divided into uneconomic holdings, fragmentation increased and rural unemployment became a problem. Increasing intensity of labour inputs met with rapidly diminishing returns. Indeed it has been argued that the Taiping rebellion of the mid-nineteenth century was due to increasing rural poverty. Certainly it halted population growth, and some parts of the Yangtse valley still have population densities lower than they did in the mid-nineteenth century.[45]

Nor were there any solutions to the problem available at that time. Chinese migration into South East Asia was on too small a scale to alleviate population pressure. European influence was confined to the coastal areas, and thus no major irrigation works were built as in the Tonkin delta, northern Java or the Punjab. In Japan industrialisation provided some relief from growing population densities, for industry drained off the rural surplus, and also, later provided

TABLE 11 *Population and arable land in China*

Year	All China				The Rice Region			
	Arable (thousand km²)	Population (millions)	Population per km² of arable	Arable per caput (hectares)	Arable (thousand km²)	Population (millions)	Population per km² of arable	Arable per caput (hectares)
1400	252.5	70	277	0.36	149.5	45	301	0.33
1600	335.3	160	477	0.21	–	–	–	–
1760–70	634.2	270	425	0.23	317.1	170	536	0.18
1873	816.0	350	428	0.23	420.1	214	509	0.19
1913	917.0	430	468	0.21	428.2	262	611	0.16
1933	989.8	500	505	0.19	–	–	–	–
1957	1131.2	647	571	0.17	460.5	376	816	0.12

Source: Perkins, 1969, 16, 18, 207, 212, 216, 240

chemical fertilisers and agricultural machinery. This did not happen in China. Nor was there any major technological breakthrough. When J. L. Buck described the wet-rice cultivators of southern China in the 1930s the intensity of farming was unparalleled elsewhere, save in the Tonkin delta and Japan. But although crop yields were high, output per man-hour was low, and the regions had all the symptoms of chronic population pressure – indebtedness, tenancy, underemployment and malnutrition.[46]

Japan

Japanese wet-rice cultivation had a very similar history to that in China until the end of the nineteenth century, although in contrast to Han China, rice was a relatively modern introduction. Rice was taken to Kyushu in the third century B.C., almost certainly from southern China, but possibly via Korea. Expansion into Honshu was slow, possibly because the characteristic terrain of Japan was that of the small alluvial basin encompassed by mountains, rather than the broad river valleys of China. The Yayoi culture, which brought wet-rice to Japan, had expanded only to the Kinki plains at the eastern end of the Inland Sea by A.D. 300. The introduction of wet-rice led to a major change in settlement location, from the foothills to the alluvial plains. Yayoi farmers grew rice in small paddies but had no plough.[47] However in about the third century A.D. there was a further invasion from the mainland and these peoples established themselves in the Kinki – or Yamato – plains. They brought the iron plough, draught oxen and knowledge of more advanced wet-rice techniques such as the use of ponds for irrigation, and green manuring. The Yamato culture expanded both westward toward Kyushu, and northward in Honshu (Fig. 14). Progress northward was slow, partly because of the terrain, partly because of the spirited resistance of the Ainu people, the pre-Yayoi inhabitants of Japan, and also possibly because of the shorter growing season. Wet-rice cultivation was established in the Kanto plains around Tokyo by the sixth century A.D., in the Ou district of the west coast by the eighth century, and reached northern Honshu in the twelfth century. Although the first Japanese settlements were made in Hokkaido in the twelfth century, it was not until the late nineteenth century that wet-rice became of any importance.[48]

By the tenth century the Kinki and Kanto plains were the centres of Japanese civilisation (Fig. 15). Already they had very high nutritional densities (Table 12), which in 1600 were almost twice those of China. China was still the paramount influence in Japanese agriculture. Tea and silk had been introduced, and in A.D. 645 the *jôri* system of land division was imposed on the settled areas. Its chequerboard pattern can still be seen in the Kinki and Kanto plains.[49] The rice frontier continued to press northward. In the Tokugawa period, especially between 1580 and 1750, there was a considerable increase in the cultivated area, particularly in the frontier zone north of Tokyo.[50] Indeed this area remains distinctive in

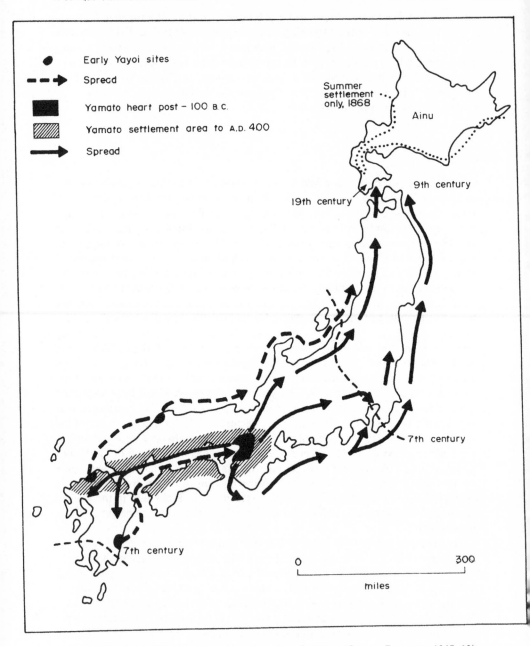

Fig. 14. Expansion of the Yayoi and Yamato cultures in Japan. |Source: Dempster, 1967, 65|

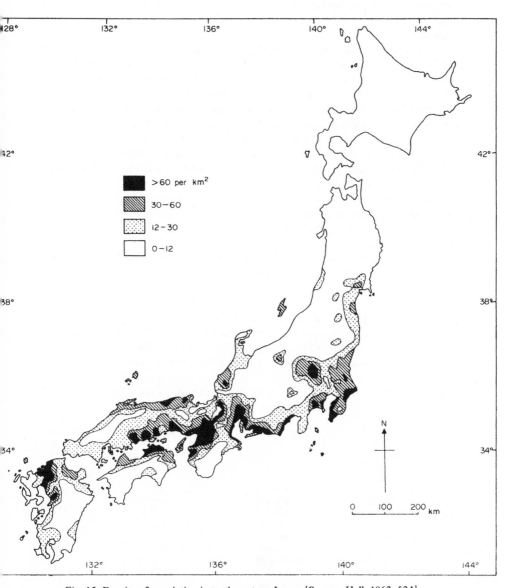

Fig. 15. Density of population in tenth-century Japan. [Source: Hall, 1962, 524]

modern Japan; settled much later than the traditional areas, it is still less commercialised, less intensively farmed, less densely populated, and with rather
larger farms. It is also the area where, since 1870, much of the new rice land has
been reclaimed.[51]

The progress of technique is more difficult to trace in Japan than in China. The
earliest wet-rice cultivators, as noted above, used the spade, not the plough; oxen
were not introduced until later, from Korea, and remained relatively unimportant, compared with hand labour, until the twentieth century. The water-buffalo
has never been introduced into Japan, although, unlike most rice-growing areas,
the horse is used in the *sawahs*. The earliest farmers used manure, night-soil, and
ploughed in grasses to maintain fertility. In the seventeenth century Japanese
farmers increasingly made off-farm purchases of fertilisers, including night-soil,
dried fish and oil-cake. Wet-rice seems to have been irrigated at an early date,
and increasingly so after the seventeenth century. The first evidence of transplanting dates from the eleventh century and the first record of wheat being grown on
the *sawahs* in winter from the thirteenth century. The double-cropping of rice,
still limited to the Kochi area by the short growing season, did not begin until the
eighteenth century.[52]

In Japan, as in China, the period between A.D. 1200 and A.D. 1700 was one of
rapid population growth, but the cultivated area seems to have expanded even
more rapidly (Table 12). Between 1720 and 1860 however the population
stagnated; then the Meiji restoration brought a renewed increase in population
and doubtless Japanese agriculture would have experienced problems as acute as
those in China had not industrialisation taken place. Although the cultivated
area has expanded since 1867 – indeed it has nearly doubled – the increase in
yields has been even more marked. This has been made possible to a large extent

TABLE 12 *Population and cultivated area in Japan, 1200–1970*

Year	Arable (km²)	Population	Population per km² of arable	Arable per caput (hectares)
1200	10 100	9 750 000	965	0.103
1580	14 948	–	–	–
1600	21 008	18 000 000	856	0.116
1700	30 300	25 000 000	825	0.121
1800	30 300	25 000 000	825	0.121
1867	32 320	27 000 000	835	0.119
1877	41 410	35 000 000	845	0.118
1905	54 237	47 000 000	866	0.115
1920	59 590	55 000 000	922	0.108
1934	60 600	68 000 000	1122	0.089
1960	57 772	93 000 000	1609	0.062
1970	55 100	103 540 000	1879	0.053

Sources: Kikuchi, 1959; Taeuber, 1958, 7, 14, 19, 20; Trewartha, 1965, 104, 106, 187,
190; F.A.O. *Production yearbook*, vol. 25, 1971

by the application of chemical fertilisers and the use of improved rice varieties. Further, although total population has increased, and the arable land per caput has declined (Table 12), the rural population has remained constant since the 1880s as industrialisation has absorbed the rural surplus (Table 13). Thus direct population pressure upon the land has not increased; indeed rural population densities have declined since the late nineteenth century.

TABLE 13   *Japan: rural population and arable land, 1877–1965*

Year	Arable land (km²)	Rural population (millions)	Rural population per km² of arable	Arable land per caput (hectares)
1877	41 410	32	772	0.129
1920	59 590	37	620	0.161
1934	60 600	37	610	0.163
1960	57 772	34	588	0.169
1965	60 040	31	522	0.195

Sources: as Table 12; F.A.O. *Production yearbook*, vol. 19, 1965; U.N. *Demographic yearbook*, 1970

Japan and southern China thus present an interesting contrast. In both countries a growing population was fed both by expanding the cultivated area and by intensifying labour inputs. In Japan however the initial nutritional densities were higher than in China, even allowing for the less reliable data available for Japan prior to the nineteenth century. But whereas nutritional densities in China have steadily increased since the fourteenth century, in Japan they remained remarkably constant until the end of the nineteenth century.

Korea, North Vietnam and Taiwan

North Vietnam, Korea and Taiwan have all been profoundly influenced by Chinese wet-rice methods, whilst the latter two countries have, in addition, been occupied by the Japanese, and North Vietnam by the French.

The Chinese occupied the Tonkin delta in 111 B.C.; there is little evidence of any advanced wet-rice technology at that time, but during the next thousand years of Chinese occupation the Annamites adopted Chinese wet-rice methods. By the end of Chinese rule in A.D. 939 they had embanked the Red River and at least partially controlled its devastating floods, and borrowed wholesale Chinese methods of growing wet-rice: green manuring, night-soil, the Chinese plough and the single draught animal, double-cropping and bucket lifts for irrigation. By the end of the period of Chinese rule, population densities were probably quite high – at least the southward migration of Annamites that began in the eleventh and twelfth centuries would support this belief, but there is little information on land use or population until after the French annexation in 1882.[53]

Wet-rice cultivation in Asia

At that time the population density in the delta was about 230 per km², but in the next fifty years the population doubled as the French improved sanitation and hygiene and death rates fell. Thus by the 1930s the nutritional density was about 600 per km². This was to some extent ameliorated by the great increase in the area which could be double-cropped, which was made possible by French construction of dams, embankments and canals, beginning in 1906 but most noticeably after the terrible floods of 1926. But the results of population growth were for the most part adverse, and were compounded by the introduction of French land law. Under this individual property rights were imposed upon a basically communal system of tenure, and this paved the way for an increase in tenancy. Farms became smaller and more fragmented as population grew, but it should be noted that they had always been relatively small; in the fourteenth century, for example, no family had been allowed to own more than 0.4 hectare.[54]

Korea. Korea, like northern Vietnam, has been profoundly influenced by China. Rice cultivation was introduced as early as the third millennium B.C., but wet-rice cultivation did not become established until the early Christian period when Korea was part of the Han Empire. At this time, as at the present, the major wet-rice areas were in the coastal valleys of the west and the south east. The first information on population distribution dates from the fifteenth century, when the population was less than a million, but the highest densities were in the rice-growing area. In the seventeenth century population rose from 1 500 000 to 7 000 000, but stagnated thereafter until the end of the nineteenth century.[55] At that time the nutritional densities in the wet-rice districts were about 500 per km², thus comparable with those of the Rice Region of China. Japanese annexation of Korea was followed by a fall in the death rate and a marked increase in population. Under the pressure of population growth and Japanese tutelage the stagnating wet-rice economy was transformed. The total area cropped doubled between 1910 and 1945, double-cropping was greatly extended, new rice varieties were introduced and chemical fertilisers began to be used. For some time a rice surplus was shipped to Japan. Less happily the commercialisation of agriculture led, as in northern Vietnam, to an increase in tenancy. Since the end of the Japanese occupation population growth has further accelerated, so that South Korea now has a nutritional density of 1200 per km². Fortunately the long Chinese tradition of farming combined with the Japanese and subsequent American influence has given the country one of the most intensive wet-rice economies in East Asia.[56] (See Table 9, p. 78.)

Taiwan. Although there were Chinese influences in Taiwan at least as early as the third millennium B.C. when rice was first introduced, the widespread adoption of Chinese wet-rice methods in the island was delayed much longer. In the modern period the first Chinese contacts were in the seventh century A.D. and in the fourteenth century the island was administered as part of the province of Fukien. But until the seventeenth century much of the island was occupied by shifting cultivators who grew millet, rice and taro. A brief period of Dutch rule led to the partial commercialisation of agriculture and the introduction of an im-

94

proved plough, horses and cattle. But the major changes came after the Chinese conquest of 1661 and the subsequent immigration from Kwantung and Fukien, by colonists who brought their wet-rice methods with them, as well as tea, poultry and water buffaloes, terracing, and methods of lifting water. But the very high efficiency of modern Taiwanese agriculture is due to more recent occupations. In 1895 the Japanese annexed the island, and after 1907 established the first large-scale irrigation systems, encouraged the use of commercial fertilisers, improved rice varieties, and encouraged double-cropping, a process extended after 1945 by American advice and aid.[57]

The Indian sub-continent

The difference between the intensity of wet-rice cultivation in East Asia, on the one hand, and India and South East Asia, on the other, has already been noted. But whereas the relatively low population densities and extensive cultivation of rice in South East Asia may be, as we shall see, attributed to the lateness of settlement, India combines early settlement with *currently* high nutritional densities *within* the rice regions, yet low yields and a low index of farming intensity (Tables 9 and 10).

As in China, the earliest wet-rice cultivation was outside the modern rice regions, in the middle and upper Ganges. Indeed Bengal does not seem to have been effectively occupied until the third century B.C., and as late as the sixth century A.D. it was still regarded as a frontier region,[58] but so too were southern China and Honshu for much of the first millennium A.D. Little is known of the deltas of the east or west coast in the early Christian period; canals had been built in the Cauvery delta by the second century A.D., there were irrigation works in Orissa, and Tamilnad was certainly settled by the third century A.D.[59] In Ceylon the first references to the irrigation works of the Dry Zone date from the fourth century B.C., but the larger tanks were not built until the first century A.D. The Wet Zone, now the centre of rice production, was largely unoccupied.[60]

It is difficult to find reliable information on the methods of wet-rice cultivation at the beginning of the Christian era. However it is significant that most of the techniques were known, if not widely practised. In Bengal rice was transplanted as well as being broadcast, although transplanting was unknown in Ceylon, and indeed remains unimportant to the present. The ox-drawn plough was used for cultivation and the sickle for reaping. Double-cropping and some irrigation were practised. Canals and weirs had been built on the east-coast deltas, and tanks in Tamilnad and the Dry Zone of Ceylon. But most irrigation works were in the drier West of the sub-continent, and not in the rice-growing areas of the East.[61]

There is little evidence on the changes which took place in Indian agriculture between Gupta times and the Mughal Empire. The flimsy evidence on Indian population suggests that the population of A.D. 1600 was little, if any, larger than that of 320 B.C.[62] Agriculture had, however, a distinctly modern flavour. The major rice-growing areas were much the same as at the present – Bengal, Bihar,

Orissa, Tamilnad and Kerala. In Ceylon, however, there had been a major shift in the location of wet-rice production. Until the thirteenth century the Dry Zone had been the major wet-rice area. But thereafter that region declined and the more humid south west assumed the importance it still retains. The decline of the Dry Zone was due to a number of factors. Tamil invasions disrupted Sinhalese rule; the irrigation system, essential in the Dry Zone, became inefficient; malaria became more common.[63]

In 1600 the population of India was probably no more than 125 000 000. The cultivated area, however, was possibly about 46 500 000 hectares, so that there was nearly 0.4 hectare of arable per head of the population. Certainly sixteenth- and seventeenth-century descriptions of India suggest that there was comparatively little population pressure. The nutritional density of 269 per km^2 was well below the figures for China and Japan at this time. Only the more fertile land was in cultivation, so that crop yields were probably not greatly below those attained at the beginning of this century. Although farms were small and often fragmented, as they had been in Gupta times, they were larger than at present. There were more livestock per farmer, and the animals had more land to graze, although there was little integration of livestock into the arable economy, save as draught animals. Little manure was used on the rice fields. Most farmers relied upon family labour, although a class of landless labourers had already appeared, drawn mainly from the lower castes who were forbidden to own land and supplemented their income by working as hired labourers.[64]

The Indian peasant of the sixteenth century might appear to have been better off than his modern descendant. And indeed he probably would have been but for the excessive rents and dues imposed. So oppressive was the Mughal governing class that in the seventeenth century there was a decline in the cultivated area as peasants fled to the towns.[65]

TABLE 14 *Population and arable land in All-India, 320 B.C.–A.D. 1968*

Year	Arable (km^2)	Population (millions)	Population per km^2 of arable	Arable per caput (hectare)
320 B.C.	–	100–140	–	–
A.D. 1600	464 600	125	269	0.37
1800	–	120	–	–
1845	–	130	–	–
1855	–	175	–	–
1871	–	255	–	–
1901	795 880	285	358	0.28
1911	868 600	305	351	0.28
1941	832 240	388	466	0.21
1961	1 515 000	570	376	0.26
1968	1 929 680	647	335	0.29

Sources: Davis, 1951, 27; Blyn, 1966, 251–350; Spate, 1956, 334–8; Spate and Learmonth, 1967, 390–6; F.A.O. *Production yearbook*, vol. 25, 1971. The figure for arable land in 1600 is an approximation based on information in Habib, 1965. All data refer to India and Pakistan combined.

TABLE 15 *Population and agriculture in Greater Bengal, 1891–1961*

Year	Population (millions)	Arable (thousand km²)	Population per km² of arable	Arable per caput (hectare)	Rice yields (kg per hectare)	% irrigated	% double-cropped
1891	74.01	217.7	339	0.29	902	–	15.9
1901	77.5	197.9	391	0.25	973	1.8	21.4
1911	82.4	211.6	389	0.25	1170	10.5	20.7
1921	83.1	208.8	397	0.25	1060	14.8	20.8
1931	90.5	197.5	458	0.21	1055	14.0	21.5
1941	108.6	195.9	554	0.18	909	17.2	21.7
1946	–	211.6	–	–	838	–	–
1951	121.7	–	–	–	838	–	–
1961	149.6	267.4	559	0.17	–	16.5	24.0

Sources: Blyn, 1966; Spate and Learmonth, 1967, 392–3

Wet-rice cultivation in Asia

At the beginning of the nineteenth century the population of India was still comparatively small and the nutritional densities low. But in the nineteenth century population began to move steadily upwards. Bengal, which in the seventeenth century exported rice, and had a remarkably diversified economy, became increasingly dependent upon rice and jute alone. The East India Company, and later the Crown, built irrigation works. In 1850 there were only 3 000 000 acres irrigated in the whole country, but by 1915 40 000 000. But most of this increase took place in the drier regions – particularly the Punjab – and not the rice-growing areas, although weirs and canals were begun on the Godavari delta in 1846 and the Krishna in 1851.[66]

At the beginning of this century the nutritional density was 358 per km^2 but the data in Table 14 refer to All-India, not the rice regions. However trends in the rice regions are reasonably well shown in Table 15, where data for Bihar, Orissa and Bengal are presented. This area includes half of the sub-continent's rice area. Between 1881 and 1941 population increase in Bengal, the east coast and the south was greater than in the north west, centre and the upper and middle Ganges. In short it was the areas of higher rainfall and rice-growing that had the fastest rate of increase.[67] This was not however matched by any increase – in Greater Bengal – in the cultivated area. The empty lands of the seventeenth century had long since been brought into cultivation, and between 1891 and 1951 the cultivated area stagnated although population doubled. The result was a marked decline in the arable per caput and a rise in the nutritional density. But this was not matched by any significant increase in the intensity of farming practices. Although the area under rice which was irrigated increased from less than 2 per cent in 1901 to 16.5 per cent in 1961, when a quarter was double-cropped compared with only one-fifth in 1901, rice yields actually declined between 1901 and 1961. The introduction of new high-yielding rice varieties in the mid-1960s thus came at a critical time.

The intensity and efficiency of Indian wet-rice cultivation are still below those of most parts of East Asia. It is by no means clear why this is so. A possible explanation may be that population growth in the Indian rice areas was much slower in India than in China or Japan. Thus, although *some* Indian farmers had long been familiar with techniques such as irrigation, double-cropping, transplanting and careful weeding, and even the use of night-soil, the relatively low densities – by East Asian standards – that prevailed until the mid-nineteenth century had allowed the persistence of relatively extensive farming methods. Indeed densities comparable with those of the Rice Region of southern China were not reached until the 1930s (cf. Tables 11 and 12). India has only had to grapple with very high densities in this century, and they have grown very rapidly. The Chinese and the Japanese had a much longer period of slowly increasing densities to combine the various techniques into a system of intensive farming.

Java

Wet-rice farming in Java is a curious outlier of East Asian techniques in South

98

East Asia. Terracing, double-cropping, transplanting and irrigation are all practised, and population densities are high, farms small and fragmented, and tenancy common. Yet crop yields are low. Further, Java has a much longer history of
wet-rice cultivation than most other South East Asian countries. Wet-rice
techniques – as distinct from rice-growing – were probably introduced into Java
by immigrants from Indo-China in the early Christian period, and certainly
before the period of Indian influence; this influence had its greatest impact on
cultural and religious life, and may have had little importance for the farmer.[68]
The wet-rice farmers were initially found, not on the coastal alluvia, but in the inner reaches of rivers, in small basins of volcanic soils in central and eastern Java;
these areas, more like the small plains of Japan than the broad valleys and deltas
of China or India, formed the basis of the state of Mataram in the eighth century
A.D. The expansion of wet-rice cultivation into the rest of Java was slow. In the
north the coastal plains were regularly flooded; to the west the Sunda highlands
had few areas of gentle slope, and the East Hook was too dry for *sawah*
agriculture without irrigation. However by the tenth century there was rice
cultivation in the Brantas valley, and the East Hook was colonised in the
thirteenth century, whilst the northern coastal plains – the *pasisir* – were occupied in the fourteenth century. But the main rice areas remained in the original
core area – *Kedjawén* – until the nineteenth century.[69]

In 1815 the nutritional density of Java was 330 per km^2, above that of All-
India in the *late* nineteenth century, but well short of Chinese or Japanese densities. But there were already signs of overcrowding;[70] the population of Java
grew explosively in the next hundred years. From 5 000 000 in 1815 it had
doubled by 1850, doubled again by 1880 and reached nearly 30 000 000 in 1900,
a rate of increase without precedent in the other areas of 'old' rice settlement in
the Indian sub-continent and East Asia. Again, unlike Japan and China, Java
was a colonial dependency, and the reaction of wet-rice cultivators to population
growth was complicated by the Dutch use of village lands to grow export crops,
particularly sugar-cane. Only in Bengal had there been a similar combination of
an industrial crop – jute – and wet-rice.

The reaction of the Javanese to such rapid population growth was various. In
the first place *sawah* agriculture expanded out of its homelands in the *Kedjawén*.
The first attempts by the Dutch to control the rivers in the *pasisir* had been in the
mid-eighteenth century[71], but the successful control dates only from the late
nineteenth century. By 1920 however there was little uncultivated land left in
Java which could be used for *sawah*. A second expansion took place in the dry
lands, or *tegalan*, throughout the island, but especially in the eastern part. Much
of this area was terraced for the first time.[72] The crops grown were nearly all
American crops introduced in the early nineteenth century: maize, cassava,
sweet potatoes and groundnuts, called collectively *palawidja*. These began to increase more rapidly than the *sawah* area after 1880, for they were grown not
only on the *tegalan*, but also as second crops on the *sawahs*. Indeed by the late
1930s the area under dry-land crops exceeded that under irrigated rice.[73]

Wet-rice cultivation in Asia

Thus whilst Java's cultivated area – including *sawah* and *tegalan* – increased four-and-a-half times between 1815 and 1920, the population of the island in 1920 was nearly seven times what it had been in 1815. By the early twentieth century the land suitable for wet-rice cultivation was exhausted. Instead the Javanese intensified labour inputs, a process described by Geertz as agricultural involution. As it was impossible to bring in new land, more and more of the increasing rural population was used to try to raise rice yields, by improving water control, by replacing broadcasting by transplanting, by more weeding, draining of the *sawahs* for aeration, using more manures, double-cropping and more careful harvesting. But little fertiliser was used, except in the areas where sugarcane was grown on the *sawahs* by sugar corporations; no new varieties were introduced. Thus the increase in yields was slow.[74]

TABLE 16   *Population and arable land in Java and Madura, 1815–1960*

Year	Arable (km²)	Population (millions)	Population per km² of arable	Arable per caput (hectares)	Rice (thousand hectares)
1815	15 150	5.0	330	0.3	848
1900	66 660	28.4	426	0.23	2787
1920	80 800	34.4	425	0.23	3151
1930	84 840	41.7	491	0.20	3272
1940	90 496	48·0	530	0.18	3434
1960	88 880	63.0	708	0.14	3514

Sources: Soen, 1968, 41, 43, 48; Geertz 1963, 69–70; Fisher, 1964a, 175, 286–9; Dobby, 1950, 23

By the 1920s the increases in cultivated land had come to a halt; indeed the present arable area is little above that in 1920, whereas the population has almost doubled. The increasing congestion in Java prompted the Dutch government to try and settle Javanese in the Outer Islands, where there was little wet-rice cultivation, and shifting cultivation or plantation agriculture predominated. This has had but limited success, if only because the migrants have rarely been more than a fraction of the annual increase in population. Thus the increasing labour inputs which characterised Javanese agriculture in the second half of the nineteenth century have had little impact on crop yields, and output per man has progressively declined. In 1960 the nutritional density was 700, a figure only exceeded elsewhere in the wet-rice regions in parts of East Asia.

South East Asia

The cultivation of wet-rice was already widely distributed throughout South East Asia 2000 years ago, and many farmers may have been using a variety of wet-rice techniques. Certainly terracing and irrigation were then known in the northern mountains of Luzon. On the mainland the position is less clear. Rice was domesticated in Indo-China at least as early as the fourth millennium B.C., but no advanced civilisations based on wet-rice developed there. Coedès[75] however believes that the Indo-Chinese grew wet-rice, used irrigation, the plough, and practised transplanting at least as early as the early Christian period, and that they carried this system south into the Malay peninsula and Indonesia. Other authorities believe that wet-rice cultivation was not introduced into Indo-China until Indians settled on the Malayan and Indonesian coasts and what is now South Vietnam in the early centuries of the Christian era.[76]

Be that as it may, later events have greater significance in interpreting the history of wet-rice in South East Asia. Three are of importance: first was the slow occupation of the deltas of the Irrawaddy, Menam and Mekong by peoples whose original homes lay further north and who had cultural affinities with the Chinese. Second was the arrival of Europeans in South East Asia, and their eventual annexation of much of the area. At first the economic consequences of European control were confined to the development of plantation crops for export, but in the middle nineteenth century rising prices for rice in Europe, and later the demand for rice in India, Japan and China, led to the development in the deltas of rice production intended primarily for export. A third important event was the very rapid growth of population, a result first of the imposition of law and order, later of the slow spread of better hygiene and sanitation, and more recently of cheap drugs and insecticides. The South East Asian states thus grew far more rapidly than the older settled rice regions (Table 17).

TABLE 17   *Population in Asia, 1830–1954*

	1830 (millions)	1954 (millions)	Increase by factor
Java	6	54.2	9.03
Other Indonesia	5	27.2	5.5
Philippines	2.5	21.4	8.5
Thailand	2.7	19.9	7.4
Indo-China	5.2	31.9	6.1
Malaya	0.4	7.0	17.5
Burma	4.0	19.2	4.8
India	130	430	3.3
China	320	640	2.0
Japan	26	88	3.3

Sources: Fisher, 1964*b*, 51; and Tables 9, 10 and 12

The Burmese people seem to have their origins in western China, but they moved south at an early date, and by the eighth century had settled the Kyautse plains in the Dry Zone of Burma, having learned wet-rice techniques from the Thai and irrigation from the Mons peoples. They had reached and conquered the coast by A.D. 1050, but although important towns were established upon the Arakan coast, the centre of the Burmese state remained firmly in the north. Such population as there was in the delta was greatly reduced by eighteenth-century wars, and when the British arrived in the 1820s it was still thinly populated; rice was grown, but only by shifting cultivation. There was no irrigation, nor had any attempt been made to control the floods of the Irrawaddy.[77]

The Thai also originated north of the present state of Thailand, possibly in the area of modern Yunnan and Szechwan; but they infiltrated slowly southwards from as early as the sixth century B.C. into the areas occupied by the Mons and Khmer people. But this movement did not become substantial until the eleventh and twelfth centuries; by the thirteenth century the Thai were well established in the northern hills of modern Thailand. By 1350 they had occupied the central plain and the Menam delta, and Ayuthia at the head of the delta had become their capital. The delta progressively became more important, and in 1770 Bangkok was made the capital. In 1855, when Sir John Bowring negotiated the trade treaty that opened Siam to western influence, the distribution of population was much the same as at present. Bangkok already had a population of 300 000. Canals and weirs had long been established, and rice was the leading crop. But population densities were low and much of the delta was unoccupied.[78]

The lower Mekong and the Tonlé Sap had civilisations earlier than the Irrawaddy or the Menam; in the second century A.D. Chinese writers described the Hindu-influenced state of Funan, which was based upon wet-rice, whilst much later Cambodia at its height, which in the ninth century A.D. produced the splendid city of Angkor, was also dependent upon rice, although much of it seems to have been produced by shifting cultivation. Both these civilisations were the products of Mon–Khmer people, but by the time Europeans arrived in Indo-China the dominant people in the lower Mekong delta were the Annamites, or Vietnamese, who had migrated south from the Tonkin delta. After the Vietnamese had gained their independence from the Chinese in A.D. 939 they moved slowly southwards along the coast and fought a series of wars with the Hinduised state of Champa in central and southern Vietnam.[79] Thus the Annamite coast immediately south of the Tonkin delta was soon settled by migrants and has retained very similar farming methods and population densities, although the latter are lower, reflecting the shorter history of settlement.[80] The Vietnamese continued to press southwards, by 1623 had established settlements near Saigon, and by the eighteenth century were settling the eastern part of the Mekong delta, pushing the Mon–Khmer people north-westwards. By the time the French annexed the lower Mekong, Vietnamese settlement had reached the Bassac river, but their farming was far less intensive than that practised in the north; population densities in the lower Mekong hardly exceeded 20 per km^2 in 1862.[81]

Burma was the first country to experience the rapid growth of rice production for export. In 1852 Britain annexed lower Burma, and during the American Civil War was cut off from the Carolinas, her main source of rice imports, whilst in 1869 the opening of the Suez Canal shortened the sea route to Europe. But the main stimulus to development was the rise in world rice prices. The main British contribution in Burma, apart from establishing law and order, was to build, between 1860 and 1930, a series of embankments to control the floods of the Irrawaddy. The rainfall of the monsoons was sufficient to provide water for the *sawahs* in the initial period. At first rice was exported unhusked, but later European and Indian capital financed the construction of mills, at first concentrated in Rangoon, but by 1900 to be found in most of the smaller towns of the delta. The colonization of the rice lands was undertaken almost entirely by immigrants from the rest of Burma, especially after 1860, who settled as peasant proprietors on farms of 3 to 4 hectares. Indian seasonal labourers also played an important role and as late as the 1930s 200000 came each year for the harvest.

TABLE 18   *Rice area and exports in Burma, 1855–1970*

	Area		Exports	
Year	All Burma (thousand hectares)	Lower Burma (thousand hectares)	Year	Exports (million tons)
1855	–	441	–	–
1866	708	567	–	–
1886	1619	1497	1881	0.5
1896	2330	2023	1901	1.4
1910	4027	3157	1911	1.7
1920	4168	3480	1921	2.4
1930	4876	4006	–	–
1941	5058	–	1941	3.5
1948	4006	2792	1948	1.2
1959–60	4290	–	1960	1.8
1970	4809	–	1970	0.6

Sources: Fisher, 1964a, 436; Dobby, 1950, 173; F.A.O. *Production yearbook*, vol. 25, 1971; *Trade yearbook*, vol. 25, 1971

The area under rice in lower Burma expanded prodigiously (Table 18), as did exports, so that by the 1930s the rice area in the delta was nearly ten times what it had been in the 1850s, and over half the output was exported. Before 1900 most of the exports went to Europe but after that to the rice-deficit areas of Asia – Japan, India, Ceylon and China became the major markets.

Much of the credit for expansion was provided by the *chettyars*, a southern Indian money-lending caste. Whilst prosperity lasted this caused few problems, but the poor prices after 1908 led to growing peasant indebtedness. By the 1930s 50 per cent of the land in the delta was owned by absentee landlords and 36 per cent by the *chettyars*. This problem of tenancy was not solved until the land reform of the 1950s.[82]

There have been few changes in farming methods; transplanting is widely practised, but irrigation is uncommon; fertilisers are rare and yields low. Nor is this surprising, for there is still unoccupied but cultivable land left in the delta and thus little incentive to intensify production. The nutritional density of all Burma in 1901 was less than 230 per km², and even now hardly exceeds 260. This density had been exceeded in China by the fourteenth century.[83]

Thailand differed from Burma in several important ways. First, the delta was already the centre of the state, and had been occupied by wet-rice farmers for at least five centuries although the population density was still low. Secondly, rainfall was insufficient to provide a secure water supply, and the success of the rice crop depended upon the floods of the Menam. Too great a flood could drown the rice fields, too little could give poor yields. Away from the area of natural inundation there was little cultivation, although the Thai had constructed some weirs and canals; nor were there any great dykes to protect the land from floods. Third, Siam, by carefully playing the French off against the English, avoided annexation, although of course the Bowring Treaty of 1855 opened up the country to European capital. Fourth, Thailand already had some tradition of rice exports, dating from at least as early as the seventeenth century.[84]

The expansion of rice in Thailand was undertaken by peasants already living there, rather than by immigrants, as in the Irrawaddy delta. It was encouraged by liberal land laws and the tax reliefs which were offered to pioneers. Labour mobility was increased by the abolition of slavery and the *corvée*,[85] whilst the construction of railways and irrigation works speeded settlement. The principal irrigation scheme was that at Rangsit, begun in 1889, and the South Pa Sak scheme, begun in 1916. But there was relatively little done to improve irrigation until after the Second World War. At first the expansion of the rice area was much slower than in lower Burma (Table 19) and exports were also smaller.

TABLE 19   *Rice area and exports in Thailand, 1850–1970*

Year	Rice area (thousand hectares)	Exports (million tons)	Total population (millions)
1850	931	–	5
1857–9	–	0.05	–
1905–6	1457	0.8	–
1915–19	2226	0.9	–
1935–9	3399	1.5	14.4
1950	5666	1.3	–
1956	6078	1.2	19.9
1959	–	1.09	21.4
1970	6727	1.08	35.8

Sources: Pendleton, 1962, 135; Fisher, 1964*a*, 174; Ingram, 1964, 109; F.A.O. *Production yearbook*, vol. 25, 1971; *Trade yearbook*, vol. 25, 1971

Indeed it is only since the Second World War, when the Burmese economy has been disrupted by internal problems, that Thai exports have exceeded those of Burma. Thai rice production is less concentrated in the delta regions than it was at the beginning of the century, with the recent development of rice production in the Khorat plateau.[86] But it is in the Central Plain that most attention has been paid to increasing irrigation facilities, most of which depend upon the Chainat barrage at the head of the delta, which was completed in 1956. Thai farming methods show Chinese influence, particularly in the ways of lifting water, and also in the use of a single buffaio in ploughing, but unlike the Chinese the Thais have no knowledge of terracing.[87] Methods are relatively extensive. Most rice is transplanted, except in areas of heavy flooding, where 'floating' rice is broadcast, but little fertiliser is used, nor is much labour expended in cultivation. Indeed from the 1920s until the mid-1950s rice yields showed a perceptible downward trend as inferior land was brought into cultivation. This has been halted by the extension of irrigation and the introduction of new rice varieties. Farms are still well above the average size for East Asia, at 3–5 hectares, in spite of the increase in population, for this has been matched by the continued expansion of the cultivated area. In 1960 the nutritional density for all Thailand was only 269 per km². Yet there are recent signs that population is beginning to increase more rapidly than output, and this may threaten Thailand's exports in the near future.[88]

When the French annexed Cochin-China in 1862 the Annamites had occupied the Mekong delta as far as the Bassac distributary (Fig. 16), but effective settlement dated only from the eighteenth century, and the average density of population was no more than 20 per km².[89] Beginning in 1870, the French constructed a series of major canals which eased the problems of flooding as well as carrying irrigation water, although only the areas near the canals were effectively irrigated. The trans-Bassac territories were then open to settlement, but whereas in Burma and Thailand colonisation was undertaken by peasant freeholders, in the Mekong delta the land was sold off in large estates of up to 1000 hectares. The estates however were divided up into farms of four to six hectares operated by share-cropping tenants, the *ta dien*. This contrasted with the smaller peasant-owned farms of between one and five hectares found east of the Bassac. In spite of the rapid growth of population in the delta as a whole, the difference between the territories to the east and those to the west of the Bassac has persisted.[90]

TABLE 20   *Rice area and exports in Cochin-China, 1880–1970*

	Rice area (thousand hectares)	Exports (thousand metric tons)
1880	486	284
1900	1052	747
1920	1821	1200
1939	2185	1454
1957	2711	812
1966	2226	–
1970	2510	–

Sources: Fisher, 1964*a*, 540, 578; Fryer, 1970, 407;
F.A.O. *Production yearbook*, vol. 25, 1971

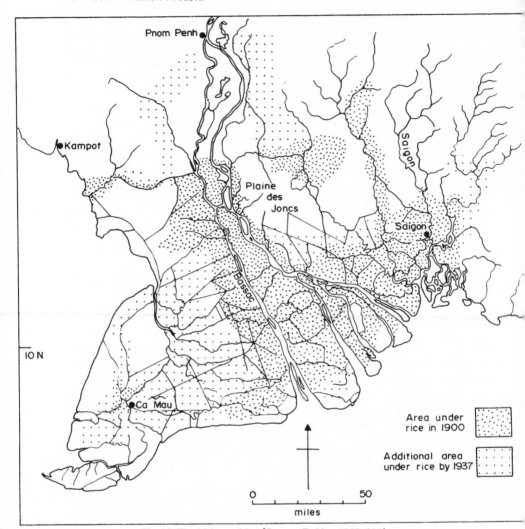

Fig. 16. The Mekong delta. [Source: Dobby, 1950, 302]

Again, as in Thailand, the expansion of the rice area in the lower Mekong was slow in comparison with the colonisation of the lower Irrawaddy (Table 20), although by the 1930s southern Vietnam's rice exports were comparable with those of Thailand. Methods were far less intensive than in northern Vietnam and yields significantly lower. Transplanting is the dominant mode of planting, although to the north of the delta where the floods are exceptionally high, 'floating' rice is grown, and in a few areas double transplanting is practised. Since 1945 some new land has been reclaimed but this has not compensated for the

106

decline in the cultivated area due to the war, and since 1964 South Vietnam has had to import rice. This is particularly tragic, not only in that the Mekong delta has much land capable of reclamation, particularly in the Plaine des Joncs, but also because the international control of the Mekong would increase the area irrigated and raise yields. The decline of the cropped area in the delta, together with population increase, the influx of refugees from the north and the unequal distribution – the Plaine des Joncs and the coastal areas have always been very thinly populated – has meant that the nutritional densities in the old settled areas of the delta are now much higher than in the Menam and the Irrawaddy.[91]

Malaya and the Philippines

Malaya and the Philippines have much in common with Burma, Thailand and South Vietnam, in that they were without wet-rice civilisations in the sixteenth century, and that they have also experienced a considerable expansion of their rice area in the last hundred years, but this has not been for export. Rather it has been to feed a rapidly growing population whose economic interests have been in the export of plantation crops, and, in the case of Malaya, tin as well.

Rice was grown in Malaya in the early Christian period; some writers believe that wet-rice cultivation was practised,[92] but it is more commonly held that only dry-rice was grown by *ladang* methods, until the sixteenth century, when wet-rice methods were introduced into Kedah from Thailand.[93] Immigrants from Sumatra also introduced wet-rice methods into Selangor in the late eighteenth century, but it was not until the nineteenth century that they were widely adopted. The development first of tin and later of rubber in Malaya attracted Chinese, Indian and Indonesian immigrants into the country in the second half of the nineteenth century, and the total population increased rapidly from 400 000 in 1835 to 2 600 000 in 1911, 4 500 000 in 1930 and 7 000 000 in 1960. This remarkable expansion has been largely a result of immigration, and not only of Chinese and Indians. In 1957 half the 'indigenous' Malay population were either immigrants from Indonesia or descendants of recent immigrants. Further, the expansion of rice cultivation has, until recently, taken second place to the expansion of commercial crops, and in particular rubber. The major rice areas are in the Kelantan and Trengganu deltas of the north east, and in Kedah in the north west, areas which are among the oldest settled in Malaya.[94] Most wet-rice cultivation is unirrigated although transplanted, and double-cropping is rare, but of growing importance in the post-war reclamation schemes.[95] These have been necessary both to settle the rapidly growing population, to reduce the substantial rice imports upon which Malaya depends, and also to try and increase the incomes of the *padi* growers who are almost all Malays.[96]

The Philippines provide an interesting case of the problems of tracing the history of rice-growing. In the northern mountains of Luzon the Ifugao peoples have long terraced hillsides and irrigated their rice, but used the hoe and not the plough. They are thought to have arrived from China perhaps 4000 years ago.

Yet the bulk of the Filipino population arrived from Indonesia in the last few centuries B.C., and possibly before *sawah* agriculture reached Java.[97] In spite of renewed contacts with Indonesia in the period of Islam hegemony, the lowland Filipinos did not acquire wet-rice techniques, and when the Spanish arrived rice was grown as a part of the *caingin* system of shifting cultivation. Although the population in the sixteenth century hardly exceeded 500 000, the Central Plain of Luzon was already the major agricultural area. Spanish influence upon the islands was not as dramatic as that of the Dutch upon Java; however, they introduced the idea of individual ownership of land – most of the Filipino communities had held their land communally – and imposed a land tax. Consequently farming became increasingly sedentary in the lowlands of Luzon, and problems of tenancy developed. The rapid expansion of the population – it was only 1 500 000 in 1800 but nearly 7 000 000 in 1899 – led to the steady expansion of wet-rice cultivation in the Central Plain of Luzon.[98] Water buffaloes and the plough were used, transplanting was practised, but, except in the area immediately around Manila where there was some irrigation, wet-rice depended upon rainfall. Unlike most other rice areas, the Central Plain lacked major rivers to give reliable inundations.[99]

Under American rule there was an extension of the irrigated area, but it did not keep pace with the expansion of the rice area, which is now six times what it was in the early twentieth century.[100] Much of this expansion however has come outside the Central Plain, and a fair proportion is of dry upland rice, not wet-rice. Only 12 per cent of the rice area is irrigated so that double-cropping is rare, for Luzon has a long dry season; rice yields are among the lowest in Asia. Nevertheless the expansion of the cultivated area has almost kept pace with the population growth and the nutritional density has not risen as dramatically as in Java, Korea or North Vietnam (Table 22), although in the Central Plain, where densities are higher, problems of overcrowding have become serious. But even there, farms are between two and four hectares in size so that the chronic subdivision of East Asia has yet to appear. Not that this means that the wet-rice farmers are prosperous. Many of them are share-croppers, permanently indebted to their landlords.[101]

Conclusions

The most striking features of the distribution of wet-rice cultivation are: first, its restriction to such limited parts of Asia; second, the very high population densities; and third, the marked contrast between East Asia and the other wet-rice areas. These facts are interconnected.

Wet-rice cultivation is only possible in a few environments. Outside areas of level ground and away from sources of water – either rainfall or rivers – the cost of terracing and moving water is prohibitive.

Second, wet-rice under Asian conditions gives a very favourable output per hectare compared with other food crops (Table 21).

TABLE 21   *Calorific value of grain crops in Asia*

Crop	Calories[1] per kg	Average[2] yield (kg per hectare)	Calories per hectare per year	Calories per acre per day
Rice	3400	1440	4 896 000	5595
Wheat	3400	820	2 788 000	3186
Sorghum	3400	400	1 360 000	1500
Maize	3400	860	2 924 000	3341

Sources:
(1) Van Royen, 1954, 84
(2) Average yield in Asia, 1948–52, F.A.O. *Production yearbook*. vol. 35, 1969

Assuming that 3000 calories are needed per day to feed a man, 0.4 hectare under rice could feed one person, with a considerable surplus, or one man and a child, or two men at a pinch. No other cereal produces so many calories per hectare; maize, the only competitor, was not known in Asia until the sixteenth century, whilst wheat cannot be grown successfully in the more humid tropics.

Thus in Asia we can envisage a number of types of farming emerging. First was tropical vegeculture; second, after about 3500 B.C., rice was domesticated. Dry-rice was grown as a part of a shifting cultivation system. Wet-rice, on the other hand, needed different conditions; it was one of the few crops that could successfully utilise seasonally inundated deltas and the lower reaches of rivers. But, as was noted above, there was no need for wet-rice to be grown intensively. Thus at some date prior to 500 B.C. extensive wet-rice cultivation was found in most of the river valleys of Asia, but it bore little resemblance to the intensive farming practices of modern times. The first millennium A.D. was the frontier period of the wet-rice cultivators. They colonised southern China, Honshu and the delta of the Ganges–Brahmaputra. At a fairly early time in this millennium most of the techniques of wet-rice cultivation were known to some farmers in most parts of South, South East and East Asia.

Nonetheless there were, by medieval times, very different levels of wet-rice techniques in Asia; it seems reasonable to suppose that this was a result of differences in population density (Table 22). By about 1400 most of the land suitable for wet-rice cultivation in China, Japan, northern Vietnam and probably Korea was already occupied; to feed the growing populations, wet-rice cultivators have been forced to intensify production. In 1400 the nutritional density of Japan already reached 900 per km² and the rice region of the Chinese South, 300.

In 1600 Japan had a nutritional density of 850, China nearly 500. At this time India, the only other country for which even the most tenuous information is available, had a nutritional density of only 269.

Although there is little reliable information on nutritional densities in South East Asia before the twentieth century, it seems certain that, except in Java,

TABLE 22 *Nutritional densities in Asia, A.D. 1400–1970 (population per km² of arable land)*

	1400	1600	1800	1900	1930	1960	1970	Rice yields (100 kg/hectare)	
								1960	1970
Japan	965	856	825	866	1122	1609	1869	50.9	52.5
South Korea	–	–	–	500	–	1200	1401	44.0	45.8
South China	301	–	536	600	–	816	–	–	–
All China	277	477	430	460	505	571	770	27.6	–
North Vietnam	–	–	–	230	670	910	906	21.9	22.8
Java	–	–	330	426	491	708	–	17.7	–
All India	–	269	–	358	450	376	354	16.1	16.8
Greater Bengal	–	–	–	391	458	559	–	–	–
Philippines	–	–	–	266	–	388	427	12.4	17.2
Thailand	–	–	–	–	–	269	313	15.8	–
Burma	–	–	–	288	–	266	–	16.0	–
Malaya	–	–	–	–	–	315	322	25.7	29.5

Sources: Tables 10 to 20 and F.A.O. *Production yearbook*, vol. 25, 1971

nutritional densities were lower than in India, and much lower than in East Asia. Although population growth has been faster in these regions (Table 17) than in East Asia or India, they still have comparatively low nutritional densities. Their cultivators have thus not yet been compelled to adopt the intensive methods of East Asia, and this is reflected in the yields and the practises of these areas (Tables 9 and 22).

By the 1960s countries in East Asia all had nutritional densities over 500 per km^2, and rice yields of 2000 kg per hectare or more; conversely the latter countries had nutritional densities of less than 500 and yields below 2000. The two exceptions are Malaya, with very high yields and a low density, and Java with a high density but a low yield. The correlation is by no means exact, but is sufficient to suggest that the date of settlement, the rate of population increase and present and past densities have been major factors in causing differences in the intensity of *sawah* agriculture in Asia.

CHAPTER 7

PASTORAL NOMADISM

The great arid belt of the Old World, from the Atlantic shores of the Sahara to the steppes of Mongolia, has been occupied by oasis farmers and pastoral nomads for at least 3000 years. But in this century the pastoral nomads have greatly declined in numbers and are now of very little significance in the world agricultural economy. There are few reliable records on the numbers of the nomads remaining. In the Sahara there are perhaps just over 1 000 000, and there are approximately 2 500 000 in the Sahel and Sudanic zone to the south and in the Horn of Africa.[1] In the Arabian desert and the steppes of Syria, Jordan and Iraq numbers have greatly declined in this century, and there may now be no more than 650 000. In the upland plateaux and mountains to the east of the Arabian desert nomads are still common, and between Anatolia and the mountains overlooking the Indus plain there are about 5 000 000 nomads, especially in the Zagros mountains of Iran and in Afghanistan.[2]

Unfortunately, there is little reliable information on the numbers in Chinese and Russian Turkestan and Mongolia, where in the 1920s they were probably most numerous. The number of nomads in Russia prior to collectivisation has been variously put at between 5 000 000 and 6 000 000.[3] Nor is it clear how far the pressure in China and Mongolia to group nomads into communes and co-operatives has destroyed the traditional economy and converted the nomads to ranchers.[4] But it seems unlikely that pastoral nomads can now exceed 15 000 000 although they still occupy very large parts of the Old World dry belt. Indeed pastoral nomads have been estimated to occupy 10 000 000 square miles of the earth's surface, nearly twice the world's cultivated area.[5] In the New World there were no indigenous cattle, sheep or goats, and the llama was used primarily as a pack animal. After the introduction of European animals livestock became an important part of the American economy, but the organisation of pastoralism resembled ranching more than nomadism even in the sixteenth century.

Although the pastoral nomad is of little importance on a world scale, he still plays an important role in some countries. Thus, for example, three-quarters of the population of Somalia are still nomadic, and whilst the Sudan census of 1955–6 estimated that 14–18 per cent of the population were nomadic, the figure may be as high as 30–40 per cent. In Iran and Afghanistan 15–20 per cent of the population are nomadic, and in Saudi Arabia nomads and semi-nomads were about half the population in the 1950s.[6] The changes in the organisation of nomadic society in Mongolia have not ended the great dependence of the country on livestock products, or apparently the traditional migrations of herdsmen.

Even where pastoral nomads have dwindled to a small proportion of the total population they often own much of the country's livestock. In Nigeria over four-fifths of all cattle are owned by the pastoral Fulani.[7]

Few though the nomads may now be, they still defy simple classification. Many writers have emphasised the differences between true nomads, who have no permanent dwellings and do not practise agriculture, and semi-nomadic peoples, who cultivate land for part of the year, and move with their herds during the dry season. Others have emphasised the difference between vertical and horizontal nomadism, and the pattern and distance of migratory movements, whilst most writers have emphasised the differences between the nomads of the Turkestan steppes, where the horse is the prestige animal, and those of Arabia and the Sahara where the single-humped camel has this role. The cattle nomads of West Africa again appear at first sight differentiated from the former two groups.[8]

Space precludes an adequate discussion of these distinctions, and only the general characteristics of pastoral nomadism can be outlined here.

Pastoral nomads rely for their subsistence upon their herds. Milk, from camels, cattle, sheep and goats, provides food. Meat is only rarely eaten, when animals die or when they are slaughtered on ceremonial occasions; then hides or skins are also obtained. Wool is an important product. Livestock are rarely sold, for they are the nomad's capital. Most nomads try to maintain as many stock as they can, regardless of their condition or the grazing available. Most anthropologists have seen cattle numbers as giving an individual prestige and playing an important social role. But it can be equally well argued that the pastoral nomad is used to drought, and in Turkestan and Mongolia, winter cold, destroying his herds. Thus the larger the herd the greater the chance of some surviving. Mixed herds, rather than herds of only one type of animal, also give an insurance against drought failure.[9] Pastoral nomads make no attempt to improve their pastures, until recently showed little knowledge of disease control, and did not practise selective breeding; indeed such empirical selection as took place has emphasised the ability to withstand drought and long journeys rather than the quality and quantity of meat, milk and wool output.[10]

But nomads do not live by milk alone, and various methods of obtaining grain have been devised. Perhaps the most common is the method of the semi-nomad. Part of the tribe – often the women and children – remain near water-holes, and sow and gather crops whilst the men migrate to pastures with the herds. This is widely practised among the cattle nomads of West and East Africa and is common on the northern edge of the Sahara.[11] Indeed throughout most of the Saharan and Arabian deserts and their semi-arid fringes, semi-nomads are more common than pure nomads. The latter obtain grain in various ways: they may exchange animal products for grain with sedentary oasis dwellers. In the past, particularly in the Sahara–Arabian realm, nomads often owned land which was cultivated by slaves or by share-croppers who were descendants of slaves. The pacification of the desert nomads since the late nineteenth century, combined with modern land reforms, has made the latter ways less common. Finally many nomadic peoples will sow grain – often millet – in recently flooded wadis and return only to harvest the crop.[12]

Both the Central Asian and the Mongolian nomads were less likely to practise agriculture and it was particularly rare amongst the upland nomadic peoples – the Khirgiz, Turks and Mongols. The nomads of the lowland Russian steppes more commonly grew crops. Yet few nomads have been completely independent of sedentary societies. They have often been described as living in a symbiotic relationship with cultivators, perhaps best illustrated by the Fulani in Nigeria who pasture their cattle on the arable stubbles of the sedentary Hausa. The relationship has rarely been so peaceful, and perhaps might more fittingly be described as predatory.[13]

Nor has the pastoral nomad's economy remained static. There has been a long-run tendency for nomadic groups to become, first semi-nomadic, and then finally completely sedentary. Thus the Nilo-Hamitic herders who pressed south in East Africa from the sixteenth century became progressively more sedentary as they entered better-watered areas, as have some of the Fulani in West Africa. In Arabia the Shammar camel-breeding nomads drifted northwards in the seventeenth century and became more sedentary in the nineteenth and twentieth centuries.[14]

Nomadic herders rely solely upon natural vegetation for their livestock's fodder, and neither sow pastures nor store forage. As they live in areas whose aridity and, in Central Asia, cold, preclude all-year grazing, they are forced to move their herds in search of new pastures and drinking water. Thus the true nomad has no permanent dwelling place and lives in tents. The movements are not, however, random. In the semi-arid areas to the north and south of the Sahara where there are seasonal fluctuations in the movement of the cyclones and the inter-tropical front respectively, there are regular north–south movements with the rains. In the deserts proper rainfall is sporadic in time and place, and movement is less ordered, but by no means aimless. In both types of migration tribal groups keep to prescribed territories, and only in years of drought do they enter the grazing districts of their neighbours. In the Fars district of southern Iran, where nomadism is vertical rather than horizontal, each group of nomads follows the same route – or *il-rah* – each year, although perhaps stopping at different places on the route to graze from one year to another. The route, from the low deserts in the south to the northern mountain pastures, is so designed to maximise the optimum use of seasonal variations in grazing.[15] Although the routes of pastoral nomads are ordered and confined to their own territories in the short-run, in the long-run many nomadic groups have displayed pastoral drift: the long-term, long-distance movement from one area to another. The slow movement of the Shammar tribes has already been noted; the Fulani originated in Senegal in the seventh century A.D. and have slowly moved eastwards, reaching the Cameroons only early in this century.[16]

The very low productivity of the grazing lands used by nomadic herders means of course that a very large area is needed to sustain the animals, varying with the precipitation available (see Table 23). One obvious consequence of this is that (human) population densities are very low in nomadic herding regions. In the Mongolian steppes the average density is 0.5 per km², in the Sahara 0.5 per km², in the Sahel 3 per km². In East Africa densities amongst the cattle nomads are higher, but rarely exceed 17 per km².[17]

TABLE 23   *Area required to feed one livestock unit*
(one livestock unit = 1 cow or 7 sheep)

Annual rainfall (millimetres)	Number of hectares per livestock unit
50–100	50 or more
200–400	10–15
400–600	6–12

Source: Ruthenberg 1971, 253

The size and composition of herds vary a great deal amongst pastoral nomads. Livestock are generally owned by families, and families grouped in tribes: but the migratory unit is generally smaller than the tribe. In the Middle East each migratory unit consists of five or six families, who each require, as a minimum for subsistence, 25–60 goats and sheep or 10–25 camels.[18]

Herd composition varies from one region to another, but throughout the whole of the dry belt sheep and goats are the most common animals, cattle the least common. Cattle need better pastures and more water to drink, and they are only the dominant livestock in the Sahel and Sudan zones of Africa, where rainfall may reach 880 mm a year. In the most arid parts of the Sahara and the Arabian desert, the camel, which can go for long periods without drinking, and will browse salty plants, is the dominant animal. In Turkestan and Mongolia sheep and goats are the most numerous; the double-humped Bactrian camel is used for transport, but the prestige animal is the horse, in contrast to the Sahara–Arabian areas, where the camel holds this position.

The origins of pastoral nomadism

Until the mid-nineteenth century most anthropologists and historians thought that mankind had evolved from hunting, fishing and gathering societies to a second stage of pastoral nomadism, followed only later by that of sedentary agriculture. Then, in the late nineteenth century, both Ratzel and Hahn suggested that pastoral nomadism was an off-shoot of sedentary agriculture, and most authorities now accept that it came later than crop cultivation. In support of this it can be argued that herding animals everywhere seem to have been domesticated by sedentary agriculturalists, whilst animals living in areas occupied by hunters and gatherers were not domesticated; that the distribution of pastoralism is peripheral to sedentary agriculture, whilst nowhere have there been pastoral nomads who were without knowledge of agriculture.[19] It must be noted however that the earliest evidence of domesticated sheep and goats in South West Asia occurs in sites lacking evidence of domesticated plants.[20]

TABLE 24   *Herd composition amongst pastoral nomads (% of total stock number)*

Group	Sheep		Goats	Cattle	Camels
Sahel[1]	——65——			34	1
Outer Mongolia[2]	55		22	8	9
Sinkiang[3]	——78——			6	6
Iran[2]	55		28	11	–
Afghanistan	55		28	11	–

Sources:
(1) Brémaud and Pagot, 1962, 311
(2) Krader, 1955, 310–13
(3) Chang, 1949, 65

The beginnings of pastoral nomadism must thus be sought in the areas where crop production was first practised. The early farmers of South West Asia grew crops and kept sheep, goats and cattle, but the two enterprises were not integrated. Livestock were herded on natural pastures near the village site. It seems quite possible that some villagers might have sought pastures at a distance from the village and eventually become specialised herders with only partial links with the village community, which a run of dry years might sever. As was seen in Chapter 2, knowledge of agriculture diffused into the Eurasian steppes by two routes; one via the Balkans into south-western Russia; here the Tripolye culture was established in the fourth millennium B.C., based on the cultivation of wheat, barley, millet and the keeping of cattle, goats and sheep; another route lay through Iran into Russian Turkestan, where both irrigation and dry farming were established.[21] The beginnings of pastoral nomadism may be traced to this latter region. The horse was domesticated from the tarpan, in the Kuznetz steppe, probably at first for meat and milk, in the third millennium B.C. The horse had spread west of the Ural River by the second millennium and south into Iran and the Near East by about 2000 B.C., where it was used to draw war-chariots.[22] At some time in the second millennium B.C. the Bactrian camel, with two humps, was domesticated in Central Asia. But it was the development of horse *riding* which was critical in the rise of pastoral nomadism in the Eurasian steppes, for not only did it make herding, particularly long-distance herding, easier, but it gave the nomads a considerable military advantage over sedentary peoples. Evidence of riding becomes more frequent in the Near East about 1400 B.C., and some believe that it diffused from there to the Turkestan steppes, whilst others hold that riding developed in Central Asia itself.[23]

At the beginning of the first millennium B.C. the steppes from the Danube east to the Altai were populated – although only sparsely – by farmer-herders. In the early part of the millennium horse-riding nomads became dominant; many sedentary farmers became specialised pastoralists, possibly as a result of increasing aridity.[24] About 900 B.C. the Scythians appeared in the Russian steppes between the Volga and the Irtysh. By the time of the Greek settlements on the Black Sea coast they had achieved hegemony over the steppe farmers of the interior, a relationship between farmer and nomad which was to be repeated from the Hungarian steppes east to northern China for the next 1500 years.[25]

The early nomads in the Russian steppes were all of Caucasoid origin; east of the Dzungarian Gap, in Chinese Turkestan and Mongolia, pastoral nomadism was a later development. Nomadic herding had developed on the edge of the oases in Chinese Turkestan and further east on the edge of the northern Chinese cultivated area, possibly as early as 3000 B.C.,[26] with cattle, sheep and goats, all of which had been acquired from South West Asia. Horse riding however was introduced in the first millennium B.C. by immigrants from Russian Turkestan, who spoke an Indo-European language; the indigenous herders, of Mongoloid origin, acquired horse riding and the bow from them and first became a serious threat to China in the fourth and third centuries B.C. By that time there had already arisen a marked difference between sedentary Chinese agriculture and the steppe society of the nomads.[27] It was then that the Great Wall of China was begun. To the north of China in the later Han period nomadic groups of Mongoloid origin were to be found, belonging to the Turkic-speaking peoples in the west, proto-Mongolian speaking in the centre and Tungu-speaking in the east. The Hsiung Nu eventually moved west into Bactria; the Huns, partly of Turkic- and partly of Mongol-speaking origin, also later moved westwards and began the Turkicisation of the nomads of the Eurasian steppe which has lasted until modern times. A series of nomadic groups moved westwards in the following centuries, generally settling down west of the Dzungarian Gap. The remarkable expansion of the Mongols, beginning in the tenth century and reaching a peak in the thirteenth century, left few Turkic-speaking nomads east of the Altai in their original homeland. They became, however, the dominant group in Turkestan, the southern Russian steppes and parts of Anatolia, Iraq and Iran.[28]

The continual movement of various nomadic groups through the Russian steppes delayed settlement there; indeed between the second century B.C. and the seventh century A.D. sedentary cultivators were driven off the steppes, and the nomads reigned supreme. Some nomads seem to have practised primitive cultivation, although their herds were their main concern. Slav settlement of the steppe began only in the tenth century but was later rebuffed by the Mongol invasions in the thirteenth century. It was not until the seventeenth century that the Russians fully occupied the wooded steppe, and the settlement of the steppes west of the Don only got under way in the late eighteenth century.[29]

Nor did the supremacy of the pastoral nomad end at the mouth of the Danube. The Hungarian plain, the westernmost part of the Eurasian steppe, was still thinly settled at the end of the Middle Ages, although nomadism had long since disappeared. The settlement of the western part of the Eurasian steppes could only really begin once advances in military methods gave standing armies supremacy over the nomads, beginning in the sixteenth century; from then the pastoral nomads retreated from the European and Russian steppes.[30]

As we have seen, the earliest farmers in South West Asia kept livestock as well as growing wheat and barley, and doubtless specialised herders broke away from the settled communities at an early date. There are references to nomadic onslaughts as early as Sumerian times, but the nomadic herders of the Middle East do not seem to have adopted the horse. It was the single-humped camel, the dromedary, which gave the herders mobility and led to their expansion. Neither the date nor the place of domestication of the dromedary is certain, but it was probably domesticated as a pack animal in South West Arabia in the third or second millennium B.C.[31] By the end of the second millennium, camel nomads were raiding Israel, and in the early part of the first millennium B.C. camel caravans were crossing the North Arabian desert. The diffusion of the dromedary out of Arabia was slow; it was introduced into Egypt in about the sixth century B.C. but was unimportant until Ptolemaic times.[32] Further west the camel was known in North Africa in Roman times, but was comparatively unimportant, as was pastoral nomadism.[33] The camel grew in importance in the early Christian centuries, but the expansion of pastoral nomadism in the Sahara is closely associated with two periods of Arab expansion. The first, in the seventh century, followed a period of drought in the Arabian desert, the vigorous expansion of Islam and the adoption of the Arabic language in Egypt and by the Berbers in North Africa.[34] These invasions disrupted the sedentary agriculture of North Africa, but comparatively few of the indigenous peoples took to pastoral nomadism.[35] One exception was those Arabised Berber groups who in the eighth century A.D. spread south across the Sahara into the western Sudanic zone, and north into Spain.[36] In the eleventh century there was a second outpouring of *bedouin* from Arabia into Africa, the Hilalai invasions. The numbers involved were far greater than in the seventh century, and sedentary agriculture declined on the coast, particularly in Cyrenaicia and Tripolitania. One group from the latter region – the Tuareg – were pushed south into the desert by the Arabs, and adopted pastoral nomadism. Arab influence in the eastern Sudan had been comparitively small immediately after the conquest of Egypt in A.D. 639, but nomads pushed south in the eleventh century, destroyed two Christian kingdoms, and from them developed the modern Baggara.[37]

Pastoral Nomadism thrived in conditions of political instability: these were rife in the Near East in the Middle Ages. In Anatolia there was no true nomadic pastoralism until the eleventh century, when Turkish pastoralists arrived. They were reinforced by further arrivals in the thirteenth century when the Mongol Empire included briefly most of the Near East and Anatolia; the warfare of this period destroyed much of Mesopotamia's irrigation works, and further north the Jezirah was deserted by sedentary farmers, to remain to the pastoralists until the late nineteenth century.[38]

The origins of pastoralism in Africa south of the Sahara are far from clear; it is often argued that there were no pastoral nomads in sub-Saharan Africa until after the eleventh century A.D. Yet there is good evidence that cattle, sheep and goats were kept long before this. During the Saharan Sub-Pluvial between 5500 B.C. and 2500 B.C. the Sahara was wetter than at present, and occupied by pastoralists who were part proto-Berber and part Negroid; they kept livestock and grew some crops. By 2000 B.C. they had largely disappeared before the encroaching desiccation, leaving a remnant and largely Negroid population in the oases.[39] There is little evidence of nomadic pastoralism in West Africa again until the eighth century A.D. The Fulani, now the major pastoral tribe, were first known in Senegal in the eighth century, and may possibly be a mixture of indigenous Negro peoples and the Arabised Berbers who spread south at that time. The Fulani began to move south in the eleventh century, at the time of the Islamisation of the West African Sudanic kingdoms; later they also moved eastwards. The long drift eastwards resulted in the sedentarisation of much of the Fulani population, so that only part of the 6 000 000 Fulani in West Africa are still pastoralists.[40]

In East Africa pastoral nomadism – as distinct from the keeping of livestock – does not seem to have been important until after A.D. 1000. The Horn and much of eastern Africa was occupied by hunters and gatherers until the Bantu pushed east and north into what is now East Africa in the second part of the first millennium A.D. Further north the only pastoralists were the Beja, who had acquired pastoralism from Arabia at a very early date. But after A.D. 1000, a number of sedentary groups living in the Ethiopian highlands, including the Afar, Somali and Galla, adopted pastoralism and moved into the dry steppes to the east and south. The Galla occupied Somalia for some centuries as pastoralists, but were pushed back into the Ethiopian highlands by the expanding Somali, and by 1600 had become sedentary farmers again. The Somali have continued to expand in the Horn. All three groups are Caucasoid in origin and speak Hamitic languages. However Negro peoples known as Nilotes acquired pastoralism at about the same time as the Afar, Somali and Galla, and pushed south from the southern Sudan into the Lakes region of East Africa after the thirteenth century A.D., where in some cases they subjected the sedentary Bantu, in other cases became sedentary themselves.[41]

The decline of pastoral nomadism

In the twentieth century pastoral nomadism has everywhere been in decline; true nomads have become semi-nomadic, and the semi-nomadic fully sedentary. But the sedentarisation of nomads is by no means new; the decline began in the sixteenth century. We must now consider why this has happened.

Until the sixteenth century pastoral nomads had a military advantage over peasants. They were mobile, on horses or camels, and their mounted archers and clever tactics were generally too much for medieval European armies. However improvements in weapons after the sixteenth century took the initiative from the nomads. It was not however until the late eighteenth century that the European steppes were finally opened to settlement when the Russians defeated the Turks in 1768–74 and 1787–92.[42] Outside Europe the nomad still had the upper hand, and retained the advantage as long as central governments were weak. Thus in North Africa and the Middle East the pacification of the nomads did not come until European powers arrived. In North Africa the French occupation in the late nineteenth century, and in the Middle East the British and French occupation after the First World War, finally brought the *bedouin* under control. Pacification removed several sources of nomad income. First, it led to the abolition of slavery. In the Sahara many *bedouin* h'ad Negro slaves who worked land which provided grain and dates. After the abolition of slavery the lot of these people – the *haratin* – was often little improved, for they became share-croppers. Only recently, under the impetus of land reform, has this relationship ended. Second, pacification has reduced tribal warfare, and more significant, the 'protection' of sedentary cultivators by the *bedouin*. Third, pacification and modernisation have ended the nomads' monopoly of transport across the desert. In the Sahara the *bedouin* had a thriving trade in slaves and gold from early medieval times: the end of their military power combined with the introduction of buses and trucks has greatly reduced income from this source. The first regular bus route across the Sahara began in 1927. Not only have the nomads lost their monopoly as carriers, but much of their trade has passed into the hands of urban merchants, who have ventured into the steppes and deserts since the end of the nomads' military power.

Once the pastoral nomads ceased to be a threat to the sedentary cultivator, colonisation of the more humid steppe areas was possible. This began first in Russia. In the early nineteenth century the Ukrainian steppes were settled, then the Kuban, and the Tatar shepherds were slowly forced into villages.[43] In the late nineteenth century Russian settlement of the northern steppes of Central Asia pushed the Kazakh herdsmen south into the arid steppe and desert, a process completed during the Virgin Lands scheme of the 1950s. In China the advance of settlement into the dry and cold nomadic areas of Mongolia and Manchuria was longer delayed. The Great Wall of China corresponds approximately to the 380 mm isohyet, and farming in this area was highly marginal;[44] further east, Manchuria, the grazing lands of both Mongol and Manchu tribesmen, was closed to settlement by the Manchu dynasty in the later seventeenth century, as was Inner Mongolia, although the extreme south of Manchuria had been part of the Chinese *ecumene* since the third century B.C. At the end of the nineteenth century Russian and Japanese interest in Manchuria finally led the Manchu government to encourage Chinese settlement; in 1907 all formal limits to settlement were lifted. Chinese migration reached a peak in the late 1920s; between 1916 and 1957 the cultivated area tripled.[45]

Growing security from the depredations of nomads also led to the expansion of cereal cultivation into the grazing lands of North Africa and the Middle East, although not on the same scale as in Russia or China. In the early nineteenth century pastoral nomadism was still expanding towards the coast in parts of North

Africa, but this tide was reversed after the French occupation.[46] Typical of the process of settlement was the course of events in Syria. The Jezirah had been partially occupied by sedentary cultivators from an early date, but was largely deserted by farmers after the Mongol invasions of the thirteenth century and occupied by nomads from Arabia in the seventeenth and eighteenth centuries. The Ottoman Empire was for long unable to provide the security which would have encouraged settlers to return. But in the 1860s the Turkish police acquired modern rifles that gave them an advantage over the *bedouin*, armed only with flint-locks; nonetheless the *bedouin* were not completely subjugated until the French mandate. But greater security coupled with railway building led to the reoccupation of the steppes; between 1800 and 1950 4 000 000 hectares of land had been brought into cultivation, and the nomadic tribes largely settled. Indeed the need to sedentarise the nomads was part of the constitution of the Republic of Syria.[47]

By no means all nomads became farmers when they gave up their old way of life, for not only has the cereal farmer expanded into their old domain, but modern industry has grown up in the desert and provided employment; in Central Asia Soviet mining development absorbed nomads, as did the building of the Turk–Sib railway.[48] More spectacularly the building of petroleum plants in Saudi Arabia, Algeria and Libya has absorbed nomad labour, just as earlier the building of the Suez Canal led to the sedentarisation of Egyptian nomads in the late nineteenth century.[49]

In the last hundred years governments of all political complexions have tried to settle the pastoral nomad; to the European colonial powers the nomads were a military irritant, and could be more easily taxed if sedentary. To the new nation states of the modern period the nomads have often been a cause of ethnic separatism as well as symbolising a backward past. In Russia and China the nomads have been not only ethnically different from the dominant people in the state, but also difficult to incorporate in a Socialist agriculture. In the Soviet Union the attempt to force the pastoral nomads of Central Asia into *kholkoz* was at first disastrous. In Kazakhstan many nomads slaughtered their animals; the number of cattle in the autonomous Republic fell from 7 000 000 in 1928 to 3 050 000 in 1938. Many Kazakhs fled to Sinkiang. In 1942 a further attempt was made to stabilise the nomads. Permanent buildings for livestock *kholkoz* had already been established, and ownership of livestock had become communal rather than individual. After 1942, under the *otgonnyi* system, attempts were made to grow fodder for winter feed, veterinary facilities were made available, and winter cattle shelters were constructed. The livestock were also allowed to be pastured on state land outside the *kholkoz* limits. But seasonal movements to pastures were still made, and allowed. Since the 1950s further efforts have been made to provide winter fodder by growing alfalfa under irrigation. In effect an attempt has been made to convert nomadism to ranching.[50]

In China the Communist government has also tried to incorporate the pastoral nomads of Sinkiang and Inner Mongolia into livestock co-operatives, but they proceeded more cautiously than the Russians had in the 1930s. Wells have been dug, and attempts made to improve the natural pastures.[51] Outer Mongolia, the last home of the Mongol nomads, is a particularly interesting case. Outer Mongolia was the first Communist state outside the Soviet Union, and in 1929 followed the Russian example and tried to collectivise its nomads. The attempt failed, and a more cautious policy was followed thereafter; as late as 1947, 99 per cent of the livestock were privately owned. But after 1957 nomads were compelled to join the *negdel*, or livestock co-operatives. The aim has been to convert the nomads to a ranching system, but the economy is still essentially nomadic, with two or three migratory moves made each year.[52]

Outside the Socialist countries the attempts to sedentarise the nomad and convert him to a rancher have been prosecuted with less vigour, but a similar trend has been apparent, particularly in Africa south of the Sahara. Thus in Kenya several efforts have been made to establish Masai families on 'ranches'. Such attempts have often foundered on the refusal of the Masai to cull their herds to a level compatible with the grazing resources available, and their reluctance to sell cattle. Similar difficulties have been met with in Nigeria.[53]

The decline of the pastoral nomad can be attributed to the modernisation and Europeanisation of the world that began in the nineteenth century. They have also retreated before more intensive systems of land use. The Great Alföld, the south Russian steppes and southern Manchuria all gave excellent pastures, but could all give good cereal crops once drought-resistant varieties had been bred and the mouldboard plough adopted. With the possible exception of parts of the West African savanna, the nomad has been pushed into those areas where crop cultivation is impossible without irrigation. In these areas it is likely that pastoral nomadism is the best use of the land. Certainly it would be prohibitively costly to cultivate these areas: and the conversion of the nomads to ranching has proved difficult. After a long history of expansion, nomadism is now the optimum method of exploiting the arid steppes and the desert. It may be wise to leave them, rather than to enforce sedentarisation.[54]

CHAPTER 8

MEDITERRANEAN AGRICULTURE

Mediterranean agriculture is that type found in the areas surrounding the Mediterranean Sea which have mild, wet winters and hot, dry summers, and also in those areas elsewhere with a similar climate – central and southern California, central Chile, the south west of Cape Province, the south west of Western Australia and the southern part of South Australia.[1] In terms of area occupied, in numbers employed or in the value of its products, it is not of major importance. Nor would all writers accept it as a valid type, for within the Mediterranean basin a variety of agricultural enterprises are pursued (Fig. 17), whilst some writers are unhappy with the assumption that similar climates give rise to similar types of farming.[2] But the agriculture of the Mediterranean has played a major role in the evolution of agriculture in the western world, and on this ground alone it justifies discussion.

Three environmental characteristics have been of fundamental importance in the evolution of traditional Mediterranean agriculture. First is the long summer drought; rainfall is confined to the winter half of the year. Unless crops are irrigated they must either be sown in the autumn and harvested by early summer, or be capable of resisting drought. Second are the comparatively mild winters and hot, sunny summers. Temperatures are such that a variety of temperate crops can be grown in the rainy season, and – with irrigation – sub-tropical crops in the summer. Thus, given adequate moisture, not only rice, sugar-cane, tobacco, citrus fruits and even bananas can be grown, but wheat, barley, potatoes and deciduous fruits as well. Third is the terrain. Mediterranean agriculture has its classic *locus* on the shores of the Sea, where coastal plains are backed by low hills which share the summer drought, and mountains which have not only more rain in winter, but some in summer too. Agriculture has both adjusted to summer drought and differences in slope, and integrated the use of these contrasting micro-environments. Thus a typical village community would grow wheat and barley in the plain, and graze sheep and goats on the stubble; it would grow olives and grapes on the lower hills, with patches of irrigated vegetables around the village; in the summer the flocks would be driven to the higher pastures of the mountains to return to the plains when the autumn rains came.[3]

But whilst such communities still exist on the shores of the Mediterranean, the agriculture of the basin is now far more complex. Nor has this traditional agriculture been transferred unchanged to the areas of Mediterranean-type climate overseas.

123

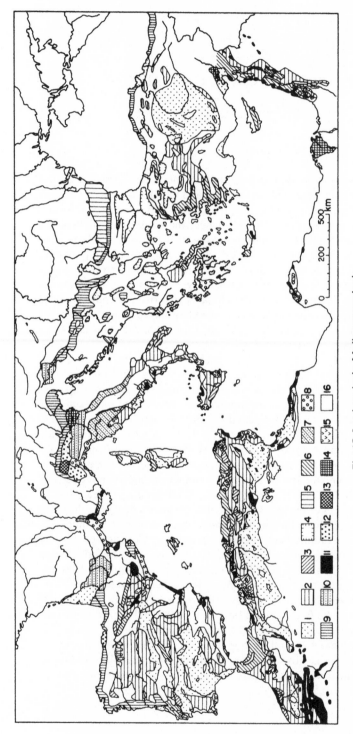

Fig. 17. Land use in the Mediterranean basin.

Key: 1. Lowland regions with little cultivation. 2. Open field: wheat, barley and fallow. 3. Open fields without fallow: wheat, leguminous crops (grain). 4. Open fields except around the villages where specialised cultures are found; wheat dominant, maize subordinate, brief periods of fallow. 5. Open fields except around the villages, maize dominant. 6. Dry Mediterranean-type polyculture. 7. Cultura promiscua. 8. Specialised Mediterranean-type shrub culture (with vines). 9. Non-Mediterranean-type polyculture based on maize. 10. Non-Mediterranean-type polyculture; wheat and fodder cultivation; no fallow. 11. Mediterranean *huertas* with irrigated cultivation predominating. 12. Intensive stock rearing. 13. Large-scale rice production. 14. Large-scale commercial farming. 15. Large-scale cultivation of wheat, fodder and sugar beet. 16. Little cultivation due to poor soils. [Source: Birot and Dresch, 1953, 104–5]

Agriculture in the Mediterranean basin

The prime feature of land use in the countries surrounding the Mediterranean Sea is the great importance of cereals, and in particular wheat. In the countries of the West Mediterranean about half the arable land is under cereals and a further 40 per cent in fallow, leaving only a tenth of the area in fruits, vegetables and other crops.[4] The crops are sown – often they are still broadcast – as soon as the autumn rains come, and harvested in early summer. Although the winter rainfall is not as variable as the summer rainfall of other wheat-growing areas such as the Great Plains or the Australian wheat belt, the total is low and yields are closely correlated with spring precipitation, the 'latter' rains. These are highly variable.[5] Little manure is used – there are few cattle to provide it – and artificial fertilisers are uncommon; methods of cultivation and harvesting are primitive, particularly east and south of the Sea in Turkey, the Levant and North Africa. Most of the wheat and barley is grown on small peasant farms, using only family labour: however, even on the large estates of southern Italy and southern Spain, worked by day labourers, methods are still poor.[6] Perhaps the most distinctive feature of cereal cultivation is the fallow. After a crop has been harvested, the land is left fallow not only for the ensuing summer, but for the following winter and summer as well, the aim being to conserve soil moisture. The fallow is generally worked to keep down weeds, although in the Levant and North Africa it may be left uncultivated and the sheep of nomads grazed on the stubble and weeds.

Although most of the arable land is devoted to cereals, much of the land used for *agricultural* purposes is for grazing. But most of this is unimproved pasture, and little cropland is used for fodder crops. Thus livestock products are a low proportion of farm income. In Britain and Denmark four-fifths of total agricultural income is derived from animals: in the Mediterranean countries the figure rarely exceeds 40 per cent and is generally only between a fifth and a third.[7] Cattle are not numerous and beef and dairy products are unimportant. Sheep and goats are the dominant animals, for they can survive on much poorer fodder than cattle. Two central problems limit the development of livestock production. First is the summer drought and the consequent absence of good grazing. The traditional response to this was transhumance: sheep and goats fed in the plains in winter and spring, and were driven to the upland pastures in summer. Transhumance – particularly long-distance transhumance – is far less important than it was in the past, but still survives in parts of Greece, Italy, Yugoslavia, Spain and North Africa (Fig. 18).[8] Second is the lack of integration between crop and stock farming in the Mediterranean. As yet no legume has been found which, inserted in the rotation, can provide feed for livestock and replenish soil fertility as does clover in temperate areas. Thus most crops grown in the Mediterranean are for direct human consumption; in contrast, in northern Europe crops as well as grass are fed to animals. Irrigated pastures do sustain dairying industries in parts of Italy, southern France and Israel; but this is uncommon.[9]

Thus in terms of land-use patterns, the Mediterranean is dominated by exten-

126

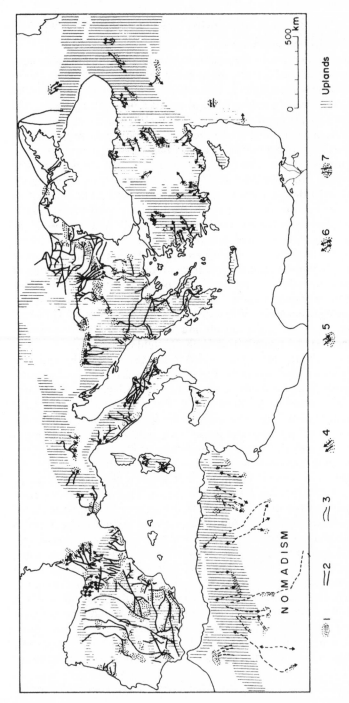

Fig. 18. Transhumant routes in the Mediterranean basin, after Müller. [Source: Braudel, 1966. 88–9]
Key: 1. Winter pastures. 2. Transhumance routes. 3. Direction of transhumance. 4. Normal transhumance (herds belonging to plains-dwellers). 5. Inverse transhumance (herds belonging to mountain-dwellers). 6. Normal and inverse transhumance. 7. Double transhumance (herds belonging to people of intermediate slopes).

sive wheat cultivation and grazing (Fig. 17); both have a low productivity. However this impoverished farming system is partially redeemed by the importance of tree crops and horticulture. The olive and the grape-vine are the most important of the tree crops, the fig being of little significance and the date-palm confined to the southern parts of the region. Olive groves are found throughout the Mediterranean basin, and indeed the limits of the olive are a good indication of the range of the Mediterranean climate. The tree will grow on steep slopes and its long roots enable it to survive the summer drought. Although it does not bear fruit for seven years after planting, it will subsequently yield for very long periods with comparatively little attention. The grape-vine will also grow on steeper slopes and is also drought-resistant, but it requires more labour. In traditional Mediterranean agriculture every village, if not every farm, would grow cereals, keep sheep and goats and have grapes for wine and olives for cooking oil and lighting. Indeed in some parts of the Mediterranean, epitomised by the *cultura promiscua* of central Italy, trees and grain are interplanted.[10] But in the last hundred years olives and vines have expanded in some areas to the exclusion of other crops. In Bas-Languedoc, which produces 15 per cent of the world's wine output, half the cultivated area of Hérault province is under vines, whilst in parts of Cordoba in southern Spain olive groves occupy four-fifths of the cultivated land.[11] Most of the grapes in the Mediterranean are grown for wine production – indeed the Mediterranean basin produces two-thirds of the world's wine. In the eastern Mediterranean, however, the grapes are also grown for table grapes, currants and sultanas.[12]

The fourth element in the agricultural landscape of the Mediterranean basin is the cultivation of fruits and vegetables. Not only can temperate fruits such as apples and pears be grown, but also sub-tropical fruits such as the peach and citrus; of the citrus fruits the orange is of special significance. The vegetables grown include potatoes, lettuce, onions, cauliflowers and peas. Both fruits and vegetables have been an important part of Mediterranean farming since at least Roman times, but as with viticulture and olives, their specialised production is a comparatively recent development. Much of the area under vegetables and fruits is irrigated, in contrast to the dry-farming of cereals, vines and olives. Thus although a very low proportion of arable land in the Mediterranean region is irrigated (about 8 per cent), it produces a high proportion of the total agricultural income. Thus only 10 per cent of Spain's arable land is irrigated but it accounts for half the value of all agricultural production. Fruits, vegetables and the tree crops, for the most part intensive crops, thus account for much of the value of production and of the labour hours expended in agriculture. Vegetables alone account for 28 per cent of Greek farm income, and about one-fifth in Turkey, the Lebanon and Morocco. In Tunisia tree crops and vegetables account for one-third of the value of output. This justifies Vidal de la Blache's assertion that in the Mediterranean the garden rather than the field is the focus of the farmer's attention;[13] this part of Mediterranean agriculture is labour-intensive, in contrast to the extensive nature of wheat cultivation and grazing.

Mediterranean agriculture

It is a characteristic feature of countries experiencing industrialisation that in the early stages the agricultural population increases, then stabilises as migration to the towns takes off the natural increase, then finally declines. Such a process has been going on in parts of north-western Europe since the late nineteenth century, and there has been a particularly rapid decline since 1950. But in the Mediterranean countries this latter phase has yet to be reached. Indeed in Portugal, Greece, Turkey, the Levant and North Africa the numbers dependent upon agriculture are still increasing. In Spain the agricultural population fell from 13 000 000 to 11 000 000 between 1950 and 1965. Indeed only in Italy and southern France have there been radical declines in the agricultural population since the end of the Second World War. One consequence of this is that the Mediterranean countries have agricultural population densities significantly higher than those of Europe north of the Alps; the number of agricultural workers per hectare of arable land is approximately double that of north-western Europe.[14] Although such densities are well below those of Asia they still have an effect upon farm structure. Farms are small; in Greece 81 per cent of the farms are less than five hectares in size, in Spain two-thirds.[15] More significant is the absence of the medium-sized farm characteristic of northern Europe. In southern Spain and southern Italy very large estates still exist, the latifundia, worked either by day-labourers or by share-croppers. But they are not characteristic of Mediterranean farms; nor indeed is tenancy, for most farmers are now occupier-owners. Where tenancy does exist the prevailing method is by share-cropping rather than by cash rent. The continuing population pressure has led not only to the constant subdivision of farms, but to their fragmentation, which greatly impairs efficiency.[16]

The areas of Mediterranean-type climate overseas

There are marked variations in farming within the Mediterranean basin, particularly between the north west – France, Spain and Italy – and the areas to the east and south of the Sea. These may be ascribed partly to the differences in the climate – which is generally hotter and drier to the south and east – and to the influence of long Muslim occupation. But at present the differences may be more immediately attributed to the degree of economic development; industrialisation, urbanisation and incomes have progressed more in the north west than elsewhere, and agriculture has become more specialised and intensive in the coastal areas of Spain, France and northern Italy. Thus although Spain still has a third of its population dependent upon agriculture and Italy a quarter, Greece, Yugoslavia and the Lebanon have half their populations still in agriculture, Algeria and Tunisia nearly two-thirds and Turkey three-quarters.[17]

And it is this degree of industrialisation that accounts for many of the differences between the overseas Mediterranean-type countries, although there are also differences in climate, position and the history of settlement.[18] Thus

Chile still has a third of its population employed in agriculture and a national income per caput rather less than Spain. The South West Cape and Western Australia, in contrast, have much lower proportions of their populations engaged in agriculture, whilst California is one of the richest areas in the world and has a very small agricultural work force.

The four overseas regions all grow much the same range of crops as the Mediterranean basin itself; there have been no major alterations of the basic complex. Even in California and Chile there is little difference, although some American crops could be grown. Thus Chile is the only Latin American country where the wheat area exceeds that of maize; characteristically American crops are only found in the *chacra,* the small irrigated vegetable crops near the farmer's house.[19] However the relative importance of the major enterprises and the manner in which they are carried out do differ significantly. Broadly speaking, the higher the national income per caput the more intensive and specialised the farming; thus the countries of the Mediterranean-type climates may be ranked roughly in an ascending scale: North Africa, the Levant, the Balkans, Chile, the North West Mediterranean basin, Western Australia, the South West Cape and California. Some authors have recently written of the Californisation of Bas-Languedoc. It could be argued that all Mediterranean-type countries aspire to the type of farming found in that state.

How significant are the four major agricultural enterprises of the Mediterranean basin in the overseas areas? In all four cereal production is important, but most noticeably in Chile. In that country cereals occupy three-quarters of the area under crops, and wheat four-fifths of the cereal area; it is sown in autumn, harvested in early summer and dry-fallowing is practised. Yields are low and variable, little manure or fertiliser is used, and even on the large *hacienda* little machinery is used.[20] In Western Australia, South Australia and parts of the South West Cape, wheat and barley occupy a large proportion of the cultivated area, but, although autumn-sown cereals predominate and fallowing is practised, and although yields are low, cereals are grown on large mechanised farms with a small labour force. In both Africa and Australia wheat production has followed in the wake of sheep rearing. In the last thirty years these two enterprises have been progressively integrated to produce a form of mixed farming. The key in Australia has been the cultivation of subterranean clover, a legume that will thrive in low-rainfall areas, provide grazing and restore soil fertility. But although this combination of wheat production and the grazing of sheep can ultimately be traced back to the Mediterranean tradition, they are more profitably considered under other heads (see pp. 281–3).

At the end of the last century California had the largest sheep flocks in the United States and was a leading wheat producer with the most advanced form of mechanisation at the time. However, since then these extensive land uses have been replaced by more intensive ones. Cereals now occupy only one-third of the arable land;[21] barley, the major cereal, is still a fallowed dry-land crop, but is mainly fed to livestock, as are the other grains except rice, which as in the Po valley, is irrigated; but in California its cultivation is also highly mechanised. Thus in the overseas Mediterranean countries there are echoes of the wheat production of southern Spain or Sicily, but the technological level is clearly very different – except in Chile.

The role of the tree crops – olives, figs and the grape-vine – is very variable. Although all three are grown in the overseas areas, figs and olives are of very minor significance. The countries of the Mediterranean basin produce all but 6 per cent of the world's figs. Olives are also largely confined to the Mediterranean basin; only 2 per cent are produced elsewhere. In the Mediterranean basin olives are found on most farms, as well as in the specialised areas such as southern Spain. Elsewhere only in Chile are olive trees widely distributed. In California and the Cape olives occupy a negligible area and are produced on specialised farms only; in California they are produced for canning, not for oil. This clearly reflects the northern European preferences of the populations of California, the Cape and Australia.[22]

The grape-vine however has been much more widely adopted, although again in California, the Cape and Western Australia it is not found on all farms but is concentrated in specialised areas of viticulture. A higher proportion of the overseas grapes are marketed fresh or as dried fruit than in the Mediterranean; such a contrast however is found in the Mediterranean basin itself, between East and West. Nowhere in the overseas Mediterranean-type climates are grapes, figs and olives part of traditional agriculture except in Chile. There most *haciendas* have some land under grapes. The only specialised area of viticulture is around Talca. Nonetheless although viticulture occupies only 100000 hectares – some 2 per cent of the cultivated area – it affords employment for nearly half the agricultural work force. Elsewhere in the overseas Mediterranean areas viticulture, olives and figs are highly specialised and highly localised, catering mainly for the local market.[23]

Horticulture is the third element in the Mediterranean complex and its importance in the economies of the countries around the Mediterranean Sea has already been emphasised. Fruits and vegetables have a remarkable importance in California. Deciduous fruits such as apples and pears, and vegetables such as tomatoes, lettuce and asparagus, are grown in the Los Angeles basin, the San Joaquin valley and the coastal valleys near San Francisco. Citrus fruits, once located primarily near Los Angeles, have increasingly been relocated in the San Joaquin valley as the Los Angeles urban area has expanded. Fruits, nuts and vegetables occupy 30 per cent of California's farmland and account for half the value of all crops grown.[24] These industries are highly specialised and carried out on comparatively small irrigated farms. They account for a high proportion of the labour employment of Californian agriculture and, in spite of advances in mechanisation, employ large numbers of seasonal labourers at harvest time, many of whom come from Mexico. Although the rapid growth of population in the post-war period has provided a growing local market, the industries originally relied upon exports to the eastern seaboard. To overcome the disadvantages of distance, the fruit and vegetable producers have had to develop co-operative marketing to ensure a high standard of quality and to process much of the produce; canned juice and fruit account for much of the citrus output.[25]

Horticulture is not as important in Chile, the Cape or Australia as it is in California. In Chile the low level of urban demand has precluded any significant specialised production of vegetables, except near the major cities, and there are few exports. Deciduous fruits are more important than citrus; exports of either are unimportant, for the seasonal advantage does not appear to have overcome the disadvantage of the great distance from the major urban markets of the northern hemisphere. Since the subdivision of property that began in 1950 there has been a slow increase in orchards and vegetables.[26]

Cape Town was originally established as a victualling station for the Dutch East India Company, and a wide range of vegetables and fruits was introduced, which are still produced on the Cape Flats and in the Stellenbosch irrigated areas.[27] Although citrus fruits were first introduced into South Africa at the Cape, South African exports come mainly from the Eastern Cape and the Transvaal, not from the area of Mediterranean climate. It is worth recalling here that the citrus fruits are indigenous to South East Asia and were a comparatively late introduction into the Mediterranean basin. Although the Cape winters are a little mild for temperate fruit, the major fruits are apples, peaches and apricots.[28]

In Western Australia fruits and vegetables are of comparatively little importance compared with wheat and sheep, and are concentrated on the coastal plains south of Perth. But most of Australia's viticulture and citrus fruit production is to be found not in the typically Mediterranean climate of the south west, but in South Australia, and particularly in the irrigated areas of the Murray River.[29]

We turn last to pastoralism. The role of sheep in the development of South Africa and Australia needs little emphasis (see pp. 250–3) and it was the merino, a Mediterranean breed, that allowed the initial exploitation of the arid interiors of both continents. Although the Boer trekkers who moved east of the Cape lived a semi-nomadic life in the eighteenth century, and practised a form of transhumance, the early sheep runs in Australia were based on English methods, and after the 1850s on techniques reminiscent of American ranching. (See Chapter 12.) Sheep raising in both areas is now increasingly done on mixed wheat and sheep farms, in sharp contrast to the pastoralism of the Mediterranean basin. It is in Chile that the tradition of Mediterranean – or more accurately, Spanish – pastoralism is most closely preserved. The central valley of Chile south of Santiago is not a continuous alluvial lowland, but rather a series of basins separated by spurs of the Andes and the coastal ranges. These are used for summer grazing by sheep and cattle, which are kept on the enormous *haciendas* of the lowlands. But a considerable proportion of the *haciendas* are not used for intensive crops, but for growing alfalfa; indeed half Chile's irrigated land is used for pasture, of which only one-third is improved. This however does not reflect the existence of intensive grazing, but the extensive use of land by owners largely uninterested in crop production. As late as the 1950s 87 per cent of Chile's farmland was divided between only 5000 *haciendas;* conversely a large population of *inquilinos* owned a minute proportion of the land. The present land reform campaigns which got under way in the 1960s may lead to a more intensive use of this land.[30]

California presents the most interesting example of changes in pastoral land use. The mountains to the east and west of the central valley provide open range for grazing cattle and sheep, and in the nineteenth century a form of transhumance was practised, although there was more cultivated fodder in the lowlands than is characteristic of the Mediterranean basin. But with the rise of more intensive farming both sheep and wheat declined. In the 1920s less than 10 per cent of California's farm income was derived from livestock products. The figure however is now 40 per cent. Since 1930 the growing population of California has demanded both dairy products and beef, and it has become profitable to irrigate alfalfa to feed cattle, as well as using the upland open range, whilst substantial dairy industries have developed in the coastal ranges north of San Francisco and near Los Angeles.[31]

But it is in farm structure that the differences between the Mediterranean basin and the overseas areas are most clear. Although fruit and vegetable farms in California, South Africa and Australia are typically small, they are nowhere as diminutive or as fragmented as those of the Mediterranean basin. The average size of farm in California is 190 hectares, and in Western Australia typical farms are about 800 hectares. In Chile of course the Spanish tradition of latifundia is oppressively clear, but it should be recalled that the latifundia of Andalusia are not typical of all Spain and even less so of other Mediterranean countries. Again, with the exception of Chile, farm population densities are low in the overseas areas, and farm incomes high; machinery is widely used and capital inputs are considerable. This is most striking in California, where over 2 800 000 hectares are irrigated, more than two-thirds of the arable land. Thus it would be difficult to group California with Algeria, or Western Australia with Greece, in any classification of modern agriculture. The common heritage will however be clear when the evolution of agriculture in these countries is dealt with.[32]

Early agriculture in the Mediterranean basin

The beginnings of modern Mediterranean agriculture are to be found in South West Asia and the eastern Mediterranean, where wheat and barley were first domesticated, as were cattle, sheep and goats. By the third millennium B.C. the ox-drawn wooden *ard* had been adopted, whilst sheep and goats were grazed by most village communities. The origins of transhumance are unclear but seem to have emerged in the second millennium. The predominance of cereal cultivation, and grazing of sheep and goats, was thus an early feature of Mediterranean agriculture; nor was it confined to the Mediterranean region *in sensu stricto.* East of the Judaean hills the Mediterranean climate and the characteristic vegetation give way to steppe and then desert, but the Fertile Crescent in Syria and Iraq has sufficient precipitation for rain-fed agriculture. Indeed the winter concentration of rainfall extends as far as Karachi in the south and the foothills of the Kopet Dag in the north.[33] The combination of extensive cereal production and transhumant grazing still persists throughout much of South West Asia today.

Neither the date nor the location of the domestication of the grape-vine, the olive or the fig has been clearly established,[34] but Greece, Asia Minor and the Levant appear to be the most likely *locus* and possibly as early as the fourth millennium B.C.; these plants were thus introduced at a later date into the western Mediterranean and eastwards into Babylon, Assyria and as far as north-western India and Turkestan. The basic features of modern Mediterranean agriculture thus arose in the eastern Mediterranean, and were probably best developed in the coastal areas; further, these elements of the farming system were all independent of irrigation.

The diffusion of the Mediterranean complex westwards along the shores of the Sea is not easy to trace. But there is little doubt that, however early the grape and olive were carried westwards, they were not fully established until the millennium before Christ. By that time a number of urban civilisations had arisen based on ports and trade, and it was the trading and colonising activities of the Phoenicians, the Greeks and later the Romans which established eastern Mediterranean agriculture – and much else besides – around the coasts of the Sea. The Phoenicians – from what is now the Lebanon – founded Carthage in 814 B.C. Greek colonisation began in the eighth century B.C., not only in southern Italy and Sicily, but also in Spain and southern France, and on the northern shores of the Black Sea, whilst Greek power reached in the fourth century into Turkestan, Mesopotamia, Egypt and as far east as the Indus.[35] The importance of sea transport in the establishment of colonies and the expansion of imperial dominions must not be underestimated, for it allowed the Greek city states and later Rome to specialise in the production of wine and olive-oil for export, and in return to import grain. Thus the Mediterranean economy became at least partly commercialised early in the millennium before Christ.[36] At its height Rome had a population of one million, a major market, which obtained its grain from southern Italy, Tunisia and Egypt, and olive-oil and wine from southern Spain. Earlier the Greeks had influenced Egyptian agriculture, which had been curiously isolated from the rest of the Mediterranean. Under the Ptolemies Greek settlers established viticulture – beer had hitherto been the national drink of Egypt – introduced new breeds of sheep for wool, and grew olives for oil rather than as a fruit.[37]

By the first centuries of the Christian era the basic features of traditional Mediterranean agriculture were well established. Wheat and barley were the main crops, invariably grown with a fallow; the *ard* was used to cross-plough, and the fallow was worked two or three times to eliminate weeds. The crop was harvested with the sickle. Cereals and fallow dominated the land-use pattern, and the growth of summer crops in rotation was only possible in the wetter areas.[38] Latifundia had already made their appearance in southern Spain and southern Italy, although the small family farm was the predominant type in both early Latium and Greece. It later gave way to the large estate, worked at first by slaves, and by the first century A.D. by *coloni,* or share-croppers; such estates were found in Sicily, southern Italy, southern Spain and also, after the Punic Wars, in Tunisia.[39]

The significance of vegetable and fruit production in Roman times is difficult to establish. Certainly the production of vegetables around the major cities was important, and they were commonly irrigated, for although they could be sown in autumn they needed irrigation in the summer. They were a significant part of Babylonian, Egyptian, and later of Roman agriculture. Onions, lettuces, asparagus, cucumbers and others were all grown, although the tomato and potato were not introduced until after 1492.[40]

Orchards were an important part of classical Mediterranean agriculture, and by the first few centuries of the Christian era apples, pears, peaches, apricots and cherries were grown. Citrus fruits – other than the citron – were not grown, although they were already known in Mesopotamia.[41]

The extent and importance of irrigation in the Mediterranean basin in classical times are a matter of controversy. It was well established in the Nile valley and in Mesopotamia, where indeed farming was impossible without it. But in most other parts of the basin it was essentially supplementary and used mainly for vegetables and fruits, although in the Levant the hillsides were sometimes terraced and irrigated for cereals. It has been argued that the irrigated area in Tunisia and parts of the Levant was far greater in Roman times than at present, but for the most part irrigation outside the Levant was not of major importance.[42]

It is perhaps appropriate here to stress the significance of Mesopotamia in the development of Mediterranean agriculture. Farming was – and is – based upon three types of crop: those which would complete their life cycle in the period of winter rain, such as wheat; those which could survive the summer drought, such as the olive; and those crops indigenous to areas outside the Mediterranean climate which grew in summer and thus had to be irrigated. These crops came from the monsoon lands of South and South East Asia, and were first introduced into Mesopotamia before being adopted in Egypt and the Levant; thus in the first millennium B.C. rice, sugar-cane, cotton and citrus fruits were already being grown in Mesopotamia but were not yet of any significance in the Levant or Egypt.[43]

There is less reliable information upon livestock husbandry in classical times than upon crop production. In Italy neither beef nor milk was of much significance, and pigs provided much of the meat. Cattle were mainly valued for draught, and rarely raised for beef; sheep and goats were almost certainly the most numerous animals. The beginnings of transhumance are by no means well established; references to transhumance occur in the middle of the first millennium B.C., but it does not appear to have taken place on the scale that was common in medieval times.[44]

The Fall of Rome to the discovery of the New World

By the first century of the Christian era the Roman Empire embraced the whole of the Mediterranean basin, and indeed more besides, and Roman farming had reached its apogee. If the agronomies of Roman writers are any guide, agricultural knowledge had reached a standard not to be surpassed until the nineteenth century. The value of manures was well known, green manuring practised, and lucerne cultivated. A minority of farmers grew legumes in the rotation, but, then as now, the dry summer made the bare fallow more common. A wide range of agricultural implements was available, and plough shares and the blades of sickles were increasingly made of iron. Dry-farming was well understood and almost universally practised. Although irrigation was essentially supplementary, a number of lifting devices were known, particularly in the Levant, where the *noria* was in use, and dams were built to conserve erratic winter rains; wells were dug, cisterns built to store rainfall in the Judaean mountains, and *foggaras* used to trap ground-water. Then as now the failure to integrate livestock and crop husbandry had a limiting effect on yields, which could have rarely exceeded 650 kg per hectare, except on the better soils.[45]

There were signs of decline even before the Fall of Rome. In North Africa and the Levant the cultivated area contracted, possibly due to overtaxation and labour shortages, whilst in southern Italy pastoralism slowly spread into areas of crop production. The latifundia increased at the expense of the peasant proprietor in the later Roman Empire.[46] This tendency continued into the Middle Ages; as insecurity grew, so peasants sought protection from a powerful lord, both in the Mediterranean basin and in northern Europe; the *coloni* gradually became enserfed.[47] Thereafter one of the principal differences between western Europe and both eastern and southern Europe was the rate at which the peasant freed himself from feudalism.

The agricultural consequences of the barbarian invasions and the disintegration of the Roman Empire are difficult to establish. Economic hegemony in Europe did not however pass north of the Alps, but rather from the West Mediterranean to the East, where the Byzantine Empire survived.[48] But even in the West Mediterranean there was no great decline in agricultural technology. The Visigoths, for example, did not disrupt the Roman system in Spain, although pastoralism may have increased in importance in the interior.[49] In Italy disruption was perhaps greater. The decline in population led to less intensive cultivation, insecurity to a greater self-sufficiency and thus less regional specialisation, whilst pastoralism grew in importance.[50] This decline is not easily documented, but there seems little doubt of its extent. Insecurity, warfare and major outbreaks of plague, particularly in the sixth century, were responsible. Thus in A.D. 350 the

135

population of the Mediterranean basin together with South West Asia was about 60 000 000, but by A.D. 600 only 40 000 000.[51]

The Dark Ages in northern Europe were a period of important technological change; the mouldboard plough replaced the Mediterranean *ard*, and the two-field system of the south was superseded by the three-field system. But the lack of rain in early summer made this impossible in the Mediterranean;[52] the *ard*, on the other hand, was probably well adapted to the light soils of the south, where moisture conservation was more significant than drainage, and too vigorous cultivation encouraged soil erosion. The Mediterranean countries were also beginning to pay the penalty of their long history of settlement. The steady deforestation of the uplands encouraged soil erosion, which in turn overburdened the streams with silt. Centuries of oversilting led to poor drainage in the lowland plains, making them a ready ground for the spread of malaria which had been introduced from Africa only in Roman times.[53]

Pastoralism certainly spread in the later part of the first millennium A.D. and reached its height in the later Middle Ages. There were a number of causes. In North Africa, the invasion of the *bedouin* first in the seventh and again in the eleventh centuries led to a decline of sedentary agriculture compared with nomadic herding, particularly in Cyrenaicia, whilst in the Levant the early Arab invasions had a similar effect, although agriculture revived later. In Italy and Spain the establishment of elaborate systems of transhumance had other causes. The use of latifundia and a shortage of labour encouraged more extensive use of the land; but there were more positive reasons. The beginnings of woollen textile industries in northern Italy, Flanders and England encouraged the growth of sheep numbers. The ease of taxing wool exports gave pastoralists the support of governments. In both Spain and Italy legislation favoured the shepherd at the expense of the farmer. In Spain migratory herding of sheep may have been extended by the Berbers who settled after the Arab conquest; certainly the merino was introduced from North Africa about A.D. 1300. The movement of sheep flocks from south to north was well-established by then, and the Mesta was formed in 1273; wool exports began in about 1300. By 1447 2 500 000 sheep were involved in transhumance and the confirmation of the Mesta's rights at the end of the century undoubtedly impeded the enclosure of land in the *meseta*.[54] In Italy transhumance was found in every part of the country in the Middle Ages, but long-distance transhumance was most marked in the south, particularly after the depopulation caused by the Black Death in the mid-fourteenth century.[55] As in Spain the pastoral organisation, the Dogana, received royal support, and the flocks grew rapidly. In A.D. 1400 there were 5 600 000 sheep involved in the Appenine–Apulia region, and 10 000 000 by 1650. Transhumance reached its peak in the fifteenth and sixteenth centuries, when routes were to be found throughout the Mediterranean basin.[56]

There were however more positive changes in Mediterranean agriculture in the Middle Ages, brought about by Arab innovations and later by the economic revival in Europe which began in the ninth century.

The remarkable expansion of Islam began in the mid-seventh century; by A.D.750 the religion of Mohammed and the language of the Arabs, as well as political control, were established in the Levant, Mesopotamia, Egypt, North Africa and southern Spain, Sicily, Crete and Cyprus, Persia, Turkestan and as far east as the Indies.[57] On the whole European historiography has emphasised the negative aspects of Islamic expansion, in particular the bedouinisation of life in Cyrenaica, North Africa, parts of the Levant and later, after the invasions of the Turks, of Anatolia and the Aegean islands. But the positive aspects of Arab conquest were also significant. In the first place the Arabs overran Mesopotamia and Egypt, civilisations dependent upon irrigation; they were thus influential in extending techniques long known in the Near East to the western Mediterranean. We have noted earlier the difficulty of establishing the importance of irrigation in Roman times, and this has led to much dispute about the significance of the Arab contribution. But in Spain at least it seems to have been paramount. They established the *huertas* of Valencia, introducing elaborate canal systems and spreading the use of the *noria*.[58] Of equal significance was the encouragement of the intensive cultivation of fruits and vegetables. But of greatest moment was the introduction of a wide range of crops already grown in South West Asia, or recently brought from India or South East Asia. First were the citrus fruits. The citron was already known in the eastern Mediterranean in Roman times; but the bitter orange only reached South West Asia in the tenth century, and was introduced to the western Mediterranean in the eleventh century. In the late fourteenth century oranges were exported from Spain to England.[59] The lemon was known in Spain by A.D. 1150, the lime in the thirteenth century. The sweet orange in contrast was popularised by the Portuguese after 1450. The Arabs were responsible for the introduction of the citrus fruits into Spain and Sicily, but the Crusaders also played an important role in their diffusion westwards in the twelfth and thirteenth centuries.[60]

Perhaps more important were a number of other crops. Sugar-cane is not known in the Mediterranean until it is recorded in Egypt in the seventh century; but it then spread slowly westwards and became an important crop in Spain, Sicily, Cyprus, Crete and the Levant, providing much of northern Europe's sugar until, first, the Portuguese African island colonies, and later the American colonies, destroyed the industry. Cotton and the mulberry tree were also Arab introductions.[61] Lucerne was originally introduced into the eastern Mediterranean about 490 B.C. but its use appears to have declined after the fall of Rome. However its value was rediscovered, and irrigated lucerne pastures were a distinctive part of Lombardy farming as early as the twelfth century. The last crop of importance, rice, brought by the Arabs to Spain, was grown in the coastal *huertas* in the fifteenth century and later introduced into Lombardy.[62]

Thus the Arabs greatly enriched the crop combinations of the Mediterranean as well as encouraging the tradition of horticulture; indeed by the later Middle Ages horticulture was the only field in which the Mediterranean retained a technological lead over northern Europe.[63] On the other hand the spread of

137

Islam, with its prohibition of the use of alcohol, had an adverse effect on the growth of the grape-vine. It was not that its cultivation was banned;[64] rather that the emphasis shifted to the production of fresh grapes, and later in the fifteenth and sixteenth centuries to the production of currants and sultanas.[65] Nor did the Levant or the other Muslim areas share in the great expansion of viticulture of the nineteenth century, except in the French colonies.[66] The prohibition of the eating of pork also deprived the farmers in Arab lands of an important source of meat. But perhaps one of the most grievous long-term effects of Islamic expansion was the introduction of Arab land law, which, later modified by the Ottoman Turks, led to the proliferation of estates owned by absentee landlords and worked by share-croppers overburdened by tax and with little interest in improving their farming.[67]

In the tenth century there were signs of a revival in economic life throughout Europe, and the Mediterranean shared in this growth. The population of Italy doubled between the tenth and fourteenth centuries, and indeed the population of the whole basin recovered: but this recovery was greatest in Italy, Spain and southern France, those parts of the Mediterranean nearest the growing commercial centres of northern Europe. By 1300 the population of the western Mediterranean was back to what it had been in the first century A.D.; that of the Muslim lands east and south remained stagnant.[68] The growth of population led to an expansion of the cultivated land and in particular the revival of irrigation in the Durance, in the Po valley, and in the *huertas* of south-eastern Spain.[69] Most progress was made in northern Italy, where agricultural advance was a response to rapid urban growth, and where, conversely, urban investment went into agriculture. The textile industries prompted the growth of new crops – mulberry trees for silk, and woad for dyeing; the land under fruits, vegetables and grapes expanded to feed the communes; the fallow declined as rotations were devised, and, most striking of all, irrigated pastures supported a dairying industry. This was the achievement mainly of small farmers, not large estates. Indeed northern Italy had by the fourteenth century the most advanced agricultural system in Europe. But it should be remembered here that the Po valley is one of the few large areas of fertile lowland in the Mediterranean basin, and further has a climate much modified by its northerly and continental position; it was thus not typical of the Mediterranean basin.[70]

By the sixteenth century the Mediterranean basin was in its last days of economic pre-eminence in Europe. The active trade that had nourished its cities still survived. Grain flowed from Sicily and southern Italy to North Africa, Spain, France and northern Italy; trade in wine and oil persisted, particularly of the sweet wines of the hotter and drier eastern Mediterranean, whilst the spice trade still flourished, in spite of the Portuguese achievement.[71] But the ascendancy of the Mediterranean in Europe was over. In the first place population increase in the sixteenth century, general throughout Europe, led to famines in the late sixteenth century; whereas in northern Europe more intensive farming methods were adopted, in the Mediterranean the farming system remained unaltered outside northern Italy; the advances of the high Middle Ages had been based on the introduction of new crops and the expansion of the cultivated area, not on the introduction of new farming methods. In the second place northern Italy, which looked set to establish 'sustained economic growth', declined in the seventeenth century before competition from northern Europe. Thereafter urban and industrial growth and all that implied became the prerogative of the north west of the continent. Lastly, the expansion of Europe and the settlement of the New World, and the bypassing of the overland routes to the East, made the Mediterranean peripheral to the great trade routes.[72]

The modern period

After the remarkable achievements of Italy in the Renaissance and of Spain in settling the New World, the Mediterranean declined – or perhaps more accurately stagnated – until the nineteenth century. There was very little technological change in agriculture, although new crops were adopted. Maize was introduced into Spain in 1493, but its cultivation was unimportant until the late eighteenth century and indeed it has had its greatest importance outside the Mediterranean region proper, in the summer rainfall areas of the Balkans and Aquitane. Tobacco, in contrast, was rapidly adopted, most noticeably in the eastern Mediterranean, particularly in western Anatolia and Greece.[73]

After the seventeenth century the progress of Mediterranean agriculture can perhaps most usefully be charted in comparison with events in northern Europe. Population began to increase in southern and northern Europe as outbreaks of the plague became less frequent; indeed the last major outbreak in Europe was in a Mediterranean area – in Provence in 1720. Subsistence crises became less common as transport improved. But the decline of the death rate began in Spain and Italy only in the 1890s, much later than in north-western Europe, and in south-eastern Europe, the Levant and North Africa, even later. The steady increase in population in the Mediterranean in the early nineteenth century meant that by 1850 all the signs of acute rural congestion were present,[74] and in southern Spain and southern Italy they were exacerbated by the unequal division of land. The increase in the rate of population increase in the 1880s and 1890s therefore produced a major crisis. One response was emigration. It was on its most massive scale from Sicily and southern Italy to the United States; but 420000 Greeks emigrated between 1890 and 1910, whilst many Spaniards left for Latin America. When the decline in the death rate reached the Levant in the 1930s there was a large-scale emigration from the Lebanon. In France the problem was less acute, but many of the settlers in North Africa came from the Midi.[75]

There was of course also massive emigration from northern Europe in the nineteenth century, but it was mainly before 1880; by the end of the century the rate of population increase in northern Europe was slowing down, whilst, more significant, industrialisation was absorbing the surplus labour on the land. The

Mediterranean did not experience industrialisation or urbanisation at the same time, although the beginnings of northern Italian industrialisation date from the 1880s. The absence of industrialisation until very recently – the Italian economic miracle is largely post-Second World War – has meant that much of the Mediterranean has suffered from acute underemployment in agriculture, a lack of easy access to machinery and fertilisers, and is without a large and wealthy urban market to stimulate a shift to animal products.

Although industrialisation has been late in Mediterranean Europe it has at last got under way; although per caput income in southern France is still only half that of northern France,[76] Mediterranean France is nonetheless part of a developed country, whilst since 1945 northern Italy has experienced a remarkable economic transformation. Even Spain has successfully reduced its agricultural population since 1950 and has the beginnings of an industrial revolution. Further, these three areas all have the advantage of nearness to the major industrial areas of north-western Europe, and thus lower transport costs for marketing agricultural produce.[77] The Balkans, Greece, Turkey, the Levant and North Africa, on the other hand, not only have the disadvantage of remoteness, but also have industrialised far less than the countries of the north-western Mediterranean. There is thus now a far greater difference between the western and the eastern Mediterranean than there ever was in the past, even in the heyday of Arab expansion and the conflict with Christian Europe.

Against this background we may examine the more recent changes in Mediterranean agriculture. First, there have been major increases in the cultivated area, particularly since 1850. Much of this has been by the reclamation of low-lying marshy land, particularly in the lower Po valley, the Campania and some of the Spanish estuaries. But in the nineteenth century there was also expansion into arid and hilly areas. Thus in Spain after 1860 much common land formerly used for grazing was put under wheat, an expansion that continued during the boom prices of the 1914–18 war. In Italy rapid population growth in the later nineteenth century pushed cultivation into hilly areas, often leading to deforestation, the silting of rivers and flooding in the coastal plains. In Algeria French colonists in the late nineteenth century pushed dry-farming of wheat into the steppe, and the wheat areas of Syria and Turkey have also increased greatly in the last hundred years. Thus over 1 000 000 hectares of new land have been added in Italy since 1860.[78] Much of the new land was devoted to wheat, in spite of the crisis of the 1880s when cheap American grain flooded the market. Nearly all the Mediterranean countries opted for tariffs to protect their wheat growers; this has meant that inefficient producers have been preserved; for whilst some artificial fertiliser has been used in wheat farms, there has been little mechanisation and few increases in labour productivity or crop yields.[79]

Not only has wheat production remained largely unmechanised – unlike that which became established in California and Western Australia in the late nineteenth century – but there has been little progress in integrating cereal and livestock production. The fallow remains common; few legumes are grown in rotation, and little manure is available to increase crop yields. Only in the wetter areas has maize or a legume been inserted in the rotation. Furthermore the expansion of the arable area has led to the decline of transhumance. The Mesta lost its power to tax in Spain in 1758. In the nineteenth century the enclosure of commons and the increase in the wheat area reduced the use of the *canadas*, and by the end of the century the dwindling number of transhumance sheep were being carried by train. In southern Italy the Dogana was abolished in 1806, and the numbers of sheep involved in transhumance between Apulia and the Apennines has fallen to less than 500 000.[80]

The major changes in the agriculture of the Mediterranean since 1850 have been in the expansion of the traditional crops of olives and grapes, of fruit trees – especially the citrus – and the development of vegetables. In addition a number of cash crops have increased – cotton, sugar-beet, rice and tobacco. All these – with the exception of sugar-beet – had been grown at least as early as the sixteenth century, but there were few areas devoted to their specialised production. Since 1850 a number of more favoured areas have ceased to grow the full range of traditional Mediterranean crops and have specialised in one or two cash crops. Much of this expansion, particularly in citrus fruits, rice and vegetables, has depended on an increase in the irrigation, and thus agriculture has become progressively more intensive: most of these crops require far more labour than extensive wheat production, and so the growing agricultural population has been more readily absorbed than in the wheat-growing areas, thus accentuating a difference in population density between the intensive coastal areas and the more sparsely populated interiors – most noticeably in Spain, Sicily and southern Italy.

TABLE 25   *Labour inputs in Mediterranean agriculture*
(number of work days per hectare per annum)

	By dry farming	By irrigation
Wheat and barley	30	–
Maize	40–50	75
Cotton	60–70	120
Vegetables	175–220	350–400
Fruit trees	80	130

Source: Chaine, 1959, 322

The shift to more specialised agriculture in the Mediterranean was only possible after a number of advances in the European economy. First in importance was the rise in real income per caput in the industrial centres of north-western Europe, creating a demand for what were, in the mid-nineteenth century, still luxury products for the majority of the population – wine, oranges, flowers and a wide range of vegetables. Internal demand was also important, particularly in southern France, which had access to the growing populations of Paris and the Nord, and in southern Italy, which after unification and the railway-building frenzy of the 1860s and 1870s had a market in the industrial cities of Lombardy and Piedmont. The improvement of transport was also a prerequisite for change. Whilst sailing ships were the only means of transport the marketing of fresh fruit in northern Europe was a chancy business; the replacement of sail by steam was thus important, as were the more regular sailings between northern Europe and the Mediterranean after the opening of the Suez Canal in 1869. The railway penetrated southern Europe slowly. Northern Italy had no link with the south until after 1865 and no effective network until 1885. Paris was not linked with Avignon until 1856, Nîmes with Lyons until 1879, whilst Valencia was connected to Madrid by rail only in 1857 and to France in 1878.[81]

Clearly the countries of the north-western Mediterranean had a great advantage in sheer nearness to north-western Europe compared with the south east, which still slumbered beneath Ottoman rule. Indeed it was the political expansion of northern Europe into the eastern Mediterranean which prompted economic growth in that region; Russia's threats to the Dardanelles, Britain's concern to control the route to India, and French activities on the Barbary coast, all led eventually to the development of export trades in the countries of the eastern Mediterranean, as did the Jewish settlement of Palestine which began in the 1890s. Thus there was little demand for Turkish or Greek tobacco until British and French soldiers acquired a taste for it in the Crimean War. Tobacco of course had the advantage of being less perishable and of very high value per unit weight. The eastern Mediterranean suffered from remoteness – and indeed still does. More recently the spread of refrigerated cars on railways, and holds in ships, and the growth of processing – canned fruits and vegetables, the extraction of fruit juices – have given the more distant areas a chance of marketing their produce. Prior to these advances the best way of marketing fruit was by drying it. The eastern Mediterranean here had the advantage of longer and hotter summers than the west; furthermore the Muslim east's lack of interest in wine prompted the production of raisins, of which Greece and Turkey had a monopoly until the appearance of California and Australia in the trade in this century.

The first signs of change then came in the western Mediterranean, and in the traditional products of wine and olive-oil. Between the fourteenth and eighteenth centuries there had been a slow increase in peasant consumption of wine in Europe;[82] in the nineteenth century the growth of population – and particularly of urban populations – in France, Spain and Italy, and also in Austria-Hungary, led to the appearance of specialised areas of viticulture. Of these the most dramatic was Languedoc. In the early eighteenth century, Bas-Languedoc was an area of traditional Mediterranean agriculture. There was extensive cereal production and transhumance between the alluvial lowlands and the Massif Central; most farmers grew some vines and had olive trees, whilst mulberry trees sustained a local silk industry. But in 1681 the Canale Royale linked Sète with Bordeaux, and the eighteenth century saw a steady increase in viticulture. In 1824 the area under vine-grapes in Roussillon and Languedoc was 238 000 hectares. In the next half century the railway linked the Midi with the North and viticulture expanded to a peak area in 1875 of 430000 hectares.[83] Most of the vineyards were small, less than 10 hectares in size, producing mainly low-quality wines for everyday consumption; little of the cultivated area was in other crops. Disaster struck in the 1860s with the arrival of the disease *phylloxera*; thousands of hectares of grape-vines were uprooted as the disease spread eastwards. This had a serious effect on French wine production, which radically declined. However in 1878 it was found that the American *Rupestris* vine was immune to the disease, and Languedoc was slowly replanted. But the American stock did not thrive on the sandy uplands where the local vines had flourished and so the new vineyards were established on the better soils of the alluvial lowlands. However the acreage has never returned to the peak of the 1870s, and nor has prosperity, for the decline of the Midi between 1870 and 1900 prompted expansion of vineyards in other countries – especially Algeria – whilst yields in Languedoc have increased steadily. By the 1930s Languedoc was suffering from low prices, overproduction and overspecialisation. Since 1945 it has been a problem region, and there have been attempts to diversify by uprooting vines, increasing irrigation, and cultivating fruit and vegetables.[84]

The late nineteenth century saw a parallel expansion of vineyards in other parts of the western Mediterranean; in Spain the area under vines increased from 400000 hectares at the beginning of the nineteenth century to three times that figure by the 1930s. Most of the exports – and Spain was the world's leading exporter of wine for a brief period after 1880 – were from the coastal regions, most noticeably the south west around Jerez de la Frontera where there were long-established trading links with Britain; but viticulture also expanded in the interior, mainly to provide the home market.[85]

The most dramatic expansion came in Algeria. The early French settlers had hoped to produce tropical crops, including coffee, sugar-cane and cotton. After some short-lived success with cotton in the 1860s most settlers turned to wheat; their methods however were little improvement on those of the indigenous farmers, whilst the indispensable wine was imported. The *phylloxera* epidemic in France was thus a rare opportunity, quickly seized. The area under vines increased tenfold between 1880 and 1930; as the Algerian wines, like those of Languedoc, were of low quality, they contributed to the problem of overproduction which has beset France since the 1900s.[86]

Italian wine production also boomed in the 1880s as *phylloxera* did not arrive until the end of the century, and the railway linked the south with the industrial north and also with markets in central Europe and France itself. One region which was transformed was Apulia, for long given over to transhumance and wheat; but the railway, falling grain prices, and the customs treaty with France in 1863, all led to the transformation of the Albe Murge and the Murge Basse, and the specialisation by smallholders in viticulture and olive groves. In the 1870s the Apulian tree crop zone had less than 100000 hectares in vines, but now has nearly 300000 hectares. Most of the wine goes to make vermouth.[87] On the other side of the Adriatic, olive trees and transhumance formed the basis of the economy, for there was little good arable land. A decline in the olive paved the way for the expansion of viticulture in Dalmatia after French production declined until by 1900 it was virtually a monoculture; then however *phylloxera* struck.[88]

Although comparatively little of the world's wine output moves into international trade, wine is still the leading agricultural export of the Mediterranean countries – although the figures for France in Table 26 include substantial exports from the non-Mediterranean areas. Much of the exports come from highly specialised areas of viticulture which existed only in embryonic form before 1850. Furthermore wine remains a product predominantly of the western Mediterranean, whilst most of the fresh grapes come from the same region. The eastern Mediterranean's exploitation of vineyards is only significant in the production of raisins.

TABLE 26   *Exports of fruits and vegetables from Mediterranean countries*

	Fruit and vegetables as a % of all agricultural exports	Exports of each country as a % of all Mediterranean exports of each product					
		Citrus	Olive-oil	Wine	Apples and pears	Grapes	Raisins
Portugal	27	–	6.5	11.4	–	–	–
Spain	52	25	27.7	10.7	0.3	34.1	2.6
France	8.4	5.9	2.3	41.9	28.0	7.2	–
Italy	58	18.6	12.3	15.7	66.7	47.2	–
Yugoslavia	10.9	–	–	1.4	–	0.9	–
Greece	31.0	3.9	24.0	1.3	0.1	4.9	58.2
Turkey	30.4	1.9	0.7	0.2	–	0.8	37.6
Lebanon	52.4	1.3	–	–	4.6	0.7	–
Jordan	76.5	0.4	0.5	–	–	–	–
Israel	80.7	19.9	–	–	–	–	–
Cyprus	75.0	3.7	0.5	1.0	–	2.8	1.1
Malta	22.0	–	–	0.2	–	–	–
Tunisia	23.0	0.7	21.2	1.3	–	–	–
Algeria	–	4.5	2.4	13.1	–	–	–
Morocco	68.9	18.9	1.3	1.2	–	–	–

Source: F.A.O. *Trade yearbook*, vol. 23, 1969

The late nineteenth century saw the expansion of the area under olive trees, and the creation of specialised areas of cultivation, particularly in Spain and Tunisia. It was in Spain however that the major advance took place, for there was a market not only in Europe, but also in Latin America, where Argentina was yet to become a significant producer. The area under olives more than doubled between 1858 and 1932.[89] Whilst the expansion of vineyards was largely in the hands of small peasant proprietors, the increased output of olives and olive-oil came from the large plantations of olive trees in the interior of southern Spain, worked by day-labourers.[90] Much the same development came in Tunisia after 1881, where large estates were created in the Sahel zone near Sfax by French proprietors but operated by Tunisian share-croppers.[91] Only in Italy, and especially in Apulia, was the increase in olive-oil output undertaken by smallholders. The output for olive-oil has not increased at the rate of the other specialised products of the Mediterranean. There has never been much demand for olive-oil in northern Europe, whilst cheap oilseeds have encroached upon the Mediterranean market. Further, Spain has progressively lost its monopoly as first Tunisia and later Greece has entered the dwindling market.[92] Thus in southern France olive groves on the better soils have been uprooted and replaced by more valuable crops, and they survive only in poorer soils. In contrast, Italy, which is a major importer, has reduced acreage but turned increasingly to the irrigation of olives.[93]

But for the most part the expansion of viticulture and olive trees was achieved without irrigation or major changes in technology. In contrast the growth of specialised areas of fruit and market gardening has been dependent upon irrigation. Apples and pears can of course be grown without irrigation, and furthermore are not confined to Mediterranean climates. It suffices to note the importance of northern Italy and the dramatic rise, since the 1930s, of the Lebanon as an apple exporter.[94] The expansion of citrus fruit production has been far more striking. There are about 600 000 hectares under citrus fruit in the Mediterranean basin[95] and the production is strongly localised. In the middle of the nineteenth century orange trees were widely distributed in the basin, but of only limited economic significance. However in the 1850s a Valencian merchant sent cases of oranges to Liverpool, and in 1860 the first steamship linked Valencia and England. Thereafter oranges expanded rapidly in the Valencian *huerta* not only replacing other crops – particularly olive trees – but prompting the reclamation and irrigation of new land. By 1873 oranges were being exported to the United States and Germany and in 1878 the railway connected Valencia with France. Between 1880 and 1900 orange exports quadrupled.[96] The other region to benefit from the steamship was Sicily, which had a long-established citrus-growing tradition in the coastal areas of the north and east, and grew lemons as well as oranges and mandarins, the crop having been introduced to Europe from China only in the early nineteenth century.[97] Both Valencia and Sicily had a climatic advantage in the production of citrus fruits, not only compared with northern Europe, but with the northern shores of the Mediterranean where temperatures were lower, and the risk of frost and the hazards of the *mistral* precluded, for the time being, specialisation in citrus fruit.[98] Until the 1920s Spain and Italy largely controlled citrus exports to northern Europe. Thereafter California, South Africa and Australia, with generally superior methods and better marketing systems, began to compete, whilst other Mediterranean producers appeared. In Palestine Jewish settlers in the coastal plain had grown oranges in the 1900s, but in 1920 there were still only 2000 hectares under the crop, but by 1938, 30000 hectares.[99] Even later came the emergence of Morocco. French settlement in Morocco after the First World War had largely been concerned with wheat production, but in the 1930s Californian experts were brought in to advise: in 1940 there were about 1 000 000 orange trees on European estates, by 1950 5 000 000, and Morocco now accounts for a fifth of citrus fruit exports from the Mediterranean basin.[100] Cyprus too has become a significant exporter only since the 1930s, and is of interest because, together with Israel, it produces most of the grapefruit grown in the Mediterranean. Four-fifths of the Mediterranean's exports of citrus fruits are of oranges, and citrus fruits together with wine are the Mediterranean countries' principal agricultural exports.[101]

There had been a long tradition of vegetable production in the Mediterranean basin, both around villages and on a more commercial scale near the major cities; indeed most of the vegetables now produced, with the exception of potatoes and tomatoes, are indigenous either to the Mediterranean or to South West Asia. But the absence of rapid transport precluded any significant specialisation until the coming of the railway, and, as with viticulture, it was internal demand within France that led to the first areas of specialisation, in the Lower Rhône. Most of the vegetables grown in the Mediterranean are also grown in northern Europe; the advantage of the south lies in the possibility of early crops, the *primeurs* of the French. This advantage increases southwards as winter temperatures rise, whilst with irrigation some multiple cropping is possible; in Malta, for example, two crops of potatoes can be grown.[102]

The earliest specialised market-gardening areas in the Mediterranean grew up in the Lower Rhône after the linking of Avignon with the north. As the tourist trade of the Côte d'Azure developed in the late nineteenth century, farmers turned to the production of vegetables and flowers for hotels; from this rose the Grasse perfume industry.[103] However the depression of the 1930s and the reduction in the tourist trade led farmers to market in Paris, while in Languedoc, where the predominance of viticulture had retarded the cultivation of vegetables, there were beginnings of interest as wine prices slumped. Southwards the irrigated areas of Roussillon could send vegetables to Paris a few weeks earlier than the Lower Rhône. In Spain the linking of Valencia and Madrid prompted the growth of vegetables in the *huertas*. Northern Italy experienced a rapid increase in vegetable production in the 1880s as imports of American grain combined with demand from the growing industrial towns to intensify farm production. The linking of southern Italy with the north by rail gave a boost to the intensive cultivation of the Campania and Sicily.[104]

As with citrus fruit the development of vegetable production in North Africa and the eastern Mediterranean came much later than in the north west; however the comparative remoteness of these areas from north-western Europe has been partly compensated for by the growth of markets in Germany and eastern Europe, and also by the growing internal demand from the western Mediterranean exporters. Italy, for example, exports only 6 per cent of her vegetable output.[105] Furthermore the more southerly regions, such as Morocco and Malta, have the advantage of early production. Statistics on the value of vegetable output are hard to discover, but it appears to be increasing more rapidly than fruit production. Thus for example in Italy in 1952 vegetables were 9.7 per cent of the total value of agricultural output, and fruit 10.9 per cent, whereas in 1964 the figures were 14.6 per cent and 12.5 per cent respectively.[106]

The development of intensive production in the last hundred years has been dependent upon the extension of irrigation. Not all irrigation has been devoted to fruit and vegetables. Rice is one major cash crop which has grown in importance since the 1860s, especially in the Lower Po valley, the Valencian *huertas* and the Ebro delta.[107] In the Levant – particularly Greece and western Turkey – cotton, which in the eighteenth century was a major export, supplying about a third of Britain's raw cotton imports before the advent of the United States, is now a major crop, although little more than a third of all Greece's cotton area is irrigated.[108] In the fifteenth century Spain and Sicily supplied much of Europe's sugar; some sugar-cane is still grown in southern Spain, but the American plantations killed the industry in the sixteenth century. However the protectionism that characterised late-nineteenth-century Europe prompted the development of sugar-beet under irrigation in several parts of the Mediterranean, but particularly in the Po valley.

The increase of irrigation resources in the Mediterranean is difficult to chart. Figures are however available for Spain. In 1858 there were 850000 hectares of irrigated land, in 1900, 1000000, in 1940, 1300000, and by 1967, 2270000.[109] In spite of the considerable expansion of irrigation facilities in all parts of the basin, particularly since the 1920s, a comparatively small part of the arable area is irrigated – in the 1950s the figure for Spain was 10 per cent, Greece 9 per cent, Italy 13 per cent and Turkey and Yugoslavia less than 1 per cent. Even Israel, with a third of its arable land irrigated, falls far short of California's figure. Nor will further expansion be all that easy. Not only is flat land in short supply, but water resources are limited, particularly in the east and south of the basin.[110]

Mediterranean agriculture has shown in the last century some paradoxical contrasts. Changes in extensive cereal production have been comparatively few. Transhumance has declined, and the integration of crops and livestock has only been achieved in either the wetter or the irrigated regions.

Viticulture and olive-oil expanded down to the 1930s but their future is limited. The low-quality wines of the Mediterranean are currently superabundant, and the market for olive-oil is stagnant. In contrast the specialised crops of the irrigated areas have provided an ever-increasing proportion of agricultural income. Much of this production is in the coastal areas, and here high rural densities are found. In contrast the interiors, still mainly under wheat, are areas of chronic underemployment and poverty.

The Spanish in the Americas

A major difference between the Mediterranean-type climatic areas of the

Americas and those of South Africa and Australia is that the former were settled by Spaniards, the latter by Dutchmen and Englishmen. As both Western Australia and South Africa have been dominated by the expansion of wheat and sheep, their history is dealt with elsewhere (Chapters 12 and 13), and this section is concerned only with Chile and California. It is thus appropriate to begin this description with some general account of the Spanish influence on American agriculture.

About half the sixteenth-century settlers of the Americas came from Andalusia.[111] They were thus acquainted with the classical Mediterranean crops and techniques – wheat and barley, raised by dry-farming methods, vine-grapes and olives; citrus fruits, sugar-cane, rice and cotton were grown in southern Spain in the fifteenth century, all with irrigation techniques introduced or elaborated by the Arabs. The techniques of cattle ranching and sheep transhumance were well developed in the south, and the role of the Spanish in the evolution of ranching in the Americas is dealt with in Chapter 13. Sugar-cane and cotton were the basis of the early plantation systems of the Americas, and are described in Chapter 12.

The first settlers in the West Indies found that wheat, grapes and olives did not thrive in the climate, although citrus fruits did.[112] Indeed it was not until the highlands of Mexico and Peru were reached that wheat could be cultivated satisfactorily. Olives and grapes were more successful in Mexico and particularly in the irrigated coastal areas of Peru. Whilst at first the Spanish authorities were concerned that the countries should support themselves, they subsequently feared that colonial olive-oil and wine would undercut the home product. Peru produced its first crop of grapes in 1551, but in the seventeenth century the Spanish Crown forbade its further cultivation. Whilst this policy of discouraging olive-oil and wine production was successful in the major centres of Spanish settlement, it was less efficient in the remoter areas. Thus both olives and vines were established in the northern parts of New Spain, in Chile and Mendoza by the end of the eighteenth century; by then the colonial authorities had given up any attempt to control their cultivation.[113]

The first settlements in California were not made until the late eighteenth century, although it had been reached in 1542, the same year as the foundation of Santiago in Chile. The earliest settlements were mission stations – at San Diego in 1769, Yuma in 1780 and Los Angeles in 1781; later forts were sited on the coast as far north as San Francisco. The missions introduced citrus fruits, olives and vine-grapes, although the major economic activity of the early settlers was ranching. In Chile settlement was much earlier – in the second half of the sixteenth century – but in neither region were there Indian agricultural civilisations comparable with those of Mexico or Peru. Thus the agricultural tradition of the Spanish was less altered by contact with the indigenes than it had been elsewhere.

In both countries the initial land grants were very large. Although the Spanish latifundia may perhaps be traced back to the Roman occupation, they were derived more immediately from conditions in medieval Spain, and particularly on the frontier of settlement during the *reconquista*. In northern Spain land was held in small peasant proprietorships, but as the Moors were pushed south in the thirteenth century the warfare and settlement were undertaken by military and monastic orders. Much of the southern part of Spain, reconquered after 1212, was thinly populated and the land was allocated by the Crown in large holdings to individuals and orders, and a pastoral economy was adopted.[114] In Spanish America all land was regarded as Crown property, and some attempt was made to protect Indian rights. However *encomiendas* – the right to tribute and labour from the Indian population – were allocated to Spaniards. In thinly populated areas Spaniards established large holdings on the public domain which were legalised by time. The decline of the Indian population in the late sixteenth century made the usurpation of Indian land more easy. *Encomiendas* were of little significance after 1600, but the introduction of *repartimiento,* a system of forced Indian labour with nominal wages, led to the rise of peonage, where Indians were tied to an estate. The precise nature of early Spanish land grants is extremely complex, but certainly in the eighteenth century the *hacienda,* the very large estate, operated by peons tied to the estate, predominated throughout Spanish America save where the plantation, based on slavery, was the rule.[115]

In Chile the establishment of *haciendas* dates from the seventeenth century,[116] and they were devoted largely to cattle; tallow and hides were exported to Lima, and later wool became an important product. In the eighteenth century however wheat began to be grown, initially for export to Peru but by the nineteenth century to other areas. The rise of inquilinage appears to date from this period of conversion to cultivation, rather than to the initial settlement.[117] In California the establishment of large estates took place at a much later date, and was preceded by the establishment of forts and missions. However in 1822, when Mexico became independent, the missions were secularised, and *ranchos* of at least one square mile were granted to Mexican citizens. Cattle were the major product of those holdings, which were found mainly in the Los Angeles basin and the coastal ranges, and not in the central valley. In 1845, three years before the United States' seizure of Mexican territories, the population of California was less than 5000, most of whom were Spanish. The gold rush and annexation altered this. By 1860 there were 379 994, mainly Anglo-Americans.[118] Some of the large estates were subdivided, but initially cattle ranching remained the major economic activity until the rise of wheat production. The cultivated area expanded rapidly, and by the 1880s there were 1 210 000 hectares under wheat in California, whilst the state had the largest sheep population in the Union.[119] Here then were the essential features of traditional Mediterranean agriculture. But wheat was not cultivated on small farms, rather on large ones with gang ploughs and horse-drawn combines; nor at first was wheat dry-farmed for the Anglo-American farmer lacked the Spaniard's experience of arid farming. Instead land was cropped continuously with a resultant loss of soil fertility and declining yields. Later fallowing was adopted for cereal production.[120]

Mediterranean agriculture

The 1880s saw a major turning-point in Californian farming. Declining wheat yields led to a reduction in the crop, and by 1904 feed barley was the leading grain. In 1913 the wheat area had fallen to only 120000 hectares. More significant was the growth of the irrigated area, too productive to devote to cereals, and the linking of California with the east coast by rail in 1869 and 1876.[121] The system was unlike that of the countries of the Mediterranean basin: olive-oil and wine played a small part in the intensification of agriculture, although both had been introduced in the eighteenth century. Instead it was citrus fruit and vegetables that took the lead. Most of the produce was exported to the east coast, where it had to compete with the market-gardening produce of the north east and the citrus fruits of Florida.

Although California was linked with the east coast by rail in the 1870s, other changes were necessary before produce could be transported economically to New York; at standard freight rates it would have been impossible to compete with Florida. However, the railway companies had the choice of freight at reduced rates, or no freight at all, and chose the former.[122] In 1887 refrigerated cars began to run, allowing the transportation of early vegetables, whilst the first shipment of refrigerated fruit was made in the following year.[123] Both fruits and vegetables from California had a seasonal advantage over areas nearer the markets of the north east which had cold winters. But Californian growers had to organise their production to ensure acceptance and overcome distance. This was done in a number of ways. First, the many small growers were organised into co-operative organisations which ensured a high standard of produce. Secondly, to reduce the weight transported, the processing of fruit was undertaken in California; two-thirds of Californian fruit is now processed.[124] Canning and the extraction of juices began in the 1880s. Thirdly, every effort has been made to reduce production costs by mechanising farm production. It is here that the major contrast with the Mediterranean basin occurs, for California has never had a dense agricultural population, and has been dependent in the past upon migrant Mexican workers for harvesting. Population densities are still very low in spite of the intensive production.[125] Fourthly, there has been a high degree of specialisation both by farm and by area. At no time has there existed in California the traditional Mediterranean farm which grew wheat and kept sheep and goats, and grew olives, grapes and figs for home consumption, if we except the early mission stations. Since the 1920s many farmers have concentrated upon one crop. The areas of crop specialisation are well-known. Fresno in the southern San Joaquin valley is an area of raisin production. Table grapes are produced around Sacramento, whilst viticulture is mainly confined to the coastal valleys near San Francisco. Citrus fruits were formerly grown predominantly in the Los Angeles basin, but are now being progressively relocated in the San Joaquin valley, pushed out by urban sprawl. Field crops such as cotton, sugar-beet and rice are grown by irrigation almost exclusively in the San Joaquin valley.[126]

Fifthly, between 1880 and 1930, when horticulture was growing in importance and extensive wheat production in decline, there was a reduction in the average size of farm. Since the 1930s this has been halted, and farms are becoming larger. Sixthly, farmers have obtained high yields by the prompt application of new methods, particularly the use of new crop varieties and the adoption of fertilisers and pesticides. Lastly, and most significant, the irrigated area has been greatly increased; in 1890 there were 400 000 hectares under irrigation in California, now there are 3 035 000.[127]

Thus since 1880 the agriculture of California has been profoundly changed. In the 1880s extensive wheat production and livestock rearing predominated. Since then, viticulture and more especially fruit and vegetables have superseded these extensive land uses. As in the Mediterranean basin, rice, sugar-beet and cotton have also become important since the 1920s; indeed cotton is now the most valuable single crop.[128]

Thus in historical perspective Californian agriculture is not so different from the countries around the Mediterranean Sea. The essential differences are in efficiency, and these in turn are linked to agricultural population density, the degree of industrialisation and thus the capacity of the market to absorb what were once luxury products.

In Chile, in sad contrast, there has been strikingly little change. Much of the central valley of Chile is irrigated, but it not used for intensive crops. (See above, p. 131.) Citrus fruits are of little importance and vegetable production is confined to the small *chacra* of the *inquilino* or to the immediate neighbourhood of the bigger cities. Nor can the unequal division of land be blamed for the backwardness of agriculture. Two factors appear important: first has been the absence of a wealthy internal urban market to stimulate the initial development of intensive farming, and second the distance of Chile from both the United States and European markets.

Summary

The development of Mediterranean agriculture is of particular interest. By classical times the eastern Mediterranean complex had spread throughout the basin. Farming methods were as good as anywhere in the world. By the sixteenth century most of the crops now grown were in cultivation. Thereafter the essential characteristic has been the shift to more intensive farming systems, carried farthest in California, but already well developed in the north-western Mediterranean. In many ways the key to the modern differentiation of the Mediterranean climatic areas is in terms of degree of industrialisation. Continued economic growth should lead to the further expansion of the irrigated intensive sectors, and the eventual absolute decline of cereal production. Here however it should be noted that California could specialise in fruits and vegetables because wheat could be produced as cheaply further east – and within the United States. It seems likely that national policies will maintain cereal production for much longer in Europe.

CHAPTER 9

MIXED FARMING IN WESTERN EUROPE AND NORTH AMERICA

Europe north of the Alps in Roman times was thinly populated, and, compared with the Mediterranean region, possessed of a backward agricultural technology. But, as has been seen in the preceding chapter, economic ascendancy had passed from south to north by the seventeenth century, not only in trade and industry but also in agriculture. Northern Europe is the home of two of the most productive of agricultural systems, mixed farming and dairying.

Mixed farming – or Commercial Crops and Livestock, as it was described by Whittlesey[1] – is found throughout Europe, from Ireland in the west through central Europe into Russia. It is also found in North America east of the ninety-eighth meridian, reaching its apogee in the Corn Belt: outliers are to be found in other areas of European settlement, in the Argentine pampas, South East Australia, South Africa and New Zealand (Fig. 1). The origins of mixed farming in Australia and Argentina are different from those in Europe, and are more conveniently dealt with in Chapter 12. In Europe Whittlesey made a threefold division; he assigned the British Isles (save the east), Scandinavia, and the coastal regions of France, Germany and the Low Countries to a dairying belt; western and central Europe he assigned to Commercial Crops and Livestock; and eastern Europe, the Balkans and European Russia north of the steppe to a subsistence sub-category of Crops and Livestock. But since the collectivisation of agriculture in Russia in the 1930s, and in eastern Europe since 1947, agriculture in these regions can hardly be regarded as subsistence, although there are still marked differences in productivity between east and west. This difference is of course not new; but its discussion would require more space than is here available. Hence this chapter describes the mixed farming of north-western Europe and eastern North America, whilst the following chapter deals with the emergence of dairying in these same two regions and also in Australia and New Zealand.

Many Europeans find it difficult to regard their farming systems as part of one major system; indeed European geographers have traditionally emphasised not only differences between countries, but between *pays* within one country. But on a world scale the farming of northern Europe has considerable homogeneity. It is perhaps salutary to recall the remarks of a visiting Chinese – perhaps apocryphal – on European diet, quoted by P. Lamartine Yates:[2]

Always the same food and how dreadfully monotonous; no variety, no contrasts. Seldom more than three dishes to a meal and frequently only two. First a plain vegetable soup. Second, a meat in slices accompanied by two vegetables, always one white and one green. Third, a dish of bread and cheese or fruit, or on better occasions, both. These Europeans have a singularly uniform approach to gastronomy.

The mixed farming of north-western Europe has many distinctive features. It is, first of all, highly commercialised. Although many writers have emphasised that the farming of the European peasantry is a way of life as much as a business, there are in fact few subsistence farms left; particularly since the Second World War farming has been dragged into the market place. Not only does the farmer raise crops and livestock primarily for sale, but he also purchases many of his inputs. The rapid increase of tractors and other forms of agricultural machinery has become a major production cost. Since the late nineteenth century artificial fertilisers have been purchased in large quantities, and again especially since 1950. The application of fertiliser per hectare of arable land is higher in north-western Europe than in any part of the world except Japan. Further, many farms – particularly in Britain and the Netherlands – purchase grains and concentrates to feed their livestock. Not only is the farmer thus involved with manufacturing industry in the purchase of inputs, but he sells his produce as raw material rather than as a finished product. Since the late nineteenth century processing industries have progressively taken over parts of the farm's activities, so that there is now little cheese or butter made on farms, sugar-beet is grown under contract to sugar refineries, potatoes are sold to distilleries and vegetables are grown under contract to freezing plants. Indeed mixed farming is essentially associated with densely populated, urbanised and industrialised societies, dependent upon high incomes for the sale of its products and upon manufacturing industry for the provision of its inputs.

This relationship accounts for a further distinctive feature of mixed farming systems. Although agricultural population densities are still high in many parts of north-western Europe – although not in the United States – the agricultural labour force is everywhere declining, as indeed is the rural population.[3] This is the result of the widening gap between farm and urban incomes, and the growth of industrial employment in the last hundred years. The decline of the agricultural labour force began first in Great Britain in 1851 but had spread to many parts of north-western Europe by the 1880s. Rural and agricultural populations partly stabilised in the 1920s and 1930s, when there was much industrial unemployment and many European countries protected their agriculture; but since 1950 there has been a further and sharper decline.

Nonetheless agricultural population densities are still high in western Europe, if not in North America. Indeed much of rural western Europe is overpopulated, not in the sense that the wet-rice areas of Asia are overpopulated, but that the rural economy is unable to provide a standard of living comparable with that in the towns. Table 27, in which agricultural population is related to arable land, overstates the density by excluding grassland, which is a major crop in many European countries. However it makes clear the differences in density between, on the one hand, the United States and Europe, and, on the other hand, within

Europe between Britain, Denmark and Sweden and the rest of north-western Europe. This reflects not only the history of industrialisation and the date of settlement, but also farm structure.

The typical farm in the mixed farming regions of north-western Europe and the eastern United States is the family farm, owned and operated by family labour. Hired farm labourers are uncommon in both continents; family workers provide 70–85 per cent of the labour force in western Europe.[4] Tenant farming is unusual; nor is tenancy associated with backward farming or oppressive landlords. On the contrary, some of the most efficient farming is found in areas with a high tenancy ratio, such as the Netherlands, Britain and the American Corn Belt, for where the tenant is protected by the law capital investment can be divided between occupier and landlord. Further, many farmers rent land in addition to owning it, to try to maximise the economies of scale gained in the use of machinery.

TABLE 27   *Agricultural population densities in Europe, 1965*
(agricultural population per km² of arable land)

Belgium	63	Sweden	31
Denmark	24	Switzerland	142
Finland	47	U.K.	27
France	40	U.S.A.	7
West Germany	54	Japan	411
Irish Republic	76	South Korea	674
Netherlands	111	Nigeria	211
Norway	76	Ghana	182

Source: F.A.O. *Production yearbook*, vol. 22, 1968

There is a difference in the average size of farm between the American Corn Belt and western Europe. The drawbacks of using the *average* size of farms are well known,[5] but the difference between the two continents is real. Family farms in the Corn Belt tend to be between 40 and 100 hectares.[6] In Europe farms are much smaller; there are a great many dwarf holdings, often worked part-time by men who have jobs in industry. But even the typical farm is small by American standards. Thus in West Germany two-thirds of the cultivated area is occupied by farms of between 10 and 50 hectares, in France about one-half.[7] The large farm is not of much importance except in eastern England and northern France. Thus most western European farms are too small to benefit fully from economies of scale, and many are too small to provide an acceptable standard of living. But fragmentation provides even more acute problems. In England, Denmark and Sweden most farms are consolidated units; elsewhere they typically consist of a number of dispersed and small plots, In spite of numerous efforts in this century and particularly since 1950, many of Europe's farms are in dire need of consolidation. This is a problem rarely met with in the more recently and more sparsely settled regions of North America.[8]

Mixed farming is carried on, then, under a variety of tenurial conditions: it is now time to turn to the more specifically agricultural characteristics of the system. The major feature of mixed farming is that farms produce both crops and livestock, and the two enterprises are integrated. This is most obvious in the land-use patterns. Few farms in western Europe or the eastern United States have *less* than a fifth of their cultivated area under grass. Some of this grass is permanent, some sown for two or three years only and then devoted to crops again. In the cooler, moister maritime regions grass occupies as much as three-quarters of the agricultural area.[9] In the better-farmed areas grass is treated with as much care as an arable crop. This alone distinguishes mixed farming from any other farming system. A variety of crops are grown. Cereals occupy much of the tilled land, the leading grain varying with climate and soil.[10] In the American Corn Belt maize is still the leading crop, although soy beans have had a startling increase in the last thirty years. But oats, winter wheat and barley are also grown.[11] In Europe wheat is the leading cereal in the drier regions and predominates on the *loess* soils. But further north on the poorer morainic soils of northern Germany, and in the shorter growing seasons of Scandinavia, it is replaced by rye or barley. Some wheat is sold for bread flour, and barley is used for malting; but in contrast to cereal growing in other farming systems, a large proportion is fed to animals on the farm, or sold to manufacturers of feeding stuffs. Maize in the Corn Belt is almost entirely fed to cattle and pigs on the farm, except for a few areas south west of Chicago.[12]

TABLE 28　*Farm structure and income in north-western Europe, 1960*

	% of farmland owner-occupied	Average size of farm (hectares)	% of total farm income from sale of livestock products
Belgium	32	8	66
Denmark	93	16	84
Finland	95	–	82
France	50	–	66
West Germany	85	12	78
Irish Republic	95	12	77
Netherlands	47.5	–	56
Norway	90	5	71
Sweden	60	13	–
Switzerland	75	–	*c.* 75
U.K.	55	27	70

Source: *World agricultural atlas*, vol. 1, 1969, 49, 50, 93, 98, 107, 136, 171–2, 186, 229, 232, 279, 297, 306, 400, 415, 416, 452, 470

In Europe a second major category of crops grown is roots. Turnips, mangolds and swedes, grown entirely as fodder, are less common than in the past, and the dominant roots are the potato and the sugar-beet. Potatoes are grown as vegetables, for feeding pigs and cattle, and in Germany for sale to dis-

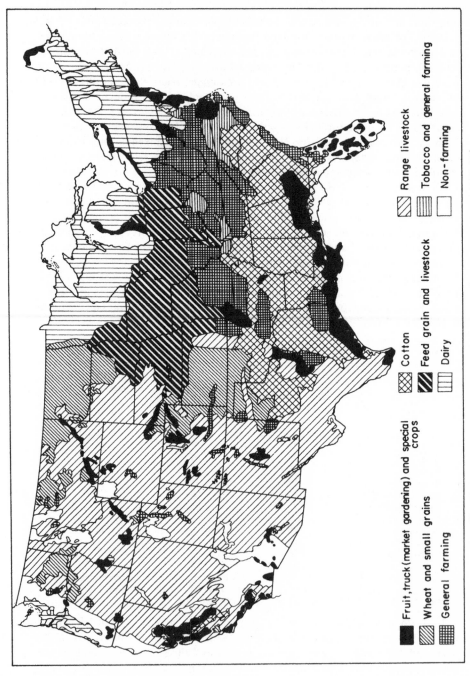

Fig. 19. Major types of farming in the United States. [Source: Marschner, 1959. 75]

Fruit, truck (market gardening) and special crops

Wheat and small grains

General farming

Cotton

Feed grain and livestock

Dairy

Range livestock

Tobacco and general farming

Non-farming

tilleries.[13] Sugar-beet, which provide a large proportion of Europe's sugar, are of course sold to sugar refineries, but the pulp is generally returned to the farm and used as cattle feed. Neither sugar-beet nor potatoes are of comparable significance in the mixed farming regions of the United States; most American sugar-beet is grown under irrigation in the arid West.

The advantages of growing a number of crops are threefold. In the first place it protects the farmer against the risk of poor prices and disease. In the second place it spreads labour requirements more evenly throughout the year, particularly where both autumn- and spring-sown crops can be grown, which is true of most of north-western Europe – in contrast to the Mediterranean areas. Third, and perhaps most important, it aids in the maintenance of soil fertility if crops are grown in rotations. Instead of growing the same crop continuously in the same field, a succession of different crops is grown. This reduces the risk of disease; further, if complementary crops are grown, different nutrients are removed from the soil. Traditionally European rotations have included roots, which not only give a rest from cereals, but allow row cultivation during the growing period as well as providing cattle feed; cereals, whose straw can be used for the preparation of farmyard manure; and temporary grasses, which not only provide grazing or hay, but also help to restore the nitrogen content of the soil.

But whilst crops are an important source of income for many farmers in the mixed farming regions, they are of little consequence compared with livestock products. Indeed much cropland is used to feed animals, as has already been noted. In western Europe only a quarter of the cropland is sown with crops intended for direct human consumption[14]. In Denmark, which will be touched upon in more detail in Chapter 10, nine-tenths of all grains are fed to livestock, and in Sweden three-quarters of all the crops are so consumed.[15] Not surprisingly a high proportion of farm income is derived from the sale of livestock products—milk, butter, cheese, beef, poultry, pigs and eggs. The relative importance of these items varies from country to country; thus in Germany pigs and milk are the main animal products, in Ireland cattle and milk, in Sweden milk and pigs, in the U.K. cattle and milk. Nowhere in western Europe are sheep any longer of much economic significance.

Livestock are fed in a variety of ways in mixed farming systems. As already noted, much of Denmark's crop output is fed to cattle and pigs; conversely in the Netherlands 67 per cent of all stock feed is obtained from grass, which in the cooler, moister parts of Europe is the cheapest feed available.[16] In the winter not only forage crops, but imported concentrates, are fed to livestock. Livestock production is clearly dependent upon the arable production of the farm and the two enterprises are interdependent. Livestock feed on crops grown on the farm, and graze the pastures. In return their manure helps to maintain soil fertility. The combination of crops and livestock further evens out labour demands during the year. Livestock require daily attention, and family labour is thus fully utilised. Livestock – particularly through milk and eggs – provide a regular weekly income, compared with the once-yearly payments of more specialised production.

Earlier the problems arising from the existence of small and fragmented farms were noted. However, whilst this helps to account for the differences in productivity between mixed farming in the United States and western Europe, the high productivity of European mixed farming when compared with other systems should not be overlooked. Agricultural productivity is difficult to define and even more difficult to calculate; and generally little can be done other than to compare physical measurements of input and output.[17] Thus in north-western Europe, crop yields are high. Wheat, which is grown in a variety of systems, is a reasonable index: it gives over 4000 kg per hectare in most of north-western Europe, but less than 2000 kg in most Mediterranean countries and in the extensive wheat-producing regions of North America, Argentina and Australia.[18] High crop yields reflect careful cultivation, the use of artificial fertilisers in large quantities, the application of organic manure, the pursuance of rotations, and the control of disease. High crop yields are matched by very high milking yields, a result of careful breeding and meticulous attention to the feeding and care of livestock. But in terms of output per man, west European farming does not compare favourably with mixed farming in the United States or with some other farming systems. Here again this reflects the persistence of small family farms and the continuing oversupply of labour, thus retarding the adoption of machinery, and indeed, other improved farming techniques. However this should not obscure the fact that there have been quite remarkable advances in west European agriculture since 1950, with not only an increase in the use of machinery, but also the widespread adoption of improved crop varieties and the greater use of fertilisers and pesticides.

In many parts of northern Europe since the Second World War traditional mixed farming, with its emphasis upon a diversity of products and the integration of crops and livestock, has been giving way to specialisation in one or two products. Thus in parts of eastern England farmers have replaced the traditional Norfolk four-course, of grains, roots and clover, combined with sheep, milk and beef, with continuous cropping of cereals. There is some logic in this. Guaranteed prices have removed the need for diversity of production, artificial fertilisers have diminished the need for livestock to provide manure, whilst steady increases in farm size have allowed the economic use of machinery.

Further, rising labour costs have made it increasingly difficult to keep a variety of livestock and grow a wide range of crops, particularly root crops. Under modern competitive conditions there is also a better return on managerial skills if specialisation rather than diversity is the key-note. However it should be noted that the adoption of continuous cereal cropping in parts of eastern England has led to a deterioration in soil structure, and there may yet be a return to the traditional combination of crops and livestock.[19]

The origins of mixed farming

As has been seen in Chapter 2, the domestication of plants and animals had spread into northern Europe at an early time. There is however, little reliable documentary evidence on farming until the ninth century A.D. The casual asides by Caesar and Tacitus on farming methods and institutions have caused more confusion than enlightenment.[20] Thus the agricultural historian is dependent upon the archaeologist for evidence of agricultural conditions until well into the Middle Ages.

The variety of crops grown in northern Europe in Roman times was much less than in the Mediterranean region. Oats, barley, wheat and rye were all grown, as was spelt, which remained a major crop until late in the Middle Ages.[21] There is evidence of peas, lentils and vetch being grown, but vegetables and fruits, so important in the Mediterranean region, were of little significance. Agricultural settlement was in villages or hamlets and farming was on an individual, not a collective, basis.[22] There was still much shifting agriculture, or at least long fallowing; where permanent settlement was found, fields were small and rectangular in shape, and a two-field system was often practised.[23] The implements were primitive. The plough, made of wood, was based upon the Mediterranean *ard* and had neither wheels, coulter nor mouldboard.[24]

Farmers thus had difficulty in cultivating the heavy, ill-drained soils which were more widespread in the north than in the Mediterranean region, but this did not confine them to the limestone uplands as was once argued, although the lighter soils were still probably the most densely populated.

Most farmers kept livestock as well as growing cereals; pigs probably provided most of the meat, for cattle were raised as draught animals rather than for beef.

Although there is some evidence of stall-feeding and the growth of forage crops,[25] livestock for the most part fended for themselves in the woods, marshes and heath which still made up much of the northern European landscape. Forest covered much the greater part of the continent, in contrast to the Mediterranean region where longer and denser settlement had already removed much of the original woodland and over-grazing by sheep and goats had prevented regeneration.[26]

In much of northern Europe – particularly in the cooler and moister north west – cropping was unimportant compared with pastoralism,[27] whilst in the east, Slav tribes still placed much reliance on hunting and collecting.[28]

The Roman impact upon this primitive world was limited. They introduced the two-handled scythe and possibly chickens.[29] In Britain and Gaul they established *villas*, large, well-equipped estates run by servile labour, producing not only for the owner but for a market; this was in sharp contrast to the small subsistence farms that predominated elsewhere in the north. On the frontier of the Empire, which ran through the Low Countries, the presence of large numbers of Roman troops may have encouraged commercial farming, and of course the establishment of towns elsewhere would have had a similar effect.[30] But Roman agricultural technology was based upon dry-farming, irrigation and crops such as figs, vines and olives, appropriate to the warm and semi-arid Mediterranean but not to cooler and moister conditions north of the Alps. Nor had the Romans experience of the spring-sown crops which could be grown in the north. Perhaps their most important introduction was the vine. New varieties were bred which could endure the shorter summers. By the third century A.D. viticulture had reached as far north as the Rhine, by the fourth century to the Moselle.[31]

Although farmers in the north grew cereals – and indeed little else – and kept livestock, their system was not one of mixed farming, for there was little integration save on some exceptionally well-farmed *villas*.

Northern Europe after the Fall of Rome

In the ninth and tenth centuries literary evidence on farming becomes more abundant, although it is admittedly mainly confined to descriptions of very large estates in northern France and the Low Countries. However the characteristic features of the medieval rural economy which emerge from these documents – the open fields, the two or three fields, the methods of ploughing, the manorial system – undoubtedly had their origins at an earlier date. The new economy and its institutions were once attributed to the migrations of Germanic-speaking peoples which took place after the fall of the Roman Empire. The Germanic peoples were first identified in about 600–700 B.C. in southern Scandinavia and Germany between the Rhine and the Oder, and subsequently spread south. By the fifth and sixth centuries A.D. they were found in the Low Countries and northern France, in England, in north west and south west Germany, as well as southern Scandinavia.[32] Few writers now accept the ethnic arguments put forward by Meitzen to account for the distribution of rural settlements and certain associated agricultural features. Nonetheless it is within this area during the Merovingian and Carolingian periods, that many of the distinctive features of northern Europe's medieval economy emerged.

The open fields and the manor

One of the distinctive features of the modern European landscape is the shape of the fields. North of the Loire, in the Low Countries and in West Germany, and formerly in England and southern Scandinavia, arable land is arranged around villages in long unfenced strips. In contrast, in southern France, western Britain, and northern Scandinavia the arable plots were squarer in shape and associated with hamlets. Around the arable strips were woodland and rough grazing which were held in common by the villagers. The origin of these differences is still obscure, although it is now commonly attributed to differences in the type of plough. Where the *ard* was used, the cross-ploughing characteristic of the Mediterranean regions was still practised; rectangular-shaped fields were thus most suitable. However when the wheeled plough, with coulter and mouldboard, was adopted, which was more difficult to pull than the *ard*, it was more convenient to plough a furlong and then turn the team.[33]

The date of the introduction of the heavy plough is still unknown; it seems to have spread slowly in western Europe after the sixth century A.D.[34] Later horses began to be used instead of oxen, after the invention of the fixed-head collar and metal shoes in the ninth and tenth centuries. But horses did not immediately replace oxen; they cost more to feed and could not be sold for meat. Their adoption was thus slow and geographically irregular; by the fifteenth century the horse had replaced the ox around Paris, but was still rare in Germany. By the end of the Middle Ages the ox still predominated in the extreme north of Europe and in the Mediterranean, but the horse predominated in the areas between, and also in most grazing areas.[35]

In the fifth and sixth centuries most arable land in northern Europe was farmed on the two-field system. The strips in one field were sown with winter or spring corn, and those in the other field were left fallow to rest the land and allow cultivation to get rid of weeds. Although the land surrounding the arable fields was held in common, there were few regulations governing the use of individual strips. The introduction of the three-field system was thus an important advance. The strips in one field were sown to winter corn, those in a second field to spring corn and the third field left fallow. Four harvests could thus be obtained from one field in six years, as against three in the two-field system. As population grew after A.D. 1000 and the expanding arable area reduced the amount of common grazing available, so more stringent regulations were imposed; the use of the common land was stinted, the stubble left open to grazing after the harvest and the farmers compelled to follow a common cropping system.[36]

The first references to the three-field system occur in the eighth century A.D. but it did not immediately replace the two-field system. Instead it spread slowly from north of the Loire into the Low Countries, Germany, Denmark and England. But in all these areas both temporary cropping and the two-field system survived until the end of the Middle Ages, especially on poorer soils and in the remoter areas. Nor does the three-field system seem to have penetrated western Britain, northern Scandinavia or southern France.[37]

There is little evidence during the Middle Ages on the comparative importance of the large estate and the small freehold farm; the accounts of tenurial conditions are coloured by the fact that the only surviving documents relate to large estates.[38] It seems likely however that during the Merovingian and Carolingian periods not only were many large estates newly created in recently colonised areas, but that many independent farmers gave up their rights to a powerful lord in return for protection in troubled times, particularly from the Vikings.[39] In return the lord of the manor, the *seigneur,* gave protection and dispensed justice.[40] The manor was thus more than a system of land tenure. Manors might consist of a whole village, several villages, the part of one village or parts of many villages.[41] The land was divided into two parts, the *desmesne,* worked directly by and for the lord; and *tenancies,* smallholdings worked by peasants. When documents on the manorial system, the *polyptyques* of the ninth and tenth centuries first become available, the *desmesne* was the greater part of the manor, worked directly by slaves or hired labourers.[42] But as the Middle Ages wore on and slavery declined, the *desmesne* was increasingly worked by villeins; they were allocated land for their family, and in return were obliged to work the *desmesne,* providing ploughs and oxen. There was thus no freehold or cash rent; the manor was a self-sufficient unit. The manorial system spread from the area around Paris north into England, Flanders, Brabant, Germany and Denmark, but not Sweden, Norway or Finland.[43]

In the eleventh century the manorial system began to change; the *desmesne* declined, and more and more of the manor was farmed by tenants, who were still obliged to cultivate the surviving *desmesne*. But after about 1200, with the growth of a monetary economy, lords began to demand cash rent rather than services from their tenants.[44]

In the early fourteenth century the medieval economy was in crisis; the decline in population after the Black Death and the consequent shortage of labour led to the further curtailment of the direct farming of the *desmesne*. By the fourteenth and fifteenth centuries the peasant holding was the dominant production unit in western Europe, with land held on lease but heritable. Further, by 1500 there was already a marked difference between peasants within a village community; a small class of rich peasants had emerged, whilst the rapid growth of population and the subsequent subdivision of farms had given rise to a class of landless labourers.[45]

The Economic Renaissance and the late Middle Ages

Direct exploitation of the land and the dominance of the *desmesne* was at its height in the ninth and tenth centuries, when farmers in the north were still predominantly cereal producers. Yields were low, the harvest rarely giving more than thrice the seed broadcast, for most of the manure was wasted on the common land. However between about 950 and 1300 there was a remarkable change in farming, prompted not only by an increase of population – which had declined in the second half of the first millennium – but also by the revival of urban life, the rise of industry, and the spread of a monetary economy.[46] The Dark Ages were past. Between the eleventh and the early fourteenth centuries the population of England doubled, as did that of the Moselle valley between 900 and 1200, whilst the population of the Rhineland increased twofold between 850 and 1150.[47] The response was both an expansion of the cultivated area and an intensification of methods.

This period was the great age of land clearance in Europe.[48] In 900 forest still dominated the landscape. In France colonisation was largely internal. Villages were widely spaced and farmers established 'assarts' and daughter villages. In the eleventh and twelfth centuries many of the isolated farms now found between the large nucleated villages came into being. Not only did villagers independently clear the woodland, but *seigneurs* organised colonisation, whilst monasteries, particularly those of the Cistercians, played an important role in land reclamation in isolated areas.[49] In the Netherlands the first dykes were constructed in the eleventh century. In England the major patterns of settlement were already established by the time of the Domesday Book, but onslaughts against heath, forest and moor continued in the following centuries. But it was German colonisation eastwards that was the most dramatic. Movements eastwards across the Elbe had begun in Charlemagne's time whilst, to the south east, Austria was settled between 800 and 1100. Vienna was founded in 1018.[50] Further north, Germans had settled in Mecklenburg and Brandenburg, and in the thirteenth century pushed into East Prussia, Moravia and Pomerania. Much of this settlement was organised by nobles who often employed *locators* to establish colonies. At first peasants were attracted to the new lands by liberal labour dues. Later however the full rigour of the manorial system was imposed, and it was in these eastern regions that it lasted longest in north-western Europe. Germans took across the Elbe the open fields, the heavy plough and the iron axe which accelerated the rate of forest clearance. By 1250 eastern Germany was exporting grain and wool to the west.[51]

During this period the major outlines of western European rural settlement were completed, save in Scandinavia. Indeed much of the land then settled, particularly in the mountain areas, was subsequently abandoned.[52] There were no major technological innovations in this period, and it is sometimes argued that crop yields did not increase.[53] But more recent evidence suggests that by the end of the Middle Ages crop yields, although well below those of modern times, were perhaps twice those of the Carolingian period, whilst the spread of the three-field system gave more harvests. The harrow came into general use, whilst the adoption of the horse and the use of larger teams for ploughing made more cultivations of the seed bed and the fallow possible; thus farming became more labour-intensive, particularly after 1250 when the supply of new land had largely run out.[54]

Thus by 1300 northern European farming had taken on many of the features it was to retain until well into the nineteenth century. The main aim of the farmer was to raise cereals; the winter-sown crops, wheat and rye provided flour; the spring-sown, oats and barley, fodder for horses, grain and malt for ale. Other crops were rare, although some pulses were grown.[55] Few fodder crops were grown, and livestock depended upon rough grazing. Stockbreeding for beef, milk or butter was thus subsidiary to the maintenance of draught animals.[56] But as population grew between 1000 and 1300, so grazing land was diminished; this reduced the number of oxen that could be kept, and so reduced the supply of manure, which in turn affected crop yields, which may have declined in the thirteenth century. By the end of the thirteenth century there were signs of overpopulation in north-western Europe, reflected in an increase in the number of famines in the early fourteenth century, and stagnation in agriculture. The key to many of the problems was the fallow. If output was to be increased the fallow had to be used.[57]

The fourteenth and fifteenth centuries were a period of agricultural depression. Prices for cereals fell and land was abandoned in many parts of western Europe, particularly in upland regions; but in some cereal-growing areas, notably eastern England and Germany, sheep raising expanded at the expense of crops and enclosure led to depopulation. The catastrophic mortality of the Black Death led however to an acute shortage of labour; thus the direct exploitation of the *demesne* diminished even further, a process which continued into the sixteenth century.[58] By 1600 compulsory labour on *desmesnes* in France and Germany had largely disappeared, and leaseholders had virtually free use of their land. Although large estates were built up again after the mid-seventeenth century, the predominance of the small and medium-sized peasant farm was not altered. In England however, although the expropriation of the small landowner may have been exaggerated by some writers, it is true that rather larger units of ownership and production were already emerging in the sixteenth century.[59]

The beginnings of modern agriculture in northern Europe

Economic historians have paid comparatively little attention to the agricultural history of the sixteenth and seventeenth centuries; but it seems true that there was little radical change in agricultural methods or institutions. However the beginnings of modern agriculture can be traced back to this period, and indeed to even earlier.

In the first place the subsistence economy of the Carolingian period began to break down. This was prompted by the growth of small market towns in the eleventh and twelfth centuries, and the rise of specialist trades such as that of the blacksmith.[60] It was even more marked in those areas where industries, and particularly the textile industries, developed. By the thirteenth century the Low Countries and northern Italy had considerable towns and industries, and an active trade, and this had important repercussions on local agriculture. By the end of the fifteenth century the Low Countries, and in particular Artois, Flanders and Brabant, were the most densely populated parts of western Europe, with a rural density of 100 to 125 per km^2.[61] The considerable urban population encouraged the production of crops for sale as well as some local specialisation. Nonetheless commercialisation was hampered by the high cost of transporting agricultural products, except in the areas immediately near to towns, or those with easy access to waterways. Before the eighteenth century no more than 1 per cent of Europe's cereal production entered international trade.[62]

Thus only products with a very high value per unit weight could withstand the cost of transport, and wine and wool were two of the few goods which did move any distance. Viticulture had spread north in the later Dark Ages, for wine was used everywhere in the Sacrament, whilst the better-off drank it instead of ale. Thus in the eleventh and twelfth centuries there were vineyards in regions well north of its present limits, in England, Flanders and Germany east of the Elbe.[63] However by the twelfth century wine-producing areas near waterways, such as the Bordeaux region and the Moselle valley, were beginning to specialise in better-quality wine for export, and as they emerged so the more northerly wine-producing regions contracted.[64]

But for the most part late medieval agriculture was still largely subsistence-orientated and dominated by the production of cereals. Between 1300 and 1800 there were three major trends which gave rise to modern mixed farming.

First was the reduction of the fallow. The year under fallow was essential, not only to rest the soil from continuous cereal cropping, but to reduce weeds by cultivation. But this was an obvious waste of arable land. A number of solutions were devised, all first practised in the Low Countries, Flanders and Brabant, and later in Zeeland and Friesland. First was the growth of turnips upon the fallow, in the fourteenth century. The turnip provided winter feed for cattle, and so increased the density of stocking, and in turn the supply of manure. Furthermore as it was a row crop, the land could be cultivated easily during growth. Second were the beginnings of convertible husbandry: two years under cereals, one year fallow, followed by three to six years under grass. When leguminous clover was sown for the long ley, not only was the soil rested from cereals, and grazing for livestock provided, but soil nitrogen was restored. Third was the growth of industrial crops, particularly hemp, woad, flax, cole seed to give oil, and, in the fourteenth century, hops for brewing. This took place near the towns in Flanders, and the reduction of fallow was matched by the purchase of night-soil, and other organic matter for use as fertiliser; in addition the growth of turnips and clover provided more fodder and thus more manure.[65]

The new methods were found on small farms, and particularly those of occupier-owners, for many farmers in the Low Countries became full owners of their land before those of much of the rest of Europe; although horses replaced oxen and the improved Brabant plough was adopted, farming was labour-intensive and the spade was much in use. By the sixteenth century farming was dominated by the production of cash crops and livestock products, and grain – 14 per cent of requirements – was imported from the Baltic. In the sixteenth and seventeenth centuries Dutch farming was the Mecca for agriculturalists from all over Europe. It was however in England that the new methods were most rapidly adopted, and indeed improved upon.[66] By the late seventeenth century turnips and clover were grown in parts of south east England, and in the early eighteenth century the classic four-course rotation emerged.[67] Turnips were grown in the first year, providing fodder for cattle in the stalls in winter. Sometimes they were eaten off by sheep 'folded' with hurdles. The land could be cultivated whilst the turnip was growing. The root crop was followed by barley or wheat, which was sold off the farm, but the straw was retained to help make farmyard manure. The cereal crop was followed by a year under clover, providing grazing and also restoring soil nitrogen, and in the fourth year barley or wheat was grown. Cattle were stall-fed for part of the year on turnips and later, in the eighteenth century, upon oil-cake, and sheep were also kept. Thus by the late eighteenth century the more advanced farmers in eastern England had integrated livestock production and crop production. A range of products could be sold off the farm – beef, wool, milk, wheat for flour and barley for malting. Furthermore the combination of crop and livestock production evened out seasonal labour demands. Thus although essential features of mixed farming appeared first in late medieval Flanders, the system matured in eighteenth-century England and thereafter became the model for the rest of western Europe.[68]

The advances which began in Flanders and flowered in England did not spread at once to the whole of Europe; indeed even as late as 1750 much of English farming still followed essentially medieval practices. In 1750 the open fields stretched from north-eastern France to the Urals; only in the better-farmed areas – generally the more densely populated – such as the Low Countries, the Rhineland and parts of the Paris basin, had the fallow been reduced or the collectivism of the medieval economy replaced by individualistic farming.

In the later Middle Ages population pressure had compelled the village community to enforce collective cropping and the stinting of commons. But this increasingly became an obstacle to the adoption of new crops and new methods, for the improving farmer was unable to free himself from the regulations governing crop selection. Further, as long as the grazing land around the arable fields was held in common there was little possibility of improving cattle or sheep breeds.

The second major trend was the extinction of common rights and the consolidation of the dispersed strips; this proceeded most rapidly in England, and later in Denmark and Sweden. Enclosure began in England at least as early as the thirteenth century, and proceeded slowly in the next four centuries. As late as 1700 half of the country's arable land was still in open field, but in the late eighteenth century Parliamentary enclosure proceeded rapidly and by 1820 it was virtually complete.[69] Enclosure of the open fields led to the consolidation of the dispersed strips into one block of land, and the end of collective rights of grazing on the stubble. The common lands used for grazing were also enclosed and the land divided up amongst the landowners in the village. In Denmark, Finland and Sweden very similar enclosures took place in the late eighteenth century, and the individual strips of a farmer were consolidated; in Denmark there was even legislation, in 1819, to prevent subdivision.[70] But in the rest of Europe, although the right to graze arable stubbles slowly disappeared, and much of the common grazing rights were extinguished, there was very little consolidation. Thus in Normandy most of the collective rights over the use of arable land had disappeared by 1750; but at no time was the consolidation of the strips considered. Indeed even the collective regulation of cropping survived well into the nineteenth century in parts of Europe, as did the periodic redistribution of strips.[71]

It is perhaps appropriate to comment here upon the problem of fragmentation in European agriculture. Although the differences between Britain and Scandinavia and the rest of Europe can be related to the specific measures for consolidation which were included in the enclosure acts of these countries, fragmentation is not simply a result of the survival of medieval land-holding. Equally important has been the rate of population increase: thus new communities established on virgin land in eastern Europe had acute fragmentation and subdivision within a few generations. Where rapid growth has been combined with partible inheritance – which was extended under the Napoleonic Code – the problem has been compounded. Most western European countries introduced legislation to consolidate at the end of the nineteenth century, but little progress was made until after 1950.[72]

As has been noted earlier, the small peasant farm had become the norm in much of north-western Europe as early as the fifteenth century. The manorial system survived in the sense that many farmers were leaseholders, although the leases were hereditable; there also survived in France, Germany and Denmark, although not in the Low Countries, many of the petty dues and obligations owed to the lord of the manor. These were largely extinguished in the period of the French Revolution, both in France and in those areas occupied by Napoleon, although the Revolution did not greatly increase peasant proprietorship in France or the adjacent territories such as the Rhineland. In eastern Germany the manorial system survived in a more rigorous form well into the nineteenth century, indeed the edicts of emancipation made in 1807–8, although freeing the peasant, compelled him to cede one-third or one-half of the land to the lord of the manor. Hence in the nineteenth century the large estates directly worked by the Junkers with landless labourers were enlarged rather than destroyed.[73]

The third major trend to be discerned after the end of the Middle Ages was a slow increase in the importance of livestock. By the fifteenth century western European agriculture was sufficiently commercialised to respond to long-term changes in prices, and a distinctive feature was the secular rise and fall in cereal prices. However, when cereal prices fell, livestock prices either stagnated or fell less. Thus in a number of periods of apparent agricultural depression there was a movement towards either the growth of industrial crops or the raising of livestock. Thus in the fourteenth century sheep rearing spread in England and Germany, and in Norway cereal production was abandoned for dairying, whilst in the mild depression between 1650 and 1750 there was some conversion of corn to grass. Viticulture also spread at this time. But it was only in the eighteenth century that specialised production of livestock became established – cattle began to be bred for meat or milk, and sheep for wool or mutton, rather than as general-purpose animals.[74]

So far the advances made in the dismantling of the medieval structure of European agriculture have been emphasised. But even by the early nineteenth century farming outside the more densely populated areas was still remarkably backward. The open fields had gone from most of England and Scandinavia, but from the Loire they stretched north to the Elbe and indeed further. Oxen still pulled a plough which had been little improved since medieval times: it was not until the iron Rotherham plough was designed in the late eighteenth century that the medieval plough began to be replaced. At the beginning of the nineteenth century the sickle was still used for harvesting, the scythe only in more advanced regions. The first seed drill was designed in Italy in 1602, and Jethro Tull published his book in 1731; but as late as 1800 Norfolk, one of the most advanced counties in England, had more land sown broadcast than with the drill, and in the rest of Europe the drill was a rarity.[75]

Not that there had been no increase in output or indeed productivity. Crop yields rose slowly, and in England may have doubled between 1750 and 1850. Even in France, where farming was slow to respond to the new changes, output of farm produce rose 60 per cent between 1700 and 1770. However it seems reasonable to argue that until the 1840s the changes which took place in European agriculture were slow. The medieval economy was slowly eroded; agricultural change was a matter of evolution not revolution. The great break came in the mid-nineteenth century and was a function of industrialisation, the challenge of the New World, and the adoption of quite new farming methods based on the application of scientific method.[76]

The Great Transformation

In the 1850s industrialisation began to gather pace in north-western Europe. At the same time the frontier in North America reached into the prairies. These two changes transformed northern European agriculture. But there had already been the precursors of change in the late eighteenth century, when throughout western Europe populations began to grow at an unprecedented rate. The causes of this upsurge are still not clearly understood, but it seems to have been due to a decline in mortality as epidemics and famines became fewer, perhaps coupled with earlier marriage.[77] At the beginning of the nineteenth century Europe was still overwhelmingly rural, and the bulk of the population was employed in agriculture. Only in England had inventions in the textile industry, the use of steam power and the introduction of the factory system led to urbanisation. The new towns grew mainly by migration from the country. But migration was still less than the rate of natural increase, so that rural populations in England rose steadily, as they did in the rest of Europe. By the 1830s there was considerable underemployment and unemployment in the English countryside except at harvest time. The mixed farming system thus matured at a time of cheap labour, and it was essentially labour-intensive. As late as the 1860s farmers could afford to employ gangs of women and children to pick stones from the fields of Lincolnshire. The new crops, particularly the turnip, required much cultivation. Few labour-saving devices were employed except the threshing machine, which was used by some farmers in the 1820s. However by the 1840s migration to the growing cities had begun to exceed the rate of natural increase in some rural areas. The labour force in English agriculture reached its peak in the 1850s and has steadily declined since. It was only then that there was the incentive for farmers to employ labour-saving machinery.[78]

A similar sequence of events occurred in the rest of north-western Europe, but with a delay, for on the continent industrialisation and the rural exodus began at later dates. Nowhere else in Europe has the agricultural labour force fallen to such a low proportion of the total work force or are there so few workers per hectare of agricultural land as in Britain (Table 29).

The lack of comparable data on the agricultural labour force in the nineteenth century, and the methodological problems of allowing for seasonal and family labour, make the precise dating of the decline difficult to calculate. But in Belgium the *active* agricultural population was just over a million in 1856, 800000 in 1880, 630000 in 1930 and just over 200000 in the 1960s. In France the *male* agricultural labour force declined after 1876, in Germany it began to decline in the 1890s, and in Switzerland and Austria slightly earlier. In Scandinavia however the increase of the agricultural population continued until the 1920s, whilst, quite exceptionally, in the Netherlands it continued to increase until the 1950s.[79]

The rate at which the labour force has declined has been essentially a function of the rate of industrial growth, and the gap between rural and urban incomes. The agricultural population has become in effect a residual. However other factors have been influential. In England in the mid-nineteenth century a substantial proportion of the labour force consisted of farm labourers, who had little incentive to stay; in contrast, in Europe, where the family farm predominated, there was more reason to remain in the family home, and the rate of the rural exodus has been much slower, and indeed has only become rapid since 1950. In Germany, for example, the agricultural labour force was halved between 1950 and 1965.[80] Further, it has been young people who have left the land; the labour force has become progressively older, and an increasing proportion of the work on the smaller farms has been done by women whilst the men have taken jobs in nearby towns. But even after a century of decline, the European agricultural labourforce remains too large; continental Europe's farmlands are, by the standards of advanced countries, 'grossly overpopulated'.[81]

The expansion of the cultivated area

The first response of farmers to a rise in population was to increase the cultivated area. After 1750 cereal prices rose steadily, reaching a peak in the Napoleonic Wars; even during the recession of the 1820s and 1830s they were well above those of the early eighteenth century. Thus the cultivated area increased substantially, probably for the first time since the thirteenth century. Upland areas were brought into cultivation in the Massif Central, for example, and in the moorlands of northern England. The reclamation of fenland in England and of polders in Holland was revived and was greatly assisted by the introduction of steam pumps. Poorer, highly podzolised soils were broken up for the first time, as in, for example, the Belgian Kempenland and the Sologne south of Paris. Later in the nineteenth century the combination of iron ploughs and pipe drainage made the cultivation of heavy clay soils a practicable proposition. In Scandinavia the

TABLE 29 Agricultural land and population in western Europe, 1900–65

Country	Active agric. pop. as a % total pop. 1965	Agricultural land^a (million hectares)			Active males in agriculture (million)				Hectares of agricultural land per man		
		1900	1950	1965	1900	1930	1950	1965	1900	1950	1965
U.K.	4	20.0	19.4	19.3	1.5	1.3	1.25	0.83	13.3	15.5	23.25
Norway	18	1.1	1.0	0.9	0.29	0.37	0.32	0.14	3.8	3.2	6.4
Finland	32	2.6	2.9	2.8	0.42	0.57	0.54	–	6.2	5.4	–
Sweden	12	4.9	4.4	3.4	0.72	0.79	0.58	0.25	6.9	7.6	13.6
Denmark	15	3.1	3.1	3.0	0.35	0.43	0.37	0.28	8.9	8.4	10.7
Netherlands	9	2.1	2.4	2.2	0.51	0.54	0.6	0.38	4.1	4.0	5.7
Belgium	6	1.9	1.7	1.6	0.57	0.49	0.36	0.189	3.3	5.0	8.4
Switzerland	10	2.1	2.1	2.1	0.57	0.36	0.32	0.25	5.7	6.7	8.4
France	18	35.5	33.5	33.6	5.8	4.5	4.0	–	6.1	8.3	–
West Germany	11	13.6	13.7	13.8	2.7	2.3	2.3	1.43	5.0	5.9	9.6
East Germany	19	6.8	6.3	6.4	0.86	0.82	0.88	–	8.0	7.2	–

Sources: Dovring, 1960, 66–67 for all except 1965 columns: F.A.O. Production yearbook, vol. 23, 1969
^a Includes rough grazing

nineteenth century saw a major expansion of settlement into quite new land: here was Europe's frontier. In Finland the cultivated area tripled between 1800 and 1900 and in Scandinavia as a whole it doubled between 1800 and 1950.[82]

But the incentives to continue expansion declined towards the end of the century. First, the rate of population increase slowed down as the birth rate began to fall; second, industrialisation and the growth of urban employment was beginning to relieve some of the population pressure on the land; third, emigration to the Americas helped further to reduce population problems in the countryside; and fourth, the import of American grains after 1880 led to two decades of depression in much of rural Europe.[83] By the end of the century the maximum cultivated area had been reached in most of north-western Europe (Table 29) and there have been few major changes since. However the ratio between grass, crops and rough grazings has changed significantly, mainly in response to price changes. Thus, for example, although the total cultivated area of Britain has not greatly changed since 1880, the area under crops declined in the last two decades of the nineteenth century and in the period between the two World Wars, and expanded in 1914–18 and since 1940, when prices have been rising or stable.[84]

The cultivated area did however continue to increase in Scandinavia and, perhaps most dramatically, in the Netherlands, where very high population densities combined with, until recently, a dependence upon agriculture, have led to extraordinary efforts to increase the land under crops. Parts of the Zuider Zee were reclaimed in the 1930s and recently the reclamation of part of the Delta region has begun. But for the most part marginal land in Europe has been abandoned in this century and capital concentrated on the better land.[85]

Industrialisation and agricultural change

The consequences of industrialisation were outlined in Chapter 4 and their significance for the mixed farming of the nineteenth century will be only briefly restated here.

First, real incomes began to rise in the later nineteenth century, and there was an increase in demand for livestock products and vegetables. It is this continuing trend which has shifted the emphasis in mixed farming in north-western Europe from cereals to vegetables and livestock products. Thus in the 1860s crops still accounted for 45 per cent of the value of British agricultural output, in 1908 31 per cent and by 1960 only 18 per cent, a trend followed throughout western Europe.[86]

Second, agriculture became increasingly dependent upon manufacturing industry for its inputs. Until the early nineteenth century farmers bought farm implements from local craftsmen and they were made mainly from wood; but in the 1770s the first all-iron plough and in 1800 the first all-iron harrow were made in Britain. By the 1840s a considerable agricultural implements industry was established, dependent of course upon a supply of cheap iron and, later, steel. Similarly such fertilisers as had been used were derived primarily from farm

171

animals, or from other natural sources such as peat, marl or night-soil. In 1839 guano – another organic fertiliser – began to be imported into Britain, but after 1880 the by-products of industry – sulphate of ammonia from gas plants and basic slag from steel-making – were in use. The subsequent rise of compound fertiliser production was clearly only possible in countries with a well-developed heavy chemical industry.[87]

Third was the slow change in the sources of power. Until the nineteenth century human and animal muscle provided all the power on farms, although water-mills had been used to grind corn since the high Middle Ages and wind-mills rather later. In the industrial revolution steam power replaced water power, but in agriculture it was less easily applied. It was used to pump dry Dutch polders and English fens at the end of the eighteenth century, and used in larger farms to work threshing-machinery in the 1820s: some ploughing with steam was done in mid-century. But the major change in the nineteenth century was the replacement of the ox by the horse, a process complete by the end of the century in much of northern but not in eastern or southern Europe. The tractor, although invented before the First World War, made little ground in Europe until the 1920s; at the same time electricity first became available on farms.

Fourth was the application of scientific knowledge to agriculture. The use of fertilisers was closely associated with advances in agricultural chemistry and plant and animal breeding with discoveries in genetics. There had been, of course, advances in breeding before; indeed the major European cattle breeds had emerged by the mid-nineteenth century: subsequent improvements however have greatly increased milk yields and beef output.[88]

Fifth was the improvement in transport. By 1850 Britain had a well-developed railway network, as had France and Germany by the 1880s. This reduced the cost of moving not only farm products, but farm inputs. Cattle no longer lost weight and value on long drives to market, and early vegetables could be sent to distant cities. The expansion of fluid milk production away from the environs of towns was of course completely dependent on the spread of the railways.

The Adoption of New Techniques

It must not be thought that the new implements and methods which became available to farmers in the mid-nineteenth century were widely adopted at first. In Chapter 4 the slowness with which the reaper was adopted has been noted. The reasons for this inertia are manifold, but the following points may be made. First was the slow decline of the rural population. As long as labour was cheap there was little incentive to adopt labour-saving methods; thus in Europe it was Britain where most progress was made because it was there that the agricultural labour force declined most rapidly. Second was the size of farms; on most of the farms of western Europe there was little point in employing tractors or reapers, let alone combine harvesters, and this of course remains a problem to the present day. Again it is significant that most progress in mechanisation has been made in those countries where farms were of moderate size and already consolidated in the early nineteenth century: Britain, Scandinavia and East Germany. Third, it should be noted that after 1880 there was little prosperity in European agriculture, for not only were prices depressed by competition from abroad, but as real income rose in the cities proportionally less and less was spent on food.[89] Thus, with few sources of capital other than their own savings, few farmers could afford the new inputs. Fourth, it should be recalled that in France and Germany high tariffs protected the farmer from competition, and may have compounded the inertia of the peasant. In 1880 one-third of French peasants were illiterate.[90] It is significant that the greatest increases in farming productivity came in the late nineteenth century in those countries where most attention was paid to rural education, the Netherlands and Denmark; in Denmark elementary education was introduced as early as 1814.[91]

It would be absurd to argue that there was no increase in farming productivity after 1850 – far from it. In Germany wheat yields doubled between 1800 and 1883 and again by 1913,[92] and comparable if less dramatic advances were made in other parts of Europe, especially in the Netherlands and Denmark. Even in France, where least progress was made, wheat yields rose by 50 per cent between 1850 and 1880, although on the eve of the First World War French crop yields were the lowest in north-western Europe.[93] But such gains in productivity were largely a result of greater inputs of labour and fertiliser per acre; there was little investment in labour-saving machinery. It is worth emphasising how dramatic the changes in productivity since the 1930s have been. Thus from 1800 onwards labour productivity rose in Europe at about 1 per cent each year, but since 1950 the figure has reached 5 per cent in parts of Europe; in the United Kingdom in 1962 the marginal value of agricultural production per worker exceeded that of the per capita product of industry.[94] This of course is partly a comment on the inefficiency of modern British industry, but nonetheless demonstrates how remarkable the advances in western European agriculture have been. Much of this has been in a period when agriculture has been protected from overseas competition, for by the 1930s even Britain and Denmark had adopted various measures of protection.

Thus western European agriculture since 1850 has become progressively more intensive, not only by shifting production to higher-value products, but by increasing inputs of fertiliser, using better seed, and cultivating the land more efficiently with improved implements. Investment in machinery, except in Britain, has been much more recent, and is still impeded by an excessive labour force and the predominance of small and fragmented farms. Nonetheless the increase since the 1930s is impressive. In 1940 there were 5 700 tractors on Dutch farms, by 1958, 66 000 and by 1967, 134 000, whilst between 1950 and 1968, the number of tractors in use in West Germany had increased seven times, and in France eight times. The combine-harvester was virtually unknown before 1940; thus for example there were none at all in Denmark in 1944, in 1960, 11 570, and 40 000 in 1968.[95]

Agricultural policies and livestock production[96]

There is little doubt that the main cause of the increasing importance of livestock production in western Europe has been the increase in real incomes; nonetheless in the 1880s the fall in cereal prices caused by growing imports of American grain depressed cereal cultivation and led to a swing to livestock farming.

Until the 1860s western Europe, in spite of the population increases of the preceding hundred years, still produced most of its own food. Even Britain was 95 per cent self-sufficient in the 1830s.[97] However grain imports increased substantially throughout the 1870s and the poor seasons at the end of the decade increased them even further. The combination of cheap land and mechanisation in the United States, and the fall in both land and oceanic freight rates, allowed the American farmer to market grain well below the price of the European product. Later, after the introduction of refrigeration on ships, livestock products could be sold in Europe; but the price of meat and dairy products did not fall as much as that of grain.

The fall in prices brought varied reactions from European governments. Although most European countries had long had some forms of control on grain imports, by the 1860s most had adopted a large measure of free trade. After 1880 Britain and Denmark held to free trade, as did for the most part the Netherlands and Switzerland; but Germany and France established tariffs on grain and livestock products.[98] Farmers in the free trade nations responded in different ways. In Britain the cereal producers of eastern England underwent a period of profound depression; land was abandoned and wheat declined. But, in contrast, livestock producers and market gardeners prospered. In Denmark and the Netherlands farmers accepted the challenge. Denmark had been a grain exporter in the 1860s, but between 1880 and 1910 completed her transformation to a livestock goods exporter. The Netherlands already had much of its agricultural land under grass, and was a major exporter of butter and cheese. Livestock production was intensified, and horticultural output increased. In both countries co-operatives were established, herd books begun and rural education promoted. The challenge of falling prices was met.[99]

In France and Germany tariffs allowed the maintenance of wheat production. In France industrialisation had made comparatively little progress, and the preservation of the peasantry was an aim of politicians of most persuasions. In Germany however the protection of grains was largely a result of the political influence of the Junker landlords of the east, and was to the detriment of both the peasantry of the west and the growing urban proletariat.[100] Protection retarded both technological advance and the shift towards livestock production in both France and Germany. In the 1930s the apparatus of protection was revived after a brief period of relatively free trade in the 1920s. But in the 1930s even Britain and Denmark introduced a measure of protection. In Britain it affected wheat and sugar-beet. Since the end of the Second World War nearly all farmers in western Europe have been sheltered from overseas competition, either by subsidies, tariffs, import quotas or guaranteed prices. It is in this period of protection that such rapid progress has been made by farmers who, sure in the knowledge of high and stable prices, have invested in machinery, fertilisers, new crop varieties and buildings. But protection has preserved many inefficient farmers, caused high food prices and led to overproduction.

Changes in Crops and Livestock

The intensification of European agriculture since 1850 by the increase in inputs such as fertilisers has been matched by intensification in land use. First has been the final elimination of fallow, although it survives on some heavier clay soils. The first crop to utilise the fallow was the turnip, but other fodder roots were subsequently bred, including the swede and the mangel-wurzel. The adoption of fodder roots, although well under way in Britain and the Low Countries by the eighteenth century, was delayed elsewhere; in France, for example, they only became of major significance in the middle of the nineteenth century and in Denmark only after the shift towards livestock production.[101]

But of most significance was the adoption of the sugar-beet, first bred in the eighteenth century. The first sugar-beet factory was established in Silesia in 1801, and the crop spread rapidly throughout Europe. The British blockade of the continent cut off supplies from the West Indies, and in 1806 Napoleon encouraged beet by granting a bounty. Later there was a boom in sugar-beet growing in Germany in the 1830s, and by the mid-century it was a major crop throughout the continent, particularly on the lighter soils of northern France, Saxony and Silesia. The very high labour costs – then about ten times those for wheat – meant it could only be grown in densely populated areas; further, the cost of moving it to the factories gave farms near waterways an advantage. The crop fitted well into a rotation with cereals, potatoes and temporary grasses, and was particularly important on the larger farms of northern France and eastern Germany. In England there was no protection for beet-sugar as there was on the continent, and it was not until the 1920s that a subsidy was granted. It rapidly replaced the turnip in the Norfolk four-course in eastern England and soon became a major source of income.[102]

The other major introduction was that of the potato, which had begun to be grown in many parts of western Europe in the mid-eighteenth century, but did not become of major significance until the nineteenth century. Like the turnip, it was grown in rows and was thus a cleaning crop, suitable for inclusion in a rotation. Not only was it grown for direct human consumption, but in Germany and the Netherlands industrial alcohol was extracted from it, whilst in Germany it was a major feed crop, particularly for pigs.[103] The potato reached its peak at the end of the nineteenth century and has subsequently declined; thus for example the area under potatoes in France in 1950 was only two-thirds that of 1900. The consumption of potatoes has declined as living standards have risen, whilst increases in labour costs have made it costly to grow, for the potato, like the fodder roots, requires a great deal of labour.[104]

Mixed farming in Western Europe and North America

The third major crop introduction, already discussed in Chapter 3, was that of the temporary grasses. The growth of such grasses dated back to the fifteenth century, but the widespread use of improved grasses and the establishment of ley farming did not get under way until the end of the nineteenth century. Even now it is only in the Netherlands and a few other smaller areas that grass is given the care it merits, and in few parts of Europe does the crop receive the attention it does in New Zealand.[105]

Cereal crops declined in importance in the later nineteenth century compared with industrial and forage crops. The reduction of cereal prices led to a further decline, except in France and Germany where tariffs kept the price of wheat up. But in most parts of Europe an increasing proportion of the grain was fed to cattle. The inferior grains gave way to wheat as incomes rose. Rye thus declined, except in areas of poor soil such as eastern Germany, and buckwheat and spelt largely disappeared. Oats held its own as a fodder crop for horses until the middle of the twentieth century, but as the tractor has replaced the horse, so the oats area has fallen. In 1950 there were 8 000 000 horses on north-west European farms, in 1968 only 2 500 000, and over the same period the oats acreage was halved.[106]

Changes in livestock numbers also demonstrate the increasing intensification of land use in western Europe. In the Middle Ages – and indeed until the eighteenth century – sheep had been of great importance as they provided the raw materials for the leading industry as well as giving meat, and in southern Europe, milk. In the early nineteenth century Britain, Germany and Spain were the leading wool producers. However the number of cattle and pigs was already beginning to increase faster than the number of sheep. Then after 1870 there was a quite dramatic decline. In Germany in 1873 there were 25 000 000 sheep but this fell to 5 800 000 in 1912 and in 1968 there were only 2 600 000 in East and West Germany combined. This decline occurred everywhere in western Europe except in Britain. There appear to be two reasons for it. First, sheep in Europe were kept upon common land and rough grazings. As these were enclosed and reclaimed the supply of feed diminished. Nowhere in Europe were sheep integrated into an arable system as they were in eastern England. Second, no attempt was made to protect wool from imports, and by the 1870s wool from New Zealand and Australia, and later from Argentina, could be marketed at prices well below those which made European wool production profitable. Sheep numbers continued to decline until after the Second World War, since when numbers have increased again in some countries. They are now found largely in mountainous areas; in Britain for example, sheep numbers in the arable east have declined, but have increased in the upland areas.[107]

Sheep rearing is an extensive use of land, and it is not surprising that it should have been abandoned in Europe in the lowland areas and displaced to mountainous regions where it is often the only form of agricultural land use possible; or to the remote areas of cheap land in Australasia. Similarly the intensification of western European farming since 1850 has seen very considerable increases in cattle and pigs. This began at least as early as the 1870s, and every western European country saw an increase in cattle – and particularly cows – between 1870 and 1910. Thus in Britain the total numbers of cattle and calves rose from 5 000 000 in the 1860s to 7 000 000 on the eve of the First World War. This increase has continued to the present. In 1950 there were 61 000 000 cattle in north-western Europe, in 1968 78 000 000. Over the same period pig numbers have doubled.[108]

Although the cultivated area in some parts of Europe continued to increase down to the eve of the First World War, and in the Netherlands and Finland down to the present day, there has not been a radical increase in the total agricultural area of north-western Europe in the last seventy years. Thus the density of stocking has risen very markedly. How has this been achieved?

First, between 1880 and 1940 there was a decline in the cereal area and an increase in the growth of forage crops and grasses. Second, an increasing proportion of the arable area has been used for feeding livestock, and cereals for human consumption have been imported from abroad. Third, yields of all crops have risen. Fourth, the standards of grassland management, which until this century lagged well behind arable farming, have risen dramatically. Fifth, farmers have imported grains and concentrates from abroad. European cattle densities are high, not only because of the high level of management, but because they utilise large areas of land elsewhere to feed their populations, both human and animal, a situation only possible in a rich industrialised society. Table 30 illustrates cattle densities in some selected regions.

TABLE 30   *Cattle densities in selected countries, 1965*

Country	No. of cattle (thousands)	Crops and grass (thousand hectares)	No. of cattle per km² of crops and grass
North-western Europe	76 500	98 000	78
All Europe	124 000	240 000	51
Denmark	3 400	3 017	112
Netherlands	4 000	2 227	179
France	21 000	33 600	62
U.K.	12 000	20 000	60
U.S.A.	109 000	435 000	25
Australia	18 000	489 000	4
South America	185 000	497 000	37
Argentina	50 000	177 000	28
New Zealand	7 700	13 600	56
Asia	275 000	606 000	45
China	62 000	286 000	21
U.S.S.R.	93 400	597 000	15
World	1 072 631	4 407 000	24

Source: F.A.O. *Production yearbook*, vol. 23, 1969

Mixed farming in Western Europe and North America

The development of the American Corn Belt

Many writers on the American Corn Belt – now variously described as the Corn – Soybean Belt or the Midland Feed Region – have stressed its uniqueness;[109] certainly there are few regions to match its productivity, a result of a combination of fertile land and an advanced agricultural technology. Yet although the Corn Belt has few counterparts in Europe – Denmark is perhaps the closest – it is a lineal descendant of the mixed farming of north-western Europe. The modern Corn Belt occupies much of the area between the Alleghenies and the Great Plains, being bounded in the north by an area of dairying, in the west by increasing aridity and wheat production and in the south – although corn (i.e. maize) persists as a major crop – by the absence of the integration of stock and livestock production and the importance of cotton. From the Dakotas and Nebraska east into Ohio, farming is based on the growth of crops to feed pigs and beef cattle; thus four-fifths of Iowa's farm income is from livestock. A very high proportion of the total land area is in farmland, and most of the farmland is in crops; pasture is of less importance than in most western European countries. Corn occupies 40–60 per cent of the cropland, a lower ratio than in the 1920s, largely owing to the rise of the soybean, a valuable cash crop. The main purpose of the crops however is to feed pigs and beef cattle, the former nearly everywhere being of greater importance. Pigs are bred on the farms; young steers however are still brought from the western range and fattened on corn and grass before going on to the meat-packing factories.[110]

Thus although the farming system is broadly similar to the mixed farming of western Europe, there are important differences. Although rotations are followed, no root crops are grown.[111] The use of artificial fertilisers is less intensive than in many parts of western Europe, but on the other hand machinery is far more commonly used. Farms are larger, and rarely are they fragmented. There is little hired labour and agricultural population densities are much lower than in any part of western Europe. The most obvious difference is in the importance of maize: maize does not thrive in north-western Europe. Only in southern Europe, Aquitaine and Hungary for example, are summers hot enough to give good yields. In contrast the Corn Belt provides the optimum conditions for its growth, and it outyields other feed crops in this region. Thus the average yield of corn in the Corn Belt in 1962 was 4500 kg per hectare, oats 2550 kg, wheat 1900 kg and rye 1100 kg.[112]

There is of course considerable regional diversity within the Corn Belt. Although four-fifths of all crops are fed to livestock there are a few areas of predominantly cash corn production, particularly to the west and south west of Chicago. There are also islands of dairying within the region, and milk production grows progressively more important towards the north as maize yields decline. Westward some corn is irrigated and up to a third of the farmland is devoted to grazing cattle. A variety of crop combinations are to be found, which include corn, oats (which has declined as the tractor has replaced the horse), winter wheat, sorghum and temporary grasses.[113]

It is not surprising that farming in the United States should resemble that of north-western Europe. In 1790 two-thirds of the population had come from the British Isles and most of the rest from the Netherlands, Germany and Scandinavia; as immigration gathered momentum in the nineteenth century the same area provided most of the migrants.[114] It was not until the late nineteenth century that migration from southern Europe became important, and by then the agricultural settlement of the United States was nearly complete. By the middle of the seventeenth century settlers in New England and New York had imported most of the crops then grown in northern Europe, together with cattle, sheep and pigs. Early in the eighteenth century potatoes were introduced into New England from Ireland. But the most important crop of the early settlers was maize; wheat was far from successful at either Jamestown or Plymouth, but the settlers were taught how to grow maize by the Indians and thereafter it was the major crop throughout the United States in both North and South. As the pioneers pushed over the Alleghenies and into the Ohio valley maize was the first crop grown and generally occupied the greater area, although wheat was commonly the cash crop. Maize had a number of advantages over wheat. Its yields were higher and more reliable, and the plant was less susceptible to disease; further, maize could be harvested over a long period, in contrast to wheat which had to be harvested rapidly. This was an important fact in a labour-short economy. On the other hand maize had a low value per unit weight and could not be transported far; it thus had to be converted into higher-value products: it was fed to pigs or cattle, or made into whisky. A further problem which became apparent in the later nineteenth century was the difficulty of mechanising sowing, cultivating and harvesting operations. Thus between 1830 and 1870 labour productivity in small-grain production increased some six times, but in maize production it only doubled.[115]

The first settlements in New England bore a considerable resemblance to those in England. Land was granted by the Crown to colonising companies, which in turn allocated land to proprietors in townships. Within the townships nucleated villages were established, and 'lots' of arable land allocated which, like the strips in the English open fields, were widely dispersed, whilst woodland and grazing were held in common. But by the end of the eighteenth century most of the common land – save the village greens – had been enclosed, and elsewhere in New England the isolated homestead was becoming the dominant mode of rural settlement.[116] Nor were the pioneers who crossed the Alleghenies in the early nineteenth century to settle the woodlands of the Ohio valley and the blue-grass country of Kentucky fettered by seignorial rights or shortage of land. Land could be acquired by purchase or by squatting. The 1841 Pre-emption Act allowed land that had been effectively occupied to be purchased at $5 a hectare, whilst after 1861 the Homestead Act allowed occupation of 64 hectares and its subsequent purchase at very easy rates. Not that all of the Mid-West was purchased in such a manner. In New York, Ohio and Illinois there was much speculation in land, and very large properties were acquired. But whatever the manner of land acquisition the first settlers had – for those times – large farms in a consolidated unit. Nor did the laws of inheritance or any subsequent population increase lead to fragmentation or subdivision. Until the 1890s there was always cheap land to the west.

Thus the differences between American and European farming largely spring from the differences in the man/land ratio. From the beginning of settlement land was abundant – if not always free – and labour in short supply. Landless labourers were uncommon, for they could always go west to get their own land. The pioneer farmer and his descendants – outside the South – have had to rely upon family labour. Ninety per cent of the farm-work in American farming today is carried out by the farmer and his family, and wage labourers have only been important in California.[117]

The relationship between the agricultural work force and the land in farms is shown in Table 31. The farm population of the United States increased until the First World War, but except for the period between 1870 and 1890 the increase in the cultivated area exceeded the increase in the farm population. After 1910 the farm population stabilised, and then in the 1930s began to decline. It is now less than half what it was in the 1930s; farmland per caput has continued to increase; so that each United States agricultural employee works on average ninety hectares, compared with twenty-three in the United Kingdom and five in the Netherlands.

TABLE 31 *Agricultural work force and area in farms of the United States, 1820–1970*

Year	Agricultural work force (thousands)	Land in farms (thousand hectares)	Hectares / head
1820	2 070	–	–
1830	2 770	–	–
1840	3 720	–	–
1850	4 900	118 623	24.2
1860	6 210	164 777	26.5
1870	6 850	189 068	27.5
1880	8 610	231 516	26.8
1890	9 990	252 226	25.2
1900	10 710	339 271	31.6
1910	11 340	355 465	31.3
1920	11 120	386 639	34.7
1930	10 480	399 190	38.0
1940	9 000	429 554	47.7
1950	8 036	468 825	58.3
1960	5 837	454 655	77.8
1965	4 836	435 613	90.0
1970	3 253	–	–

Sources: U.S. Bureau of the Census, 1960, 1964; F.A.O. *Production yearbook*, vol. 23, 1969

Although the *total* agricultural work force of the United States did not begin to decline until the 1930s, there were pronounced regional variations in the numbers of the rural population. Thus much of New England and New York State had reached their maximum before 1870 and have subsequently declined. Most of the Corn Belt reached its maximum by 1880, or at the latest 1910, and has since stagnated or declined, whilst the wheatgrowing areas of the Great Plains did not reach their peak until the First World War or later, and declined only after 1930.[118] This reflected three factors; first were the industrialisation and migration to the farms in the North East, which as early as the 1830s were leading to the abandonment of marginal land in the interior of New England; second was the opening up of new land beyond the Appalachians, and the improvement of communications; in particular the completion of the Erie Canal in 1825, which allowed Ohio farmers to undercut New England grain and wool producers; third was the fact that whilst the present Corn Belt had been largely occupied to its western limits by 1860, infilling continued to the end of the century as immigrants from the North East as well as from Europe continued to arrive.[119]

Thus whilst the decline of the rural population in the Corn Belt was a comparatively late phenomenon compared with Britain or Belgium, and even with parts of France and Germany, it should be recalled that even the peak densities never matched those of western Europe, and this had important consequences for the evolution of mixed farming. In 1920 the total farm population of eleven Corn Belt states was only 8 316 000, a density per square kilometre of land in farms of only two, of improved land of eight; in 1965, after seventy years of decline, the agricultural population per square kilometre of agricultural land in north-western Europe was twenty-five.[120]

The lower densities of population, a function of the very recent settlement of the United States, have thus been a major factor in accounting for differences between the mixed farming of the United States and western Europe. The dominance of comparatively large and consolidated farms has already been noted. But the shortage of labour also accounts for the unimportance of root crops in the United States and particularly in the Corn Belt.[121] Further, it helps to explain the relatively rapid mechanisation of corn production. In 1840 corn was grown in much the same way as it had been in the seventeenth century, planted by hand, covered with hoes and cultivated with a shovel plough. Corn production was mechanised more slowly than wheat production, but by 1860 farmers had available corn-planters and improved cultivators, and in 1864 the check-rower, a machine that planted corn in equi-distant hills, was patented. The first effective combined corn-shucking and fodder-shredding machine was not developed until 1890, and the corn-binder in 1892. Farmers often overcame the problems of harvesting by letting pigs eat off the cobs.[122]

Unlike that of Europe, the mixed farming of the United States was established at a time when the frontier of settlement was constantly moving onwards, and indeed the corn–hog economy was partly a function of frontier conditions. There is

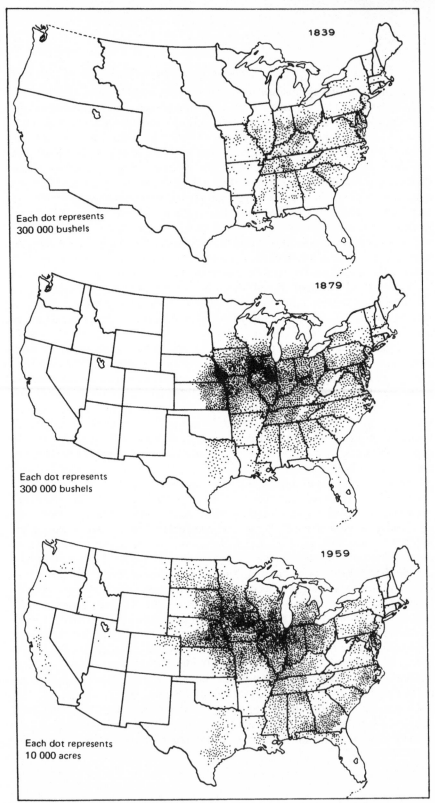

Fig. 20. Distribution of corn output in the United States, 1839, 1879 and 1959. [Source: U.S. Department of Agriculture, 1922, 171–2; *U.S. Census of Agriculture*, 1959, vol. 2, 654]

some controversy as to where it first arose.[123] Maize had been grown and pigs kept throughout the United States since the earliest colonial times, before pioneers crossed the Alleghenies into the upper Ohio valley and the Kentucky blue-grass country. In the early decades of the nineteenth century they were primarily subsistence farmers. Wheat was the first cash crop, although it was costly to transport over the mountains to the east-coast cities until the building of the Erie Canal in 1825. Farmers near the Ohio River however could ship corn south to the cotton plantations; but cattle and, to a lesser extent, pigs could be driven on the hoof. Everywhere on the frontier there was abundant grazing, and surplus maize could be fed to animals. By the 1830s a number of districts specialised in fattening cattle and pigs on grass and corn and driving them east: the Kentucky blue-grass country, the Scioto valley, and the middle Wabash. In 1840 the main centre of corn and hog production was in the border states of Kentucky, Tennessee and Virginia. Cincinnati was the first meat-packing centre.[124]

After 1840 the frontier of settlement pushed westwards out of the woodlands on to the prairies of Indiana, Illinois and Iowa. Here farmers were presented with quite new conditions. At first they settled only in the wooded valleys, and left the treeless interfluves, particularly those that were badly drained, unsettled. But the adoption of the chilled steel mould-board and the breaking-plough led to the rapid settlement of all but ill-drained land, which awaited the introduction of pipe drainage after 1870. By 1860 the frontier of settlement had reached the present western limit of the Corn Belt, although much of the land was still only partially settled or held in large ranches.[125]

The first farmers in the prairies grew a wide range of crops; wheat was generally the first cash crop. As late as the 1860s there were still a number of very large pastoral holdings where cattle were reared and grazed on grass and corn. But as immigration continued and land values rose, so the big holdings were broken up into smaller farms, and more of the prairie was put beneath the plough. Ranching was displaced westwards into the Great Plains, as was wheat production.[126]

Between 1840 and 1880 the major features of the modern Corn Belt developed. As the railways reached westwards into the prairies, so the great drives were eliminated. At first live pigs were sent east on the railway. After 1857 pork could be sent in ice, and by 1868 there were refrigeration cars. But most of the hogs went comparatively short distances to local meat-packing plants in Chicago, Omaha and St Louis. The breed of pig was improved after the 1840s; the lean razor-backed, half-wild pig that could be driven long distances was replaced by imports from England and China, and large lard-producing animals were bred. Cattle were also improved in quality, particularly by the introduction of Shorthorns. As the area under grass diminished, so farmers ceased to breed cattle, and imported young steers from Texas and, in the 1870s, from the northern Great Plains; cattle were thus reared on the range, and then fattened on corn and wild hay on Corn Belt farms. Between 1850 and 1900 pigs increased in numbers at a greater rate than beef cattle, and by 1900 cattle were subsidiary to pigs.[127]

The farming methods of the emergent Corn Belt were poor; rotations did not come into general practice until the end of the century and the best use of cattle manure was not made; artificial fertilisers were rarely used. Farmers believed in the inexhaustible fertility of the prairie soils. But by 1900 the classic Corn Belt rotation of corn, wheat, oats and hay had appeared in many parts of the region, whilst the first silo had been built in 1875.[128]

Between 1820 and 1880 the frontier of settlement moved from the upper Ohio valley west to the Great Plains. The centre of corn and hog production also moved westwards (Table 32). In 1840 pigs and corn were to be found throughout the United States, but there was a marked concentration in Tennessee and Kentucky and the adjacent parts of Ohio and Virginia, to the south east of the modern Corn Belt; farmers in this region could ship corn down the Ohio to the cotton plantations or send cattle on the hoof across the Alleghenies to the growing urban markets of the east coast. But as settlement pressed westwards so did the centres of corn and hog production, and also of wheat. On the eve of the Civil War, Indiana, Illinois, Missouri and Iowa were producing a third of the corn and a quarter of the hogs. By 1880 Iowa was the leading producer of corn and hogs, a position it has not lost since. By the end of the century eastern Nebraska and eastern Kansas had a corn–hog economy. The last significant shift was in the inter-war period into South Dakota, Minnesota and southern Wisconsin. Table 32 shows the percentage of corn and hogs produced in each state. But the absolute figures are of interest; the total output of corn in the United States doubled between 1840 and 1860, doubled again between 1860 and 1880, and yet again between 1880 and 1960, although the area under corn in fact declined between 1920 and 1960.[129]

It is worth noting that the corn–hog economy originated in the wooded areas of Ohio and parts of Kentucky, where soils are podzolised; most of the Corn Belt now lies well to the west on prairie soils. As the frontier has pushed west, so extensive ranching was displaced further and further west, and in its turn areas once devoted to large-scale wheat production have now been invaded by the corn–hog economy, a result of rising land values, and the need to utilise land more intensively. The outlines of the modern Corn Belt were clear by the 1880s; but the methods of farming were not very good. Indeed there was little increase in the average yield between the 1860s and the 1920s. But since about 1930 there has been a radical change. Poor farming methods had led to widespread erosion and conservation techniques were adopted; rotations were more widely pursued. Artificial fertilisers have been increased. But most striking has been the adoption of hybrid corn, which in 1933 was grown on only 1 per cent of the corn area, by 1960 on 94 per cent. The rural exodus which began in the 1920s prompted mechanisation and an increase in the size of farms. Corn yields doubled between 1935–9 and 1960–2, whilst the man-hours required to produce 30 hectolitres fell from 108 to 12; the comparable figures for wheat were 67 and 12. Thus the mechanisation of corn, which lagged behind that of wheat in the nineteenth century, is now on a par with it.[130]

TABLE 32 *Corn production and hog numbers, by states, 1839–1960 (% of national output of corn and of numbers of hogs)*

	1839		1859		1880		1899		1919		1960	
	Corn	Hogs	Corn	Hogs	Corn	Hogs	Corn	Hogs	Corn	Hogs	Corn	Hogs
Tennessee	11.9	11.1	6.2	7.0	3.5	4.5	–	3.1	3.0	–	1.3	2.3
Kentucky	10.5	8.7	7.6	6.9	4.1	4.6	2.7	–	3.0	–	1.8	2.4
Virginia	9.1	7.5	4.5	4.7	–	–	–	–	–	–	–	1.1
North Carolina	6.3	6.2	–	5.6	–	–	–	–	–	–	2.0	2.4
Georgia	5.5	5.5	3.6	6.0	–	–	–	–	–	–	–	2.7
Ohio	8.9	7.9	8.7	6.7	6.3	6.5	5.7	5.0	6.3	5.1	5.5	4.5
Indiana	7.4	6.1	8.5	9.2	6.5	6.6	6.7	5.9	6.7	6.3	8.4	7.8
Illinois	5.9	5.3	13.7	7.4	18.5	10.8	14.9	9.4	12.1	7.8	17.2	12.1
Missouri	4.5	–	8.6	7.0	11.5	9.5	7.8	7.7	6.2	6.5	5.1	7.0
Iowa	–	–	5.0	–	15.6	12.6	14.3	15.4	15.8	13.2	20.0	21.7
Nebraska	–	–	–	–	3.7	–	7.9	6.5	6.8	5.7	7.9	4.7
Kansas	–	–	–	–	5.9	3.7	8.5	5.7	–	–	1.7	1.9
Texas	–	–	–	–	–	4.1	4.1	4.2	4.6	3.7	1.0	1.7
Minnesota	–	–	–	–	–	–	–	–	3.0	4.0	8.4	6.9
Wisconsin	–	–	–	–	–	–	–	3.2	–	–	3.1	3.6
South Dakota	–	–	–	–	–	–	–	–	–	3.2	2.7	3.0

Sources: U.S. Department of Agriculture, 1922, 187–91; 1923, 171–3; U.S. Bureau of the Census, 1964

Mixed farming – an appraisal

Mixed farming as practised in both North America and Western Europe can be clearly traced back to the early village sites of South West Asia, where both livestock and crops were kept by farmers. The significant moments in the evolution of modern mixed farming were, first, the introduction of the heavier plough and the three-field system in the early Middle Ages; second, the reduction of the fallow and the cultivation of roots and grasses as fodder, beginning in the late Middle Ages; and third, the intensification of farming and the progressive shift to the livestock products since 1850. The initial changes have all come in areas near to urban areas; thus in the Middle Ages in the Low Countries, and in the eighteenth century in south-eastern England. But it is perhaps as well to remember that the intensification of farming has only been possible because the industrial strength of western Europe and the eastern United States has not only led to higher incomes and higher demand, and provided fertilisers and machines, but by exporting manufactured goods has allowed these regions to import from distant areas products produced by more extensive means. Earlier in this chapter the effect of imported American grain on European farming was noted. New England had experienced such competition even earlier, and had turned from wheat and wool to more specialised products such as vegetables and milk as early as the 1840s. The latter specialisation must now be considered.

CHAPTER 10

DAIRYING

We have seen in the preceding chapter how farmers in Europe and North America progressively shifted their attention to livestock products after 1850; of these, milk and other dairy products became by far the most important. In the European Economic Community, in the United States and in the United Kingdom, milk makes up one-fifth of the value of the total agricultural output and in some countries the proportion is even higher; in Finland it is 60 per cent, in Switzerland 36 per cent, and in Luxemburg 35 per cent.[1] Although dairying has a long history, the modern dairy industry is a product of the last hundred years, and perhaps, more than any other branch of agriculture, has been dependent upon the growth of urban incomes, improvements in transport, and advances in science and technology.

Table 33 shows how closely dairy production is associated with areas of European settlement.

Five-sixths of the world's milk is produced in Europe, Russia, North America and Australasia, nearly nine-tenths of the butter, over four-fifths of the cheese, and virtually all the condensed, evaporated and dried milk. Further, much of the dairy production of Afro-Asia and Latin America is produced in outliers of European settlement such as South Africa and Argentina.

Until the 1850s dairying took place only on the farm. Fresh milk was only consumed by the farm family or in villages and towns within a close distance. Cheese and butter were made by the farmer or, more commonly, his wife. In some very large towns urban dairymen kept cows in stalls, fed upon hay and brewer's grains. However in the second half of the nineteenth century the spread of railways allowed large cities to draw upon distant regions for fresh milk. This was only made possible by the rise of wholesale firms which contracted with farmers for the delivery of milk, and resold to retail roundsmen within the cities. Further, the application of power to churning and the invention of the cream separator transferred the making of cheese and butter to factories, whilst the manufacture of condensed, evaporated and dried milk has always been a factory process. About a third of the milk produced in the European-settled areas is consumed fresh, a third made into butter, 13 per cent into cheese, less than a tenth into other manufactured products, whilst the remainder − 8 per cent − is fed to animals.[2]

Milk has always been produced on the majority of farms within the mixed farming systems of Europe, North America and Australasia, and indeed is still very widely produced within these areas. However the rising demand for milk since

TABLE 33   *World output of dairy products, 1965 (thousand metric tons)*

	No. of cows (thousands)	Milk	Butter	Cheese	Condensed, evaporated and dried milk
North-western Europe	34 500	100 000	1790	2200	3300
Southern Europe	5 000	14 000	130	720	100
Eastern Europe	15 000	35 300	570	514	160
Russia	40 100	75 000	1177	444	–
North America	56 000	62 700	720	1255	2760
Australasia	14 000	13 300	460	183	370
Africa	30 000	10 000	107	295	60
Asia	80 800	26 500	590	156	170
Latin America	31 600	21 100	95	300	240
World	306 900	357 960	5640	6067	7160

Source: F.A.O. *Production yearbook*, vol. 23, 1969

the 1880s has led to the emergence of regions specialising in dairy production, and it is thus possible to identify a specific type of agriculture (Fig. 1). In North America much of Ontario, New England, New York State, and parts of Ohio, Michigan, Wisconsin, Iowa and Minnesota are devoted mainly to dairying, with a marked difference between the East, where milk for the cities is the main product, and the West, where with less urban demand more of the milk is manufactured (Fig. 19). In Europe milk production is more widely spread; but some areas of specialisation can be identified. The western parts of England, much of Wales, Scotland and Ireland; Brittany and Normandy in France; southern Holland and Friesland in the Netherlands; the northern Germany coastal areas; Denmark; and most of the agricultural areas of Norway, Sweden and Finland, whilst the mountain areas of Austria, Switzerland and northern Italy, are also largely given over to milk production. Dairying is also found near to the major cities in northern Europe. In the southern hemisphere North Island, New Zealand, and parts of the coastal regions of south-eastern Australia have important dairying industries.

Characteristic features of dairy farms

It must be re-emphasised that milk production is an enterprise on many different types of farm in Europe, America and Australasia. The specialised dairy farmers however have a number of features in common. First of all their farms are small, particularly those in western Europe. In Friesland the average size of a dairy farm is 15 hectares, in southern Holland only 7. In Britain and Denmark dairy farms are rather larger than in the rest of Europe. In Denmark, for example, four-fifths of dairy output comes from farms of between 10 and 120 hectares. In North America and Australasia farms are larger, as might be expected, but are still smaller than mixed farms. Thus in the Dairy Region of the United States the average farm is about 80 hectares, of which however about 20 hectares are in woodland or waste. In New Zealand the average dairy farm is 60 hectares. As a cow needs 0.6 to 0.8 hectares to provide feed for the year, even under the best farming conditions, typical herds are small. The average size of a dairy herd in the European Economic Community is only five cows, and herds are as small in much of the rest of western Europe. In Finland, for example, 80 per cent of all cows are in herds of less than four whilst in the Netherlands, although the average herd is twelve cows, a quarter of all herds have less than five. In Germany the average herd has six cows.

The larger herds are found, not unnaturally, where dairy farms have larger areas. In Denmark the average herd is 24, in Great Britain 26 and in the United States over 20. The largest herds are in New Zealand – 80 – where also stocking densities are high.[3]

Cows need to be milked twice a day most days of the year – assuming they are being adequately fed in winter – and thus dairy farming is labour-intensive, for even with milking machines, automatic feeding devices and field machinery, there is no slack period. This unremitting toil partly accounts for the decline in the number of dairy farmers – particularly the marginal producers – in western Europe and the United States since 1950. However in the past dairy farming had many advantages for the small farmer. He received regular cash payments throughout the year, and milk prices have, on the whole, not shown as great fluctuations as other products. Indeed in the last forty years most western countries have established marketing schemes that aim at stabilising prices. For the very small farmer dairying gives a better return per hectare than most other possible enterprises. Thus in Northern Ireland, where four-fifths of the farms are less than 20 hectares, the net returns per hectare for different enterprises are: pigs and poultry, £69; dairying, £64; cash crops and stock, £61; mixed livestock, £51; cattle feeding, £37. Returns per man-hour are not good however, and most dairy farms depend upon family labour. In the American Dairy Belt four-fifths of all farmers are occupier-owners. Few tenants are prepared to give cows the attention they need, and tenancy is thus uncommon.[4]

A modern dairy farm not only needs long hours from the farmer but a great deal of capital. Good breeds of milk cows themselves represent a very high outlay, whilst milking machinery, special buildings for milking, and barns or silos for the storage of winter fodder are also expensive. Further the farmer will also need the usual field equipment for an arable dairy farm, and hay-making machinery on grass farms. Milking machines hardly pay unless the dairy herd exceeds twenty or more cows; in spite of this many small dairy farmers do have milking machinery. In Finland, for example, 50 per cent of the machines in use are on herds with less than ten cows. Thus, as in most western farming systems, the average size of farm and herd has risen in order to utilise fully the economies of scale which are then possible. In the United States the average herd was only four cows in 1910, sixteen in 1950 and over twenty in 1960. In every dairying region there has been a significant decline in the number of small dairy farms since 1950, and a concentration of milk output not only on the larger farms, but in the most suitable areas.[5]

Although many farmers in the dairy regions produce only milk, dairying is frequently combined with other enterprises on the same farm. In eastern England dairying increased in importance after 1930 on large mixed farms; roots and grains could be fed to dairy cows in the winter to take advantage of the higher prices given for winter milk. In Denmark and the Netherlands the classic combination has been of dairying and pigs, for in regions where most of the milk is manufactured, the skimmed milk can be used as feed. In France milk production is everybody's business and nobody's occupation, and is combined with a wide range of other enterprises, including even viticulture. In South Australia milk production is invariably on mixed enterprises, whilst in New South Wales it is more commonly confined to specialised farms. In the Great Plains ranchers keep some dairy cows and send milk to the centralisers, whilst conversely there has been a significant revival of the urban dairy in the last twenty years, where cattle are fed in stalls on imported hay and concentrates. But even specialised dairy farmers have side-products. Young calves which are not needed as replacements are sold for veal, whilst in England the dairy farms provide most of the young steers which are fattened for beef on other farms.[6]

Perhaps the most important regional differences in dairy farming are, first, the way in which the cows are fed, and, second, the utilisation of the milk.

A major factor in the economics of dairying is that the consumer – particularly of fresh milk – requires an even flow of milk throughout the year, whereas the cow produces a maximum yield after calving and at the time of maximum grass growth, generally in spring or early summer. Prior to the nineteenth century there was little consumption of fresh milk, and the summer flush of milk was made into cheese or butter. Cows were inadequately fed in winter, and so gave very little milk. However, with the rise of a large urban demand for milk, farming systems had to be devised which provided sufficient feed throughout the year. The ideal system is based upon grass, which is generally the cheapest of all cattle feeds, but only exceptionally is grass growth sufficient to maintain herds in milk for the whole year. The principle exception to this rule is North Island, New Zealand, where grass does grow throughout the whole year although the rate of growth declines in the winter months. Thus the New Zealand dairy farmer buys hardly any concentrates, grains or roots and relies upon grazing and hay. In addition the winters are so mild that cattle can be kept out, a significant saving on the cost of buildings. On the other hand the New Zealand farmer is extremely careful with his grass – all imported European varieties – applies fertilisers and controls his grazing patterns.

No part of north-western Europe has a grazing season as long as that of New

Zealand. However in a number of the specialised dairying regions grass provides grazing for six months or more in the summer and hay is cut for winter consumption. Thus the heavy soils of Cheshire and Somerset, the polders of Friesland and southern Holland and the pastures of Brittany and Normandy provide much of the feed for dairy cows. It should be noted that few of these areas are very suitable for crop cultivation. This is even more true of Norway and Finland, where grass occupies more than four-fifths of the cultivated area. In parts of lowland Switzerland grass produces most of the feed, but this is cut and taken to the cows in stalls either as fresh cut grass or as hay. In the mountain areas the alps are still used for summer grazing. In the American Dairy Region there is a marked difference between the feeding patterns of the East and the West. In New England and New York State, which have cool moist summers and long cold winters, cows are grazed on grass in the summer and fed in stalls in the winter on hay, grain and concentrates. But the eastern milk producer grows little of his own fodder: it is generally cheaper to purchase grain grown in the West. The western milk producers who have summers more favourable to crop growth have a larger proportion of their farms under grains and provide more of their own winter feed.[7]

However in all these regions winter grass growth is negligible, hence the art of the successful dairy farmer is to provide the cheapest combination of winter feeds to maintain milk yields. Thus at one extreme is the New Zealand dairy

TABLE 34   *Utilisation of milk in selected countries, 1965*

	Per cent of total milk used for:					
	Liquid and cream	Butter	Cheese	Dried, evaporated and condensed milk	Feed and waste	Total manufactured
Austria	34.7	30.7	9.9	4.8	19.6	45.4
Belgium	25.5	53.7	6.0	6.9	7.7	66.6
Denmark	15.3	60.7	13.6	6.0	4.2	80.3
Finland	37.6	49.9	6.9	4.0	1.4	60.8
West Germany	25.8	52.7	6.4	6.2	8.9	65.3
France	20.5	36.1	20.5	4.3	18.4	60.9
Irish Republic	21.3	49.3	5.1	7.9	16.1	62.3
Netherlands	23.9	31.4	22.1	18.5	3.8	72.0
Norway	52.9	24.4	18.3	1.3	4.4	44.0
U.K.	68.1	7.7	9.5	7.6	6.9	24.8
Canada	33.1	43.4	10.8	8.2	4.2	62.4
U.S.A.	47.3	23.3	12.6	14.9	1.6	50.8
Australia	23.1	62.3	8.3	6.1	–	76.7
New Zealand	8.2	71.6	14.8	2.6	2.5	89.0

Source: F.A.O. *Production yearbook*, vol. 23, 1969

farmer, with grass growth for much of the year; at the other the Danish farmer who stalls his cows most of the year and devotes most of his land to feed crops.

Although milk is the primary product of all dairy farms there are significant variations in its utilisation.

In most countries at least one-fifth of all milk production goes to the liquid market; the United Kingdom is exceptional in that over two-thirds is directly consumed and a small proportion is manufactured; the only comparable fluid consumption is in the eastern United States, for whereas one-half of all U.S. milk is consumed liquid, in the north-eastern states most of it goes into the liquid market. However more typically between one-half and two-thirds of all milk is manufactured. Exceptionally high proportions are manufactured in the Netherlands, Denmark, Australia and New Zealand. All these countries have specialised in dairy production for export and clearly this necessitates manufacture. Only 6 per cent of all dairy produce goes into international trade; these four countries account for half the butter exports and 40 per cent of all cheese exports.[8]

The early history of dairying

The first evidence of milking in South West Asia dates from the fourth millennium B.C., when cows were milked in both Mesopotamia and Egypt. At a later date the nomadic groups of Arabia and Central Asia milked not only cows but camels, sheep and goats. Butter and cheese appear to have been made by the time of the third millennium, the latter from the milk of sheep, goats and camels as well as cows. Dairy products were not however very important in the Mediterranean of classical times. Fresh milk was a rarity, and butter-making, which the Greeks are thought to have learnt from the Scythians, not much practised; both the Greeks and the Romans used olive-oil instead, and butter was used for anointing rather than food. Cheese however was more common, made from the milk of sheep and goats rather than cows.[9]

Milking and the use of dairy products may have been introduced into India by the Aryans in the second millennium B.C. Certainly the milking of cows, water buffaloes and goats was practised by the end of the first millennium B.C. and *ghee*, the distinctive clarified butter, was already being made. In contrast, there is no evidence of milking in early Chinese history, and it has remained of negligible significance down to the present day; indeed it is unimportant throughout the area of Chinese influence, in Korea, China, Japan and eastern Indo-China. In western Indo-China, milking was extended during the period of Indian expansion in the first millennium A.D. In Africa milking may have been independently discovered by nomadic peoples in the Sahara in the fourth millennium, but it was not carried south into humid tropical Africa and remains unimportant in West Africa, the Congo basin and the tsetse fly belt of southern Africa; it is possible that the practice of milking did not penetrate into eastern and southern Africa until after A.D. 1000. In the Americas milking was unknown until the arrival of Europeans.[10]

Dairying in Europe before the nineteenth century

Milking and the making of butter and cheese were known in northern Europe at least as early as the second millennium B.C., if not before, and Roman authors give the impression that dairy products were much more important to the north of the Alps than to the south. By the later medieval period, when more documentary evidence becomes available, it is clear that dairying was widespread in northern Europe, but only locally was it of major significance. Cattle were kept primarily as draught animals, and secondarily for their meat. Milk was of very little importance in comparison, and the consumption of fresh milk was unusual. The summer surplus was converted into cheese or butter. Butter was still a luxury, and beef fat and lard were used instead.

There were no specialised milk breeds in medieval times, and milk yields were very low. The medieval farmer had a chronic shortage of fodder, and such winter keep that he had went to feed oxen and beef cattle. Thus cheese and butter making was a seasonal activity, and flourished in the areas of good summer grass growth. In the fourteenth and fifteenth centuries some of the modern areas of cheese and butter production already had some reputation. In thirteenth-century Norway arable areas declined, grain was imported from the Baltic, and fish and butter were exported. The *saeter* system expanded in both Norway and northern Sweden after the ninth century A.D. Both Sweden and Denmark exported butter to Lubeck, and indeed in Sweden Crown taxes were paid in butter, an indication of its importance. Dutch cheese was exported from Groningen as early as the twelfth century. Brie already had a reputation for cheese, as did Normandy, whilst the Alpine areas were already producing dairy products in the late Middle Ages.[11]

Butter and cheese were made principally in those areas where crop production was difficult, for example on the badly drained soils of the Dutch polders, or the very heavy clay soils of Cheshire, in wetter areas such as Norway, or in mountain areas where the preponderance of steep slopes made cereal cultivation uneconomic. Conversely most of these areas had good grass growth. But even in the areas with good grass there was little fodder for winter feed and so annual yields were low; in medieval England they have been estimated at 540–680 litres. Changes in dairying in the sixteenth and seventeenth century were few. However the first urban dairies appeared in London in the seventeenth century, providing fresh milk for the better-off; the numbers increased in the eighteenth century, whilst dairying became established on the edge of the built-up area. In 1800 London had a ring of meadows which maintained cows that supplied the city with milk; the dairy farmers fed their cattle in stalls in winter on turnips, hay and brewer's grains.[12]

Throughout the sixteenth, seventeenth and eighteenth centuries the new fodder crops – temporary grasses, turnips and mangolds – were very slowly adopted by farmers in western Europe, and this made it possible to maintain milking through the winter, although the grass areas retained their pre-eminence.

Better feeding led to better yields, and by the end of the eighteenth century the average cow in England was giving 1300 litres a year. Hay making was also becoming easier; the scythe was improved, and the horse-drawn hay-rake invented.[13]

As late as the mid-nineteenth century dairying was still a secondary occupation for mixed farmers in most parts of western Europe and North America. True, some areas did specialise in butter and cheese making, still of course carried out only on farms. Very little fresh milk was consumed; in England in 1865 consumption per caput was only 0.1 litres a day. There were good reasons for this. Milk was highly perishable, and before the coming of the railway could not be carried far for sale. In the eighteenth century milk was carried ten miles on horseback into Liverpool and Manchester, and this was about the limit. The urban dairies had a poor reputation and the adulteration of milk was common. Although some of the specialist dairy breeds had already emerged, most milk still came from dual-purpose cattle: in England the Shorthorns which were just beginning to replace Longhorns. In the United States the Devon was still the most popular dairy cow. Nor was demand sufficient to prompt improvement; few industrial workers in Britain could afford milk or butter, although cheese was cheaper and more widely consumed.[14]

The Dairying Revolution: fresh milk

Since 1850 a series of interlocking technical changes have transformed the dairying industry in the United States, western Europe and Australasia. Milk is now the most valuable single farm product in nearly every country in these three regions. The most important underlying factor has been the relative improvement of prices for dairy products compared with those for grains. This began, not, as is sometimes argued, after 1873 when the opening up of the western United States produced a flow of cheap grain, but much earlier. The shift towards livestock production was under way in New England in the 1840s, in England in the 1850s and in much of western Europe by the 1860s. Denmark is frequently cited as an example of a grain-exporting country changing to dairy production because of the import of cheap American grain. Yet exports of livestock products exceeded those of grain by 50 per cent in 1873, before the fall in grain prices. The subsequent decline in grain prices and the smaller decline in the price of livestock products made it profitable to feed grain to animals, a quite fundamental change in farming.[15]

The increase in the urban population was a major factor in causing an increase in the output of dairy products; for example the population of the New York metropolitan area rose from 1 260 000 in 1860 to 6 500 000 in 1910, creating a vast market for the dairy farmers of New England and New York State. But the mere increase in population was not in itself sufficient to create an effective demand for milk. First there had to be a rise in real income: in the middle of the nineteenth century few industrial workers could afford fresh milk or butter and thus consumption was low. In England the weekly consumption per caput of milk in the 1870s was about 0.8 litres; it increased to 1.68 litres in the 1930s and 2.8 litres in the 1950s. This long-term increase in fresh milk consumption was not only a result of rising incomes. In the 1850s and 1860s milk sold in towns from urban dairies was not only adulterated, being frequently mixed with water, but carried germs. A series of legal measures greatly improved the quality of liquid milk. In 1856 Boston passed laws to prevent adulteration, and the major American cities quickly followed suit. In Britain the Sale of Food and Drugs Act of 1875 helped to reduce adulteration, and an Act of 1885 enforced minimum standards of hygiene in dairies. In 1882 Koch discovered that tuberculosis could be carried by milk from infected cows, but it was not until the 1920s that the testing of cattle and their slaughter – if found infected – became compulsory. Pasteurisation – the heating of fresh milk to destroy germs – was adopted in some wholesale dairies in the 1890s but did not become general practice in Britain or the United States until after the First World War. Similarly, although milk bottles were first used in the 1890s, much milk was still delivered in cans until the 1930s. By the 1920s the nutritional value of milk became more widely known and the provision of milk at reduced prices in British schools dates back to 1927.[16]

The growth of milk output for liquid consumption was not only dependent on a wealthier population and better hygiene. In the mid-nineteenth century fresh milk could only be carried – at the most – ten or twenty miles to its market, and so the large cities depended upon urban dairies or a narrow zone of dairy farmers on the outskirts of the cities. However the spread of the railway allowed farmers at ever increasing distances to sell milk in distant cities. Thus in the 1840s milk was taken 48 kilometres to Boston, by 1870 104 kilometres and by 1900 the 'milkshed' extended 440 kilometres, whilst on the eve of the First World War fresh milk was being supplied to New York City from over 480 kilometres away. In Britain London was by far the most important market for milk; in 1861 only 4 per cent of the capital's milk was supplied by rail, by 1891 83 per cent. Much of this came from up to 200 kilometres away. In the late 1920s milk was delivered to London from as far away as southern Scotland. The great cities of western Europe also drew upon increasingly distant supplies. In the early 1930s milk came into Berlin from up to 700 kilometres away.[17] The rise of the liquid milk industry was dependent not only on the spread of the railway, but on the provision of adequate roads for taking milk from the farms to railway-stations, pasteurisation, methods of keeping milk cool in transit and the rise of wholesale organisations which collected milk from farmers and re-sold – after treatment – to retailers. Although it was the railway that allowed the great cities to draw upon distant areas for their milk supplies, the motor lorry became important in the 1920s, first to convey milk from farms to the railhead, and then increasingly, as milk-tankers were produced, they took over much of the long-distant transport of milk to city consumers in the United States and Britain.

The Dairying Revolution: manufacturing

In 1850 cheese and butter were made entirely on the farm, generally from the summer 'flush'. Both were made by hand methods. Cheese was made from fresh whole-milk which was allowed to ripen, and then rennet, part of the lining of a calf's stomach, was added; this caused the curds to coagulate and sink to the bottom; the whey was drained off and fed to pigs. The curd was then cut into smaller lumps, put into moulds or 'vats' and put under presses. The cheeses were allowed to ripen for varying periods of time. Cheese could keep for up to four years, and could be accumulated on the farm and taken to market only two or three times a year. It was thus possible to produce cheeses in remote areas. Butter was also made from whole-milk which was left to settle so that the cream rose to the top, and was then taken off with a ladle. The cream was churned until butter formed, salt and colouring were added, and the butter was packed in wooden firkins, sealed to exclude air. Nonetheless butter would go rancid fairly rapidly and had to be sold off the farm more frequently than cheese.[18]

In the late 1840s a number of cheese factories were established in Ohio, and in 1851 one was opened in New York State. Not only could the factories use power and more expensive machinery than the individual farmer, but they could draw upon a large number of cows in the district, use the most skilled cheese-makers, cut costs and produce a standard product. Cheese factories were slow to get started, but by the 1860s and 1870s their numbers were expanding rapidly, from New England to Wisconsin, and American cheese was imported into Europe, prompting the expansion of factories in most parts of western Europe and also in Australia, New Zealand and Canada. The first cheese factory in England opened in Derbyshire in 1870. Factory cheese-making was slow to get under way in New Zealand; in 1882 there were only five factories but by 1893 there were fifty-five. Factory production of cheese began in western Europe in the 1880s but farmhouse production remained a substantial proportion of all cheese until after the Second World War, although it is now a very small proportion of total output.[19]

Butter factories, or creameries, were a later development, the first appearing in the United States in 1861. Indeed the major invention in the production of butter was not made until 1879 when Laval in Sweden and Nielsen in Denmark patented cream separators. Hitherto cream had been separated by gravity, but the machine used centrifugal force. The separator was first used in factory production, but in 1885 a hand separator, which could be used on farms, was made. Power was applied to the churning of cream. The factory process thus had more significance for butter production than cheese; butter factories were rapidly established in the United States, Canada, western Europe and Australasia. However farm butter was not immediately superseded. In the United States half

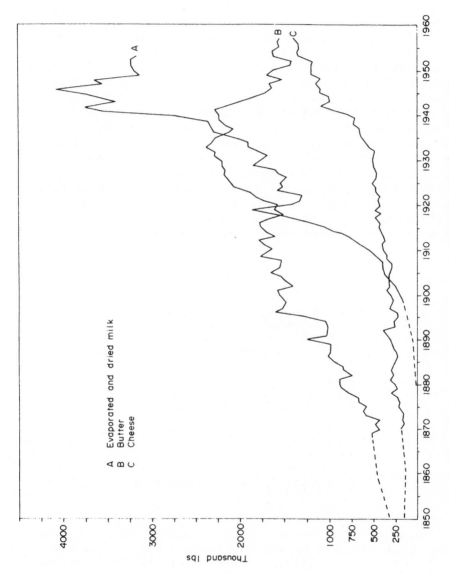

Fig. 21. Output of butter, cheese and evaporated and dried milk in the United States, 1850–1957.
[Source: U.S. Bureau of the Census, 1960]

A   Evaporated and dried milk
B   Butter
C   Cheese

of all the butter made still came from farms in 1899, and as late as 1930 one-quarter.[20]

In 1850 the output of butter in the United States was three times the output of cheese (Fig. 21). Both butter and cheese output subsequently increased rapidly, but by 1900 butter output was nearly five times that of cheese and remained at roughly that ratio until the 1930s. Since then butter consumption has declined in the United States, mainly due to the competition of margarine. In 1936 consumption per caput of butter per year was 7.5 kg, of margarine 1.4 kg. By the 1950s butter consumption was about 3.6 kg, as was that of margarine. Cheese output however has continued to increase, and is now approximately the same as that of butter. The rise of evaporated and condensed milk and ice cream is more recent. Ice cream had been made since at least 1600, but it had been difficult to preserve; advances in refrigeration led to the beginning of wholesale manufacture in New York State in 1851, whilst in 1856 Gail Borden patented a method of making condensed milk; this not only reduced the volume of milk by 75 per cent – milk is 86 per cent water – but sterilised the milk so that it would keep. However the output of evaporated and condensed milk in the United States was small until the beginning of this century; in 1905 however it exceeded cheese output, and in 1936 butter output, and by 1956 was greater than the output of butter and cheese combined.[21]

Comparable figures are not available for other countries, but the relative importance of cheese and butter in world trade shows the same trends (Table 35)

TABLE 35   *World exports of cheese and butter (thousand metric tons)*

	Cheese	Butter
1854–8	56	37
1884–8	150	127
1909–13	253	325
1924–8	333	459
1934–8	280	615
1952–6	396	488
1964–8	649	723
1970	960	903

Source: Stern, 1960, 61; F.A.O. *Trade yearbook*, vol. 23, 1969, 92–6; vol. 25, 1971, 93–8

for although in the 1850s there was a greater international trade in cheese than butter, largely because of the difficulty of preserving butter for long periods, world butter exports had passed those of cheese by the 1890s. Since the 1950s however butter exports, although continuing to increase, have felt the effect of competition from margarine. The trade in butter was only possible, of course, after the introduction of refrigeration on railways in the 1870s, and after 1882 in ships. This allowed countries as remote as New Zealand to market butter in London, which then, as now, was by far the most important market for butter and cheese.

The Dairying Revolution: on the farm

The great increases in both fresh milk and manufactured dairy products were a result of a series of radical changes in economics and technology. These were matched on the farms of western Europe, where not only did many farmers become specialised dairy farmers, but in North America, Australia and New Zealand they expanded into newly farmed lands.

The great increase in milk was achieved both by an increase in the number of cows and by an increase in the yield of milk per cow.

The increase in the number of cows in milk was greatest in the overseas territories where new land was still being brought into cultivation. In the United States cow numbers doubled between 1870 and 1890; in New Zealand the cows in milk quintupled between 1890 and 1925. In Europe there were few increases in the area under crops and grass, and so increases in cow numbers were less dramatic, but still striking. Thus in England and Wales the number of cows in milk doubled between the 1860s and 1940, in Holland the number of cattle doubled between 1870 and 1938, and in Denmark between 1860 and 1925.[22] But the increase in milk output was not achieved by an increase in numbers of cows alone. Thus, for example, between 1860 and 1960 cow numbers in Great Britain doubled but milk output trebled. This was a result of an increase in milk yield per cow.

Reliable data on milk yields are difficult to find, not only because milk recording only began in the late nineteenth century, even in the advanced dairying countries, but also because they are recorded by weight in some countries and by volume in others. Table 36 shows that on the eve of the First World War the highest yields were obtained in the intensively farmed countries of north-western Europe. These countries have increased their yields even further in the last half century, but not as dramatically as the increases obtained in the countries which had lower yields in 1914.

Information on average yields before 1900 is fragmentary. However in Britain the average yield in the mid-nineteenth century has been estimated at about 1800 litres. It has thus doubled in the last century. In Denmark figures are available since 1861, when the average yield per cow was 1000 kg; it had doubled by 1893 and is now nearly four times the figure for 1861. At the beginning of this century Dutch milk yields were already high – about 2720 litres per cow – but have nonetheless increased since then by 50 per cent.[23]

How were these increases in milk yields achieved? There were a variety of reasons. First, cows were fed much better. In the seventeenth and eighteenth centuries more roots and grasses were grown, and hay yields were increased. By the 1840s the better farmers were feeding oil-cake. But much of this increased forage was fed to beef cattle and the milch cows took second place. But in the later nineteenth century when milk prices rose and beef prices fell, although less than grain prices, more attention was paid to dairy cows. This was particularly true of Britain and the north-eastern United States, where demand for fresh milk was growing; demand was as great in winter as in summer. At the same time the first reliable knowledge on the value of different cattle feeds became available and cows could be fed by ration, rather than intuitively. The fall in world grain prices after 1880 meant that in western Europe not only was it profitable to feed local grain to cattle, but it was possible to import maize from Argentina and the United States. Oil-bearing plants were imported and crushed in mills at the ports, the oil-cake providing protein. Better feeding not only helped to increase output but also lengthened the period of lactation.[24]

TABLE 36   *Milk yield per cow, 1914 and 1965 (kg)*

	1914	1965
Netherlands	3400	4207
Switzerland	3130	3370
U.K.	2670	3797
Denmark	2560	3946
Germany	1970	3642
Canada	1700	2896
U.S.A.	1700	3767
Norway	1650	3240
Sweden	1630	3531
Hungary	1315	2214
Australia	1220	2264
Japan	1040	4284
Italy	990	2000
Chile	680	1700

Sources: U.S. Department of Agriculture, 1923, 321; F.A.O. *Production yearbook*, vol. 22, 1968, 395–7

But grass still provided much of the feed for livestock either from grazing in summer, when growth was rapid, or for hay, which was cut in June, cured and stored for winter feed. Hay-making was labour-consuming, the only implements available being the scythe and the pitchfork. But by the mid-nineteenth century farmers had horse-drawn hay-mowing machines, and later the tedder, which turned the cut grass in the field. In western Europe experiments in silage were under way in Germany and Hungary in the 1860s. Fermenting the grass – and maize – in pits and later in towers allowed the storage of larger quantities, made it more palatable to cattle, and increased the vitamin content. Silage methods were introduced into the United States in the 1870s and were rapidly adopted in the Corn Belt, but were not generally adopted by dairy farmers until the 1920s. In Britain it was an uncommon method until after the Second World War.[25]

The improvement of grass varieties was of major importance. English varieties were introduced into the United States in the seventeenth century, and into New Zealand in the late nineteenth century. In the latter country and also in the Netherlands, where grass provides 67 per cent of all feed compared with only 17 per cent in Great Britain, much attention has been paid to the selection of improved varieties, controlled grazing, and the application of fertiliser. In the Netherlands the application of nitrogen fertiliser quadrupled between the 1930s and the 1950s. In New Zealand the growth of white clover in the pastures ensures a high nitrogen level, but superphosphate is necessary; since 1949 much has been applied by aerial spraying.[26]

Perhaps more spectacular has been the improvement in breeds, although it is possible that the importance of this has been overestimated. The early history of cattle breeding was touched upon in Chapter 3. By the mid-eighteenth century distinctive regional breeds had emerged in western Europe, but they were still essentially multi-purpose animals; their prime function was to provide draught, second to provide beef, and their milking qualities were a poor third. In eighteenth-century England Robert Bakewell attempted to select qualities by inbreeding, and was successful with the New Leicester sheep which gave wool and mutton. He was less successful in cattle-breeding, but in the early nineteenth century the Collings brothers in North East England bred the Shorthorn from stock in Lincolnshire and Norfolk which undoubtedly had Dutch blood. But the Shorthorns were primarily beef cattle, and it was not until the 1830s that the Dairy Shorthorn was bred. The first good milker in Britain was the Ayrshire, bred near Glasgow and first exhibited in the 1820s. Before this Alderney cattle – a general name for the Guernsey and Jersey breeds of the Channel Islands – had been brought to England in the eighteenth century, but they were of little importance. On the continent the two main dairy breeds were the Brown Swiss and the Holstein. In the eighteenth century outbreaks of cattle plague had destroyed most of the cattle in the northern Netherlands, and they were replaced by cattle from Holstein, subsequently called Friesians in Britain and the Netherlands, and Holstein in the United States.[27]

In the late nineteenth century much attention was paid to the improvement of dairy cattle. Herd books were begun; milk-recording made a slow start, and gave factual evidence on yields; Stephen Babcock's butter-fat test allowed creameries to pay farmers for the butter-fat content of milk deliveries, and farmers in turn began to select for high butter-fat content. European dairy cattle were taken to the United States, Australia and New Zealand to form the basis of dairy herds. In the United States dairy cattle were still of very poor quality in 1850, although improved varieties had already been imported. In New Zealand the first dairy herds were mainly of Shorthorns. The spread of the Friesians and Jerseys was slow. In Britain, for example, Shorthorns which were essentially dual-purpose beasts, formed two-thirds of the national herd in 1908; the only specialist dairy breeds were Ayrshires, Jersey and Guernsey, which together were only 7 per cent of all cattle. Friesians were hardly known, and the British Friesian Herd Book was not started until 1909. Shorthorns were still the leading milch cows in the 1930s, but thereafter Friesians had a meteoric rise; by 1955 they were 44 per cent of all dairy cows in Britain, by 1968 64 per cent. The Friesian gives a very high yield of milk and also an acceptable beef; but it has a low butter-fat content. Thus in New Zealand, where butter was the leading dairy product, the early Shorthorns have been replaced by the Jersey, whose milk gives a very high butter-fat content although a rather lower yield. They are now 81 per cent of all cows in milk in that country. Even in Denmark, which for long relied upon the upgrading of the indigenous Danish Red, the Jerseys are now rapidly increasing in numbers.[28]

The careful breeding of cows has resulted in increases not only of yields, but also of butter-fat content; thus, for example, the butter-fat content in New Zealand rose by 20 per cent between 1930 and 1960, and in the Netherlands by 26 per cent between 1910 and 1957. Breeding has been made easier by the widespread adoption of artificial insemination, which first began in the U.S.A. in 1938, in Britain in 1942; by 1960 half the cows in New Zealand and the Netherlands were served by artificial insemination.[29]

In the mid-nineteenth century there was very little machinery used in dairy production. The making of cheese and butter required equipment – churns, pans, vats and presses – but it was mainly carried out by manual labour, although for a while dog-powered churns were used on some American dairy farms. By the beginning of this century much of the production of cheese and butter had been transferred to factories, although farm butter was still important in some western European countries on the eve of the Second World War. Since 1900 the main changes on the dairy farm have been the introduction of tractors, the improvement of hay-making machinery and the slow introduction of milking machinery. The first machine for milking cows was patented in the United States in 1862, but an efficient machine was not available until 1895 when a Scotsman, Alex Shields, patented the Thistle machine. Its adoption was remarkably slow, except in New Zealand. In 1920 in Taranaki, one of the major New Zealand dairy regions, 70 per cent of all herds were milked by machine. By contrast, in Great Britain in 1939 only 15 per cent of the herds were machine-milked, although the figure has now reached 90 per cent. Even in the United States the adoption of milking machinery was slow; in 1910 there were only 12000 milking machines in use, in 1920 55000 and in 1930 100000, but by 1950 653000. This slow rate of adoption is not difficult to explain. First, most dairy herds – especially in Europe – were small, but machines were uneconomic except with herds of twenty-five or more cows. Second, milking was carried out mainly by women and children; the opportunity cost of their labour was low. Third, the early machines were both expensive and unreliable. Thus the general adoption of milking machinery has come only since the 1940s. Since then the number of dairy farmers in most countries has stagnated or declined, whilst yields have continued to rise; the average size of herd has increased, making the use of machinery more economic. The result has been an increase in productivity; labour efficiency doubled on United States dairy farms between 1940 and 1958.[30]

Regional Variations in Dairy production

Some of the regional differences in dairy practices have already been discussed. But perhaps the most striking differences are, first, between those regions where milk mainly enters the fresh milk market – Great Britain and the north-eastern United States – and the remaining regions where the bulk is manufactured; and second, between those countries which provide mainly for their home market, with some exports, and those which export a high proportion of their dairy products (Table 37).

TABLE 37 *Dairy exports, 1965*

	Total value of butter and cheese exports (million $)	% of national output exported:	
		Butter	Cheese
Australia	91	46	49
New Zealand	290	83	86
Canada	11	–	19
U.S.A.	33	–	2
Denmark	168	66	60
Finland	28	34	51
France	110	22	12
West Germany	47	–	–
Irish Republic	30	63	82
Netherlands	141	124[a]	63

[a] including re-exported imports
Sources: Commonwealth Secretariat, 1972, 5; F.A.O. *Trade yearbook*, vol. 23, 1969, 90–5

Some of the essential facts about milk and dairy products in the United States are shown in Table 38. Milk is the most perishable of the dairy products and cannot be transported more than the distance which can be travelled by lorry or train overnight, although longer journeys may be made under special circumstances. Thus, for example, fresh milk in cartons is regularly sent from Minneapolis to Phoenix, Arizona, a distance of 1770 km.[31]

This accounted for the presence of urban dairies and the narrow zone of milk producers around the cities in the pre-railway era. However the price received by the farmer for fresh milk has generally been well above that paid by factories. Thus when the railways came, urban milksheds could expand into areas where dairy farmers could hitherto only market their milk as butter or cheese; on the other hand in areas which were remote from urban markets fresh milk could not be produced in large quantities unless it was converted into butter or cheese. These products are less perishable than fresh milk and, further, have a higher value per unit weight. With the introduction of refrigeration it became possible to send butter and cheese very considerable distances to market, provided that the product was of high quality and production costs below those in the areas near the market. In New Zealand, Australia and the western part of the United States environmental conditions were suitable for dairy farming, land was cheaper than in western Europe or the eastern United States and farms and herds thus larger and costs lower per unit of output.

TABLE 38   *Milk and milk products; some facts*

	A (metric tons)	B (%)	C (cents per kg)
Butter	39	2.5	140
Cream	82	7.5	–
Cheese	99	4.0	100
Dried milk	124	–	–
Condensed milk	372	–	–
Fresh milk	–	36–38	24

A: weight of product obtained from 1 000 000 litres of fresh milk
B: freight cost Wisconsin–New York, as a percentage of value of product, 1950
C: price per kg, U.S.A., *c.* 1955

Sources: Chisholm, 1962, 100; Higbee, 1958, 260; Alexander, 1963, 132

One might expect, then, to find dairy production zoned around major cities; near to the market would be fresh milk, then processed milk and further out cheese and finally butter production. Regional contrasts in dairying do in fact show some correspondence to this hypothetical zonation, especially in the United States, although of course other factors distort the pattern. Variations in the environment – particularly the quality of grass and the length of the growing season, in the tradition of cheese and butter-making, and the presence of other land uses all affect the location of dairy production. Furthermore in many countries marketing boards have standardised transport costs for milk deliveries, and this has not only allowed remote producers to compete but also obscured the zonation of dairy production.[32]

The United States

The traditional Dairy Region of the United States is still a distinctive area, although in the last thirty years there has been an increase in milk production in other parts of the country, particularly in California and the South. The Dairy Region has two wings; in the East, New England, New York State, south-eastern Pennsylvania and New Jersey produce almost entirely for the fresh milk markets. Westward there is an area of low dairying intensity before the western wing of Minnesota, Wisconsin, north-eastern Illinois and north-eastern Iowa is reached, which produces some fresh milk for Chicago, Milwaukee and Minneapolis, but mainly produces for butter and cheese manufacture. Most of this region has relatively cool summers and long cold winters which do not preclude crops but do give good grass yields.[33]

Butter and cheese were widely produced by colonial farmers in New England, New York State, New Jersey and south-eastern Pennsylvania, but this was subsidiary to the production of cereals and cattle. Only Rhode Island had developed any specialisation in dairying by the end of the eighteenth century. However in the first half of the nineteenth century New England began to feel the impact of imported grain from west of the Appalachians, and dairying spread from southern New England into the mountain areas, and furthermore New England farmers moved into the northern lowland areas of New York State as early as the 1800s. In both areas the specialised production of butter and cheese emerged.[34]

As settlers moved westwards in the nineteenth century they tried a variety of farming systems in the newly colonised areas. As we have seen in an earlier chapter, the corn–hog economy came to dominate much of the Mid-West by the 1880s, but north of this region summers were too short to give good yields of corn and wheat was the preferred cash crop.[35] But as new lands were opened up ever westwards, so the wheat frontier moved on. Farmers then turned to dairying – in northern New York, north-eastern Ohio, Michigan, north-eastern Illinois, Wisconsin, Iowa and Minnesota. Thus the area of milk production constantly expanded (Table 39). In 1869 New England, New York State, New Jersey and Pennsylvania – the old settled area – produced nearly 90 per cent of all

TABLE 39 *Milk sold off farms in the United States by states, 1869–1959 (per cent of United States total)*

	1869	1879	1899	1919	1939	1959
New York	57.6	43.7	20.8	22.6	13.7	8.9
Ohio	9.4	8.8	3.9	5.4	5.6	4.1
Massachusetts	6.4	5.5	3.1	2.1	1.4	0.69
Pennsylvania	6.1	6.8	8.0	9.9	7.3	7.69
Illinois	3.9	8.5	11.0	6.3	5.5	3.4
Connecticut	2.6	2.3	–	–	1.1	0.69
New Jersey	2.2	2.9	–	2.2	1.7	0.96
Vermont	1.6	–	2.6	–	2.3	1.6
California	1.5	2.3	2.6	3.0	6.7	5.8
New Hampshire	0.9	–	–	–	–	–
Wisconsin		4.7	11.8	18.7	18.6	15.5
Iowa		3.0	10.0	–	1.2	4.6
Minnesota		–	4.8	–	2.3	8.4
Michigan		–	–	5.1	5.1	4.4
Washington		–	–	2.5	2.0	1.6
Indiana		–	–		3.2	2.4
Missouri					1.8	2.5

Sources: U.S. Department of Agriculture, 1923; *U.S. Census of Agriculture*, 1959

American milk production. In the next thirty years milk production rose from 7 702 000 000 litres a year to 76 000 000 000. Output increased in every state, but the centre of production shifted westwards. At the beginning of the twentieth century the 'old settled' Dairy Region still produced over 40 per cent of American milk but the western states of Illinois, Iowa, Wisconsin, Michigan and Minnesota equalled this proportion; by 1939 the western wing produced more than the eastern as dairying penetrated north into Minnesota and west into Nebraska. Since 1939 the most striking feature of the distribution of milk production in the United States has been the growing importance of regions outside the traditional Dairy Region not only in the adjacent Corn Belt but on the west coast and in the South. One-third of the milk produced in the United States now comes from outside the traditional Dairy Region compared with one-quarter in 1919.[36]

The location of cheese and butter production has also shifted westwards. Thus for example in 1849, before the introduction of cheese factories, four-fifths of all cheese was made in New England and New York State and much of the rest in Ohio. But after 1849 the expanding milksheds of New York city, Boston and other eastern towns cut into the areas supplying milk to cheese factories and creameries; the factories could not offer prices as high as the fresh milk suppliers, and factories began to close; but further west dairy farmers lacked the urban outlets of the east coast, and their milk went to the creameries and cheese factories, whose products, after the introduction of refrigeration in 1872, could be marketed in the East. New York State reached its peak as a cheese producer in 1892; yet by the 1920s Wisconsin produced three-quarters of all American cheese, and by the 1950s cheese factories had virtually disappeared from New York State. Butter production had also moved west; in 1919 43 per cent of American butter was still made on farms throughout the United States, and indeed even within the dairy region itself farm-made butter was significant in Michigan and Ohio; but over half the factory butter was made in Minnesota, Wisconsin, Iowa, Illinois and Michigan. The Butter Belt lay west and north of the cheese production areas, and with the spread of the hand separator and the centraliser, which could convert sour cream into butter, production of cream extended well beyond the Dairy Region into the Great Plains. By the 1950s, when farm butter had virtually disappeared, the Tri-state butter region dominated American output, with nearly half the total, whilst the centraliser belt to the west produced a further 16 per cent from farms in the Dakotas, Kansas and Oklahoma. In the East both butter and cheese production has become insignificant; in Pennsylvania for example, only 5 per cent of all milk used goes for manufacturing.[37]

The history of American dairying location confirms the principles outlined at the beginning of this section. The great cities of the east coast now absorb virtually all milk production. A similar phenomenon can be seen on a smaller scale in Wisconsin, where the expansion of the Chicago milkshed has led to the decline of the once celebrated cheese region of south-eastern Wisconsin, whilst butter production has been displaced further north and west.[38]

Western Europe

In the mid-nineteenth century dairy farming was only well established in those regions where environmental conditions either favoured good grass growth or were unfavourable to cereal cultivation owing to excessive rainfall, high altitudes and steep slopes. The Netherlands and Switzerland were the most advanced of the dairying regions. In the latter country milk yields were probably twice as high as in any other part of Europe. In the Netherlands the damp polders of Friesland and southern Holland gave an excellent grass, and the Friesian cattle gave high yields. In the 1850s the Netherlands produced half the world's exports of cheese and over a third of the butter.[39]

The dairying revolution had varying effects upon the countries of western Europe. In the United Kingdom the rise of the urban population and the expansion of the railway not only encouraged dairy farming in areas where it had not been practised before, but attracted fresh milk from the traditional farmhouse cheese and butter regions of Somerset, Wiltshire, Cheshire, Lancashire and Derbyshire. Fresh milk was one of the few commodities in which the British farmer had complete protection – by distance – in the depression years of the 1880s and 1890s; and not only did cattle numbers increase in the late nineteenth century, but the numbers of cows in milk increased faster than beef cattle. But there was little development of either cheese or butter production; for example, Derbyshire cheese declined as milk was diverted to the fresh market. By the 1870s 40 per cent of all milk was going to the fresh market, 40 per cent for cheese and 20 per cent for butter; but by the 1930s three-quarters of all milk was going to the fresh market. After the reorganisation of milk marketing in 1933 the cost of transport to market was standardised, and all producers were paid a 'pool' price, which varied according to the surplus produced above urban demand. One consequence of this has been the expansion of fresh milk production into areas once too remote, a process accelerated by the motor lorry.[40]

In western Europe milk production for the urban market increased near the great cities, but much of the expanded milk output went into cheese and butter production. However, perhaps of most interest have been the differing ways in which farmers produced more milk. In the traditional dairying nations of the Netherlands and Switzerland much of the land was already under grass, and there was little decline in crops. Traditional dairying practices were intensified. In Denmark there was a different sequence of events.

A feudal society had survived in Denmark until the end of the eighteenth century; bondage was not abolished until 1788. Thereafter enclosure acts destroyed the traditional village, leading to a dispersion of settlements on the newly consolidated farms.[41] The small farmer was protected and laws were passed to prevent subdivision and fragmentation. In the first half of the nineteenth century there was a considerable expansion of the cultivated area, particularly in the heaths of western Jutland; grain, live cattle and pigs were exported. On those larger estates which had survived butter production was important; indeed in the

207

Dairying

1850s Denmark was second only to the Netherlands as a butter exporter. Thus, as was noticed earlier, Denmark was shifting towards livestock production long before the agricultural depression of the 1880s. But with falling grain prices the Danes turned even more to livestock production and, in particular, dairying. But this was not achieved by laying down land to grass. Rather the Danish farmers increased the cultivated area; they drained their heavier clays and limed the heath lands. Cereal areas increased and, more dramatically, the area under roots expanded. These crops were fed to an increasing number of cattle and pigs, whilst concentrates were imported. Grazing and hay played a relatively small role in the economy and cows were stall-fed for much of the year. Butter was the main product, and skimmed milk was fed to pigs, which initially were sent to Germany but after 1887 were bred for the British bacon market.[42]

But perhaps the most distinctive features of the Danish rural economy in the late nineteenth century were the comparatively large farms and the careful organisation. The first credit co-operative had been formed in 1851; but in 1882 co-operative dairies were established; the factories which produced butter, cheese and later bacon were thus owned by the farmers who supplied the raw materials. Indeed progress in dairying in north-western Europe was highly correlated with the degree of co-operation; it dominated farming in Scandinavia and the Netherlands, but was slow to get under way in Belgium, France and, curiously, Britain, where it had first begun.

Danish dairying and bacon production expanded until the late 1920s, when Denmark provided 29 per cent of world butter exports and a third of the pork, bacon and ham exports. Britain and Germany provided the major markets, and Danish agriculture suffered from the protectionism of the 1930s. Since the Second World War Danish agriculture has changed yet again. In spite of the continued prohibition of amalgamation and subdivision of holdings, the average size of farm has increased, the farm population has declined and mechanisation has progressed. Further, the root area has declined and barley has become the major feed for cattle. The number of dairy cows has declined since the 1930s but output has risen because of the increase in yields.[43]

New Zealand

Both the Netherlands and Denmark were well placed for the major markets of western Europe, Britain and Germany. In 1880 Australia and New Zealand could hardly have been more remote, and their only important exports were wheat and wool. But in 1882 frozen meat was successfully shipped to Britain, which led not only to the development of beef and mutton exports, but also to the first shipments of dairy produce in the 1890s. In 1880 South Island still had the greater proportion of New Zealand's population and was economically more important, but henceforth it was North Island that took the lead, although the first dairying took place in South Island. New Zealand was able to compete in distant markets for a number of reasons. First, grass growth continued all the year round, although the rate of growth was reduced in winter; thus the cost of overall production and particularly winter production was low. Second, the summer flush came in the northern hemisphere's winter, a fact more important in the nineteenth century than at present. Third, the mild winters made expensive housing unnecessary. Fourth, the major dairying regions – Taranaki, Hauraki, the Waikato and the Bay of Plenty – were still largely under their natural vegetation; improvements in the brush-burn techniques of clearing the woodland allowed their rapid settlement between 1880 and 1920, whilst Acts of 1892 and 1894 subdivided large estates and made close settlement possible. Farms and thus herds were substantially larger than in western Europe, whilst the land was cheap. But as in Denmark it was the organisation of marketing which gave New Zealand a competitive edge. Co-operative dairying got under way in the early 1880s and by 1893 there were over 200 factories on North Island. New Zealand also gained from the experience of Wisconsin's factories. By the 1920s cheese and butter factories were significantly larger than those in Denmark or the Netherlands, and New Zealand has remained in the forefront of dairy technology both in the factories and on the farm. The country has relied heavily on the British market and continues to do so, although in the late 1960s 30 per cent of dairy exports had found markets elsewhere.[44]

CHAPTER 11

PLANTATIONS

The major industrial centres of the world lie in cool temperate areas. On the other hand a number of valuable crops can only be grown in the tropics – such as cacao, bananas, coconuts, jute, sisal, hemp, rubber, coffee, oil-palm – or the sub-tropics – such as sugar-cane, cotton, tea, groundnuts and tobacco. All these crops had been cultivated by the inhabitants of the tropics long before the arrival of Europeans, and indeed spices had reached Europe from the Moluccas and Malabar at least as early as Roman times. However the expansion of European settlement and trade led to the production of these crops specifically for export to Europe. In the Americas, where, away from the Indian cultures in Mexico and Peru, there were very low population densities, the early settlers established the plantation system, based upon an abundance of land and imported slave labour, to produce high-value goods such as sugar and tobacco for sale in western Europe. Africa, however, was bypassed; its lack of good harbours, the prevalence of disease, and later the overwhelming importance of the slave trade, meant that there were few attempts to produce export crops until the late eighteenth century. In Asia the Portuguese and Dutch, the most active of the early explorers, were more interested in trade than settlement. They found dense populations and more advanced civilisations than there were in the Americas or Africa. Thus at first they were content to buy agricultural products, such as spices in the East Indies or tea in China, from the indigenous producers. It was not until the nineteenth century that Europeans took an active part in the production of these crops.

Thus from the very beginnings of the cultivation of tropical crops for export there were two types of producer: the European-owned, financed and managed plantation, at first characteristic of the Americas; and the small subsistence farms which only secondarily produced cash crops for sale. The plantation however was pre-eminent until the middle of the nineteenth century, when the abolition of slavery led to the collapse of many of the classic cotton, coffee and sugar-cane plantations. Many plantations were subdivided into tenancies; these farmers often continued to produce plantation crops. In South East Asia the cultivation of rubber spread rapidly amongst smallholders in the early twentieth century, in emulation of the plantations. In Malaya in particular many smallholders grew only a cash crop, rather than a cash crop with food production. In West Africa peasants dominated the production of export crops from the beginning, and the plantation was – and still is – of lesser importance.

Because so much of tropical cash crop production is by smallholders, the idea of the plantation as a major type of farming is no longer satisfactory. Most modern writers prefer to deal instead with the production of plantation crops, and emphasise the contrasts between plantations and smallholders. Such a 'type' is far from satisfactory on most of the criteria of agricultural classification; on the other hand, because of the connections between the two in the past, they are conveniently dealt with together in a study in historical geography.

Plantation crops

Because so many of the crops grown in the tropics for export are produced by smallholders, data on area and output are far from complete. Table 40 is an attempt to indicate their relative importance.

Tropical export crops occupy at the most 95 million hectares, about 10 per cent of the world's cropland. But of this figure, much of the cotton is grown outside the tropics, whilst substantial proportions of the area under tea, groundnuts and tobacco are grown on peasant farms for local consumption. Thus the areas devoted to specialised production for export are small and difficult to locate on a world map. Nonetheless in the 1960s the annual value of the exports of these crops exceeded $12 000 000 000, nearly twice the value of the exports of all cereals. Furthermore the value of these crops is often a very high proportion of all export income in many tropical countries.

The classic plantation crops are tree crops – rubber, coconuts, oil-palm, sisal, cacao and coffee.[1] All are confined to the tropics; more significant, there is a period of some years between planting and the first yield. Thereafter there is another period before the crop reaches its maximum yield, and then a further period when yields decline; thus the life of a tree may be up to 100 years in the case of coconuts, or little more than seven years in the case of sisal. The economic implications are several. First, the crop will be grown either as a secondary crop on a food farm, or by a large corporation which can afford to wait out the period between planting and production. Second, the decisions to make extra plantings are taken five to ten years before the crops begin to bear, thus accounting for the violent fluctuations in supply. Third, the decision to replace ageing stock is of considerable importance.

To this group of crops may be added bananas and tea. Bananas are largely a product of the humid tropics; however the plant is a herbaceous and not a woody perennial. After the fruit has been harvested the growth above ground is cut off; the root systems resprout and grow without further planting, so that the crop can be regarded economically as a perennial. Tea, which gives almost continuous production of leaves for many years, is *not* exclusively a tropical crop, being grown in areas with cold winters.

Cotton, jute, tobacco and groundnuts are all annuals, and thus supply can be adjusted more easily to demand. Of these only jute is exclusively tropical. These crops do however require considerable labour at limited times of the year, and

TABLE 40 *Plantation crops, 1964–9*

	Area (million hectares)	Value of exports (million $)	Americas a	Americas b	Asia a	Asia b	Africa a	Africa b	Oceania a	Oceania b
Cotton	31	2300	35	42	37	14	9	25	–	–
Groundnuts	18	402	15	–	53	9	30	82	–	–
Sugar-cane	10	2090	50	50	39	17	7	8	4	7
Rubber	6	1250	1	–	90	89	7	5	–	–
Coffee	6	2280	66	69	6	5	27	25	–	–
Cocoa	5	536	24	19	–	–	72	79	–	–
Tobacco	4	1070	31	62	46	16	5	10	–	–
Jute	2.9	170	–	–	96	94	–	–	–	–
Bananas	1.6	433	61	76	25	11	5	9	–	1
Tea	1.2	666	–	–	87	81	7	10	–	1
Coconuts	–	406	8	3	77	83	5	1	6	1
Palm-oil	–	246	–	–	25	–	69	–	–	–
Sisal and other agaves	1.2	120	48	–	3	54	49	39	–	–

a: % of weight of output
b: % of value of exports

Sources: F.A.O. *Production yearbook*, vol. 23, 1969; *Trade yearbook*, vol. 23, 1969; Commonwealth Economic Committee, *Plantation crops: a review*, 1970

thus have problems which tea and rubber, whose labour requirements can be spread out through the year, do not have. The last crop to notice is sugar-cane, which, like the banana, is a herbaceous perennial; after the cane is harvested, the growth is cut to ground level, and a 'ratoon' crop resprouts the following year without any replanting. However yields fall off with each succeeding ratoon, and replanting becomes necessary after two or three years.

The concept of a plantation

The plantation has been an important institution in the production of tropical crops for 500 years; its characteristics have obviously changed over such a long period. Furthermore the plantation has attracted the attention of historians and sociologists, as well as geographers, because of its great importance in the history of the Americas. There is thus considerable disagreement on its characteristic features.[2]

Plantations specialise in the production of one or possibly two crops which are tropical or sub-tropical. Parts of the plantation may be used for growing food crops for the resident labour force. Livestock are not kept, except as draught animals. Plantations are generally large and are found mainly in thinly populated areas.[3] The size varies; the Harbel plantation of the Firestone Company in Liberia covers 56 560 hectares; but in Malaya there are many rubber estates of only 40 hectares.[4] Part of the variation is because the optimum size for production varies from crop to crop. But in spite of the large area, a large, disciplined but not skilled labour force is necessary. Because plantations have usually been established in sparsely populated areas labour often has to be imported and provided with housing, food, and educational and medical facilities. In the past, slavery was the solution to the problem, and later indentured labourers – particularly Indians – went to sugar plantations in various parts of the British Empire. Indians also provided much of the labour in the Malayan rubber plantations and the Assam and Ceylon tea plantations.

The technical and managerial staff have invariably been European, although in many ex-colonial plantations they have now been replaced by local people. European managerial staff have been necessary in the past, for although the labour force has been large and much of the cultivation unmechanised, the standards of farming have been good and new methods rapidly adopted. Thus in spite of the predominance of manual labour, yields per hectare and also returns per hectare are high, particularly in the case of bananas and sugar-cane. Labour costs are high, generally at least half and sometimes four-fifths of total production costs.[5] Whilst in the past the cheap labour of the tropics was undoubtedly an important location factor, social legislation, the growth of trade unions and higher wages have partly eroded this advantage.[6] Most of the production of plantations is exported to either Europe or North America, and most of the capital for the establishment of the plantation is derived from these areas. The early plantations in the Americas were generally family-owned, but in the nineteenth

213

century the joint-stock company slowly replaced the family unit. At the turn of the century the scale of operations in rubber and banana plantations and the very substantial investment necessary in land clearance, planting and processing, housing and building harbours and railways, led to the rise of the corporate plantation. Many plantations have been expropriated by newly independent countries in Africa and Asia since 1945. Nonetheless new plantations in the tropics are still generally financed from the United States or Europe, although companies are now often established in collaboration with the local government.

Many – indeed nearly all – plantation crops have to be processed before leaving the plantation, and furthermore processed rapidly after harvesting. There are a number of reasons for this. First, the yield of many crops declines quickly after harvesting; second, processing gives a product of higher value per unit weight that can be transported over long distances; third, many products are perishable in their unprocessed form, but not after processing. The need for processing has thus been recognised as a characteristic feature of plantation production, although the degree of processing varies from crop to crop. The more complex the process, the more likely the crop is to be produced on plantations rather than on smallholdings.[7]

This relationship between factory and farm helps to explain some other characteristics of the plantation economy. One aim is to utilise fully the capacity of the factory throughout the year; this means that the area planted must be large, or alternatively the company must control a large area of the crop, grown either by contracted smallholders or by tenant farmers working company-owned land. The ideal crop for the processing unit is one where harvesting is continuous, such as rubber tapping, or plucking tea leaves; or where the climatic conditions are such that a number of harvests can be obtained within a year. This not only fully employs the factory's capacity, but smooths out labour requirements on the land.

Thus annual crops are less suited to the plantation system than perennial tree crops, since the latter need far less cultivation – for after planting they yield for many years – and do not have marked seasonal labour peaks. It is no coincidence that whilst tobacco, cotton and sugar-cane were the earliest plantation crops grown in the Americas, all were cultivated as annuals, and are now grown mainly by smallholders. The exception to this is sugar-cane, which is still grown on plantations in those areas where there is no risk of frost and a reliable supply of water; then the cane can be ratooned for up to eight years and planting phased to give more continuous harvesting. In the last hundred years the plantation system has retreated from the sub-tropics, and been applied increasingly to tropical tree crops, leaving the production of sub-tropical annuals in the hands of smallholders.[8]

Many writers regard the plantation as an institution rather than a specific type of farming. Thus Thompson has seen the plantation as essentially a frontier institution rather than a specifically tropical type of farming.[9] More recently Gregor has argued that the organisational characteristics of plantations are possessed by many large farms in temperate areas, although Courtenay has pointed out that large-scale corporate production in temperate areas is concerned with annual crops with marked seasonal peaks of labour needs, and are generally mechanised with a relatively small labour force.[10] Perhaps equally pertinent is that many of the definitions of the plantation are based in one area or one period; the classic American plantation is very different from those established in the Far East in the late nineteenth century. Since the early twentieth century the plantation has given ground to the peasant producer.

The Smallholder

The heyday of the New Plantation System – the modern corporate plantation – was at the turn of this century. But since then smallholders have grown an increasing proportion of tropical exports. The advantages of the smallholder were particularly marked in the depression years of the 1920s and 1930s. Large plantations were vulnerable to low prices. They had high fixed costs and could not easily switch to the production of other crops. The smallholder, in contrast, grew cash crops as a subsidiary to food production, and had no large labour force to support.[11]

Arguments about the relative merits of plantation and smallholder production have continued to the present day, without being resolved satisfactorily. Smallholders rarely attain the high standards of farming found in plantations, the quality of their products often leaves much to be desired, and they are slow to adopt new methods. They are at a particular disadvantage where the crop must be processed soon after picking or where very large amounts of produce must be processed. Yet even tea and sisal, which have these characteristics, are produced by smallholders. The disadvantages of the smallholder can however be overcome to some extent by group farming or by co-operatives.[12]

The relative decline of the plantation has not however been solely due to economic reasons. Since 1945 plantations have been subject to harassment in newly independent countries. In some cases they have merely changed ownership, but elsewhere they have been subdivided into smallholdings. The present political climate makes the return of the plantation to pre-eminence unlikely.

The term smallholder covers a multitude of types of farmer. Many smallholders are subsistence farmers who produce a cash crop only incidentally. But in parts of Malaya smallholders grow only rubber and in Ghana only cacao.

The origin of smallholders is worthy of note. In the Americas most smallholders arose only after the end of slavery, where they took land on the subdivided plantations, or fled to seek new land in unoccupied areas. In contrast the smallholders of Asia pre-date the plantation, as they do in Africa, although in parts of East Africa former European-owned estates have been broken up into small farms since independence.[13]

Plantations in the Americas

The plantation system had its beginnings in the islands off the African coast in the fifteenth century, and from there may be traced back to the Mediterranean and even Persia, where the first sugar mills were established. But it was in the Americas that it came to maturity.[14] Until the middle of the nineteenth century the Americas dominated the trade in tropical crops. Africa produced little other than palm-oil; Asia, admittedly, was more significant but only Java and Ceylon had any importance in trade, particularly in coffee. Since that time plantations and smallholders in Asia, Africa and Oceania have taken more and more of the world trade in tropical products. But 40 per cent of the world's exports of tropical produce still originates in the Americas, compared with 27 per cent from Asia and 16 per cent from tropical Africa.

It is impossible to deal fully with the history of the plantation in the Americas; but some general tendencies can be recognised. First has been the change in organisation; until the 1830s the plantation dominated the production of export crops and the smallholder had very little significance. The American plantation which developed between 1500 and 1850 was not exceptionally large. In the United States in 1860 the average size of farm in the cotton-growing states was 161 hectares. Of the 470 000 farms in the South only 15 000 were more than 200 hectares.[15] In Barbados in the late seventeenth century the *largest* estate on the island was 368 hectares, whilst in Jamaica in the late eighteenth century, the heyday of the sugar plantations of the Antilles, the *average* size was about 360 hectares.[16] The sugar plantations of north-eastern Brazil were rather smaller than this. The eighteenth-century tobacco plantations of the Chesapeake Bay area were between 80 and 200 hectares.[17] Most of these plantations were owned by families, who were often absentee; indeed many of the West Indian estates were owned by people who lived in France or England, where they formed powerful political lobbies to continue the military and financial protection of the sugar isles. The estate was run by an overseer, and attorneys dealt with the financial affairs of several estates.[18]

The distinguishing feature of the classic plantation was the use of slaves. True, the early crops of tobacco and sugar-cane in Virginia and Barbados were produced by indentured white labour, but the smallholder was soon displaced by the plantation. The first African slaves were taken to Hispaniola from Spain in 1501; in 1518 the first *asiento* was granted.[19] The slave trade was declared illegal by Great Britain in 1807, but it continued until the 1870s. Between 1500 and 1870 about 10 000 000 Africans were taken to the Americas, of whom 6 000 000 were transhipped between 1701 and 1810. Nearly 40 per cent were taken to Brazil and 50 per cent to the Caribbean.[20] Only one-twentieth went to the United States, one of the few places where slave numbers grew by natural increase; elsewhere the death rate exceeded the birth rate, and the plantations had to import their labour continuously.[21]

Labour demands upon the plantations were heavy; not only did tobacco, sugar-cane and cotton, the major plantation crops before 1850, require sowing, weeding and harvesting, but the primitive sugar mills and cotton gins required an inordinate amount of manual labour. Most of the field cultivation was undertaken with the hoe and *machete;* the plough and draught animals were uncommon even in the United States until the mid-nineteenth century, and the use of manure was rare.

Plantations for the most part concentrated on the production of one crop; but by no means the whole area would be under the cash crop. Plantations were generally in thinly populated areas, where there had previously been little cultivation; the natural vegetation therefore remained; indeed in the tobacco and cotton plantations of the United States woodland and crop were often rotated, soil fertility being restored by a sort of long bush-fallow.[22] Further, some part of the plantation had to be devoted to growing food for the slaves. In the American South many plantations were equally divided between woodland, cotton and corn.[23] In the Brazilian sugar plantations exhausted cane-land was allowed to rest under a forest fallow. Cane was grown by *lavradores,* share-cropping tenants, who each had six hectares of cane and about twenty slaves, whilst *moradores,* free tenants, worked as labourers and also grew food. The *señor de engenho* owned the mill and the land.[24] The West Indian sugar plantations were also characteristically divided between woodland, cane and 'provisions' land, on which the slaves were allowed to grow food crops in their rare moments of spare time. Nonetheless the British West Indies could not provide enough food and relied upon imports from the North American colonies – fish from New England, corn and beans from the mid-Atlantic states.[25]

The abolition of slavery had varied consequences for the American plantations. In the United States some plantations were subdivided and sold to smallholders. More commonly the plantations were worked by share-croppers, who were provided with mules, implements, seeds and fertiliser, and directed by the plantation owner. Share-tenants provided more of the factors of production, and received a half rather than a third of the crop. A typical cropper had ten to twenty-five hectares, of which six to eight hectares would be under cotton, the most a family could pick. Four to eight hectares would be under corn. By 1913 31 per cent of the farmers in the South were black tenant farmers, 30 per cent white tenants, 7 per cent black owners and 32 per cent white owners. The average size of the production unit in the South thus declined from 1860 to 1913. But since then migration from the land, particularly of blacks, has led to an increase in the average size of farm, a decline in the number of tenants, and a great decline of black labour. In 1859 90 per cent of the labour force were slaves; in 1964 only 15 per cent of the farmers in the South were black. Mechanisation has led to the reappearance of large plantation-like farms, but nevertheless two-thirds of all cotton producers still have less than six hectares under the crop.[26]

In Brazil the abolition of slavery in 1886 also changed the organisation of production. The coffee plantations in the Paraiba valley used slaves, but after 1886 the main coffee areas were to the west in São Paulo. Between 1886 and

Plantations

1936 there were 2 800 000 migrants into São Paulo State, mainly from Spain and Italy, and the coffee *fazenda* took on its modern form. *Coloños,* often recent immigrants, were hired for a year to cultivate a number of coffee trees for a wage and sometimes were allowed to grow maize and beans on a separate plot. On the frontier the *coloño* cleared the forest and planted coffee trees with food crops between the rows; after five years, when the first berries appeared, they moved on to another *fazenda*. But as the coffee frontier moved west into Parana the *fazenda* and the *coloño* gave way to the *sitio* or small landowner.[27]

The effect of the abolition of slavery on the sugar plantations was complicated by two other parallel changes, the rise of the large steam-powered *centralo,* and the long-term decline in sugar prices, due to competition from both cane-sugar in the East Indies and beet-sugar in Europe. In 1814 sugar stood at 97 shillings a quarter, in 1831 23 shillings. There was yet a further decline from 30 shillings a quarter in 1872 to 5 shillings in the 1930s.

In the larger islands of the West Indies many of the freed slaves established themselves as smallholders on vacant land, whilst some estates were subdivided. But in the more densely populated islands such as the Barbados the freed slaves had little alternative but to remain on the plantations as wage-labourers. However in Trinidad and British Guiana, which had only recently become part of the British Empire, most freed slaves established themselves as smallholders. The estates turned to India for labour. Over 370 000 Indians came to the two territories between 1838 and 1917.

Since the mid-nineteenth century the plantation with its own sugar mill has been progressively replaced by the large *centralo* which gets its cane either from smallholders under contract, or from tenants on company land. This tendency was particularly marked in Cuba. Although steam was introduced into the mills in 1817, and the first *centralo* established in 1831, the structure of the industry was based on family-owned plantations and mills until the 1880s. Then slavery was abolished and narrow-gauge rails were introduced, which allowed much larger mills to be operated; the family plantation disappeared. In 1877 there were 1190 sugar mills, in 1899 207. American investment in the island after 1899 led to an even further reduction in the number of mills, to 185 in 1927. To ensure a steady supply of cane the mills bought out the small family plantations, which had relied on free labour after 1886; cane was either supplied by share-cropping tenants – *coloños* – or was worked by labourers. A similar sequence occurred in Puerto Rico, where the *centralo* replaced the small mill and the corporation the family plantation. Many small planters were forced to become *coloños*. Thus whilst sugar-*cane* is now increasingly a product of the smallholder in the Americas, sugar is a product of the large mill.[28]

At a time when the plantation was being replaced by the smallholder throughout the Americas, the production of bananas followed an opposite course. The first bananas exported were produced by smallholders in Jamaica, but by the 1890s the major producers were massive plantations, often worked with imported West Indian labour, on the Caribbean coast of Central America,

218

and later on the Pacific coast. Bananas have to be moved very rapidly after harvest, as they perish unless kept at low temperatures; furthermore, to maintain a flow of produce throughout the year, planting and harvesting have to be staggered. Thus the plantation, and in particular the large corporate plantation, was the ideal organisation for handling the crop. Indeed smallholders were of little importance until after the Second World War. Since 1947 banana production by smallholders in Ecuador has had a phenomenal increase, providing a quarter of world exports in the 1960s. At the same time American companies such as the United Fruit Company have withdrawn from some of their plantations, mainly because of the political problems involved in maintaining them, and now purchase fruit from smallholders, a policy they have pursued in Jamaica since the 1930s. The banana in the Antilles has always been primarily a smallholder's crop.[29]

Thus throughout the Americas the smallholder has gained in importance since the mid-nineteenth century. One other important characteristic of the American plantation must be discussed, the constant migration of production. This may be interpreted at three levels. First, as was noticed before, many planters used to rotate woodland and crop in a form of shifting cultivation within the plantation. This has become less common as land has become scarce and more intensive methods have been adopted. Second, in the United States and Brazil plantations have moved progressively westward in the last 150 years, taking up new land as the frontier has moved on. Thirdly, the location of the leading producers of bananas and sugar-cane has changed over time, reflecting a variety of circumstances, including the availability of land, prices and the presence of disease. The major plantation areas will now be examined.

Cotton in the United States

In the late eighteenth century cotton growing was comparatively unimportant. Europe, the main market for textiles, obtained its raw cotton from the eastern Mediterranean and its high-quality textiles from India. However the demands of the Lancashire textile industry prompted the expansion of cotton growing in north-eastern Brazil and later the West Indies, which in 1790 provided 90 per cent of Britain's imports.[30] Although cotton was grown on the south-eastern seaboard of the United States, it was not of great importance until a number of circumstances led to a striking expansion. First was the growth of Lancashire's demands. In the 1770s only 7 000 000 bales were imported annually, but by 1792 26 000 000 and in 1800 56 000 000. Second was Eli Whitney's invention of an improved cotton gin in 1793; with this, one man could gin 22 kg of cotton a day, compared with 0.45 kg a day with earlier gins. Third was the introduction of new varieties of cotton. The indigenous cottons, George Green Seed and Creole Black Seed, had seeds which were difficult to separate from the lint. Two new varieties were introduced. Sea Island was introduced to the islands off the Georgia coast in 1786, and was the major export until 1792. More significantly

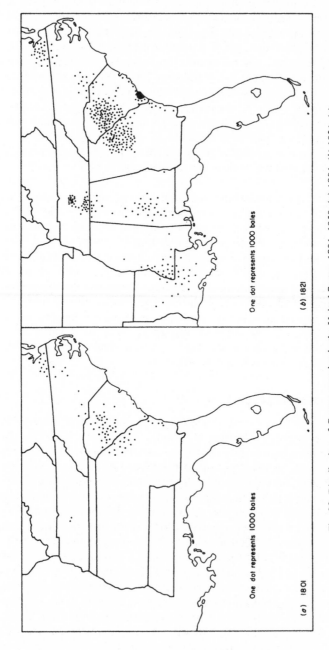

One dot represents 1000 bales

(b) 1821

One dot represents 1000 bales

(a) 1801

Fig. 22. Distribution of Cotton growing in the United States, 1801–1959. (a) 1801, (b) 1821, (c) 1859, (d) 1919, (e) 1959. [Sources: Gray, 1933, 684: U.S. Department of Agriculture, 1922, 331, 333; U.S. Census of Agriculture 1955, vol. 2, 657]

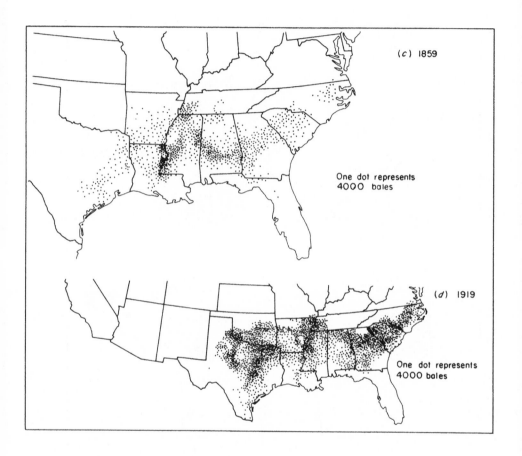

(c) 1859

One dot represents
4000 bales

(d) 1919

One dot represents
4000 bales

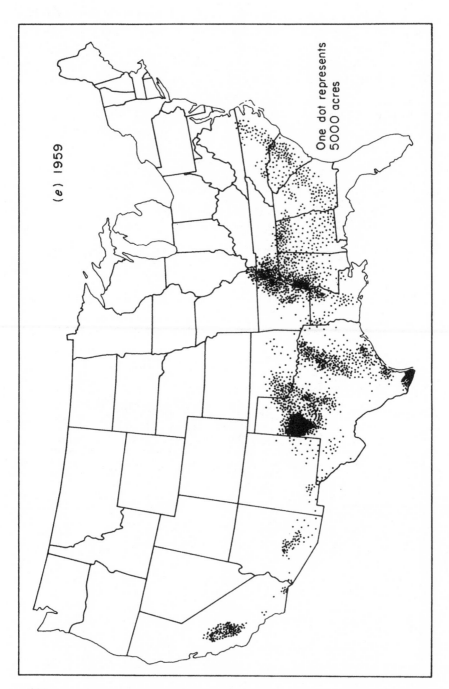

(e) 1959

One dot represents
5000 acres

Mexican varieties were crossed with local varieties; the hybrid could be picked more easily, had a longer staple and was less susceptible to disease.[31]

Cotton growing was first established in Georgia and South Carolina, when in the 1790s the sparsely populated piedmont was occupied by planters with their slaves.

The earliest expansion was north into North Carolina and Virginia, but after 1815 it was westwards into the Mississippi valley. In the first period of expansion planters practised a crude system of farming, and often moved on after soils had been exhausted. By mid-century the plough was becoming widely adopted, the drill was in use, and manure was being used.[32] The Old South, with its exhausted soils, was compelled to turn to the use of artificial fertilisers as the frontier swept even further westwards. In 1919 Georgia, South Carolina and North Carolina spent $147 000 000 on fertilisers, the other cotton-growing states less than a fifth of this sum.[33]

The westward move of production can be seen in Table 41 and Fig. 22. In the 1820s the Carolinas and Georgia were the major producers; on the eve of the Civil War the lower Mississippi valley. By the end of the century Texas was the leading producer. In the 1920s when the peak area was reached, more than half the output came from west of the Mississippi and production under irrigation was beginning in Arizona, New Mexico and California.

The changes in land tenure after 1862 have already been noted. The abolition of slavery did not halt the expansion of the area. In 1839 there were 1 800 000 hectares under cotton, in 1859 5 200 000, in 1890 8 500 000, and by 1910 12 750 000.[34]

The peak was reached in 1930, but major changes had set in before then. The boll weevil first appeared in Texas in 1894 and soon reached most parts of the Cotton Belt; it caused farmers to reduce their cotton area and turn to other crops; the low prices of the 1930s further caused a decline in cotton, whilst attempts to reduce widespread soil erosion prompted the U.S. government to subsidise the growing of legumes and the adoption of conservation methods. Farmers now grow sorghum, peanuts and soy beans as well as corn and cotton, and there has been a remarkable increase in pasture and beef. The area under cotton has declined greatly – from 17 000 000 hectares in 1930 to 4 050 000 hectares in 1968. The Cotton Belt has contracted to a number of small regions. Cotton production however has not contracted sharply, owing to the doubling of yields since 1940, whilst the decline of the labour force has led to growing mechanisation.[35]

The quite remarkable expansion of the cotton industry in the first half of the nineteenth century was the result of a number of circumstances. The trade links with Britain were undoubtedly significant, as was the availability of cheap land, and the fact that the plantation system was already in existence, for it had been perfected in the Old South for the growth of tobacco, rice and indigo. By 1820 the United States was the leading producer, and by 1860 all other producers save India were dwarfed by its output (Table 42). In the late nineteenth century the

TABLE 41 Production of cotton by states, 1839–1964 (% of U.S. total)

	1839	1859	1879	1899	1919	1954	1964
North Carolina	6.5	2.7	6.8	4.6	7.5	2.8	2.5
South Carolina	6.8	5.5	9.1	8.9	12.5	3.7	3.7
Georgia	20.4	13.0	14.1	13.5	14.8	4.5	4.2
Alabama	14.8	18.4	12.2	11.5	6.3	5.4	5.7
Mississippi	24.4	22.4	16.7	13.7	8.5	11.5	14.5
Louisiana	19.3	14.5	8.7	7.4	2.6	4.2	3.8
Arkansas	0.8	6.6	10.5	7.4	7.6	10.0	10.2
Tennessee	3.5	5.5	5.7	2.4	2.6	3.6	4.5
Missouri	–	0.7	0.3	–	0.5	3.1	2.6
Texas	–	8.0	13.7	27.5	26.2	27.4	26.5
Oklahoma	–	–	–	0.7	8.9	2.1	1.8
Arizona	–	–	–	–	0.5	6.6	5.6
California	–	–	–	–	0.4	11.3	11.4
New Mexico	–	–	–	–	–	2.3	1.7
Other	3.5	2.7	2.2	2.4	1.1	1.5	1.3
	100	100	100	100	100	100	100
East of Mississippi	80	70	66	57	54	32	35
West of Mississippi	20	30	34	43	46	68	65
of which irrigated states	–	–	–	–	0.9	20.2	18.7

Sources: U.S. Department of Agriculture, 1922, 331–3; U.S. Census of Agriculture, 1964, vol. 2, 422; U.S. Census of Agriculture, 1959, vol. 2, 828

TABLE 42 Cotton production, 1791–1860 (million kg)

	1791	1801	1811	1821	1831	1840	1850	1860
Brazil	9.98	11.79	15.88	14.51	17.24	13.61	18.14	16.33
West Indies	5.44	4.54	5.44	4.54	4.08	3.63	1.36	2.72
Egypt	–	–	0.45	2.72	8.16	11.34	13.61	15.42
Rest of Africa	20.41	20.87	19.9	18.44	16.33	15.42	15.42	15.88
India	58.97	72.58	77.12	79.39	81.56	83.83	95.2	204.1
Rest of Asia	86.18	82.58	86.23	61.2	52.16	49.9	54.5	60.8
Mexico and South America	30.84	25.40	25.85	19.96	15.88	15.88	18.14	28.85
Other	–	6.8	4.99	3.63	1.81	5.9	6.80	45.36
U.S.A.	0.91	21.77	36.29	81.65	173.2	294.9	449.1	726.0

Source: Bruchey, 1967, 7

225

South provided three-quarters of world exports, but since other producers became established in the Civil War, its importance has declined, although a third of all exports still come from the United States.

Coffee in Brazil

Coffee was introduced into the Americas in the early eighteenth century, but production was limited to plantations in the Antilles until the end of the century. In 1774 it was being grown near Rio de Janeiro. Thereafter the industry displayed a remarkable expansion west across southern Brazil; its progress was in fact very similar to that of cotton in the United States, and it is only in these two countries that plantation crops have extended so far into the interior of the continent. In the late eighteenth century St Domingue was the leading American producer of coffee but the revolution in 1799 left a gap in the European market. Coffee was grown at first on slave-worked estates in Brazil in the humid areas inland from both Santos and Rio de Janeiro, where, however, there was no dry season. Suitable climatic conditions were met with in the Paraiba valley, where the slave-run *fazenda* dominated coffee output in Brazil until the 1880s. However farming methods were poor; woodland was cleared, coffee planted, and the *fazenda* moved on after the soil was exhausted.[36]

The first coffee to be grown in the interior of São Paulo in the 1830s was near Campinas. By the 1850s the coffee frontier was pushing towards Ribeirão Prêto. By 1883 São Paulo's output exceeded that of the Paraiba valley, which declined. The great expansion after 1895 was north towards the Rio Grande and west towards the Rio Parana; in these areas the *coloño* replaced the slave (see above, p. 218).

The rapid expansion of the coffee belt was greatly expedited by the building of railways, largely British-financed, particularly after 1880. Coffee output doubled between 1895 and 1910, and the first problems of overproduction were met by the prohibition of further planting; in 1906 valorisation was introduced. But neither this nor the catastrophic fall of prices in 1929–31 could halt the continued expansion of the coffee frontier, although it did prompt diversification; in the post-Second World War coffee shortage the State of Parana became the new frontier, and by the early 1960s Parana was producing half Brazil's coffee, and São Paulo only a third.[37]

As the coffee frontier moved westwards, so the type of organisation changed. In the Paraiba valley the slave-run plantation was the typical production unit, in São Paulo the *fazenda*, operated by *coloños*, whilst in Parana the *sitio*, the small landowner, is the predominant type. The frontier regions have always had the advantage of virgin soils and lower costs, so that the bypassed regions have been compelled both to intensify their production and to diversify. The Paraiba valley was the first area to adopt modern farming methods; it now grows little coffee but produces dairy products, fruits and vegetables for the Rio market. Further west in São Paulo coffee is still important, but occupies a small part of the cultivated land. Pasture for beef, cotton and sugar-cane, together with maize and beans, are the major crops. Only in the frontier regions of Parana is coffee still a monoculture, although most *sitios* also grow rice, beans and maize between the rows of coffee trees,[38]

Sugar-cane in the Americas

Sugar-cane does not have a frontier history like that of coffee or cotton. In contrast with them, the early areas of production remain producers today. But for a variety of reasons supremacy has passed from one region to another.

The Portuguese established sugar plantations worked by African slaves on the islands off the West African coast and from there Columbus brought sugar-cane to Hispaniola in 1494. In 1503 a sugar mill was built and in 1515 Canary Islanders were brought to improve the methods of manufacture. The first exports to Spain were made in 1522. Sugar was the ideal product for the early Americas. It had a high value per unit weight, was not perishable, and had an expanding market in Europe. Yet although the Spanish planted sugar-cane and imported slaves to work the plantations in nearly every one of their colonies in the early sixteenth century, few became important.[39]

There were a number of reasons for this; in the first place sugar-cane was grown in Granada, and the Spanish were reluctant to encourage competition from their colonies; nor did the monopoly of trade encourage exports, even less the *flota* system with its irregular sailings. For much of the sixteenth century the Spanish were seduced by the lure of gold and silver, whilst at home their economy stagnated.[40] The first major producer was not in the Spanish colonies but in north-eastern Brazil, where the Portuguese settled in the 1530s. Nor was this surprising for the Portuguese already had plantations on their African islands, and controlled the slave trade, whilst there was an abundance of land near the Reconcavo and Recife, the principal settlements. But it was the Portuguese connections with the Dutch which were critical. By the 1490s the Dutch had replaced the Venetians as the main distributors of sugar in north-western Europe. They easily overcame the Portuguese Crown's trade restrictions, and provided much of the early capital for the industry. Indeed the Dutch occupied the Brazilian sugar districts between 1624 and 1654, the period of Brazilian dominance.

After the middle of the seventeenth century the Brazilian trade declined as the French and British Antilles grew in importance, not, it should be noted, because of lower costs in the Antilles, for Brazilian production costs were a third below those of the English islands, but because British and French possessions had a rapidly expanding and well-protected market. The Antilles were settled by the French and English in the early seventeenth century, beginning with St Kitts in 1623. Private companies comparable to those in Virginia attracted white indentured servants. The first crops were tobacco, cotton, ginger and cacao, grown by smallholders, but without any great success.[41]

Plantations

The Dutch were finally expelled from Brazil in 1654 and were then influential in establishing the sugar industry in Barbados, the Guianas and Martinique. The small farmers were bought out, and the large slave-run plantations came to dominate the islands. The *Pacte Colonial* of 1627 and the Navigation Laws of 1650 gave tariff protection to sugar, and exports were confined to French and British ships. The eighteenth century saw the ascendancy of the Antilles. On the smaller British islands sugar became a monoculture, although there was more diversity of cropping in the French islands and also in Jamaica. The islands not only had the advantage of protection, but were relatively close to the European market, had only short hauls from the mills to a port, and – of some importance – did not suffer from escaped slaves, as did Jamaica, Demerara and Berbice. By the end of the eighteenth century the Lesser Antilles dominated the sugar trade – St Domingue was by far the biggest exporter. The islands were constantly fought over, and the English islands made a significant contribution to British wealth and industrial investment.[42]

But in the nineteenth century the initiative passed to the Spanish islands of Cuba and Puerto Rico, and to a lesser extent to the sparsely populated Guianas and Trinidad. In 1799 the slave rising put St Domingue, henceforward called Haiti, out of action, and indeed the fleeing planters were important in establishing the sugar industry in Cuba. The abolition of slavery in the British islands in 1833, together with the end of protection in the same year, gave British possessions in the East, and also Dutch estates in Java, an entrée into the sugar market of Britain. Nor did British or French producers adopt new methods as rapidly as the Cubans.

In the mid-eighteenth century Cuba was still largely given over to ranches, whilst tobacco and coffee were grown by smallholders. The British occupation of 1762 brought planters with some 10 000 slaves, in the expectation that the island would be retained after the war. It was not to be, but by the end of the century Havana had become a free port. The American revolution severed trading links between the British West Indies, and the fall of St Domingue left a gap in the European market, whilst the boom in sugar prices in the early nineteenth century led to a rapid expansion of sugar plantations. This had important consequences; in 1790 there were 96 000 Europeans in Cuba and only 44 000 slaves. Over half a million slaves were imported between 1810 and 1870, and indeed slavery was not abolished until 1886. The growth of the *centralo* and the importance of American investment after 1899 have already been touched upon (see above, p. 218). There was a staggering increase in output between 1898 and 1930, from 500 000 to 5 000 000 tons. In the nineteenth century the mills had largely been in the centre of the island, but then they expanded into the east and west. By the 1950s Cuba was a sugar-dominated island. Sixty per cent of the total cropland was under cane, three-quarters of all exports were sugar, and nearly half the island's food had to be imported.[43]

No explanation of the changing location of sugar production in the Americas can neglect the significance of its politics. All the sugar-cane areas in the

Americas established in the past are still producing. Their changing importance reflects, however, changes in political rather than economic facts. The rise of the British and French Antilles was due largely to protected markets. French interest declined after the fall of St Domingue, partly due to the establishment of beet-sugar factories at home. Cuba and Puerto Rico were the sole remaining Spanish colonies after the mainland colonies became independent in 1822, whilst after 1898 both benefited from a guaranteed market in the United States. The revival of the British West Indian sugar production at the beginning of this century was again related to the rise of imperial preference after half a century of British commitment to free trade. The Cuban revolution and the severance of links with the United States have led to a renewed interest in sugar-cane on the Pacific coast of the Americas, not least in Peru, which has an efficient plantation economy dating mainly from the late nineteenth century.

Bananas in the Americas

The banana was introduced into the American tropics from the Canary Islands in 1516 and was rapidly adopted as a food crop. But it was not grown for export until the late nineteenth century. The banana must be shipped within a fortnight of harvesting; it must be kept cool during the voyage and the voyage must be as rapid as possible. The development of the trade thus awaited the construction of railways, the development of refrigeration in ships, and the replacement of sail by steam.[44] The first bananas from Jamaica reached Boston in 1870, and from Costa Rica to New Orleans in 1879. In the 1880s banana plantations were established in the sparsely populated Caribbean coastlands of Costa Rica, Nicaragua and Panama, using imported West Indian wage labour. The companies had to build not only railways and harbours but often hospitals and schools.[45]

The banana boom carried on into the 1920s as Britain and western Europe joined the United States as importers and new plantations were opened in Honduras, Guatemala and Mexico. But the inter-war period saw the rapid spread of two diseases, Panama and *sigatoka*. First detected in Central America in the 1880s, Panama disease was virulent on the Caribbean coast. The disease, combined with exhaustion of the soil and the movement of the plantations away from railheads, forced banana companies to abandon the Caribbean plantations and move to new sites on the Pacific coast; by 1942 the United Fruit Company had largely abandoned its holdings on the Caribbean coast. Yet by the 1950s Panama disease was raging on the Pacific coast, and in 1956 the Quepos–Parriba site in Costa Rica was out of production.[46]

Until the Second World War Central America and the West Indies dominated the world trade in bananas. The most striking feature of the post-war period has been the emergence of Ecuador as the world's leading exporter. Production began in the Guayas lowland in 1947 and spread north into Esmeraldas and south to El Oro. Unlike Central American production, most of Ecuador's bananas are produced on peasant holdings. It may well be, however, that in future the location of production will be more stable; the dominant variety grown in the Americas has been Gros Michel, which is highly susceptible to Panama disease. But Dwarf Cavendish is immune, and by 1965 much of the Central American areas were being replanted with this variety. *Sigatoka* can be controlled by spraying, although this is expensive.[47]

Plantations in Asia

In the middle of the nineteenth century Europe imported a wide range of agricultural products from Asia: coffee from Ceylon, India and Java, sugar from Mauritius, Bengal and Java, cinnamon from Ceylon, spices and gambier from the Straits settlements, as well as some coconuts and copra, indigo from Java and Bengal, tea from China – and so forth. But the volume and value of this trade was much less than that from the Americas, still dominated by United States cotton and West Indian sugar. Indeed the only British import from the Asian tropics of comparable significance was tea from China. In 1854 20 per cent of all Britain's imports came from Asia, 37 per cent from the Americas and less than 5 per cent from Africa. Fifty years earlier the American trade had been even more important. In 1808 over one-third of Britain's imports were from the British West Indies.[48] Nor had Asia more than a handful of plantations; most of the crops raised for exports were produced by indigenous smallholders, in most cases as an incidental part of their production of food; but in Java peasants were compelled to devote part of their *sawah* land to sugar-cane, and the *ryot* of Bengal was forced to grow indigo and later jute. Thus there was no development in Asia of what has been called the *Old* Plantation System, where family-owned estates of moderate size were worked by slaves.[49]

A number of causes accounted for the pre-eminence of the Americas in tropical trade and the relative unimportance of Asia. First, Europeans had colonised the Americas in order to settle. Finding a relatively sparse population with few products for trade, they had perforce to produce for themselves goods which could be sold in Europe in order to obtain imports. In much of Asia, in contrast, the early European explorers found densely populated areas with comparatively advanced civilisations. The indigenes already produced a wide range of tropical goods; therefore Europeans confined themselves to trading in these goods, not in producing them. Nor was there much interest amongst Europeans in organising production until the nineteenth century, when demand for tropical goods in Europe began to increase steadily. The progress of industrialisation and the accompanying rise in incomes meant that more people could afford the luxuries of tobacco, coffee, sugar and tea, whilst industry created new mass demands for cotton, jute, vegetable oils and, later in the century, rubber.

In the middle of the century the American plantation system was under stress, as the abolition of slavery, beginning in the British colonies in 1833 and culminating in Brazil in 1888, removed the main prop of the system. Further,

British liberalisation of trade left the British colonies in the West Indies un-
protected, and encouraged the exploitation of Asia. But as demand grew, the
supply was not necessarily forthcoming, and the European powers gradually
turned to organising agricultural production themselves, first in Java, later in
Bengal and Assam, whilst the Chinese pioneered in the Straits settlements. This
in turn led to the end of Asian independence, as first Holland, then Britain, took
political power to control trade, both to produce more raw materials and
foodstuffs but also to create markets for their exports.

Even so it was not until the late nineteenth century that the development of the
Asian tropics really got under way. This was to some extent due to changes in
transport. The American tropics had always had the advantage of nearness to
western Europe. In 1869 the Suez Canal was opened, whilst steam slowly
replaced sail, bringing Asia much nearer in travelling time.

The rise of the Asian trade in tropical goods thus coincided with a new mass
demand resulting from the industrial revolution, particularly for rubber and
vegetable oils. The plantations established in Asia reflected this change. The New
Plantation System was quite different from the Old Plantation System. Plantations in Asia were generally larger than those in the Americas; they were
financed by companies in London, Paris or Berlin; they were directed by
expatriates rather than by local families; they sponsored research in agriculture
and prompted advances in processing the crops. Like the American plantation
they depended upon imported labour, for they were established in sparsely populated areas. Thus Tamils went to Ceylon to pick tea and to Malaya to tap
rubber trees, whilst Biharis migrated to Assam and Chinese went to Sumatra.
Unlike the American planters, the New Planters did not have absolute control of
their labour force, but the system of indentured labour gave the plantation
manager considerable control, whilst the penal sanctions applied to labour in the
early years of Sumatran development fell little short of slavery.

The plantations, as in the early American period, were near to the sea; indeed
even today most export production in South East Asia is within 80 km of the
coast.[50] But the plantations have occupied a far smaller area than in the
Americas, and had comparatively little impact upon the existing indigenous
farmers. The smallholders who have, since 1919, taken over so much of Asiatic
production of export crops, were not freed slaves who took up free land on subdivided plantations, but subsistence farmers who have incorporated cash crops
into their farming system. The demise of the plantation has of course also been
associated with the end of colonialism, particularly in Sumatra, where the Dutch
plantations were occupied by squatters. Elsewhere in India and Ceylon, many
plantations have simply changed ownership.

Plantation crops in Indonesia

From 1621 to 1799 Java was under the control of the Dutch East India Company, but thereafter it became a Dutch colony, and from 1830 was exploited for

the benefit of the Dutch government, at that time in parlous straits at home. In 1830 the Governor, J. Van den Bosch, imposed the Culture System upon Java. Under this peasants were required to deliver a number of crops to the colonial government; in return taxes were remitted. The peasants were also required to labour on public works for part of the year. The crops were processed in factories operated by Europeans or Chinese under contract to the government, and all trade with Holland was handled by a state monopoly. Private enterprise was not forbidden, but was not encouraged.[51]

Sugar-cane, tobacco and indigo were all grown on the *sawahs* of central and eastern Java in rotation with rice, and, in the case of sugar-cane, by far the most important crop, delivered to the contracting mills. Peasants were not supposed to have more than one-fifth of their land in export crops at any one time. Coffee, tea and pepper could not be grown on the *sawahs,* but were comparatively easily incorporated into the swidden agriculture of the western highlands and the East Hook. Until the 1860s sugar and coffee were the main exports, output was largely confined to Java and production was by smallholders, not by plantations.[52]

In the 1850s government monopolies began to be relaxed, and in 1870 an Agrarian Law ended the system of forced deliveries. Its two most important provisions were to allow companies leases of up to seventy-five years in sparsely populated areas and to abolish forced labour. However until 1919 the concessions sometimes included the right to the use of local labour. The system of forced deliveries from *sawah* lands was abolished. Instead sugar-cane was now to be grown on land leased from the village community; the land furthermore had to be returned to the peasant after harvest to prevent ratooning and thus reduction of the rice area, and labour in the factories had to be paid wages. The state contractors were replaced by private companies.[53]

The companies extended the area under irrigation, and introduced the use of fertiliser, both of which benefited rice crops as well as sugar-cane. There was little change in the location of sugar production, which remained in the most densely populated areas of central and eastern Java. However the concession system not only extended the growth of coffee and tea in western Java, but prompted the rapid expansion of production in Sumatra, hitherto sparsely populated and occupied only by swidden cultivators. In 1863 Jacob Nienhuys obtained a concession near the Deli River to grow tobacco; this he grew by using land for only one year in eight. Labour was acquired from both Java and China.

Nienhuys' success in producing a high-quality cigar-wrapper leaf attracted other tobacco planters, but very soon other crops were grown in the *cultuurgebied* of north-eastern Sumatra, not only by Dutch companies, but by British, French and American firms. The immediate beneficiaries of the 1870 reform had been individual planters, but after the poor prices of the 1880s and the spread of *Hemileia vastatrix* or coffee rust, and *sereh,* a disease of sugar-cane, the corporation progressively replaced the individual planter in both Sumatra and Java. In Sumatra tobacco was joined by coffee after 1891, rubber in 1907, and later tea, oil-palm and sisal. This remarkable expansion meant that whereas in 1870 the Outer Islands accounted for only 13 per cent of the Dutch East Indies exports, in 1930 they accounted for 56 per cent; and whereas there were no more than a handful of estates in 1870, by 1937 there were 1177 estates on Java, averaging 900 hectares in size, and 1212 in the Outer Islands, averaging 1160 hectares.[54]

The growth of plantations was not confined to the Outer Islands; they were particularly numerous in the thinly populated western highlands of Java, where tea and coffee estates were numerous at the end of the nineteenth century. The spread of coffee rust in the 1880s not only led to attempts to replace *Coffea arabica* by *C. robusta,* but prompted planters in Java and Sumatra to try rubber. In 1902 there were only 175 hectares under rubber, by 1914 239000 hectares.[55] At that time the estate dominated the East Indian agricultural exports – only 10 per cent came from smallholders. But the success of estate rubber prompted smallholders to grow the crop – it fitted reasonably well into the swidden cultivation system in the Outer Islands. Thus throughout much of this century smallholders have produced an increasing proportion of Indonesia's products; by 1938 they accounted for 40 per cent of exports, including 60 per cent of the rubber, half the coffee and a quarter of the tea, virtually all the copra, whilst the old-established spices also remained, as they had begun, a product of the indigenous farmers.[56]

The Japanese occupation, the wars of independence and the later appropriation of Dutch and other plantations have all dealt the plantation crop exports of Indonesia severe blows. Indeed, except for rubber, the output of all crops is below what it was in 1938, due to the loss of protected markets, European capital and supervision, and growing indiscipline amongst plantation workers.[57]

Malaya

Malaya in the early nineteenth century did not have the well-established agricultural civilisations of Java; wet-rice cultivation among the Malays was comparatively recent in both the north east and the south west, where there had been immigrants from Sumatra in the eighteenth century. The first production of crops for export was undertaken largely by immigrant Chinese, who produced pepper, gambier, cloves, sugar-cane and coffee in a modified swidden system.[58] The turning point was the introduction of *Hevea braziliensis* into Singapore in 1877. There it was grown in the Botanical Gardens by H. N. Ridley, who urged the English planters who had arrived in the 1870s to try it. They were for the most part more interested in growing coffee – some had come from Ceylon – but in 1879 *Hemileia vastatrix* attacked the coffee estates. In the mid-1890s some planters interplanted rubber with coffee, but as late as 1900 there were only 2020 hectares of rubber in the whole of South East Asia, although in 1897 Ridley had devised an improved method of tapping the trees.[59] The boom came after 1905. On the west coast of Malaya there was already a network of railways to service the tin workings; land was granted, at first on perpetual lease, and British, French and American companies established plantations to grow rubber; the labour to tap the trees and cultivate came not from the Chinese or the Malays, but from indentured labourers, brought from India. From 137 hectares in 1897, 20000 in 1905, the area rose to 117000 in 1909 and by 1919 Malaya supplied half the world's rubber exports. In spite of the slump in 1920–2 and the restrictions of the Stevenson scheme, there were 1400000 hectares under rubber in 1940.[60] The plantations had produced most of the rubber before the First World War, but smallholders rapidly increased their share of the output. Malays found it easy to grow some rubber on the slopes above their valley-bottom rice holdings, whilst many Chinese smallholders grew only rubber. Smallholdings – defined rather arbitrarily as holdings of less than 40 hectares – now produce half Malaya's rubber output.[61]

Although rubber occupies 60 per cent of Malaya's cropland, it is not the only plantation crop grown. The crops grown in the nineteenth century – sugar-cane and coffee – are no longer of any importance, but oil-palm has experienced a boom. The first trials were made in 1903, but it was not taken up seriously until the early 1920s, when rubber prices were low and some rubber estates were converted; it was also grown on virgin land in Johore. It again increased in area in the late 1950s.[62]

India and Ceylon

1857 was not only the year of the Indian mutiny but also the centenary of the East India Company's rule in India, whilst Ceylon had been a British possession since 1798. In this period Indian trade had profoundly changed, as exports of manufactured goods were replaced by primary products. The main agricultural exports in mid-century were cotton, which went almost entirely to China, and financed England's import of tea, indigo which went to the Lancashire textile mills, sugar from Bengal and small amounts of coffee and tea. Cotton and sugar-cane were produced entirely by peasants, as was indigo, but the latter crop was produced in a manner similar to the Dutch Culture System in Java. Indigo was grown on small peasant farms in Bengal, but the dye was abstracted in European-owned mills by 'planters' who advanced credit and supervised production. Indebtedness to the 'planters' led to a system of quasi-forced labour which eventually led to serious riots. A similar method of production was adopted as jute became an important crop after the Dundee mills were cut off from Russian supplies of flax and hemp during the Crimean War.[63]

But the crop which was to assume great significance in the later nineteenth century was tea. Until the 1830s it was cultivated only in China and Japan on small subsistence farms. There had been attempts to grow tea in Bengal, Java and Ceylon in the late eighteenth century, but without success. However, in 1833 the East India Company lost its monopoly of trade with China and sought to cultivate tea in India. The early history of tea in Assam is still a matter of controversy, but it seems certain that imported Chinese varieties were unsuccessful, as they were in the Nilgiris, and that the first tea estates in Assam used local varieties. By 1841 there were 1052 hectares under tea in Assam; by the middle of the century it was being grown in Sylhet and Darjeeling. The great period of expansion was between 1880, when the area in Assam was 51 600 hectares, and 1913, when it had reached 147 000 hectares. In 1888 British imports of tea from India exceeded those from China for the first time. By 1900 less than a tenth of British tea imports were from China, by 1930 only 1.6 per cent.[64]

In the middle of the nineteenth century the Brahmaputra valley was thinly populated, and the development of the tea industry depended not only upon improved transport – a steamer service began in 1847 and a railway was built in 1885 – but upon imported labour. The tea tree is kept to the height of a shrub by pruning and continuous plucking of the leaves. Labour requirements are high. In Assam and Ceylon there are about 3.5 workers per hectare under tea. The early labourers for the Assam estates came mainly from Bihar, on five-year contracts. Estates were generally large and British-owned.[65]

But Assam was not the only area of tea production in the Indian subcontinent. Plantations were established in the Nilgiris and in Ceylon in the 1830s to grow *arabica* coffee. But after 1870 the rapid spread of *Hemileia vastatrix,* combined with the competition of Brazilian coffee, made its production uneconomic, even when replanted with *robusta.* In 1878 there were 8990 hectares under coffee in Ceylon, by 1895 only 1400. Tea underwent a remarkable expansion, partly on the old plantations, partly on virgin land, the area rising from 437 hectares in 1875 to 154 000 in 1900.

The labour force came not only from the local population, but also from Tamilnad. Tamils had been brought in to work the coffee plantations as early as the 1830s, but after 1844 direct recruitment became more common.[66]

Although the smallholder is of considerable significance in Ceylon, in contrast to Assam, the Indian and Ceylonese tea output is still produced mainly on estates. In Ceylon, for example, over half the area under tea is on estates of more than 200 hectares.[67] Indeed the tea industry exemplifies most of the characteristic features of the modern plantation industry. Initially most of the capital was British and the major market Britain, although in both India and Ceylon a substantial proportion of the estates are now owned by Indians or Ceylonese. Labour makes up two-thirds of the production costs, and much of the labour is still recruited from outside the estate area. Plucking of leaves is continuous the year round, and the tea factories are thus used to full capacity. The scale of operation allows new methods of cultivation to be adopted rapidly, and indeed much of the increase in output in the last thirty years has come from greater yields, which in India and Ceylon are 50 per cent greater than in Indonesia.[68]

Plantation crops in Africa

The two distinctive features of plantation crop production in tropical Africa are the lateness of its development and the relative unimportance of the plantation both in the past and in the present.

Although tropical Africa now provides about 16 per cent of the world's exports of tropical crops, in the middle of the nineteenth century its contribution was negligible. When Europeans first reached the Guinea coast in the fifteenth century they did not find any substantial agricultural civilisations producing crops for trade; tropical Africa's earlier trade with Europe, in both Roman and medieval times, had been mainly in gold, ivory and slaves.[69] Nor is this perhaps surprising. Of the ten principal agricultural exports from tropical Africa in 1968, only two were from indigenous crops – coffee and the oil-palm. Cocoa, ground-nuts, tobacco, sisal and rubber are American crops, unknown in the Old World until after 1492, whilst tea was not introduced from Asia until the late nineteenth century. Although bananas may well have been known in West Africa in the sixteenth century they could not of course be exported, and the bananas of commerce have all been introduced. Although all three varieties of coffee are indigenous to Africa, coffee drinking was unknown, and coffee was not cultivated in the continent until the nineteenth century, whilst the cottons now grown are of American origin. Of the indigenous products the pepper of West Africa was different to that of the East Indies, already well known, and did not appeal to European tastes; nor was there at that time any demand for kola-nuts or any appreciation of the value of palm-oil.[70]

The first explorers of the West African coast thus found few commodities which could be traded. However both the Spanish and the Portuguese introduced sugar-cane into the off-shore islands – Cape Verde, the Canaries, São Tomé and Fernando Po – and until the Brazilian sugar industry got under way in the mid-sixteenth century the islands provided an increasing proportion of Europe's sugar. Once sugar-cane had been introduced into the Americas and the plantation system established, Europeans came to West Africa for slaves and this trade dominated the coast until the early nineteenth century.

Even had there been no slave trade Europeans were unlikely to have exploited the area on the scale which they did the Americas or later South East Asia. There were few good harbours on the coast, and it was difficult to penetrate the interior to where the more advanced African states were to be found; the coast's unsavoury reputation for disease was at least partly justified, as was found in the nineteenth century when a few attempts at European settlement were made. Thus until the early nineteenth century there was little trade between West Africa and Europe, other than in slaves.

Three events led to the development of exports. First was the abolition of the slave trade, by Denmark in 1803 and Britain in 1807. This led British traders in particular to seek alternative items of commerce. Second was the industrial revolution in Europe and the growing demand for vegetable oils for lubricants, soap, candles and cooking oils. Third was the scramble for Africa in the late nineteenth century, when Britain, France and Germany established colonies. In all three cases the colonies were expected to provide agricultural products for the mother country. Thus the great expansion in African trade came only at the beginning of this century.

When expansion came it was not the plantation which was the spearhead of change, as it had been in the Americas in the eighteenth century, or was in South East Asia in the late nineteenth century. There were several reasons for this. First, the age of slavery was over, and Africans were reluctant to work as labourers on plantations. Second, European capital was flowing steadily into South East Asia, where the rubber boom was about to get under way. Third was the policy of the colonial powers. In British West Africa the early colonial authorities were opposed to the alienation of land to foreigners, either as settlers or in the form of plantation companies. Thus for example Lever Brothers were unable to obtain concessions in southern Nigeria, and turned instead to the Belgian Congo. The French, after unsuccessful attempts to settle Europeans in Senegal in the 1820s, relied increasingly upon peasant production of export crops, although they did not exclude plantations.[71] Thus in West Africa only the German colonies of Togo and the Cameroons were dominated by plantation production. In the Congo different attitudes prevailed. The Congo Free State, established in 1884, sold concessions to foreign companies, who ruthlessly exploited the native population, compelling the collection of wild rubber and the cultivation of other crops. International opinion forced the Belgian government to take over the control of the Congo in 1908, but many concessionaires remained. Until the 1930s the Belgian colonial authorities encouraged the establishment of plantations – notably *Huilieries du Congo*, a Unilever subsidiary – but in the 1930s they began to encourage peasant farming. In Tanganyika the Germans established plantations, and in Nyasaland large areas were alienated to Europeans, as they were in Kenya and Rhodesia. But in the latter two countries it was not only the corporate plantation which the authorities sought to attract but the permanent settlement of European farmers. Indeed in Kenya not only did Europeans grow export crops on large estates, but they sought to prevent Africans growing the crop, both to prevent a decline in quality and to ensure a supply of labourers for their own estates. In Uganda the colonial authorities were not initially hostile to planters, as were those in British West Africa, but few planters came and after 1916 land could no longer be alienated to foreigners. Further south the Portuguese had little control over the interior of either Mozambique or Angola until the first decade of this century; subsequently they have encouraged both Portuguese settlers and plantations, the former on some scale in Angola.[72]

The pattern of early colonial land policies persisted until the 1950s. But as Africans have gained independence, policies have changed. In Kenya and Tanzania the result has been a decline of the European estate and the growing importance of the African smallholders. In Nigeria, in contrast, the policy towards plantations was reversed in 1952, and foreign companies have been encouraged to establish estates in partnership with the state.[73] One last institution must be mentioned; in the Sudan and in the French savannas large settlement schemes were undertaken by the colonial authorities. They provided the irrigation works, established the farms, and provided the supervisory control of cotton-growing. The cotton was grown however by Africans on small farms. Much of Africa's cotton is produced in this way.

The consequence of these varying policies is that African production is dominated by the smallholder and the plantation is of little importance. Cotton, which makes up 23 per cent of Africa's agricultural exports, is almost exclusively grown on small farms. Coffee, the second most important export, is grown on surviving European estates in Kenya, and on medium-sized European farms in Angola; in the Ivory Coast, the leading coffee producer in Africa, the first coffee was grown on plantations in the 1890s but the African smallholder has grown steadily more important. Groundnuts are pre-eminently a smallholder's crop, and the bulk of the export of palm products comes from peasants, although there were oil-palm plantations in the Congo and more recently in Nigeria. Some crops however are still produced mainly on large estates: sisal in Tanzania is the best example, but much of the tea in East Africa is still estate-produced, as are bananas in West Africa and the increasingly important rubber-growing industry.[74]

In the 1820s the decline of the slave trade led British and later French traders to seek new goods from West Africa. They found the answer in groundnuts in Gambia and Senegal and the oil-palm in Nigeria; both provided vegetable oils, for which there was a rising demand in Europe. The first exports of groundnuts were from Gambia and later, in 1842, from the lower Senegal valley. Most of the exports went to Marseilles which had a well-established industry based upon olive-oil. Until the 1880s production was confined to the coastal areas and the lower river valleys, but the building of a railroad in 1885 from Dakar to St Louis, and the eastward extension of the railway after 1908, led to the expansion of the crop into the hinterland. The railway increased production, but the discovery of hydrogenation in 1903, which made it possible to convert oils to fats, greatly increased the demand at the turn of the century.[75]

Groundnuts had been grown in Senegambia as a food crop since the sixteenth century and they were already widely grown in the nineteenth century. The oil-palm in southern Nigeria and other parts of West Africa flourishes in the hot, humid environment, but does not thrive in the shade of the upper layers of the tropical forest. It is thus most common in areas where bush fallowing has replaced the primary forest with a lower forest cover. The oil-palm, although indigenous to West Africa, seems only to have been grown in southern Nigeria after the southward movement of the Ibo in the seventeenth century. The oil-palm was used in Africa for a variety of purposes, but palm-oil from the fruit was the first export. Liverpool traders obtained it from the delta area where it was collected from the self-sown oil-palm fruits; there was no planting of oil-palm in Nigeria, although the Krobo people of the Gold Coast did plant the tree. Palm-oil replaced gold as the leading export in 1853. Later in the century machinery which extracted oil from palm-kernels was invented, and this gave a further fillip to the trade, which stagnated in the second half of the nineteenth century. Nonetheless the oil-palm was still only rarely sown until plantations were established in the Belgian Congo after 1912. The collection of palm-oil has serious disadvantages compared with plantation production, for both the yield and the extraction rate are lower. West African smallholders have thus found it difficult to compete, not only with the plantations of the Congo, but also with those established in Sumatra and Malaya in the 1920s.[76]

At the end of the nineteenth century rubber briefly became a major export from West Africa. It was obtained from two indigenous plants, a tree, *Funtumia elastica,* and the creeper *landolphia,* both occurring in much the same regions as the oil-palm. But the exploitation of these plants by tappers was rash, often leading to their destruction. Although rubber was an important export from the Congo, Nigeria, Ghana and Sierra Leone, from 1885 to 1905, the attempts to plant *Hevea braziliensis* were not successful. However in the 1920s plantations were established in Liberia and other parts of the West African coast, and since the 1950s rubber exports have been of growing importance.[77]

But the great upsurge in tropical exports from West Africa came at the end of the century with the establishment of colonial regimes which built railways, distributed the seed and in some cases compelled the cultivation of cash crops. The significance of the railway was most noteworthy in the Kano district of northern Nigeria; groundnuts and cotton had been grown in northern Nigeria in the past, and indeed the latter was the basis of a local weaving industry Once the link to the coast had been created, the growth of groundnuts in the north and cotton in the south expanded rapidly, but within the intensive bush fallowing system that prevailed. Groundnuts occupy a comparatively small part of the cultivated area, compared with Senegal, where groundnuts are grown by peasants in a bush-fallowing system, but where the crop may occupy two-thirds of the farmer's land: the cotton grown for export was not the local variety but American Upland, introduced in 1912.[78]

But it was the introduction of cocoa into south-western Nigeria, Sierra Leone and, above all, Ghana, that had the most spectacular results. In the 1880s South America was still the major cocoa producer; the Bahian plantations in Brazil were just replacing Ecuador as the leading exporter.[79] Cocoa was introduced into both Nigeria and Ghana in about 1879, but it was in the 1890s that expansion got under way. It was first grown in the Gold Coast by the Akwapim people, who were already experienced in the palm-oil trade, but had little land available for growing cocoa. However further north the forests of the Akim people were thinly populated and the Akim chiefs were prepared to sell land. The Akwapim and other tribes migrated into the forests and cleared the land for cocoa. They acquired land in groups, either of relations or in 'companies' of friends. From the profits of cocoa sales, they often acquired plots of land further north and west, and by this process of 'leapfrogging' cocoa cultivation has now reached the westernmost borders of southern Ghana. In Ashanti, which was pacified by 1900, this 'leapfrogging' of immigrant farmers has been far less significant.

Nonetheless by 1911 the Gold Coast was the world's leading cocoa producer, and its output in the inter-war period steadily increased. However in the late 1930s 'swollen shoot' disease began to spread. As the only effective measure of control, many cocoa trees have had to be rooted up and destroyed. Thus many areas in the south east, where production first began, no longer grow cocoa. They have not, however, reverted to subsistence agriculture; instead food crops are grown for the Accra market. It is important to note that cocoa growing was not merely an extension of bush fallowing. It required capital and enterprise, and often farmers grew only cocoa rather than mixing food crops and cocoa. Furthermore profits were frequently re-invested in the acquisition of more land.[80]

The history of coffee growing is of some interest in Africa, for it has followed a sequence comparable to that in the Americas. *Coffea arabica*, although originally an African plant, was re-introduced into West and East Africa in the nineteenth century. *C. canephora*, or *robusta*, was discovered in the Congo basin in 1880 and has become the major species grown in Africa. Initially coffee was an estate crop, grown in the Ivory Coast, Angola, Nyasaland, Kenya and Tanganyika not on large plantations but in European estates of 120–200 hectares. Labour, often forced, was African. Coffee had very mixed success; it was replaced in Malawi, for example, by tea and tobacco. In the inter-war period Africans began to grow coffee in smallholdings, and since 1950, with the decline of white settlement and the post-war coffee famine, it has expanded at an extraordinary rate. Thus in 1953 there were only 1600 hectares of coffee grown by African farmers, by 1963 28000 hectares.[81]

We may conclude this section on Africa by contrasting West and East Africa. In West Africa the plantation never got a firm foothold, nor were there European settlements. Peasant production of export crops has been encouraged. Because the end of the colonial era was relatively peaceful, due to the absence of white settlers, the plantations that survive have not been, for the most part, nationalised or subdivided; indeed in Nigeria there has been an attempt to encourage plantations. In East Africa European settlement has left less happy memories and not only have plantations been nationalised, but former estates have been subdivided amongst African smallholders.

CHAPTER 12

RANCHING

Ranching, or extensive commercial grazing, has many points of resemblance to pastoral nomadism, and indeed at first sight it appears to be merely a more economically advanced form of it. Yet it has a different distribution and a different origin.

Ranching now occupies a smaller area than it did 100 years ago. Since then the humid margins of the semi-arid and arid areas in which ranching is now found have been occupied by farmers who not only produce beef cattle, and sheep for mutton and wool, but grow fodder crops and cash crops, for example in the Great Plains of the United States, the wheat-alfalfa belt of the humid pampa of the Argentine, the wheat-sheep belt of Australia, and the Canterbury Plains of South Island, New Zealand. The extensive occupation of ranching has been displaced by more intensive forms of land use, and ranching has, in most areas, been pushed into drier regions where it is generally the best use of the poor vegetation and soils.

Ranching is largly confined to the areas of recent European settlement, and was unknown in the Old World, except in South Africa, until recently. In the last thirty years however there have been attempts to convert nomadic pastoralists in Central Asia and parts of Africa into ranchers. (See above, Chapter 7.) The major ranching areas are: (i) the western United States, with the adjacent parts of Canada and Mexico; (ii) the *llanos* of Venezuela; (iii) the *sertao* of Brazil, the pampa of Uruguay, the south east of the Argentine pampa, the Chaco and Patagonia; (iv) the Karoo of South Africa; (v) the arid interior of Australia; (vi) the high country of South Island, New Zealand (Fig. 1). All these regions are occupied by European settlers, and all except the humid pampa and South Island are semi-arid.

Ranching has frequently been described as a 'child of the Industrial Revolution'.[1] As we shall see, it has a much longer history than this, but it is nonetheless true that ranching emerged as a major agricultural system only in the second half of the nineteenth century. The major factor was the growth of demand for beef and wool in the urbanised areas of the eastern United States and western Europe, and in particular Great Britain. The establishment of export-orientated grazing systems in areas as remote as New Zealand and Patagonia was made possible not only by the reduction of oceanic freight rates (see Chapter 4) but also by the introduction of refrigeration into ships and railways and the advances in meat-canning. Until the 1880s ranching was relatively primitive, with few capital inputs other than the livestock themselves. Thereafter the grazing areas were transformed by the advance of wheat farmers into the semi-arid regions, by the demand for better-quality beef and mutton, which led to the improvement of sheep and cattle breeds, and the intensification of ranching; the latter included fencing, the provision of winter feed, better breeds, and bore-wells for water supplies. In some areas such as the humid pampa and parts of New Zealand the natural pasture was replaced with lucerne or sown grasses and so ceased to be areas of ranching proper. One result has been that ranching areas now rarely provide a majority of the stock raised in a country. Thus in Australia three agricultural zones are recognised: the pastoral zone, the area of ranching proper; the wheat–sheep Belt; and the high rainfall coastal areas. The pastoral zone, found only in the drier parts of eastern Australia, now produces only 20 per cent of Australia's sheep. One hundred years ago the pastoral zone covered virtually all of occupied Australia.

Ranching is, in nearly every part of the world, a large-scale operation, a natural consequence of the low productivity of the land used for grazing. In Australia sheep stations average 8000 hectares, cattle ranches in the north are even larger, and the average in the South Island of New Zealand is 5600 hectares.[2] One hundred years ago ranches in the United States and Australasia were generally on open range; the rancher held the freehold only of the land around his ranch buildings, and perhaps some of the water points. Now freehold is far more common, particularly in the Great Plains. But in the western United States 60 per cent of the land used for grazing is Federal land and ranchers pay for grazing rights. In Australia the early sheep stations were on Crown land, the grazier paying only an annual licence fee to graze: now long leases are the dominant mode of tenure, whilst in South Island 'runs' are still on Crown lands. In Latin America, in contrast, ranches have been in large private holdings from the earliest times.

Herds and flocks are also large, in contrast to those of mixed farming areas. One reason for this is the fear of stock losses in drought; the larger the herd the greater the chance of survival. This is a policy that ranchers share with pastoral nomads, and has led to overstocking and overgrazing. Only since the 1930s has there been a move towards conservation policies and attempts to adjust stock numbers to the land's carrying capacity.[3] The risk of drought is one of many hazards faced by ranchers. Another is the dependence on one product, and the consequent vulnerability in times of poor prices. Ranching is highly specialised, generally with only one product, beef or wool.[4] Only in Uruguay and parts of Australia are cattle and sheep normally raised on the same unit. The sheep runs of Australia and New Zealand raise merino sheep for wool. In contrast, in the more humid mixed farming regions, or the intensive sheep regions of New Zealand, crossbred sheep are raised on sown pastures for mutton and wool. In the United States and Brazil the ranching regions have become highly specialised, producing only young steers which are fattened elsewhere.[5]

Few ranchers grow crops either for subsistence or cash and only limited amounts of forage – roots, hay or grain – are grown for winter feed. The livestock depend almost entirely on natural pastures; indeed, where sown grasses have been introduced, or grain fed to cattle, then ranching ceases and the mixed farmer takes over, a process to be seen on the margins of all the ranching regions. The productivity of the range is low. Thus in the desert areas of the western U.S.A. at least 40 hectares of sagebrush are required to maintain a steer, and even on the grasslands of the Great Plains, 6–10 hectares, whilst in the high country of South Island, one sheep needs 3 hectares. The only exception to this is the humid pampa. In much of the pampa a more intensive farming has displaced ranching; lucerne is grown, with a year under wheat every five years; only 0.8 hectares of lucerne are needed for one steer. But in the south-eastern humid pampa where natural forage is relied upon, 1.6 to 2.8 hectares are needed and similar carrying capacities are attained in Uruguay. In both these areas soils are good and rainfall adequate for crop cultivation.[6]

One consequence of the low carrying capacity of the range is the very low population densities of ranching areas; another is low labour inputs per acre and, in comparison with mixed farming, per animal. Both cattle and sheep runs rely on hired labour, often seasonal, for round-ups, mustering and shearing. Capital inputs per acre are also low, but the initial outlay is high; thus many ranches are run by companies rather than individuals. In the past much of the investment in ranching itself and in the ancillary services of meat-packing came from outside, particularly from Britain.

Returns per acre are low, and vulnerable both to climatic and price fluctuations, so that over the last hundred years there have been major changes in ranching. In the higher rainfall areas – save the humid pampa – sown grasses, cash crops and the use of fertilisers have converted ranching to mixed farming; in the drier regions this has been impossible, and it is here that ranching survives. Not surprisingly the only large area of humid land still devoted to ranching, the Argentine pampa, has a considerable cost advantage in the beef market.[7]

The origin of ranching in the Americas

The Americas have a third of the world's cattle and 15 per cent of the sheep, and much of the continent is given over to grazing.[8] Yet the pre-Columbian populations had no herding animals other than the llama; the ranching industries are thus a recent development. The Spanish and Portuguese first introduced cattle and sheep, and probably also brought with them many of the characteristic features of modern ranching. It is in medieval Iberia that the origin of these techniques must be sought.

Between the eleventh and the fourteenth centuries economic and political life in Iberia was dominated by the *reconquista*, the slow southward advance against the Moors, and the settlement of the depopulated areas. In northern Iberia livestock keeping, as in the rest of Europe, was subordinate to crop growing: cattle were kept on small farms as draught animals and to lesser extent for their milk and meat. But as southern Iberia was reconquered in the twelfth and thirteenth centuries, a quite different livestock economy emerged. The constant warfare meant that settlement was nucleated, in fortified towns and large villages, and municipal territories were large. Crops were grown near the towns, but were not of major economic significance because of the shortage of labour and the risk of loss from Muslim raids, whilst the semi-arid environment did not encourage farming, although not precluding it. Cattle and sheep, which were mobile and thrived on the natural grass and shrublands, came to dominate the agricultural economy in the Middle Ages. They were grazed in common on the municipality's pastures, and were looked after by mounted herders, who also drove them long distances overland to summer pastures in the uplands. Twice a year cattle were rounded up, calves branded and cattle for slaughter cut out: the cattle themselves were a cross between cattle brought from the north, and the southern *Bos taurus ibericus*, the longhorns which were the ancestors of the modern fighting bull. Cattle were valued less for their stringy beef than for their hides and tallow. On the frontier of settlement half-wild cattle were hunted with lances – from which arose bull fighting. The mounted herdsmen had spurred boots, the Moorish saddle, the bolero jacket, tight-fitting trousers and low-brimmed hats. It is less clear whether the cattle were grazed on large private estates. There were two categories of cattle owners in medieval Iberia. First were the townspeople who had small herds which were grazed by hired herdsmen, who were freemen; second, the nobles and military orders, whose large herds were certainly grazed upon the public lands but may also have been kept upon private estates as well.[9]

In the fifteenth century southern Iberia was the only part of Europe with a ranching economy, and it is significant that Andalusians were a high proportion of the early settlers in the Americas. Cattle were taken to the Indies by Columbus, where they often became feral and rapidly increased in numbers. They multiplied equally quickly in Mexico. Ranching remained the leading economic activity in Cuba until the early eighteenth century.[10] In Brazil cattle spread into the *sertao* in the late sixteenth century; they were introduced into the Venezuelan *llanos* in 1548 and rapidly multiplied. The grasslands around the Rio de la Plata received cattle from two directions. Cattle were brought from Peru, across the Andes, and down to Buenos Aires, which was founded in 1580; whilst at the beginning of the seventeenth century cattle were brought into what is now Uruguay from Brazil.[11]

In Latin America cattle ranching was an important part of the agricultural economy from the beginning of European settlement, and played a major role in expanding the frontier.[12] In Brazil the earliest Portuguese settlements were on the north-eastern coast, where sugar plantations were the basis of the economy, but in the late sixteenth century cattle raisers moved into the *sertao* via the lower São Francisco valley. Here enormous if ill-defined cattle *fazendas* were established, in spite of the government's attempts to limit the size of the holdings. Cattle were raised on the natural pastures of the *sertao*, looked after by semi-nomadic *vaquieros*. Once a year the cattle were rounded up, the calves branded and those ready for market driven to the coast. Their stringy meat was sold to the plantations. But hides were perhaps more important; some were shipped to Europe.[13]

Further south in what is now Argentina and Uruguay the humid pampa was an ideal environment for the rapid growth of cattle numbers. Until the early eighteenth century wild cattle were hunted by *gauchos*, and the hides sold in Buenos Aires, and later in Montevideo. But by the mid-eighteenth century much of the pampas had been broken up into estates, often with ill-defined boundaries, and hunting had been superseded by the round-up and branding. But hides remained the major product, although a market for dried meat was found in the Brazilian plantations.[14]

Much further north the *llanos* of Venezuela had been unoccupied when the Spanish arrived in the mid-sixteenth century. The alternation of drought and flood had made cultivation difficult for the pre-Columbian populations and they lacked animals to exploit the grasslands. Thus the *llanos* were only occupied after the arrival of the Spanish. A century later over 140 000 cattle were kept on the *llanos* by the semi-nomadic *llaneros*, and by the late nineteenth century over 8 000 000 cattle were grazed on the open range.[15]

More critical developments were taking place in Mexico, where cattle, horses and sheep were introduced soon after the Spanish conquest of the Aztecs. The Indians adopted sheep, but not the half-wild cattle. At first livestock raising developed in the densely populated Valley of Mexico, often driving out the Indian farmers. But from the 1530s the Spanish cattle raisers moved north into the semi-arid lands occupied by the Chichimec. Northern Mexico was colonised by ranchers and miners in the late sixteenth and early seventeenth centuries; by the early eighteenth century there were ranches in what are now California, Arizona, New Mexico and Texas. The Spanish brought with them to Mexico the characteristic features of medieval Iberian ranching. Some new features were added. The lasso replaced the lance and leather *chaparreros* were developed as a protection against the thorny shrubs, which, together with *grama* grass, made up the natural forage; more significant, the cattle were increasingly raised not on the open range but on haciendas. The first Crown grants were of grazing rights and of the use of Indian labour – and not ownership of land. But later payment of nominal fees converted these rights to full ownership, and the rights to labour became the debt-slavery of peonage. The almost continual warfare with the Apache, Comanche and other Indians, who had acquired horses, made the *hacienda* centre invariably a fortified building, and, unlike the American ranch, it was largely self-sufficient, growing its own food and selling cattle hides and tallow. Large numbers of cattle were driven south to Mexico City.[16]

The first Spanish settlement in Texas was made in 1716, and by the end of the century there was a thriving cattle industry; the first cattle drive east to New Orleans was made in 1779. Anglo-Americans did not arrive in Texas until 1821, but they soon outnumbered the Spanish. By the time that the Texas Republic, after its brief period of independence, had joined the United States, immigrants from the East had learnt the techniques of ranching from the Spanish and often seized their ranches in the 1830s. The number of cattle in Texas rose from 100000 in 1830 to nearly 5000000 in 1860.[17]

The rise and fall of the open range cattle industry in the United States

In 1860 the Great Plains were the only grasslands in the Americas without stockraising. Most of the region was still occupied by the bison and the Indian. The frontier of agricultural settlement had however reached the easternmost prairies, and in 1853 Chicago had been linked to the East by railway.[18] In Texas there were great herds of Texas Longhorns, often half-wild, which were still marketed mainly in New Orleans. A steer sold in Texas brought $3 or $4. But in Chicago, where there were already meat-packing plants and a rail link to the markets of the East Coast, it fetched $30 or $40. Thus the great northward drives of Longhorns began in 1867, and continued until the 1880s. Cow-towns were established at the railheads at Dodge City and Abilene, and the cattle were taken by rail from there to Chicago. These drives diminished in importance in the 1870s, as the homesteaders pushed westwards, and blocked the drovers' routes. More important, they became less necessary as ranchers moved into the central and northern Great Plains and established ranches on the open range, stocking them mainly with Longhorns from Texas. By the 1880s much of the foothills of the western Great Plains were used for livestock raising from Texas in the south to Alberta in the north.[19]

Nowhere in this area was it necessary to buy land; ranchers moved into the public domain and built their homes and buildings at a water point. Cattle fed on the grasses of the open range, and farther west on the desert sagebrush. Little effort was made to provide fodder in the winter, and particularly cold winters, such as that of 1886–7, led to disastrous losses. The cattle were mainly Longhorns, giving a poor stringy meat, but whilst the cattle of several ranches shared the open range, there was little chance of upgrading the cattle. Cattle were rounded up twice a year, and the calves branded and the steers ready for market, generally at four or five years old, cut out. Family labour was insufficient and the hired hand was essential.

In the 1870s there were great profits to be made from the open range, for beef prices were high and the land was still free. Nonetheless the capital outlay for cattle was often beyond the individual; company investment was characteristic from the earliest times. In 1875 chilled beef reached England from New York for the first time, and a yet larger market encouraged further ranching expansion. Indeed overcrowding and overgrazing were apparent by the late 1870s. In Wyoming in 1871 there were less than 100000 cattle; by 1886 1250000.[20] A combination of events led to the transformation of ranching in the last twenty years of the nineteenth century. Most important was the westward expansion of agricultural settlement. Ranchers had no legal claim on the open range; as homesteaders pushed into the Great Plains cattlemen were compelled to buy land, or illegally fence the range. Alternatively they could effectively control a large area by homesteading or purchasing only the water points, or by buying alternate sections.[21] In the mid-1880s the combination of falling beef prices and several bad winters crushed many ranchers, now burdened with mortgages.[22] As urban incomes rose, there was increasing dissatisfaction with the poor beef obtained from the Texas Longhorns, and they were slowly replaced by, or cross-bred with, Herefords.[23] These animals needed far more care than the hardy Longhorns. It was essential to fence the pastures to prevent indiscriminate breeding; the cost of fencing fell radically after the adoption of barbed wire, first marketed in the 1870s. The Herefords needed winter feed, and the rancher had increasingly to gather hay, grow grain or alfalfa, or purchase concentrates.[24] In the drier areas the prime need was for water, for the Herefords could not be driven long distances without loss of weight. In the Great Plains wells were bored to tap underground water, and windmills used to lift the water. The spread of railways into the West eliminated the need for the long cattle drives which had been characteristic of the 1860s and 1870s.[25]

The intensification of ranching required more and more capital; only large ranches could survive in these conditions. There was also more regional specialisation. Increasingly cattle were bred in the southern Great Plains, and sent north for fattening, whilst the northern Great Plains produced steers which were sent for fattening on maize in the Corn Belt.[26] The expansion of farming into the Great Plains meant that ranching was increasingly confined to the rougher lands of the interfluves,[27] or pushed into the Rockies or the arid intermontane basins. By the beginning of this century the era of the open range was over in the Great Plains. In the Rocky Mountain states the rancher could still graze the summer pastures of the public domain, and indeed was not charged for this until the Taylor Grazing Act of 1934; even then, it was not, until 1947, more than a nominal fee.[28]

This century has seen further changes in ranching. Breeding improvements have slowly spread; attempts to halt overgrazing have been made, by controlled grazing, by reseeding pastures and by limiting the numbers grazed. Trucks have replaced both the overland drive and the railways as the means of marketing livestock. The Pacific coast has become a major market for beef, and so the flow of livestock is no longer exclusively eastwards. While the range industry still mainly rears steers for fattening in the Corn Belt or on lusher pastures than those of the range, commercial feedlots using irrigated crops and concentrates have appeared within the ranching areas.[29]

It is possible to argue that most of the characteristics of the open range industry were acquired from Texas, and thus ultimately from Mexico and medieval Spain. It should be noted however that there are other views. As the American frontier advanced westwards, agriculture invariably pushed cattle raising further west, as the more intensive land use displaced an extensive land use. As early as the eighteenth century cattle were being driven from the Shenandoah valley to the towns of the Atlantic coast, and cattle raising was important in the Ohio valley in the early nineteenth century and in the Illinois prairie in mid-century. It has been claimed that branding and the *rodeo,* or round-up, were practised in the Carolinas in the eighteenth century, and that the techniques of ranching were independently developed in the eastern United States, and subsequently carried westwards into Texas. This may be so, but currently it would seem that the burden of evidence still favours the Hispanic origin of most ranching techniques.[30]

Ranching in the Rio Plata region

There were few changes in ranching techniques in the rest of the Americas until the period after the Second World War: there were some exceptions. In the early twentieth century American and British cattle companies introduced into Mexico Herefords, fencing, water-drilling and the other techniques which had transformed the American industry.[31] But for the most part the livestock industry remained unchanged. The major exception to this was the humid pampa of Argentina and Uruguay, which, like the western United States, was transformed by the rising demand for beef in the late nineteenth century.

In the middle of the nineteenth century both Argentina and Uruguay were largely devoted to the grazing of sheep and cattle. Such arable cultivation as there was took place near Buenos Aires and Montevideo. There were however important differences between the livestock industries of the United States and Argentina. In the first place much of the pampa used for ranching was comparatively humid, and could well have been used for crop cultivation, whilst the mild winters precluded disastrous losses of cattle such as occurred in the northern Great Plains, although drought could be a hazard. Secondly, whereas the livestock industry in the United States developed in the public domain, most of Argentina and Uruguay was already divided up into large private holdings. In the United States land legislation favoured the small farmer, and indeed was intended to implement the development of an independent yeomanry.[32] Little provision was made in Argentina or Uruguay for such a class. Indeed land continued to be allocated in large holdings. When the Indian wars of 1879–83 finally opened up the lands south of the Salado for occupation, they were sold off in very large units. Thirdly, there was no significant market for beef in Argentina and Uruguay, which in 1850 had a very small population. The impetus for improvement came, more than in the United States, from overseas. The nearness of the cattle holdings to the coast was clearly a considerable advantage for exporting.[33]

As late as 1860 the major products of the La Plata countries were hides and wool. Only salted beef could be sent any distance, although live cattle were shipped to England until 1900. Most of the cattle were descendants of those introduced by the Spanish and the Portuguese and thus were related to the Texas Longhorns; sheep, which were as important as cattle in mid-century, were mainly of merino origin.[34] The transformation of the La Plata industry got under way with the establishment of the Liebig meat-extract plant at Fray Bentos in 1864. In the 1870s the use of smooth wire fencing, introduced in 1848, began to spread, and Shorthorns from Britain began to replace the indigenous breeds. Herefords were also imported, but were only important on the drier margins of the pampa. In 1876 the first chilled beef reached Europe from Buenos Aires, and this was followed by heavy British investment in meat-packing plants and railways. The southern limit of settlement in Argentina, for long confined to the north of the Salado trough by hostile Indians, had pushed south to the Rio Negro by 1879. Sheep, which were far more important in Argentina and Uruguay than in the United States, were also changed. At first the major market had been for wool, and so the merino was predominant. But with the establishment of packing plants and the introduction of refrigerator ships, mutton became important, and English mutton breeds, particularly the Lincoln and the Romney Marsh, supplanted the merino.[35]

In the mid-1880s most of the pampa in Argentina and Uruguay was divided up into very large ranches, carrying large herds of sheep and cattle, although still fed on natural forage. England was the major market, and provided the bulk of the investment in railways and meat-packing plants. Fencing, the provision of wells and other improvements were all under way. But little of the pampa was cultivated, for not only were the great landowners uninterested in crop cultivation, but the population of Argentina and Uruguay was too small to sustain any considerable agriculture. However change was imminent. The grasses of the pampa could be grazed all the year round, and the carrying capacity was far above that of the range in the United States. The introduction of alfalfa changed this. Half a hectare of alfalfa could support one steer, whilst even the best natural pastures could only support one steer on every two to three hectares. One sowing of lucerne could provide grazing for five years or more.[36] Though the *estancia* owners lacked the labour to undertake the cultivation, this was provided by Italian and Spanish immigrants who came into Argentina in the last decades of the nineteenth century. They rented land on the *estancias,* grew wheat for a number of years, and then planted lucerne before moving on to another tenancy. In this way wheat became a major product in Argentina, although largely as a by-product of ranching. One consequence of the expansion of arable land was the declining importance of sheep, which not only fell in numbers, from 51 000 000 in 1889 to 12 000 000 in 1922,[37] but were displaced from the inner parts of the humid pampa to the drier margins, and particularly to Patagonia. Subsequently maize and flax and later dairying and market gardening have become increasingly important in Argentina; although the wheat acreage is well below its peak in 1929, comparatively little of the pampa is devoted to ranching *in sensu stricto.* The south-eastern pampa, where the climate is cool and drainage conditions are poor, remains predominantly a grazing region, with little cropping, and specialisation in breeding cattle and producing mutton and wool.[38] Here the Aberdeen Angus, which provides the leaner meat that modern tastes demand, has progressively replaced the Shorthorn as the main breed. Further north in Uruguay, crop cultivation is confined to the area around Montevideo; alfalfa and wheat have not been as important as in Argentina, and most ranches run sheep and cattle. In northern Uruguay the range remains unfenced and the cattle are largely creole.[39]

Sheep in the Southern Hemisphere

Although sheep were the most important animals in medieval Spain, it was cattle that dominated the ranching systems in the Americas; in contrast in the other areas settled by Europeans – South Africa, Australia and New Zealand – sheep played the leading role.

Table Bay was settled in 1652 as a way station for the Dutch East Indies Company. In the early eighteenth century Dutch settlers crossed into the Little Karroo and established large pastoral holdings. By 1770 they had reached as far east as Graaff Reinet. They acquired their livestock from the Hottentots, nomadic pastoralists who had crossed the Orange river before the fourteenth century and occupied most of the South West Cape by the time the Dutch arrived. The sheep were long-legged, fat-tailed and without wool. They were prized for their tails which gave lard, and tallow for candles and soap, whilst mutton found a ready market in Cape Town for victualling ships. The cattle were zebu, predecessors of the modern Afrikander, and were kept by the Boers largely as draught or *trek* animals. Land did not have to be bought; grazing licences were granted by the Company. Most Boer families had two large ill-defined holdings, one in the arid Karroo, the other in the uplands where summer pastures were to be found. They thus lived a semi-nomadic life, often supplementing their diet by hunting, isolated from Cape Town, and indeed from each other.[40]

In 1799 merino sheep were introduced into Table Bay, but the Boers preferred their fat-tailed sheep; the British who settled in the hinterland of Algoa Bay in 1820 did however adopt the merino, and it spread westward into the Karroo. Its adoption was accelerated by the British acquisition of the Cape in 1815. There was a ready market for wool in the rapidly growing Yorkshire woollen textile industry, whilst the soap manufacturing industry in Lancashire was turning to vegetable oils. The Cape sheep thus became a minority, found mainly in the west of the Karroo. Under British administration land tenure was altered. All land became Crown property, and after 1831 it had to be purchased by auction. This, among other things, triggered off the Great Trek of the Boers north on to the grasslands of the High Veld. Here cattle became increasingly important, although mainly as draught animals.[41]

The Karroo and the fringes of the Kalahari however remained mainly devoted to sheep and, in some areas, goats. The Angora goat was introduced into South Africa in 1838, and the country was the major mohair exporter until overtaken by Texas in the 1920s. The improvement of sheep ranching however came later than in the United States or Argentina. Fencing did not begin until 1897, and its use was held back by the Boer War; it did away with the need to kraal both sheep and cattle at night, thus reducing labour needs; dipping, made compulsory, reduced diseases, whilst in 1910 Australian merinos were introduced to upgrade the quality of the stock; bore-wells slowly spread into the Karoo and the Kalahari. Little however was done to prevent overgrazing of the desert vegetation, and the carrying capacity has declined. There has been no wheat frontier, as in Argentina, the United States or Australia, to encroach on the pastoralists' land, nor has there developed a mixed farming system producing sheep and cereals. Thus over half South Africa's sheep are kept on large ranching units in the Karoo, whereas in Australia less than 30 per cent of the sheep are kept on sheep stations proper; over 40 per cent are found on sheep and wheat farms.[42]

Australia

The Australian pastoral industries are much more recent than those of the Americas, or indeed of South Africa, for the country was not settled by Europeans until 1789. In 1797 John McArthur brought merino sheep from Cape Town and crossed them with sheep of Bengal and Irish origin. There were further imports of merinos in 1804, and of Saxon merinos in the 1820s.[43] Until the 1870s the Australian economy was dominated by sheep and wool. In the early nineteenth century Australia had a very small population and little agricultural labour, although convict labour was cheap. Wool was one of the few products which had a high enough value to bear the costly journey overland to the coast and then the 12 000 miles to Britain. The times were fortuitous, for the inventions in the woollen textile industry gave rise to a greatly increased demand for wool in Britain, at a time when English wool, as a result of cross breeding for mutton, was declining in quality and when the Spanish sheep industry was in decay.[44] Nor was early agriculture in New South Wales a great success. Indeed, even as late as the 1860s there were little more than 400 000 hectares under crops in the whole continent, and wheat was imported from Chile, India and Tasmania.

It was thus pastoralists in search of grazing who spearheaded the exploration and settlement of eastern Australia. In 1813 Gregory Blaxland crossed the Blue Mountains to the Bathurst plains, whilst there was expansion southwards towards Lake George and the upper Murrumbidgee. In 1835 Melbourne was founded and the following year the first overland journey from Sydney was made. Pastoralists rapidly occupied Victoria, moving north from Portland and Geelong, until by 1863 only parts of the Mallee in the north west and Gippsland in the south east were still unoccupied.[45] Expansion north was equally rapid. The Liverpool ranges were crossed in 1827, the first sheep station on the Darling Downs was established in 1840, and the River Buddekin was reached by 1860, by which time the arid interior of New South Wales had been occupied.[46]

The first sixty years of the nineteenth century saw not only the rapid occupation of eastern Australia for sheep rearing, but naturally a great increase in sheep numbers and wool exports. In 1813 there were about 50 000 sheep in Australia, by 1860 21 000 000 and in 1890 100 000 000. Wool exports, which began in 1807, had reached 2 500 000 lb in 1830, 35 000 000 lb in 1860 and 641 000 000 lb in 1891.[47] Until the 1860s sheep rearing methods were based largely on British experience, although the farms were much larger. There was no fencing, and one station was divided from another by tacit agreement and natural features. Flocks were large, but generally operated in mobs of 400–600 sheep, looked after by one shepherd. They were centred on outstations. The sheep were driven into folds around the outstation each night, and then were taken out to the pastures during the day. The shepherds undertook most of the shearing, and the wool was taken to the coast by ox-drawn carts. Winters were mild, so there was little need for sheds, in contrast to Australia's main competitor as a wool exporter, Germany. The sheep were grazed on natural forage and relied on streams for their water.[48]

The 1860s were a turning point for the sheep industry. The gold discoveries in Victoria and New South Wales attracted rural labour into the towns and shepherds became few and expensive. Pastoralists turned to fencing their runs and mounted boundary riders replaced the shepherd, whilst shearing was increasingly undertaken by itinerant shearers who, late in the century, used powered shears.[49] After the 1860s the sheep 'runs' advanced into the arid interior, and earthen dams to collect water became essential, whilst in 1884 the first bore-well tapped the Great Artesian Basin in Queensland. Sheep were increasingly dipped to eliminate disease. Sheep breeds were improved; in 1858 the Australian merino was bred by G. Peppin, and later English breeds were imported and crossbred to produce sheep that gave wool and mutton.[50]

There were far-ranging changes in land tenure. The whole of Australia was Crown land, and until the 1830s the government of New South Wales tried to prevent settlement outside the Nineteen Counties. This they could hardly do, and the pastoralists 'squatted' on Crown lands. This could not be prevented, but the state governments realised that such pastoral occupation would prevent closer settlement by farmers. Little was done to encourage agricultural settlement until the 1860s however, except in South Australia. Before 1847 squatters had to do no more than pay an annual licence for grazing. Thus although land costs were negligible, they had no security of tenure. An Order in Council of 1847 introduced in New South Wales long leases of up to fourteen years. However the 1860s also saw the introduction of 'selection' acts, the Australian equivalent of the American Homestead Act. The pastoralists reacted in similar ways to the American cattlemen, building up large holdings by semi-legal interpretations of the 'Selection Acts'. Thus pastoralists got free land by getting their employees to file applications for home-steads, or by filing applications of imaginary people. This was called 'dummying'. In very dry areas a large area of grazing land could be controlled if the water-points were owned by a pastoralist. So he applied for lots of land with water – taking the 'eyes' of the land, or 'peacocking'.[51]

Although the acreage under crops increased between the 1860s and the 1890s, land use was still dominated by pastoralism; indeed the area used for sheep runs made its maximum advance into the interior at this time. But the system was being undermined. Rabbits, introduced into Geelong in 1859, had multiplied to become a major menace, reducing the grazing capacity, although sheep numbers continued to soar. In the 1890s wool prices collapsed, and then from 1897 to

1903 there was a series of terrible droughts, which halved Australian sheep numbers. Although there was a quick recovery, total sheep numbers did not move above the 1890s figure until after the Second World War.[52]

The disasters of the 1890s led to the bankruptcy of many pastoralists, and many large holdings were subdivided, a process which had begun with the 1884 Act. Other more powerful changes were under way. By the 1890s the wheat belt was emerging in a great arc from South Australia to Queensland. Although at first this zone had wool and wheat farms as separate enterprises, the last half-century has seen the emergence of mixed farming, whilst in the coastal areas, dairying and intensive sheep production for mutton has replaced extensive sheep rearing for wool. Thus ranching survives in the drier interior; here sheep still depend upon the natural forage, for it has proved possible neither to grow cereals and legumes nor to sow introduced grasses, and it is economically impossible to use fertilisers on pastures as has been done in the higher-rainfall zones. The pastoral zone has carried proportionally less of Australia's sheep. In the 1930s it had 37 per cent of Australian sheep, by the early 1960s only 29 per cent.[53]

The sequence of land-use changes in Australia thus bears a striking similarity to that in the American West. Until the 1860s extensive, relatively primitive shepherding techniques were practised on what was, in effect, the open range, but thereafter 'runs' were fenced, stock improved and water facilities extended. Bad prices and bad weather led to a crisis in pastoralism; thereafter much of the better-rainfall areas moved towards wheat and later wheat and sheep farming, leaving only the driest parts of the country practising ranching.

New Zealand

Sheep are ubiquitous in New Zealand, and the country is still reliant upon the exports of mutton and wool. Extensive sheep rearing however is now confined to the high country of South Island.

The first settlers arrived in New Zealand in 1840. At first Edward Wakefield's principles of colonisation were pursued, and land was sold. But in the 1850s the letting of Crown lands on licence, similar to the procedure in Australia, was introduced. In a very short period much of South Island was filled up with large sheep runs. Many of the early squatters came from Australia and brought merinos with them, and also Australian methods. Runs were rarely fenced, the sheep relied upon natural pasture, and were looked after by mounted shepherds and their dogs. Extra labour was hired to muster the sheep and shear them.[54] By 1860 New Zealand was one vast ranch providing wool for Bradford, and so remained until the 1870s when the Canterbury Plains began to be ploughed for wheat. However it was not until the 1880s that radical changes got under way. In 1882 the first refrigerated ship reached London from New Zealand, carrying frozen mutton. By the 1890s it was possible to send dairy products. This, combined with an increasing immigration and the Liberal Party's land policy encouraging closer settlement, led to the rapid intensification of land use. Small dairy and intensive mutton production replaced extensive sheep grazing in the lowland areas of both North and South Island. By the beginning of this century extensive sheep grazing survived only in the high country of South Island and more limited areas in North Island.[55]

The upland areas west of the Canterbury Plains consisted of deep valleys and many steeply sloping areas, affording few areas where arable cultivation was possible. By 1860 much of this area was held in pastoral holdings of 15 000 acres on which were run flocks of merino sheep. From the 1860s the runs were ring-fenced with smooth wire, although the fencing of paddocks was much later. This reduced labour needs. The tussock grasslands which were the dominant flora were burnt off before the sheep were run, and the green herbs and sedges so revealed provided good feed. Many flocks migrated between mountain pastures in the summer, and valley pastures in the winter.[56] The great transformation of the late nineteenth century largely passed this area by. Sown grasses were impracticable, and although some English breeds were crossed with merinos the area has remained mainly a producer of wool, and store sheep for the lowlands. Continued burning combined with the depradations of the rabbit led to a reduced carrying capacity, soil erosion and the degradation of pastures. Only in the last thirty years have there been moves towards conservation practices, and the fencing of paddocks, the growing of winter fodder, and some aerial sowing of introduced grasses.[57]

Summary

The history of ranching can be divided into a number of clearly defined stages. In the beginning cattle, half-wild, were run on the open range by mounted herdsmen, who lived a semi-migratory life. The great advantage of pastoralism in frontier regions was that the livestock could be marketed on foot. Until the 1850s hides and wool were the major products, with dried or salted meat of subsidiary importance. The rise of urban demand for meat did not immediately transform the open range in America. Indeed it was labour shortages combined with the demands for agricultural land that transformed the techniques of shepherding in Australia and New Zealand, and cattle ranching in Argentina and the United States. By the late nineteenth century ranching was being transformed in two ways. First the humid margins were experiencing the subdivision of large holdings and the rise of mixed farming; second, the ranchers who remained inviolate in the arid areas, where mixed farming was impossible, intensified their own methods, and far greater capital inputs became necessary.

The increasing intensification of ranching has been paralleled by major changes in the role of ranching in the economies of the countries. In the nineteenth century all the countries concerned were in the early stages of economic development, and food and wool exports to Europe were a major source of income. In this century industrialisation has got under way; one consequence of this has been higher urban incomes at home, and a consequent greater demand for beef and dairy products. The United States ceased to be a major beef exporter at the beginning of this century, absorbing most of its own output; and even Argentina now only exports 14 per cent of its own beef. The rise of large urban markets in Australia and Argentina has led to the intensification of farming near these markets, and displaced extensive pastoralism. Equally significant, the intensive systems produce an ever-increasing proportion of national beef and wool output. The pastoralists, in the drier margins, now find themselves in an increasingly precarious situation.

CHAPTER 13

LARGE-SCALE GRAIN PRODUCTION

In most agricultural systems based upon cultivation, grains are the major crops grown, and of these wheat and rice are of most importance. Rice is, however, with a few exceptions, the product of only one farming system, whereas wheat is a major crop in a number of systems. It is, for example, a staple crop in the small-scale, labour-intensive farms of northern India and northern China; it is grown as part of mixed farming systems in western Europe, and in the Mediterranean lands, whilst in parts of South West Asia it is grown in a manner hardly changed for the last four millennia. But the concern of this chapter is with the commercialised, mechanised and large-scale production of grains.

Wheat is still the major cash crop grown in large-scale grain production, and was of even more importance in the nineteenth century. Wheat and rye are the only crops from which bread flour can be made, and wheat flour is also used for a wide variety of pastries, cakes and pastas. It is more palatable than rye flour, and has always fetched a higher price; oats and barley have more limited uses for human food, and are grown mainly as fodder crops and for brewing. Prices for wheat are high compared with other grains, and in the long term, comparatively stable, for in the nineteenth century it was a major food for European populations, and it has become so for an increasing proportion of Asians in the last thirty years. Compared with other food crops it can be stored without spoiling, and transported over long distances fairly easily. Its relatively high value per unit weight has made it possible to sell it in remote markets. It has thus been the pre-eminent frontier crop and played a major role in the expansion of settlement in the last hundred years.[1]

Three major areas of large-scale grain production are to be found in North America (Fig. 19): first, the spring wheat region of the Dakotas and eastern Montana, together with the adjacent part of the Canadian prairies, particularly Saskatchewan; second, the winter wheat belt, centred in Kansas but including parts of eastern Colorado and Oklahoma; third, the smaller area of the Palouse country in Washington. In Latin America it is only in Argentina that large-scale grain production is carried on, in a crescent crossing the humid pampa from Cordoba and Santa Fe in the north to Bahia Blanca in the south (Fig. 1). In the Old World large-scale grain production is far less common, and is only really found in the Soviet Union. West of the Volga wheat is a major cash crop on large mechanised farms, but is generally grown as part of a mixed farming system. East of the Volga, however, grains – particularly spring wheat – form a higher proportion of the cropland and livestock are less commonly kept. In western

Siberia the Virgin and Idle Lands scheme has brought into being a farming region devoted to grains, grown on very large *sovkhoz*, which have few livestock, are highly mechanised, all in a region of very low and variable precipitation. This region conforms most nearly to the stereotype of large-scale grain production, for elsewhere wheat farmers have increasingly intensified their production and incorporated livestock into their farming system. The last, and the most remote, area of large-scale wheat production is in Australia, both in the south east and the west. The main wheat belt runs from South Australia south-eastwards into Victoria and then in an arc north-eastwards into Queensland.

Large-scale grain production is of course orientated to the sale of grains off the farm, in contrast to the subsistence wheat producers of China or northern India. Further, with the exception of Russia, a considerable proportion of the output is exported. Wheat has been the major food product (by volume) in international trade since the mid-nineteenth century. The United States and Canada account for two-thirds of the exports; Australia and Argentina contribute smaller proportions. Russia and eastern Europe, which were major exporters until the First World War, are now net importers. In the nineteenth century western Europe was by far the most important market for wheat, and as late as 1953 took half all wheat exports; but with the increase in wheat production in western Europe since then, and the appearance of China and Russia as wheat importers, western Europe's share of wheat exports has fallen to only 22 per cent.[2]

The units of production are typically large. In Russia the majority of the wheat-producing farms in western Siberia are *sovkhozes* – state farms – and average 4000 hectares. Wheat farms in North America are smaller than this; in Oklahoma farms in the wheat-growing counties averaged 650 hectares in 1950, whilst in the Dakotas *all* farms averaged 260 hectares. In Argentina wheat-producing farms range from 150 hectares to 400 hectares in size.[3] Crop yields however are low in most of the wheat-growing belts. In the Virgin Lands the average yield is 630 kg per hectare, in the Canadian Prairies 1300 kg, in the American winter wheat belt 1300–1700 kg, in Australia about 1300 kg.[4] This compares with an average yield in western Europe of 3300 to 4000 kg per hectare. The reasons for these low yields are various. First, much of large-scale grain production is carried on in areas of very low rainfall, which is furthermore very variable from year to year. Second, inputs are small; only in the last thirty years have fertilisers been used, and this combined with conservation methods and the introduction of grasses and livestock has increased crop yields in these areas. Thus the gap in wheat yields between the extensive grain producers and the mixed farmers of western Europe, although still large, has diminished.[5] The main aim of the extensive wheat farmer is to maximise output per man, for in most of these regions labour is scarce and expensive, whilst land is abundant. The farms are thus highly mechanised. In parts of North America it now takes only 9 man-hours to carry out all the operations needed to grow and harvest a hectare of wheat, compared with 148 man-hours in 1830 and 37 in the 1890s. But although expenditure on labour and fertiliser is low, the capital cost of machinery which is used for only a small part of the year is very high, not only necessitating large-scale operations, but making the wheat farmer particularly vulnerable to fluctuating prices.[6] Because the operations on wheat farms are confined to short periods of the year, it is now possible for some farmers to live at a distance from the farm, or alternatively to operate two farms well apart and with different seasonal rhythms.[7]

Large-scale grain production has been frequently described as a monoculture; and certainly this has been true of some districts in the past, where wheat alone was grown for year after year. This is now, however, comparatively rare. In most of the wheat belts there has been a marked trend towards diversification since the 1930s. By 1930 the wheat frontier had reached its outermost limit in North America, Argentina and Australia – although not in the Soviet Union. A combination of drought and poor prices led to widespread attempts to withdraw land from cultivation in the drier regions, to introduce farming methods that conserved soil moisture and prevented soil erosion, and to integrate livestock and wheat production both to improve soil fertility and to make the farmer less dependent on one product. This has been particularly successful in Australia where most wheat is now grown on farms that combine wheat and sheep production. In Canada much of the Park Belt is now devoted to mixed farming, and in Argentina there has been a trend towards integrating wheat and livestock production. Thus only in western Siberia is there still a very large area devoted almost solely to grain production. In North America the Palouse territory remains highly specialised in wheat, if only because the low rainfall precludes other enterprises. In Canada Saskatchewan has become the centre of wheat production; in the 1960s much of the province south of Saskatoon had more than 80 per cent of its cropland in wheat.[8] In the Dakotas a similar specialisation in grain is still apparent, but further south in the winter wheat belt of Kansas there has always been more diversification, and this has become more marked since 1946. In the latter year, however, 88 per cent of the cropland of the northern and central Great Plains was in grain, half in wheat.[9]

In spite of attempts to diversify the agriculture of the traditional wheat belts livestock still plays a comparatively minor role; the exceptions to this are Argentina and Australia. In the former country wheat production was formerly undertaken by tenant farmers who share-cropped parts of large pastoral *estancias* for five or six years. They grew wheat for five years, then planted alfalfa and moved on to another holding. Wheat and livestock production were thus loosely integrated. In Australia until the 1920s wheat and sheep production were generally separate enterprises; but the falling yields and poor prices of the 1930s persuaded farmers to introduce ley farming on wheat farms; this restored soil fertility, increased wheat yields and provided grazing for sheep for fat lamb and wool production.

All the major wheat-producing areas lie in regions which were very sparsely populated in the mid-nineteenth century; all have been occupied by immigrants of European origin since then. But the regions remain thinly populated, partly because of the extensive nature of farming, partly because the rainfall conditions have always precluded labour-intensive farming. All except Russia have experienced rural depopulation since the 1920s. At first sight this would appear to be due to the combined effects of drought and poor prices in the inter-war period; but it should be borne in mind that all these countries have experienced urbanisation and industrialisation in this century, and the wheat-farming areas have simply shared in the widespread trend of rural populations to move to the cities in economically advanced countries. But it has reinforced the need for highly mechanised agriculture.

The origins of large-scale grain production

Large-scale grain production, like ranching, was a product of the great economic and technological changes of the nineteenth century, which have already been touched upon (see above, pp. 45–50, 54–6). Thus the development of grain farming in Russia, the United States, Argentina, Canada and Australia has a number of features in common.

In the first place the growth of urban populations in the eastern United States and western Europe provided a market; the increase of income per caput allowed a consumer change from rye to wheaten flour, although even as late as 1925 a third of people of European origin did not eat wheaten bread.[10] Second, the repeal of the Corn Laws in Britain in 1846 made it easier for overseas producers to sell wheat in the then major market. Third, the decline in oceanic freight rates made it possible for the Russian and then the American wheat producer to undercut the British farmer. This of course would not have been possible unless production costs in America, Australia and Argentina had been low; they were low because of the cheapness of land; the rapid mechanisation of wheat farming, which was partly forced on the American and Australian farmer by the chronic shortage of farm labour; the fertility of the largely virgin soils; and the rapid spread of a railnet and an elaborate marketing system. The railway was an important factor, not simply in settling the new regions, for farmers were prepared to settle well ahead of the railways, but in providing the bulk transport that could get grain to the coast and convert subsistence farmers to commercial farmers. It is significant that in the 1860s the main wheat exports were all from coastal regions – California, Chile, South Australia and the Ukraine. They were subsequently displaced by low-cost producers in the interior of continents where the railway was an indispensable link. By the end of the century it was increasingly important in locating wheat production; in Canada, Argentina and Australia it was not thought possible for wheat production to be carried on profitably more than 25 km from a railhead.[11] Even today it costs approximately the same amount to move wheat 32 km by truck, 800 km by railway and 4800 km by sea.[12] Equally important was the development of efficient grading and bulk handling and the rapid exchange of information on prices and quantities. The latter was only possible after the introduction of the telegraph and later the telephone.

In the old-settled areas of Europe, European Russia and even the eastern United States, population densities were high in the mid-nineteenth century, and so too were land values. Migration into the thinly settled new lands was not a result simply of population pressure in the older areas, but certainly until the 1920s there was new land available at relatively low prices, thus allowing extensive production of grains. The settlement of these new lands thus resulted in an unprecedented expansion in the world's cultivated area at a time when there was little suitable land left in Europe, India or China proper. In Table 43 the total areas in the major wheat-growing countries are shown; not *all* the newly cultivated cropland was in the lands unsettled in 1860, but the great majority was. Nor of course was all new land sown to wheat, or indeed cereal crops. There was a steady increase in the wheat area of all five countries until 1930 (Table 44). Since then areas have stagnated or declined except in Russia, where the Virgin and Idle Lands scheme of 1953–6 brought a vast new area into cultivation, much of it devoted to spring wheat.

This great expansion took place in very similar environments. European farming, and that of the eastern United States, European Russia and the early settlements in Australia, had developed in forest regions, with generally an adequate rainfall. The new lands were grasslands, with progressively more arid climates as settlement moved out from the core areas.

In Russia the major vegetation and soil belts trend approximately east-west. The Russian state had its origins in the mixed forests around Moscow, and it was not until the sixteenth century that the wooded steppe to the south was colonised.[13] Beyond this lay the steppe proper, with chernozem soils; most of the Ukraine, the middle Don valley and the Kuban have between 400 mm and 500 mm of rainfall a year, but east of the Don rainfall declines and winters become longer. The chernozems occur only in a narrow belt and are succeeded southwards by the chestnut soils and a semi-desert vegetation. West of the Volga soil and climatic conditions can sustain an intensive mixed farming system, but eastwards rainfall variability makes such farming increasingly hazardous.

In the United States the major soil and vegetation belts are oriented north and south; the grasslands form a great triangle with its apex near Chicago, its most northerly point in Alberta and the southernmost in Texas. It is conventionally divided into the prairies, with an annual rainfall in excess of 450 mm and a natural vegetation of tall grass; and the Great Plains, with less than 450 mm, a high degree of variability, and predominantly short-grass. The chernozems form a narrow zone between more extensive areas of Brown Forest Soils in the Prairie region and the Chestnuts of the Great Plains.

In South America the humid pampa was once a great plain of tall grass, giving place in the west to the *monte*, an impoverished scrub woodland. Near Buenos Aires there is an annual rainfall of just less than 1000 mm, well distributed throughout the year; west and south the rainfall diminishes and becomes concen-

TABLE 43 *Expansion of cropland, 1860–1960 (million hectares)*

	1860	1870	1880	1890	1900	1910	1920	1930	1960
United States	65.8	76.3	75.9	100.1	128.8	140.1	162.4	166.8	158.3
Russia	49.2	–	102.6	112.3	–	114.3	–	109.4	195.9
Canada	–	4.4	6.06	7.6	8.4	14.1	20.2	23.4	25.0
Argentina	–	0.3	–	–	5.6	19.3	–	24.2	22.2
Australia	0.4	0.8	1.6	2.0	3.2	4.4	6.0	10.1	11.7

Sources: Urquhart and Buckley, 1965, 352; Ferrer, 1967, 99; Schwarz, 1967, 58; Lyaschenko, 1949, 450; *Official yearbook of the Commonwealth of Australia*, No. 54, 1968, 859; U.S. Bureau of the Census, 1960

trated in the summer months;[14] this contrast resembles the difference between the prairie and the Great Plains in North America. However few parts of the humid pampa have winters as cold as the central and northern Great Plains, the Canadian prairies or the Russian steppes.

Australia shares with Argentina the absence of a significant cold season. The hilly coastal regions of south-eastern Australia have a mean annual rainfall of 635 mm or more, have podzolic soils and were formerly covered with sclerophyll forest. The zone where modern wheat cultivation has taken place was once covered with a scrub woodland, with, in the south west, an area of *mallee*, low eucalyptus trees. Most of the wheat belt lies between the 250 mm and 635 mm isohyets, and in the western part of the belt there is a winter maximum. Over much of the belt rainfall variability is about 20 per cent.[15]

TABLE 44   *Expansion of the wheat area, 1860–1960 (million hectares)*

	U.S.A.	Russia	Canada	Argentina	Australia
1860	–	–	0.6	–	0.2
1870	8.4	–	0.6	0.1	0.48
1880	15.3	11.6	0.9	–	1.2
1890	14.7	13.7	1.09	1.01	1.3
1900	19.8	20.2	1.6	3.2	2.06
1910	18.4	25.0	3.5	5.8	2.9
1920	25.1	–	7.3	–	2.5
1930	25.2	26.6	10.0	9.2	7.2
1960	19.7	59.7	9.8	5.6	6.4

Sources: Urquhart and Buckley, 1965, 362; Falkus, 1966; James, 1969, 646–7; Scobie, 1967

The farmers who entered these areas in the nineteenth century were thus faced with a number of new farming problems. In the American prairie the lack of woodland at first persuaded the settlers that the soils were infertile; later they found other difficulties. The lack of wood made fencing expensive, a problem which was not resolved until the production of barbed wire, patented in 1873.[16] The thick sod was extremely difficult to turn, but this problem was solved by the introduction of a breaking plough in 1837, drawn by six oxen. But the cast-iron shares of the ploughs soon became coated with the heavy, sticky soils of the prairies. This however was overcome by John Deere's invention of the self-scouring, chilled steel blade. The great advantage of the grasslands compared with the forests was the ease with which they could be cleared for cultivation. In 1850 it took, on average, 81 days to clear a hectare of forest for cultivation, but in the grasslands only 3.7 days; this was clearly a major reason for the rapidity with which agricultural settlement advanced west in the United States.[17] In Australia the well-watered forest areas were much more costly to clear than the drier scrublands;[18] but within the latter area the *mallee* proved particularly intractable, for not only did the eucalyptus trees form tabular masses at ground level but tney regenerated rapidly after clearing. This was overcome by a special roller invented by Mullens and the use of the stump-jump plough, which allowed a crop to be sown before the stumps had been completely cleared.

The development of large-scale grain production depended upon the availability of land and the invention of machinery. The system of land disposal varied between countries. In Argentina most of the pampa had been allocated in large private holdings; after the final defeat of the Indians in the 1880s most of the newly acquired land was again sold, or given as a political reward, in very large units. Although there had been attempts to settle European migrants in colonies in Santa Fe Province as early as the 1860s, these had not been continued. Thus when Italian migrants began to arrive in large numbers in the 1880s they found no free land to settle and had little alternative but to become sharecroppers on the large *estancias*. This was not a system conducive to good farming. It is only in the last thirty years that there has been a beginning of subdivision of the large estates and the growth of freeholding farmers.[19]

In Australia, the United States and Canada unoccupied land was the property of the state, and their varying methods of disposing of land make an interesting study. All three aimed at creating an independent yeomanry by allowing 'homesteaders' to take up land at a very low price. Unfortunately the maximum amount of land allowed was generally well below that necessary in the drier areas for the economic production of wheat. Thus in Australia the 'selection' act in New South Wales allowed up to 128 hectares, that in Victoria 259 hectares. In the United States the Homestead Act of 1862 allowed only 64 hectares, which was quite inappropriate to the dry conditions of the Great Plains. In Canada the 1872 Land Act allowed each homesteader 64 hectares, but he could buy a further 64 hectares at $0.8 a hectare. In 1904 the Act was amended to allow the acquisition of larger units and comparable Acts were also passed in the United States.[20] Fortunately in both countries it was possible to buy land directly either from the government or from the land grants made to railway companies; it was therefore possible for the prosperous farmer to build up a large unit. Nonetheless many small farms were taken up, and their owners broken in the periodic droughts. In Canada, the United States and Australia the average size of farm has steadily increased in this century. Thus in North Dakota in 1880 it was 109 hectares, in 1950, 250 hectares, in Kansas 60 hectares and 150 hectares, and in Nebraska 60 hectares and 180 hectares.[21]

In Russia the settlement of the drier steppes along the Black Sea only got under way in the late eighteenth century. Catherine II attracted landlords by allocating very large estates to anyone who would settle serfs. This attracted not only Russians but Serbs, Greeks, Czechs, Germans and Poles, and along with the numerous peasant farms the area was farmed in very large estates. In western Siberia, which was not settled on any scale until after the abolition of serfdom in 1861, there was no landlord class. But the settlers took with them the collective *mir* which precluded the acquisition of very large individual holdings; nonetheless farms were larger than in European Russia. The large farms of the present are a result of colonisation in the 1950s when the state farm was adopted as the main means of settlement.[22]

The fact that land could be acquired comparatively cheaply was clearly a necessary prerequisite in the development of large-scale production. Equally necessary was the invention of suitable machinery. This was necessitated by a number of factors; labour was significantly more expensive than in the densely settled areas; even in Russia labour costs in Siberia were 25–30 per cent higher than in European Russia at the end of the nineteenth century.[23] Most of the new inventions were made in the United States and Australia, and imported into Argentina and to a lesser extent Russia at a later date. The major breakthrough was McCormick's design of a practical reaper in the 1830s; by 1860 80000 of his machines had been sold, for they were easily used in the flat level land of the prairies. In 1858 the Marsh brothers added a platform to allow a man to tie the bundles of grain; in 1873 the automatic binder was added using wire, and after 1878 twine. Steam threshing was developed in the United States in the 1830s by J. and H. Pitts; the machine was expensive and threshing was often undertaken by migratory contract workers who moved with it from farm to farm. The combination of reaping, binding and threshing in one machine was the next step; an early combine was designed in Michigan in the 1830s and taken to California in 1853, but it was not common until the 1880s and was not used east of the Rockies until after 1900. Indeed it did not become general until the inter-war period, by which time it was no longer hauled by great teams of horses but driven by a petrol-engine.[24]

The preparation of the seed bed was also rapidly mechanised; in 1864 the sulky plough – which gave the ploughman a seat – was patented, and gang ploughs were introduced, together with the spring-tooth and the disc harrow; the seed drill was a surprisingly late adoption and was not in general use in the prairies until after 1870.[25]

Although most of the new machinery was invented in the United States, parallel advances were made in Australia, and particularly in South Australia. The stripper, invented by John Bull but marketed by, and named after Ridley, was patented in 1849 and was in widespread use in the 1850s. In the 1860s two-thirds of South Australia's wheat area was reaped with this machine. In 1884 H. V. Mackay patented a harvester, adapted to Australian conditions, which reaped and winnowed. The consequence of mechanisation was greatly to reduce labour costs. Thus Ridley's stripper, which cut the heads off and left the straw standing, reduced harvesting costs from 2s. to $3\frac{1}{2}$d. a bushel.[26] In the United States in the 1830s, with broadcasting, an ox-drawn plough – horses only became dominant after 1860 – a scythe and flail, it took 148 man-hours to cultivate and harvest one hectare of wheat; but by the 1890s this figure had fallen to 37 hours in Illinois, and in California, where the combine was in use, to only six hours. This greatly increased the area which one man could handle. With sickle and flail one man could grow three hectares of wheat, but by the 1890s one man could handle 43 hectares or more. The horse became the major draught animal, pulling not only ploughs and harrows but also, in great teams, the early combines.[27]

By the 1880s farming in the United States, Canada and Argentina had pushed well into semi-arid areas, as it had in Russia at an earlier date. The lack of surface water not only made farming a chancy business, but the absence of drinking water hampered settlement until it was possible to bore deep wells, and use the steel windmill to pump up water from a depth.[28] New varieties of drought-resistant wheat were needed. The most celebrated new variety was *Federation,* bred by William Farrer in Australia and first marketed in 1902. But earlier Mennonites from South Russia had introduced a hard red winter wheat into Kansas. Further north *Red Fife* had allowed wheat cultivation in the short growing season of the Canadian prairies, and in the early twentieth century *Marquis* allowed further northern extension.[29] The successful cultivation of spring wheats had been dependent on new methods of milling flour which were imported into Minneapolis from Hungary in 1870.[30]

By the 1880s farmers in Canada, the U.S.A. and Australia had suffered from a series of droughts. This led to the development of 'dry-farming', a number of techniques aimed at conserving soil moisture, including fallowing, the creation of a mulch and repeated working of the soil after rainfall. It was advocated in Canada by Angus Mackay, in the United States by H. Campbell, and was introduced into Australia in the 1890s.[31] The belief that dry-farming could successfully take wheat-farming even further into the dry regions was no doubt one factor in the continued expansion of wheat-growing in the first three decades of this century. The disasters of the 1930s have however led to a reappraisal of methods of dry-farming. In Canada in particular new practices have been adopted. The bare fallow is no longer thought advisable, the disc and the Noble blade have replaced the mouldboard plough, and a variety of methods to reduce soil erosion have been adopted. Yet in the 1950s the Russian push into the arid steppes of Kazakhstan repeated many of the mistakes made in North America and Australia earlier this century.[32]

Russia

We may now turn to the development of large-scale grain production in each country. It was not until the sixteenth century that Russian settlers moved out of the forests where Muscovy had its origins, into the steppe. Until then nomadic pastoralists had made permanent settlement hazardous. Between 1600 and 1750 the wooded steppe was slowly colonised by Russians from the north and Ukrainians from the west, and by 1724 the wooded steppe had a quarter of Russia's population.[33] The drier steppes along the Black Sea did not become open to settlement until the Turks had been defeated; the grass steppes were thus not open to farmers until the end of the eighteenth century. In the first half of the nineteenth century the drier steppes east to the Volga and across the Don into the Kuban were taken up by farmers. Both large estates, often owned by foreigners, and small peasant farms, operated by serfs, were established. Serfs found the *barschina*, the payment of dues in labour, less onerous then *obrok*, payment in money or kind, and the former prevailed in the south. A market-orientated agriculture developed, with wheat and sugar-beet the main cash crops, although on the frontier of settlement cattle and merino sheep, introduced in the early nineteenth century, were the major products.[34] At first wheat moved mainly north to Moscow; later some was exported to western Europe from the Baltic ports. But by 1850 90 per cent of wheat exports were going through the Black Sea ports, especially Odessa.[35] In the 1860s railways linked the south with Moscow, and in the 1870s railways from Odessa and Rostov linked these ports with the wheat-producing regions. By the 1880s most of the 'new' lands in the European steppe were taken up; indeed there was a chronic shortage of land in the black earth regions by the 1870s.[36] The first half of the nineteenth century was thus a period of remarkable expansion in southern Russia; over 20 000 000 hectares of new land were brought into cultivation in the Ukraine and the Volga provinces between 1800 and 1860,[37] on farms which were markedly larger than those further north, using hired labour; after the abolition of duty on imported agricultural machinery in 1806, such implements that were available at the time were used. By mid-century Russia was a major wheat exporter, second only to the United States. Britain took from one-half to two-thirds of the grain. Grain exports were 36 per cent of all Russian exports.[38]

TABLE 45   *Migration to Siberia, 1801–1914 (thousands)*

	Total	Annual rate
1801–50	375	8
1851–60	191	19
1861–70	114	11
1871–80	248	25
1881–90	419	42
1891–1900	1208	121
1901–10	2282	229
1911–14	723	180

Source: Treadgold, 1957, 33

In the last two decades of the nineteenth century the steppes east of the Urals began to be occupied. In 1858 Siberia already had a population of 3 000 000, made up of 'old settlers' who had fled to escape serfdom, and political exiles. After the abolition of serfdom in 1861 it was easier for peasants to migrate, particularly after the building of the Trans-Siberian Railway in the 1890s, reaching the Ob river in 1896 and Irkutsk in 1898; often whole villages undertook the journey, from the great arc of overpopulated country in the middle Volga and the central agricultural region. They settled not in dispersed farmsteads, as did the American, Canadian and Australian farmers, but in villages, and retained the communal land-holding of the *mir*. Thus although the farms established in western Siberia were larger than those of European Russia, there were none of the great bonanza wheat farms of North America; nor was there monoculture of wheat or the use of machinery; and livestock remained an important part of the farming system.[39]

The flow of migrants east halted in the First World War, and the troubled conditions of the 1920s saw few leave European Russia. In 1930 individual colonisation was forbidden. Thus it was not until the 1950s that the West Siberian steppe saw a further expansion, although this was on an unparalleled scale. In 1954 the Virgin and Idle Lands programme was announced, to plough up land between the Urals and the Ob river. Most of the chernozems in West Siberia were already in cultivation, so the new lands were on the chestnut soils to the south, where the growing season is no more than 130 days, and mean annual rainfall on the southern frontier no more than 250 mm. Most of the new land was farmed in *sovkhozes* rather than in *kholkoz*, and was highly mechanised; some 36 000 000 hectares were added to Russia's sown area. The new farms were mainly put under grain, especially spring wheat. In such a climatically marginal area it is not surprising that there have been violent fluctuations in yield; the hazards of the climate were compounded by the refusal, until the mid-1960s, to use modern dry-farming techniques. Nonetheless the area east of the Volga now produces 50 per cent of Russia's grain and 70 per cent of the wheat.

Further west the farms in the European steppes have been intensified, continuing a tradition of mixed farming that was apparent in the early nineteenth century; maize and sunflowers have been added to wheat, sugar beet and potatoes. Thus the major wheat-producing region has shifted progressively east since the late eighteenth century, whilst the former wheat regions have intensified and diversified their farming system. Wheat is now the major crop in areas where the climate allows few alternatives, a pattern which has been repeated in other wheat-growing centres.[40]

The United States

The period following the Civil War saw a remarkable expansion of the cultivated area of the United States, made possible by the economic and technological changes noted above.

Most of the land brought into cultivation after 1860 was west of the Mississippi, in the prairies and the Great Plains. The advance of the frontier, however, was neither continuous nor regular. Between 1850 and 1860 most of the new land was in the prairies west of Chicago (Fig. 23a), in the 1870s in eastern Nebraska, Kansas and east Texas. In the 1880s the plough moved into the eastern Dakotas (Fig. 23b). In the first decade of this century the new land was mainly in the Dakotas, Nebraska, Oklahoma and Texas (Fig. 23c), but the last great push of the arable frontier, which lasted into the 1920s, was mainly in Montana, Wyoming and Colorado (Fig. 23d).

Large-scale grain production

Although wheat was by no means the only crop grown in the new lands, its total area rose rapidly in the late nineteenth century, reaching a peak in 1930. The centre of production moved steadily westwards, not so much because of a decline in area in the East, although this did occur, but because of rapid expansion in the West. Once the railways had penetrated the Great Plains the combination of cheap land and low labour costs made it difficult for eastern farmers to compete. Also the semi-arid areas could grow high-protein hard wheats in contrast to the soft wheats grown in the more humid East. Furthermore, as the frontier advanced into the semi-arid areas in the 1890s there were few alternative crops which farmers could grow. Fig. 24 and Table 46 trace the westward shift of wheat production. In 1815 the heart of American wheat production was in south-eastern Pennsylvania, in 1839 Ohio was the leading producer, but on the eve of the Civil War the prairies around Chicago were the centre (Fig. 24a). In 1889 the Red River Valley of the Dakotas had emerged as a major producer (Fig. 24b), as had California and Kansas. But it was not until after 1890 that the winter wheat belt or the Palouse district took on their modern form (Figs. 24c, d).

TABLE 46   *Total cultivated area and wheat area in the U.S.A.*
(million hectares)

	Cropland	Wheat
1850	45.6	3.2[a]
1860	65.8	5.4[a]
1870	76.3	8.4
1880	76.3	15.3
1890	100.1	14.7
1900	128.8	19.87
1910	140.1	18.4
1920	162.4	25.1
1930	166.8	25.2
1940	161.1	21.4
1950	165.2	24.8
1960	158.3	20.9

Source: U.S. Bureau of the Census, 1960, 278, 296–7
[a] Estimated from production figures

The present distribution of wheat-growing in the United States thus emerged only in the 1890s and had taken on its major distribution features by 1909. Other essential characteristics developed earlier. The large mechanised farm, growing wheat almost to the exclusion of other crops, appeared first in California in the 1860s. Farms of over 12 000 hectares were found here in the 1870s and 1880s. Many farmers grew wheat continuously for fifteen years or more. The land was ploughed with gang ploughs, harvested with a header, and by the 1870s a combine harvester, and migratory labour was used. Summer fallowing and mulching were practised in the 1870s. Similar farming practices developed in the Red

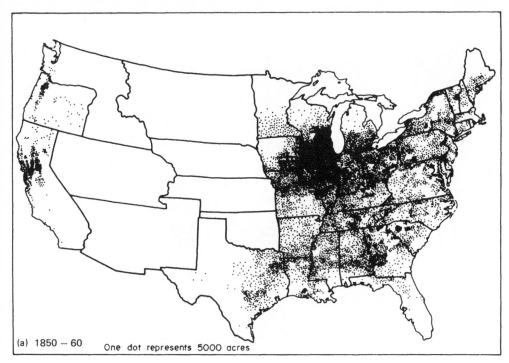

(a) 1850 — 60   One dot represents 5000 acres

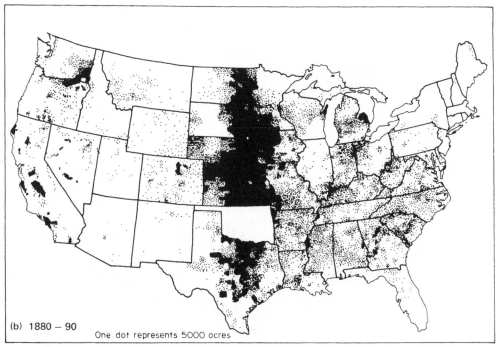

(b) 1880 — 90
One dot represents 5000 acres

Fig. 23. Location of new improved land in the United States. 1850–1920. [Source: Paullin, 1932. Plates 145–6]

269

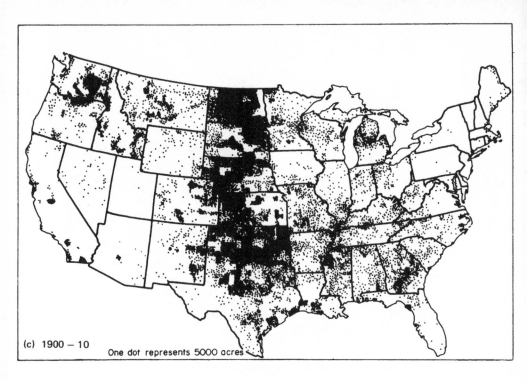

(c) 1900 – 10   One dot represents 5000 acres

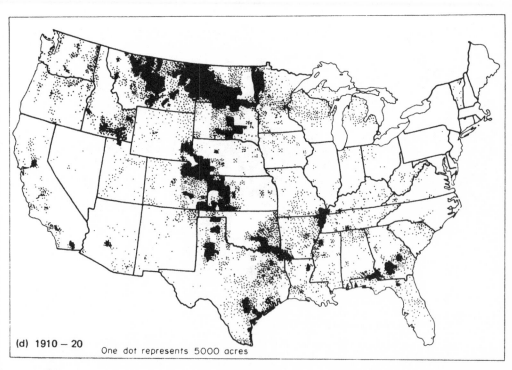

(d) 1910 – 20   One dot represents 5000 acres

270

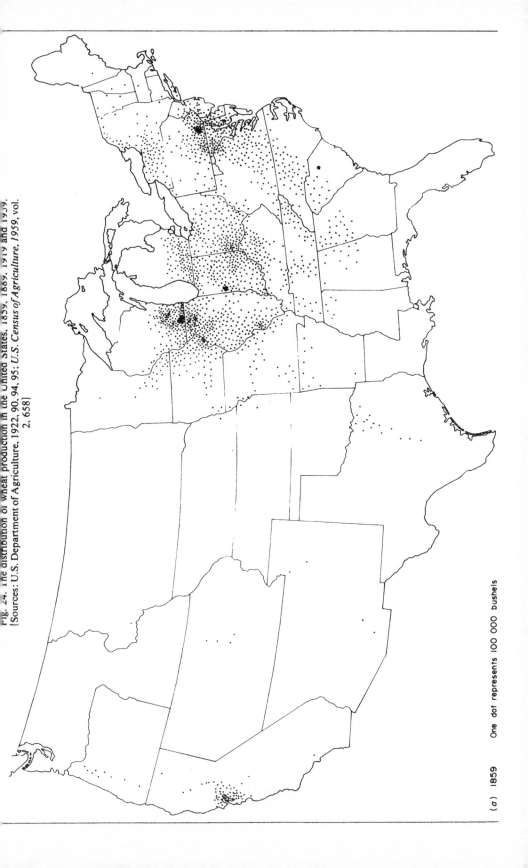

Fig. 24. The distribution of wheat production in the United States, 1859, 1869, 1919 and 1959. [Sources: U.S. Department of Agriculture, 1922, 90, 94, 95; *U.S. Census of Agriculture, 1959*, vol. 2, 658]

(*a*) 1859   One dot represents 100 000 bushels

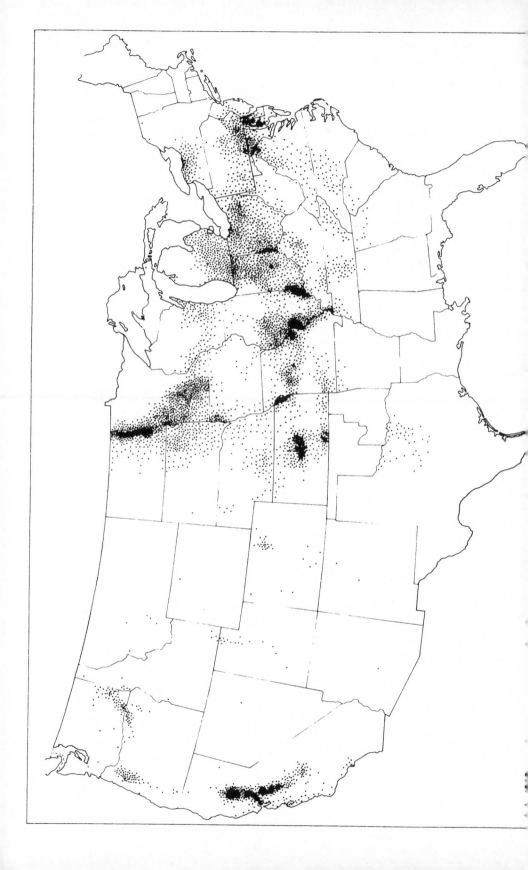

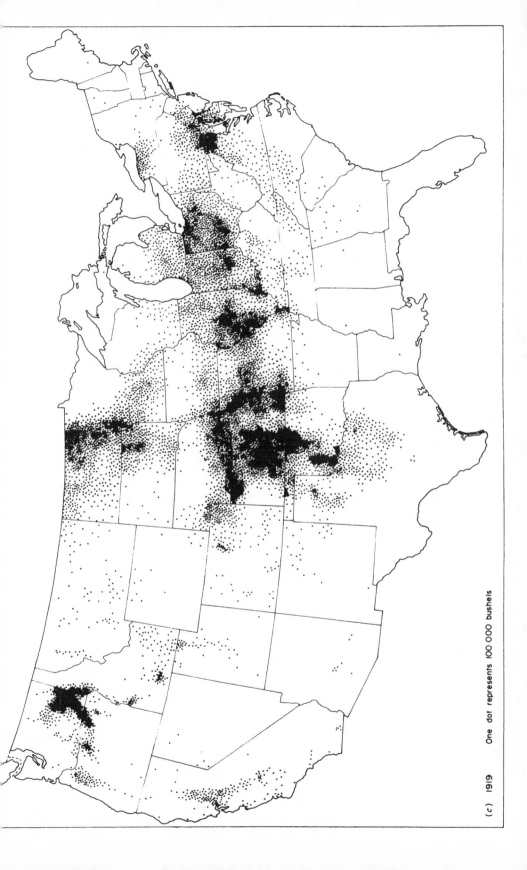

(c) 1919   One dot represents 100 000 bushels

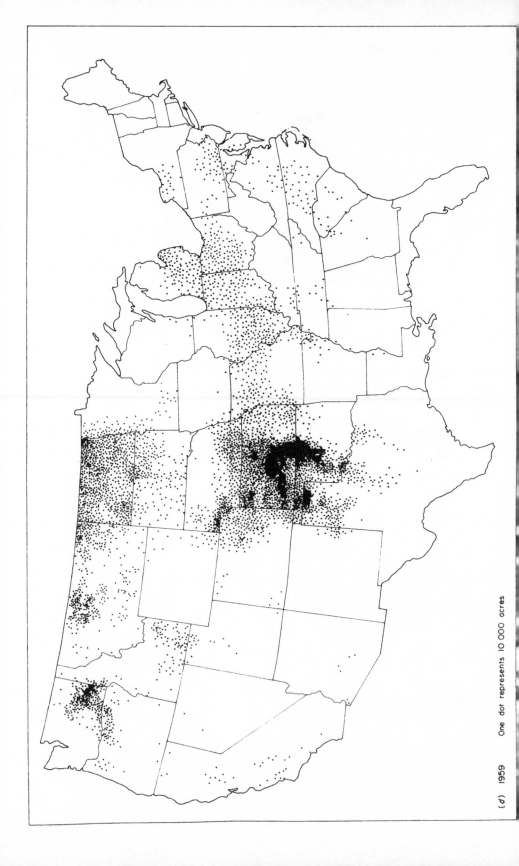

(d) 1959   One dot represents 10 000 acres

River Valley in the 1870s. Here were the 'bonanza' wheat farms, often owned by businessmen resident in the East, and like those in California, they were highly mechanised and highly specialised; wheat formed a high proportion of the cropland; 70 per cent of Minnesota's arable was in wheat in the 1870s. Crop yields were low – about 890 kg per hectare in California in the 1880s – partly because of the low and variable rainfall, but also because of the failure to use fertiliser and the unimportance of livestock and hence the lack of manure.[41] Few, however, of the bonanza farms of the Dakotas survived the poor prices and droughts of the 1880s, when most of them were subdivided and sold. A third area of large, mechanised wheat farms grew up in the Palouse country of Washington, an area needing dry-farming. Here the caterpillar tractor made its first appearance in 1904.[42]

TABLE 47   *Percentage of U.S. wheat output, by regions, 1859–1962*

	1859	1869	1879	1889	1899	1909	1962
North Atlantic	14.2	12.2	7.4	6.8	5.1	4.4	1.8
South Atlantic	16.6	7.8	6.2	5.9	4.8	3.9	1.5
East North Central	46.1	44.3	44.5	31.4	20.5	17.7	14.8
West North Central	8.8	23.4	27.1	37.4	46.6	56.2	45.4
South Central	9.9	5.0	5.3	5.2	9.4	4.7	11.5
Western	4.4	7.3	9.4	13.5	13.7	13.0	24.8

Sources: Schmidt, 1925*b*, 374; U.S. Bureau of the Census, 1964, 655

North Atlantic: New England, N.Y., Pa., N.J.
South Atlantic: Va., N.C., S.C., Ga., Fla., W. Va., Del., Md.
East North Central: Ohio, Ind., Ill., Wis., Mich.
West North Central: Iowa, Minn., Mo., N. Dak., S. Dak., Kans., Nebr.
South Central: Ky., Tenn., Ala., Miss., La., Ark., Okla., Tex.
Western: Mont., Idaho, Wyo., Colo., N. Mex., Ariz., Utah., Nev., Calif., Oreg., Wash.

But such large-scale, highly mechanised and highly specialised farming enterprises were not typical of all the wheat-producing areas in the nineteenth century, least of all in Kansas and Nebraska. Here the early settlers in the 1860s had 64 hectares or less, raised wheat as a cash crop but also grew potatoes and corn, and kept livestock. Indeed corn occupied the largest area even after the 100th meridian had been passed, and it was not until the 1890s that wheat began to replace corn in western Kansas.[43]

In the 1920s wheat made its final push into the marginal lands of the western Great Plains. The disasters of the 1930s, when land was abandoned throughout the Plains, and the population fell by 300 000, led to a retreat, but the better rainfall of the 1940s, together with the better prices of the War, again led to the ploughing of marginal land.

But this war-time expansion was temporary; since 1935 there have been major changes in large-scale wheat production in the United States. The droughts of the 1930s led to a retreat of wheat-growing from the drier areas, a move which was encouraged by the Department of Agriculture; land was seeded down to grass and grazing re-established. Since the Second World War the increase in wheat yields has led to large wheat surpluses; limitations on area imposed by the government have further reduced the area sown to wheat, which is now well below the peak of 1930. In the more humid parts of the Great Plains crop rotations have been encouraged and livestock integrated with wheat production. This has been most noticeable in the winter wheat belt, where wheat has never dominated the farming system to the extent that it did in the Palouse or the Dakotas. In the drier wheat-producing areas, where the growing of rotational crops, and particularly legumes, is difficult, new methods of dry-farming have replaced those practised from the 1890s to the 1930s. Whilst fallowing is still widely practised, a stubble cover is kept; deep ploughing is no longer practised and indeed the mouldboard plough has been replaced by the Noble blade, whilst various conservation devices such as contour ploughing and strip cropping are practised. Mechanisation has even further reduced the labour needed. In 1920, at the height of the classical wheat frontier, only 5 per cent of American wheat was harvested with a combine, by 1938 50 per cent. Little is now not combined, whilst the tractor has finally driven the horse from the American farm.[44]

In spite of these changes, which reflect a trend to the intensification of production, the three major wheat-producing areas are still those described by O. E. Baker forty years ago – the spring wheat belt of the Dakotas, the winter belt of Kansas, and the Palouse country of Washington. Together they produce three-quarters of American wheat output.[45]

Canada

The development of large-scale grain production in Canada came much later than in the United States. Wheat was of course grown in the East but the Prairies were colonised much later than the American West. This was partly due to the separation of the prairies from Ontario by the Canadian shield, whilst the United States exerted a continual attraction on the Canadian population. On the other hand the Canadians could learn from American experience. By 1900 there was a considerable body of knowledge on dry-farming and the use of machinery, whilst the provincial governments modelled both their rectangular survey and the Land Act of 1872 on American practice. The Canadian Pacific Railway received 10 000 000 hectares of land in return for the construction of the transcontinental line, emulating a practice introduced in the United States. By 1900 there was little good land left in the United States and between 1900 and 1920 250 000 Americans settled in the prairie provinces.[46]

Although Lord Selkirk had established a settlement in the Red River Valley in 1812, it did not flourish. In 1869 the Dominion government bought the land of the Hudson Bay Company, and the way was open for settlement. The Canadian prairies are the northernmost part of the North American grasslands; three zones are usually distinguished. The Park Belt, an area formerly of tall grass with clumps of trees, of which the aspen is the most common, curves in an arc from Winnipeg to Saskatoon and then south-westwards. With 350 to 500 mm of rainfall and deep black soils this is the most favoured part of the prairies. South of the Park Belt lies a zone of short grass and brown soils, with less rainfall, but carrying most of the present wheatlands; in south-western Saskatchewan and south-eastern Alberta is a semi-arid region of gramma grasses, but with some sage and cactus. Precipitation in the prairies only exceeds 500 mm in the extreme east, and of this 30 per cent is snow. However all except the south west have at least 200 mm between April and September, the effective growing season, so wheat growing is possible, but vulnerable to the high variability, which increases to the south and west.[47]

The settlement of the Canadian prairies did not really get under way until the beginning of this century. In 1900 crop production was still mainly confined to the Manitoban Park Belt, although the first wheat shipped out of Winnipeg had gone south to St Paul in 1877. But in 1885 the first transcontinental line was completed, linking Winnipeg, Regina, Calgary and Vancouver, and by 1905 Edmonton was linked to Winnipeg. By 1921 few parts of the prairie provinces were more than 16 km from a railway. The first two decades of this century saw the rapid settlement of the prairies (Table 48). In 1901 the prairie provinces had only 10 per cent of Canada's arable land, by 1931 67 per cent. In the latter year the wheat area reached its peak, and wheat was grown on two-thirds of the prairie provinces' cropland; oats and barley occupied much of the rest. In Saskatchewan over three-quarters of the cropland was in wheat. Not surprisingly this province suffered acutely in the poor years in the 1930s, when income per caput in the state fell by 72 per cent.[48]

TABLE 48 *Population and land use in the Prairie provinces, 1881–1961*

	Population (millions)	Improved land (million hectares)	Field crops (million hectares)	Wheat (million hectares)
1881	0.12	0.1	0.1	–
1891	0.25	0.5	0.48	–
1901	0.419	2.2	1.45	1.0
1911	1.3	9.0	7.1	4.0
1921	1.9	18.0	13.0	7.7
1931	2.3	24.1	16.1	10.3
1941	2.4	26.4	15.4	9.0
1951	2.5	29.0	18.3	9.8
1961	3.1	32.8	19.0	9.9

Sources: Mackintosh, 1934, 2; Richards, 1968, 411–13; Urquhart and Buckley, 1965, 352

Since the 1930s prairie farming has gone through changes comparable to those in the Great Plains. In the east the Manitoban Park Belt has progressively become more devoted to mixed farming, whilst in south-western Saskatchewan and south-eastern Alberta the drier lands have returned to ranching.

Saskatchewan has become the wheat province *par excellence,* with increased farm size, more mechanisation, improved dry-farming methods, the use of pesticides and some fertiliser; crop yields have risen in response. Outside southern Saskatchewan farmers have turned more and more to beef cattle as well as wheat. But in the drier parts of Saskatchewan the farmer has fewer opportunities to diversify, and is burdened by the problem of overproduction, the victim of his own efficiency.[49]

Argentina

In much of the humid pampa physical conditions are suitable for either ranching or crop production, but until the 1860s the region was almost exclusively pastoral. There were several reasons for this. The area had been divided into very large estancias at an early date, and the return on capital to landowners was high. Traditionally Argentinians had little enthusiasm for arable farming, and the rural population was too small to undertake intensive crop production over a large area. In the south hostile Indians made permanent settlement impossible, and it was not until the war of 1879–80 that they were finally defeated; the land thus made available for settlement was laid out by the government in large holdings for ranching rather than in small units for agricultural colonisation. Lastly the lack of adequate transport made the marketing of crops prohibitively expensive; ox-drawn carts were the only means of transport until the first railway was built in 1857. Cattle and sheep, on the other hand, could be driven on the hoof to Buenos Aires, which was already the major centre of domestic consumption and export.[50]

In the 1870s and the 1880s the Argentine cattle industry underwent rapid changes. The imported English cattle needed better feed than the natural grass of the pampa, and efforts were made to grow lucerne; the *gaucho* however was neither willing nor able to undertake cultivation. On the other hand the numerous Italian and Spanish immigrants arriving in Argentina in the 1880s and 1890s could not obtain homesteads because the available land was already in private *estancias.* A system of share-cropping tenancies emerged which satisfied both *estancia* owner and immigrant. Large farms – many as big as 200 hectares – were granted to tenants. They grew wheat for four or five years, and in the last year of their tenancy planted lucerne. Lucerne would last for up to ten years before it needed sowing again. The tenants then moved to another holding and repeated the cycle. In such impermanent conditions substantial investment could hardly be expected, and farming methods were primitive. Wheat was grown continuously, with perhaps an occasional year of flax, and fertilisers were unknown. Until the 1890s machinery was unusual; the farms were tilled with ox-drawn ploughs, and the crop harvested with sickle and scythe. Threshing was done by horses. Slowly, however, machinery was adopted. Steel ploughs replaced wooden ploughs, the horse superseded the oxen, and in 1900 the reaper was introduced. The steam thresher had been first used in 1858, but it was slow to spread. Most tenant holdings were operated by family labour, but as farms were quite large, part-time labour was needed at harvest. Part of this was supplied by the *golondrinas,* 'the swallows', migrant labourers from Italy and Spain who came for four or five months each year, and then returned home. From 1870 until the outbreak of the First World War the number of *golondrinas* rarely fell below 50 000 a year.[51]

The Italian sharecroppers were not the first to grow wheat in Argentina. It had been grown near Buenos Aires in the eighteenth century and in the 1850s a number of agricultural colonies were established in Santa Fe province, where immigrants bought the land from colonisation companies. Their cash crop was wheat; this was only possible with the expansion of the railway network (largely financed by British capital), as was the subsequent expansion of the wheat belt southwards by tenant farmers. The result of this expansion was an extraordinary increase in the cultivated area; in 1875 the combined grain and forage crop area was only 340 000 hectares; in 1913 it was 20 000 000 and by 1929, the height of the boom, 25 000 000 hectares. The value of agricultural exports in present-day values rose from $260 000 000 in 1875 to $460 000 000 in 1913 and $2 000 000 000 in 1929. Down to 1930 between 50 per cent and 70 per cent of the pampas' total output was exported each year. In 1871, when the first wheat was exported, virtually all Argentina's exports were pastoral. But by 1900 wheat was Argentina's leading export, and the country was the third exporter in the world.[52]

Wheat was not the only crop grown in Argentina. In the 1890s maize began to be grown, also by tenant farmers; it began to displace wheat in the region near Rosario, where maize yields were much higher than those of wheat. Away from this warm, relatively humid area, however, wheat was a more reliable crop. Most of the maize was exported for feeding, particularly for poultry, to Europe. After the First World War production of vegetables, dairying, and other intensive forms of agriculture developed near Buenos Aires. The heyday of Argentina's agricultural boom was reached in 1929; it has been remarkably stagnant since. The depression of the 1920s, the Second World War, which cut Argentina off from its major markets, and after the war the growth in agricultural output in Europe, have all reduced the opportunities for Argentina's exports. The arable area and crop yields have changed little since 1929, and the land remains in the hands of a relatively small number of landowners. Not only are agricultural exports lower than they were in the 1920s, but only about 30 per cent of the pampas' output is now exported.[53]

Thus the modern map (Fig. 25) of farming in the pampas represents the events not of the last thirty years, but those of the turbulent expansion from 1865 to 1930. South east of Buenos Aires lies the pastoral district, where 80 per cent of the agricultural land is still used for grazing cattle, but the largest part of the humid pampa falls within the alfalfa–wheat zone. This is still mainly a pastoral area; the *estancia* owners are primarily cattle producers, and wheat is still mainly produced by tenant farmers. However partible inheritance and financial failure

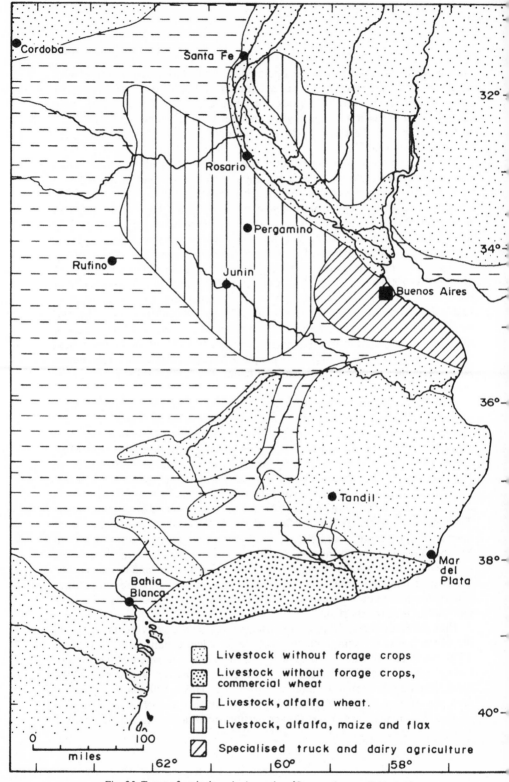

Fig. 25. Types of agriculture in Argentina. [Source: James. 1950, 310]

Legend:

- Livestock without forage crops
- Livestock without forage crops, commercial wheat
- Livestock, alfalfa wheat.
- Livestock, alfalfa, maize and flax
- Specialised truck and dairy agriculture

have led to some subdivision of large holdings, and a class of owner-occupier farmers is emerging, who are practising a genuine mixed farming system.[54]

Australia

For the first half of the nineteenth century the Australian economy was dominated by sheep, and few crops were grown. In 1860 wheat was still imported, from Tasmania and sometimes from India and Chile; only in South Australia had commercial wheat production got under way. The colony had been founded on Edward Wakefield's principles of colonisation, and both taxation and land tenure systems favoured the farmer rather than the pastoralist. In 1860 South Australia grew nearly half of Australia's 249 000 hectares of wheat. Elsewhere wheat was grown only in coastal districts, in the hills in the hinterland of Sydney and Melbourne (Fig. 26).[55]

In the 1850s there were over 600 000 migrants to Australia, attracted mainly by the discovery of gold in Victoria; but once the fervour had subsided they sought land. Both Victoria and New South Wales passed legislation in the 1860s to make agricultural settlement easier; that in Victoria was more successful than that in New South Wales, where the pastoralists still controlled the interior in the 1880s. But even in Victoria settlers were forced to leapfrog the pastoral uplands into the Wimmera and the Victorian Riverina, where wheat farming began in the 1860s. The advance into the drier lands was aided by the breeding of drought-resistant wheats, such as Purple Straw, and later the import of American and South African varieties. Further the stripper, and later in the 1880s McKay's header, were widely adopted. In the 1870s wheat farming in South Australia pushed north into very marginal land, and indeed there was a retreat during the droughts of the 1880s.[56]

By the 1890s the modern distribution had become apparent (Fig. 26). Most of the wheat farming after 1870 was undertaken on medium-sized farms of 120–160 hectares and was well mechanised, for the rural population began to decline as early as the 1880s. Wheat was grown continuously, and farming methods were often slovenly. Thus yields fell in the last thirty years of the century. In the 1890s dry-farming methods began to be adopted, based on fallowing and deep ploughing. Perhaps more significant was the detection in 1879 of a phosphorus deficiency in many wheat soils and the subsequent use of superphosphate. Yields rose again between 1900 and 1920, although there was not a great expansion of the area under wheat. The last push came in the 1920s, reaching a peak in 1930. Then in the 1930s the wheat belt suffered many of the difficulties experienced in Canada.[57]

The consequence was a slow integration of wheat and sheep farming. The value of subterranean clover had been discovered in the 1870s but was only adopted in the 1930s. Wheat was grown for three years, followed by four years of ley, on which fat lambs were produced. The older methods of dry farming were, as in Canada, shown to be harmful, and were replaced by improved

281

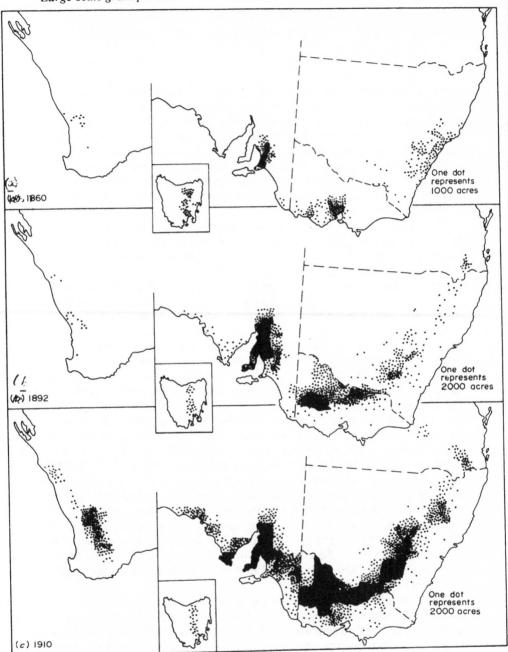

Fig. 26. Wheat acreage in Australia, 1860, 1892 and 1910. [Source Dunsdorf, 1956]

methods. Thus since the 1930s the specialised wheat farms have largely been superseded by mixed farms, although some traditional wheat farms are still to be found, particularly in northern New South Wales where substantial additions to the wheat area were made as late as the 1960s; this brought Australia's wheat area back to the 1930 level; however as yields are now higher, total output is well above that of the past.[58]

Summary

Thus although extensive wheat production can be ultimately traced back to Europe, and particularly to the Mediterranean basin, it will be apparent that large-scale wheat production is a product essentially of the late nineteenth century when changes in farming methods, transport costs and rising urban demand in Europe brought the new system into being. A number of points are worthy of note. In the first place the major belts of wheat production have constantly been displaced away from the major market areas, a consequence of rising land values as population has grown and expanded outwards from the eastern U.S.A., Buenos Aires, coastal Australia and the Ukraine. The movement has, by chance, been into progressively more arid regions. Thus wheat production has been displaced by more intensive mixed farming systems, and has in its turn invaded areas occupied by even more extensive systems – ranching or nomadic herding. By the 1930s wheat production had stabilised in areas where rainfall was so low that the farmer had few alternative production opportunities. The crises of the 1930s have led to two divergent trends. One was the abandonment of the drier lands and their reversion to ranching. The other was an attempt to diversify wheat production by introducing rotations incorporating leys and raising beef cattle and sheep. The stereotype of the large mechanised wheat monocultural farm has thus had a short history: indeed it now survives in but a few places.

CHAPTER 14

CONCLUSIONS

The most important factors in explaining the present distribution of the major types of agriculture are, first, the slowness of technical change in agriculture until the nineteenth century, and, second, the very limited areas in which the new techniques of the nineteenth and twentieth centuries have been adopted. Thus the simplest and perhaps the most useful classification of modern agriculture is into those countries which have experienced economic development in the last century and those which have not.

Until about A.D. 1600 there was probably very little difference in agricultural productivity between Europe, India and China. Thereafter the reduction of fallow, the elimination of medieval institutions and the introduction of roots and grasses gave significant increases in crop yields. But the major break came in the nineteenth century with the introduction of labour-saving machinery, the use of steam and later electricity on the farms, and the petrol-driven tractor, the use of inorganic fertilisers and the application of scientific knowledge to plant and animal breeding. Although most of these advances came in the later nineteenth century they have not been widely adopted until the last forty years. This period has been a real agricultural revolution in western farming.

This was a direct result of industrialisation; although the earlier agricultural revolution of the eighteenth century had made possible the industrial revolution in Europe, it was industrialisation that caused the major changes in agriculture which began in the later nineteenth century. Higher incomes led to a shift in demand from grain to livestock products, vegetables and specialised tropical products, whilst factory industries generated a demand for cotton, wool, jute, rubber and vegetable oils. Although population increased rapidly in nineteenth-century Europe, factory employment increased so rapidly that by the 1880s migration to the towns was causing a decline in the agricultural population, compelling farmers to adopt labour-saving devices. The railway and the steamship together reduced freights so that even grain could be shipped long distances to markets, and this allowed specialisation on both a local and an international scale. Manufacturing industry provided the new inputs which increased yields and lowered labour costs. In the mid-nineteenth century it was possible to find farmers whose methods and implements had hardly changed since medieval times; thereafter change was rapid and comprehensive in Europe itself, and brought into being new types of agriculture overseas – the large-scale grain production of the Red River Valley, the ranching of the Great Plains and the pampas, and the New Plantation System of Asia.

No such break has occurred in the continuity of agricultural tradition in Asia, Africa or much of Latin America; true, Indians in the Americas adopted the plough, as have some African cultivators; new crops were certainly adopted quickly in both Africa and Asia, where they fitted easily into the existing farming systems. But there has been little change in farming methods. Yet population has increased at an unprecedented rate in the last half-century, with no parallel increase in urban employment to relieve the increasing rural congestion which has given rise to the subdivision of holdings, increased fragmentation, underemployment and malnutrition. Farmers in these countries have not had access to the new inputs which have transformed western agriculture in the last hundred years. They have resorted to the traditional methods of increasing output, and these have proved inadequate. First fallow land has been reduced, and where possible multiple cropping introduced: land use has been intensified. Second, more labour has been spent in preparing the seed-bed, weeding and harvesting. Third, new land has been brought into cultivation, but nowhere are there large areas of good land like those occupied by Europeans in the second half of the nineteenth century. It may be, of course, that the widely heralded Green Revolution in Asia is the beginning of fundamental change in the peasant farming systems of that continent. Only time will tell.

Thus the peasant farming systems of Afro-Asia and Latin America bear the mark of the past more strongly than those of the western world, for two simple reasons. First, until 1850 there were no agricultural revolutions, but everywhere evolution; change was slow, so that the descent of modern farming systems is clearly traceable back to the Neolithic. Second, the western world has experienced industrialisation, which has provided the new inputs necessary to make the break with the past. Even so, the past is still firmly imprinted on the landscape of Europe, if less now upon the mind of the farmer than it was thirty years ago.

APPENDIX
REGIONS OF PLANT DOMESTICATION,
AFTER C. D. DARLINGTON, 1963

1. *China*
Aleurites moluccana, Tung Oil; *Avena nuda*, Naked Oat; *Glycine max*, Soy Bean; *Stizolobium hasjoo*, Velvet Bean; *Phaseolus angularis*, Adzuki Bean; *Phyllostachys* spp., Small Bamboos; *Zizania latifolia*, Manchurian Rice; *Brassica chinensis* etc., Pak-choy; *Allium fistulosum* etc., Welsh Onion; *Raphanus sativus*, Radish; *Prunus armeniaca*, Apricot; *Prunus persica*, Peach; *Citrus nobilis* etc., Orange; *Broussonetia* sp., Paper Mulberry; *Morus alba*, White Mulberry; *Camellia (Thea) sinensis*, China Tea.

2a. *Indo-Burma*
Oryza sativa, Rice; *Cajanus cajan*, Dhall; *Phaseolus aconitifolius*, Math Bean; *Phaseolus calcaratus*, Rice Bean; *Dolichos biflorus*, Horse Gram; *Vigna sinensis*, Asparagus Bean; *Amaranthus paniculatus*, Amaranth; *Solanum melongena*, Egg Plant; *Raphanus caudatus*, Rat's Tail Radish; *Colocasia antiquorum*, Taro Yam; *Cucumis sativus*, Cucumber; *Mangifera indica*, Mango; *Gossypium arboreum*, Tree Cotton; *Corchorus olitorius*, Jute; *Piper nigrum*, Pepper; *Acacia arabica*, Gum Arabic; *Indigofera tinctoria*, Indigo.

2b. *South East Asia*
Coix lachryma-jobi, Job's Tears; *Dendrocalamus asper*, Giant Bamboo; *Dioscorea* spp., Yam; *Zingiber* spp., Ginger; *Citrus maxima* etc., Pomelo; *Musa* spp., Bananas; *Cocos nucifera*, Coconut; *Elettria cardamomum*, Cardamoms; *Myristica fragrans*, Nutmeg; *Curcuma longa*, Turmeric.

3. *Central Asia*
Panicum italicum, Millet; *Fagopyrum esculentum*, Buckwheat; *Cannabis indica*, Hemp; *Phaseolus aureus*, Mungo Bean; *Brassica juncea*, Indian Mustard; *Spinacia oleracea*, Spinach; *Ocimum basilicum*, Sweet Basil; *Pyrus communis*, Pear; *Pyrus malus*, Apple; *Juglans regia*, Walnut.

4. *South West Asia*
Triticum diococcum, Emmer; *Triticum vulgare*, Bread Wheat; *Hordeum sativum*, Hulled Barley; *Linum usitatissimum*, Linseed; *Lens esculenta*, Lentil; *Pisum sativum*, Pea; *Cicer arietinum*, Chick pea; *Brassica campestris*, Rape; *Papaver somniferum*, Opium Poppy; *Cucumis melo*, Melon; *Daucus carota*, Carrot; *Ficus carica*, Fig; *Punica granatum*, Pomegranate; *Prunus avium*, Cherry; *Prunus amygdalus*, Almond; *Vitis vinifera*, Grape Vine; *Pistacia vera*, Pistachio Nut; *Diospyros lotos*, Persimmon; *Phoenix dactilifera*, Date Palm; *Crocus sativus*, Saffron.

5. *Mediterranean*
Avena strigosa etc., Hulled Oats; *Vicia faba*, Broad Bean; *Brassica oleracea*, Cabbage etc.; *Brassica napus*, Swede Rape; *Olea europaea*, Olive; *Ceratonia siliqua*, Carob; *Allium sativum*, Garlic; *Lactuca sativa*, Lettuce; *Beta maritima*, Beet; *Asparagus officinalis*, Asparagus; *Pastinaca sativa*, Parsnip; *Rheum officinale*, Rhubarb; *Humulus lupulus*, Hop.

6. *Ethiopia*
Eragostis abyssinica (for bread flour); *Eleusine coracana*, Finger Millet; *Dolichos lablab*, Lablab Bean; *Guizotia abyssinica*, Niger Seed; *Ricinus communis*, Castor-oil Bean; *Coffea arabica*, Coffee; *Hibiscus esculentus*, Okra.

7. *Mexico and Central America*
Zea mays, Maize; *Phaseolus vulgaris*, Kidney Bean; *Maranta arundinacea*, Arrowroot; *Capsicum annuum* etc., Red Pepper; *Gossypium hirsutum*, Upland Cotton; *Agave sisalana*, Sisal Hemp; *Psidium guayava*, Guava; *Curcubita* spp., Squash, Pumpkin, Gourd, etc.

Appendix

8a. Peru

Ipomoea batatas, Sweet Potato; *Solanum tuberosum*, Potato; *Chenopodium quinoa*, Quinoa; *Phaseolus lunatus*, Lima Bean; *Canna edulis*, Canna; *Lycopersicum esculentum*, Tomato; *Gossypium barbadense*, Sea Island Cotton; *Carica papaya* etc., Papaya; *Nicotiana tabcum*, Tobacco; *Cinchona calisaya*, Quinine.

8b. Chile

Bromus mango, Mango Grain; *Madia sativa*, Chilean Tarweed.

8c. Brazil–Paraguay

Manihot utilissima, Tapioca; *Arachis hypogaea*, Groundnut; *Phaseolus caracalla*, Caracol; *Theobroma cacao*, Cocoa; *Ananas comosus*, Pineapple; *Bertholletia excelsa*, Brazil Nut; *Anacardium occidentale*, Cashew Nut; *Passiflora edulis*, Passion Fruit; *Hevea brasiliensis*, Para Rubber.

9. West Africa

Sorghum vulgare, Millet; *Cola acuminata*, Kola Nut; *Elaeis guineensis*, Oil Palm; *Sesamum indicum*, Sesame.

10. Europe

Avena sativa, Oats; *Secale cereale*, Rye; *Ribes* spp., Currants; *Rubus* spp., Raspberries.

11. U.S.A.

Helianthus annuus, Sunflower; *Helianthus tuberosus*, Jerusalem Artichoke.

NOTES

Chapter 1

1. Duckham and Masefield, 1970; Laut, 1968*a, b*; Jones and Darkenwald, 1954; Dumont, 1957; Kayser, 1969; Faucher, 1949; George, 1963; Klages, 1942; Symons, 1967
2. Grigg, 1965, 1967, 1969*b*
3. Coppock, 1964; Weaver 1954*a*; Weaver, Hoag and Fenton, 1956; Birch, 1954, 1960; Blaut, 1959; Belshaw and Jackson, 1966
4. Whittlesey, 1936, 209
5. Barnes, 1965; Helburn, 1957; Kostrowicki, 1964, 1966, 1968, 1970; Kostrowicki and Helburn, 1967; Varjo, 1965
6. Grigg, 1969*b*
7. Courtenay, 1965, 1970; Gregor, 1965; Spencer 1966; Watters, 1960; Conklin, 1961
8. Boserup, 1965; Clark, C., 1967; Dumond, 1965, 302–24; Geertz, 1963; Gleave and White, 1969, 273–300
9. Butzer, 1964; Howells, 1960, 113–27
10. Turner, 1920
11. Clark, C., 1967, 98
12. Grigg, 1969*a*, 329; 1970, 51–6

Chapter 2

1. Ames, 1939; Sauer, 1952; Harris, 1969*a*, 9–14
2. Gorman, 1969, 671–3; 1971, 300–20
3. Chang, 1970; Gorman, 1969, 1971; Solheim, 1967; Fazle Khan, 1960; Sauer, 1952
4. Sharp, 1961, 349; Clark, 1949; Merrill, 1940, 629–39; Shutler, 1961, 209–11
5. Burkhill, 1962
6. Clark, J. D., 1970, 205–6
7. Lathrap, 1970, 45–67; Rouse, 1962, 37–49; 1964, 499–513; Willey, 1966
8. Lathrap, 1965, 796–8; Cutler, 1968, 13
9. Perkins, 1964, 1565–6
10. Harlan and Zohary, 1966; Zohary, 1969, 47–66
11. Mellaart, 1967, 4–5; Kenyon, 1969, 144–60
12. Braidwood and Howe, 1962, 133–42; Perrot, 1962, 147–64; Mellaart, 1964, 94–104; 1967; Hawkes and Woolley, 1963, 220–42; Rodden, 1965, 82–92; Masson, 1961, 203–7; Kirkbride, 1968, 263–74; Duprée, 1964, 638–40; Kenyon, 1969, 144–60
13. Helbaek, 1959, 371; Hawkes and Woolley, 1963, 523
14. Simoons, 1971, 431–9; Reed, 1969, 361–80
15. Hole, 1966, 605–11; Flannery, 1965; Hole and Flannery, 1957; Adams, 1962*a*, 26–9
16. Arkell and Ucko, 1965, 147; Hester, 1968, 497
17. Butzer, 1964, 424
18. Van Zeist, 1969, 44; Wright, 1968, 334–9
19. Clark, 1969, 188; Baumgartel, 1965; Wilson, 1951, 37; Westermann, 1919, 158–64
20. Jacobsen and Adams, 1958, 1251–8; Adams, 1962*a*, 26–9
21. Clark, 1957, 11; Helbaek, 1959, 367; Jacobsen and Adams, 1958, 1251–8
22. Hamdan, 1961, 123–5; Laessøe, 1953, 5–26
23. Masson, 1961, 203–7; Lisitsina, 1969, 279–88; Frumkin, 1970; Kovda, 1961; Lewis, R. A., 1966, 467–91

24. Catling, 1957, 8–9
25. Murray, 1970
26. Whitehouse, 1968, 188–93; Daniel and Evans, 1967, 36
27. Clark, J. D., 1970, 188–96
28. Murray, 1970, 40
29. Murray, 1970, 49; Clark, J. G. D., 1952, 109; Helbaek, 1959, 371
30. Murray, 1970, 102–3, 106
31. Murray, 1970, 82, 102; Clark, J. G. D., 1952, 116–26
32. Burkhill, 1962
33. Allchin and Allchin, 1968, 258
34. Wheeler, 1968, 2–3, 84–5; Dales, 1966, 92–101; Lambrick, 1964, 75–7; Piggot, 1950, 265; Mason, 1963, 17; Allchin, 1969, 323–5; Agrawal, 1964, 950–2; Raikes, 1965
35. Sankalia, 1962, 74–6; Allchin and Allchin, 1968, 161–70, 261–4; Dogget 1965, 50–60
36. Allchin and Allchin, 1968, 208–17; Allchin, 1969, 325
37. Chang, 1959, 136–8; 1962, 180–1; 1963, 94; 1965, 511; 1968a, 522; 1970; Chang and Stuiver, 1966, 540; Chêng, 1960, 196–7; 1966, 33; Ho, 1969; Isaac, 1970
38. Allchin, 1969, 325; Chang and Stuiver, 1966, 540; Ho, 1969; Gorman, 1969, 671–3
39. Grist, 1959; Ho, 1969; Kihara, 1959, 68–79; Chatterjee, 1951, 18–22
40. Ho, 1968, 173–89
41. Gorman, 1969, 1971; Solheim, 1967
42. Murdock, 1959; Vavilov, 1949–50
43. Hugot, 1968, 483–8; Davies, O., 1968, 479–80; Clark, J. D., 1962a, b; 1967; Seddon, 1968, 489–94
44. Bushnell, 1961, 287
45. Adams, 1960b, 274
46. Willey, 1960, 73–86; MacNeish, 1965, 87–94
47. MacNeish, 1964, 531–45; Willey, 1966, 109, 117
48. Lanning, 1965; 1967; Collier, 1960, 19–27; Lathrap, 1965, 796–8

Chapter 3

1. Laufer, 1929, 239
2. Purseglove, 1963, 105–22; Wickizer, 1958, 171–80; Vavilov, 1949–50, 44
3. Isaac, 1959
4. Webber, 1943, 2–17; Smith, 1966, 440–3; Jones, 1966, 376
5. Adams, 1962a; Heichelheim, 1959, 129–31; Smith, 1967, 150–2
6. Parain, 1966, 136–7
7. Hourani, 1951, 61; Chittick, 1965; Dale, 1955; Greenway, 1944; Webber, 1943, 7–8; Masefield, 1950, 9
8. Murdock, 1959, 213–15; Burkhill, 1951; McMaster, 1962; Coursey, 1968, 12–15; Simmonds, 1966, 311–12; Hornell, 1934; Seddon, 1968
9. Needham, 1954, 107–11
10. Candolle, 1904, 148; Simmonds, 1966, 310; Burkhill, 1951; Purseglove, 1968, vol. 2, 430
11. Hutchinson, 1962, 8; Candolle, 1904, 168; Hagerty, 1940
12. Nishiyama, 1961; Barrau, 1958, 47–8; Heyerdahl, 1964; Carter, 1950
13. Salaman, 1950, 206; Hawkes, 1967; Masefield, 1967, 300
14. Willet, 1962; Masefield, 1967, 277
15. Jenkins, 1948; Luckwill, 1943
16. Hendry, 1923
17. Hartley, 1963; Edwards, 1948; Hartley and Williams, 1956; Frankel, 1954
18. Schwaritz, 1966, 150; Darlington, 1963, 167
19. Miracle, 1966, 87–96; Willet, 1962
20. Burkhill, 1951; Murdock, 1959, 204–11, 213–14; Jones, 1957; Coursey, 1968, 2–22
21. Grist, 1959, 2; Johnston, 1958, 26–174
22. Waibel, 1943, 121; Purseglove, 1968, vol. 1, 225; vol. 2, 571–2; Masefield, 1950, 29, 50–5
23. Masefield, 1950, 9, 107–8

24. Wellman, 1961, 38–9; Purseglove, 1968, vol. 2, 460–89
25. Hutchinson, Silow and Stephens, 1947, 88–90; Masefield, 1950, 100, 107–8; Hutchinson, 1962; Chowdhury and Buth, 1970
26. Wellman, 1961, 17, 38; Spate, 1956, 227–8; Buchanan, 1966, 69; Purseglove, 1968, vol. 1, 149; Masefield, 1950, 60
27. Hutchinson, 1962, 5–15
28. Ho, 1955, 196–201; 1959, 176–89
29. Geertz, 1963, 91–2; Robequain, 1944, 229–31
30. Purseglove, 1968, vol. 1, 149; vol. 2, 466, 482, 572; Wellman, 1961; Geertz, 1963, 52; Masefield, 1950, 29; Ooi, 1963, 197; Robequain, 1944, 198–9; 1954, 352
31. Geertz, 1963, 112; Purseglove, 1968, vol. 1, 151; Hartley, 1967, 15; Pendleton, 1962, 202; Masefield, 1950, 148
32. Masefield, 1950, 17; Parry, 1963, 283; Haring, 1947, 252; Grist, 1959, 7; Swan, 1957, 68
33. Rodrigues, 1962, 56, 63; Masefield, 1967, 285–6, 290
34. Haring, 1947, 253; Parry, 1966, 103; West and Augelli, 1966, 281; Brown, R. H., 1948, 85; Amerine, 1969, 259–60
35. Carrier, 1968; Webber, 1943, 19, 25–6, 32; Collins, 1951
36. West and Augelli, 1966, 282; Haring, 1947, 252; Masefield, 1950, 22–3, 284; Rich, 1967, 345; Galloway, 1964, 37
37. Jeffreys, 1963b; Simmonds, 1966, 313
38. Wellman, 1961, 18, 35; Parry, 1967, 192
39. Masefield, 1950, 29–30; Baker, 1964, 114
40. Hutchinson, 1962, 8–9; Stephens, 1944
41. Polharnus, 1962, 16, 21
42. Moodie and Kay, 1969
43. Carrier, 1968, 80–1, 86–7, 124, 204, 244; Brown, 1948, 36, 39–41
44. Carrier, 1968, 134, 142, 149, 154–5, 244, 251; Brown, 1948, 33–5; Ball, 1930; Fussell, 1965, 216
45. Carrier, 1968, 151, 239–45; Edwards, 1948, 17; Graumann and Hein, 1962
46. Primmer, 1939, 205–21
47. Clark, C. M. H., 1962, 84, 134; Barnard, 1962, 64–5
48. Hungerford, 1954; Wadham, Wilson and Wood, 1967, 207, 219, 237, 244, 246, 251, 254; Spurling, 1963; Cochrane, 1963
49. Clark, 1949, 45, 48, 55, 61, 63, 293, 295–300, 338, 354
50. Yawata, 1961
51. Barrau, 1960
52. Ward, 1965, 17–35; Barrau, 1958, 12, 15, 23, 47–8, 50, 60; 1960; Fox and Cumberland, 1962, 131–47; Johnston, 1953
53. Higgs and Jarman, 1969, 39–40
54. Reed, 1969, 373
55. French, 1966, 13–14; Zeuner, 1963, 211
56. Payne, 1964
57. French, 1966, 14
58. Payne, 1964; Gwynne, 1967, 40; Joshi, McLaughlin and Phillips, 1957, 17, 23, 33
59. Wheatley, 1965a; Williamson and Payne, 1965, 138–40
60. Masefield, 1950, 15; Epstein, 1955; Bowling, 1942; Lemmer, 1947, 79–83; Joshi and Phillips, 1953, 33, 39, 126, 133, 163, 192
61. Zeuner, 1963, 246–51
62. Zeuner, 1963, 155, 160, 197–8
63. Harris, 1961; Payne, 1969
64. Lyddeker, 1912, 221, 246–51
65. Lyddeker, 1912, 122–6, 128
66. Clark, 1949, 179–217

Chapter 4

1. Curtin, 1969, 87, 88–9, 268
2. Schlebecker, 1960, 190; Davis, 1960
3. Stern, 1960
4. Clough, 1959, 391; Kenwood and Loughheed, 1971, 33–4; Youngson, 1965, 173; Courtenay, 1965, 33
5. Polharnus, 1962, 29; Waibel, 1943, 125–7; Masefield, 1950, 40, 56; Hartley, 1967, 12, 31
6. North, 1958, 541–6; Scobie, 1967, 10
7. Graham, 1968, 57, 71; Mackintosh, 1934, xi; Masefield, 1950, 58; Malenbaum, 1953, 39
8. Morris, 1958, 46–8; Youngson, 1965, 172; Borgstrom, 1967, 419, 422; Shann, 1948, 343; Simmonds, 1966, 318
9. Woodruff, 1966, 119, 121, 150; Hall, 1963, 9; Jenks, 1963, 331; Stern, 1960, 46; Simon, 1968, 25; Segal and Simon, 1961, 574–6; Sheridan, 1963, 13; Brayer, 1949; Rippy, 1959, 161
10. Fussell, 1958, 18; Borgstrom, 1967, 421–3
11. Ball. 1930, 58; Gray, 1933, vol. 2, 674
12. Sach, 1968
13. Anderson, 1936, 159; Lee, 1921, 59; Shannon, 1961, 131; Poole, 1951, 36; Foster, 1960, 50, 67–8; Morrisey, 1957, 24; West and Augelli, 1966, 243; Gray, 1933, vol. 1, 217
14. Hopkins, 1935, 711; Chang, 1962, 181; Hawkes and Woolley, 1963, 232, 319; McNeill, 1965, 238; Butzer, 1964, 416, 441; Hugot, 1968, 484–5; Seddon, 1968, 490; Clark, J. D., 1967, 611, 613; Chêng, 1963, vol. 3, 246–7, 294; Matsuo, 1959, 1; Beardsley, 1955, 324, 332, 341, 345; Evans, 1970, 1–9
15. Beyer, 1953, 393; Kelley, 1965, 336; Bose, 1942, vol. 1, 94; Semple, 1931, 298, 386, 408, 414–15, 416, 434, 440; Adhya, 1966, 42–3; Forbes, 1955, 10; Lee, 1921, 150; Clark, J. G. D., 1952, 126; Fussell, 1965, 24–5, 30; 1967, 21–2, 24; Lévy, 1967, 36; Stevens, 1966, 99; Parain, 1966, 145–6; Needham, 1954, vol. 4, 331–2, 339, 352, 356; Reifenberg, 1955, 37, 53
16. McNeill, 1965, 325
17. Slicher van Bath, 1963, 16, 63, 69–70, 289, 290; Clark, J. G. D., 1952, 100, 104, 105; Fussell, 1965, 86–7, 89, 93, 131, 135; Curwen and Hatt, 1961, 69, 71; Stevens, 1966, 96–9, 107–8; Aberg, 1957, 172–81; Parain, 1966, 136–9, 142–3, 150, 153; Needham, 1954, vol. 4, 317; White, L., 1940, 144–54, White, K. D., 1967, 10–16
18. Collins, 1968; 1969, 74–92
19. Slicher van Bath, 1963, 299; Spence, 1960
20. Dovring, 1965; Rasmussen, 1962, 587
21. Collins, 1968, 456; Kemmerer and Jones, 1959, 141–5, 421; Gates, 1960, 181, 285–6; Fussell, 1960, 105–7
22. Dovring, 1965, 642; Borgstrom, 1967, 421
23. Thompson, 1968, 70; Dovring, 1965, 654–5, 659; Fussell, 1958, 12; Peterson, 1967; Borgstrom, 1967, 413; Russell, 1966, 95
24. Bell, 1968, 147–8; Ball, 1930, 62; Russell, 1966, 333–60
25. Slater, 1961; Duckham, 1959
26. Gray, 1933, vol. 1, 184, 217, 281; West and Augelli, 1966, 278–80; Foster, 1960, 50, 67–8

Chapter 5

1. Watters, 1960, 64; Spencer, 1966, 23–5; Pelzer, 1945
2. Morgan and Pugh, 1969, 66–8, 511; Malcolm, 1953, 57; Masefield, 1962, 96–8; O'Connor, 1966, 18; Mortimore and Wilson, 1965; Johnston, 1964, 173; Stamp, 1962, 87
3. Watters, 1960, 88; Spencer, 1966, 149–50; Pelzer, 1945, 16–17
4. Allan, 1965, 257; Whittlesey, 1937, 148; Spencer, 1966, 129
5. Nye and Greenland, 1960, 3; Morgan, 1959b, 142; Watters, 1960, 72–5
6. Gourou, 1966, 35–6; Haney, 1968, 8–9
7. Allan, 1965, 44; Spencer, 1966, 87–94; Pelzer, 1945, 18; Haney, 1968, 25
8. Watters, 1960, 70; Allan, 1965, 58; Cook, 1921, 313
9. Allan, 1965, 337; Pelzer, 1945, 24–5; 1958, 129; Morgan, 1969

10. F.A.O., 1957, 160
11. Wikkramatileke, 1957, 81; Watters, 1960, 65
12. Morgan, 1969; Gleave and White, 1969; Ruthenberg, 1971
13. Nye and Greenland, 1960, 42–3, 73–89; Tosti and Voertman, 1964; Watters, 1960, 78; Soma, 1959, 470–4; Stewart, 1956, 122; Spencer, 1966, 14
14. Smalley, 1968; Chang, 1962, 180; Hawkes and Woolley, 1963, 238, 514
15. Narr, 1956, 144; Clark, 1961, 23; Butzer, 1964, 439, 445, 458
16. Evans, 1956; Bartlett, 1956; Clark, J. G. D., 1952, 92–6; Hawkes and Woolley, 1963, 283
17. Allison, 1957; Slicher van Bath, 1963, 58; Parain, 1966, 136–7
18. Linnard, 1970; Montelius, 1953; Darby, 1956, 202, 208–10; Mead, 1953, 46
19. Mather and Hart, 1954, 165; Hammond, 1966, 75–6, 81, 83–4; Gates, 1960, 135; Gray, 1933, vol. 1, 217, 281; vol. 2, 700
20. Stein, 1953; James, 1938 and 1953; Waibel, 1950
21. Spencer, 1966, 16–17
22. Ho, 1968, 179–80
23. Spencer, 1966, 116–20
24. Watters, 1960, 88; Pelzer, 1945, 20
25. Spencer, 1966, 11; Pelzer, 1945, 23–5; Geertz, 1963, 115–23
26. Morgan, 1969
27. Murdock, 1960; Morgan, 1969, 252–3
28. Morgan, 1969; Mortimore and Wilson, 1965; Wills, 1962; Murdock, 1960
29. Guthrie, 1962
30. Wrigley, 1960
31. Inskeep, 1969, 32, 39
32. Wilson, 1969a, 40–1, 55
33. Wilson, 1969b, 131–8
34. Ogot, 1968, 127–32
35. Murdock, 1959, 193–5, 306–7, 342–3
36. McMaster, 1962; Murdock, 1959, 213–15, 222–5
37. Coursey, 1965, 75; Fage, 1969, 12
38. Johnston, 1958, 175; Morgan, 1959a, 53; Dickson, 1969, 119–20; Miracle, 1965, 45, 51–2
39. Cole, 1961, 164–5; Kay, 1970, 80
40. Murdock, 1960, 530
41. Coursey, 1965, 81
42. Dickson, 1969, 47; Morgan, 1959a, 53; Miracle, 1964
43. Fage, 1969, 84
44. Gleave and White, 1969; Boserup, 1965
45. Dickson, 1969, 74–6
46. Morgan, 1959a, 52; 1969, 254
47. Wrigley, 1957, 70–3; Allan, 1965
48. Johnston, 1964, 170, 173
49. Palerm, 1967, 29, 30–5, 46; West and Augelli, 1966, 318, 322–3; Lewis, 1949, 117
50. West, 1957, 127–30
51. Allen, 1947, 575–7; Carneiro, 1960, 229–33
52. Cook, 1921; James, 1969, 469; Dion, 1950; Watters, 1971, 211–34
53. James, 1969, 715–17, 732–3; Waibel, 1950, 532–6
54. Willey, Ekholm and Millon, 1964; Coe, 1964
55. Harris, 1969a,
56. Steward and Farion, 1959, 52–3
57. Nye and Greenland, 1960
58. Cook, 1921, 309; Allan, 1965, 69
59. Ho, 1968; Clark and Haswell, 1970, 46–7; Morgan, 1969, 249; Gourou, 1966, 52; Dumond, 1961, 303; Spencer, 1966, 25
60. Pelzer, 1945, 127
61. Dumond, 1965; Boserup, 1965
62. Boserup, 1965, 15

63. Gleave and White, 1969
64. Clarke, 1966; Palerm, 1967

Chapter 6

1. Dobby, 1962, 62; Van Royen, 1954, 83; Grist, 1953
2. Goor, 1966
3. Grist, 1953, 172–3; Goor, 1966, 307, 312; Büdel, 1966, 296–7; Fisher, 1964a, 495; King, 1911, 279; Ruttan, Soothipan and Venegas, 1966, 19; Sato, 1968, 829; Ahmad, 1958, 175; Grigg, 1973; Frankel, 1971
4. Hill, R. D., 1970, 95
5. Duckham and Masefield, 1970, 340; Pendleton, 1962, 154–5; Buck, 1964, 181; Farmer, 1960
6. Trewartha, 1965, 186; Buck, 1964, 292
7. Schwartzberg, 1963; Habib, 1965, 120
8. F.A.O., 1966, 1
9. Dobby, 1950, 296; 1955, 83; Teulières, 1966, 385
10. Naval Intelligence Division, 1943, 217–20; Gourou, 1952, 109; Ahmad, 1958, 273–5; 1961, 285; Spate and Learmonth, 1967, 675
11. F.A.O., 1962
12. Fisher, 1964b, 58; Dobby, 1950, 184, 279
13. Vince, 1952, 61–2; Ginsburg, 1958, 568–9; Buck, 1964, 47
14. Hill, R. D., 1970, 94; Trewartha, 1938, 109; Fisher, 1964a, 436, 495, 540; Pendleton, 1962, 149; Islam, 1965, 4; Spate and Learmonth, 1967, 245, 576, 601, 654, 669, 672, 675, 730–5; Bhatia, 1965; Kuriyan, 1945, 76–84; Bennett, 1961, 78; Geertz, 1963, 93; Wernstedt and Spencer, 1967, 98; Huke, 1963, 215; Ghose, Ghatge and Subrahmanyan, 1960
15. Hill, 1966; Dobby, 1950, 177, 272; Kuriyan, 1945; Fisher, 1964a, 436–7, 537; Pendleton, 1962, 137–40; Fryer, 1970, 44; Robequain, 1944, 219; Spate and Learmonth, 1967, 730, 731, 735, 739, 759, 796–7
16. Kakiuchi, 1964
17. Grist, 1953, 137; Reksohadiprodjo and Soedarsono, 1961; Fisher, 1964a, 532; Ginsburg, 1958; Barton, 1963, 414; Trewartha, 1945, 204; Spate and Learmonth, 1967, 566, 576; Pelzer, 1945, 50–1; Trewartha and Yang, 1948, 278
18. Pelzer, 1945, 44; Terra, 1954, 33–43
19. Trewartha, 1965, 198–201; McCune, 1957, 92; Fryer, 1965, 79; Pendleton, 1962, 156; Gourou, 1948, 229; Aartsen, 1954, 58; Spencer and Hale, 1961, 3; Buck, 1964, 34
20. Aartsen, 1954, 58; Jack, 1957, 486
21. Dumont, 1957, 137; Trewartha, 1945, 244
22. Asakawa, 1929, 80–96
23. Alexander, 1963, 55; Bishop, 1923, 53; Hall, 1968
24. Grist, 1953, 115
25. Kemmler, 1962, 179
26. Trewartha, 1945, 206; 1965, 208; King, 1911, 194–200; Cressey, 1934, 137
27. Fisher, 1964a, 243, 437–8; Volker, 1966
28. Van Royen, 1954, 83; Chang, J., 1968
29. Dumont, 1957, 139; Fryer, 1970, 57; Ho, 1968
30. Buck, 1964, 247
31. Shaw, 1938, 381–8
32. Gourou, 1948, 232
33. Fryer, 1970, 50; Naval Intelligence Division, 1943, 284; Trewartha, 1945, 243; Gourou, 1948, 231, 233; Dumont, 1957, 143; Wheatley, 1965a, 577–83
34. Fisher, 1964b
35. Tuan, 1970, 79
36. Wheatley, 1965b, 131; Yang, 1945–6, 163–4; Wiens, 1954, 49–54
37. Needham, 1954, 331, 339; Chang, K., 1968b, 524; Chêng, 1963, 246–7, 297; Waley, 1948, 803; Lee, 1921, 45, 150; Ballas, 1968, 161; Tuan, 1970, 63, 81–4; Lao Kan, 1956, 87–90; Ch'ao-Ting Chi, 1936, 108

38. Chêng, 1963, 119, 122; Hsiang-Lin, 1967, 140
39. Ch'uan Han-sheng, 1956, 222–6; Ho, 1959, 17, 177–9; Tuan, 1970, 96, 127
40. Perkins, 1969, 6, 64; Ch'ao-Ting Chi, 1936, 42–3
41. Ho, 1956, 210–12; 1959, 175–7; Ch'uan Han-sheng, 1956, 224; Tuan, 1970, 98; Perkins, 1969, 70; Chêng, 1963, 126
42. Durand, 1960; Pritchard, 1963, 18
43. Perkins, 1969, 6; Ho, 1959, 169
44. Perkins, 1969, 38, 45, 47, 64; Ho, 1959, 117, 153, 178–9, 206
45. Ho, 1959, 273
46. Buck, 1964
47. Beardsley, 1955, 332, 341
48. U.N.E.S.C.O., 1958, 114, 115, 120; Taeuber, 1958, 12; Beardsley, 1955, 330–1, 341–6; Trewartha, 1965, 103; Bishop, 1923, 41, 62; Sweetser, 1962, 353; Davies, 1934
49. Tanioka, 1959; Dempster, 1967, 161
50. Dempster, 1967, 92; Taeuber, 1958, 19, 27
51. Trewartha, 1965, 195, 215, 241; Kakiuchi, 1964
52. Perkins, 1969, 70; Matsuo, 1959, 1–4, 37; Bishop, 1923
53. Fisher, 1964a, 531; Cotter, 1968, 14–16; Dumont, 1957, 126; Wheatley, 1965b, 128, 131; Naval Intelligence Division, 1943, 165
54. Fisher, 1964a, 515, 531, 545–6; Naval Intelligence Division, 1943, 212, 270; Adams and Hancock, 1970, 90–1; Dumont, 1957, 129
55. McCune, 1957, 27, 57–8; Fisher, 1954, 285; Trewartha and Zelinsky, 1955, 4, 7
56. McCune, 1957, 85, 86; Fisher, 1954, 290
57. Hsieh, 1964, 125, 135, 140–56, 162–72; Hung, 1958, 47–55
58. Chatterjee, 1963, 164–6; Saraswati, 1937, 13; Ghosh, 1959, 48–9
59. Stein, B., 1967, 179; Anstey, 1952, 161; Adhya, 1966, 39
60. Farmer, 1957, 10–17; Murphey, 1956, 181–5
61. Maity, 1957, 39, 74, 76, 92; Bose, 1942, vol. 1, 63; Murphey, 1956, 191; Davis, 1951, 24; Adhya, 1966; Habib, 1969a, 381, 384
62. Davis, 1951, 26–8; Datta, 1962, 286; Moreland, 1920, 22, 289
63. Moreland, 1920, 102, 104; Farmer, 1957; Murphey, 1956, 181–6
64. Habib, 1965, 120, 121; Moreland, 1920, 102, 111; Maity, 1957, 74
65. Habib, 1965, 324–6; 1969b, 46, 51
66. Ahmad, 1968, 88; Randhawa, 1962, 78–82
67. Davis, 1951, 26; Trewartha and Gosal, 1957; Geddes, 1941
68. Terra, 1958, 165; Kroef, 1951, 19, 21, 23
69. Niel, 1964; Geertz, 1963, 38–46
70. Geertz, 1963, 78–81
71. Pelzer, 1945, 54
72. Spencer and Hale, 1961, 35
73. Geertz, 1963, 93; Fisher, 1964a, 258
74. Geertz, 1963, 35, 77–8
75. Coedès, 1966, 26
76. Forde, 1950, 430
77. Luce, 1940; Andrus, 1957, 14; Fisher, 1964a, 433–4; Kirk, 1947–9; Stewart, 1921; Cheng, 1968, 3–4
78. Naval Intelligence Division, 1943, 170; Pendleton, 1962, 5–6; Fisher, 1964a, 82, 487–533; Zimmerman, 1937, 384–90; Sternstein, 1966, 66–9
79. Hall, 1968, 25; Majumdar, 1955, 2; Braddell, 1956, 8
80. Fisher, 1964a, 532; Cotter, 1968, 16
81. Fisher, 1964a, 533, 539; Naval Intelligence Division, 1943, 215; Cotter, 1968, 18
82. Christian, 1941; Fisher, 1964a, 438–9
83. Scott, 1921, 256; Fisher, 1964a, 174, 436, 455; Cheng, 1968; Andrus, 1957, 14–17, 52–9
84. Pendleton, 1962, 140–1; Ingram, 1964, 102
85. Ingram, 1964, 110
86. Fryer, 1970, 139–40

295

87. Fryer, 1970, 143; Barton, 1960, 157; Pelzer, 1945, 47
88. Pendleton, 1962, 135; Fryer, 1970, 139–44; Fisher, 1964a, 489–97, 505–11; Van Roy, 1967, 473–4
89. Fisher, 1964a, 533, 539
90. Naval Intelligence Division, 1943, 229–30
91. Fisher, 1964a, 564–6; Fryer, 1970, 403–12
92. Wheatley, 1961, xxxi
93. Burkhill, 1935, 1600; Ooi Jin-bee, 1963, 224
94. Vlieland, 1934, 64–70; Ooi Jin-bee, 1963, 106–7, 117–18, 126, 133
95. Hill, 1970, 15; Rutherford, 1966; Ho, 1965
96. Fryer, 1970, 256–65
97. Beyer, 1953; Fisher, 1964a, 698–9; Gourou, 1952, 110
98. Wernstedt and Spencer, 1967, 126, 128, 181
99. Fryer, 1970, 177–8; Dwyer, 1964, 239–40
100. Fryer, 1970, 177
101. Dwyer, 1964; Fryer, 1970, 165–6

Chapter 7

1. Capot-Rey, 1962, 302; Davies, 1966, 195; Brémaud and Pagot, 1962, 311; Silberman, 1959, 559; Stenning, 1959, 1
2. Awad, 1962, 325–9; Barth, 1962, 341
3. Patai, 1951, 403; Tursunbayev and Potapov, 1959, 511
4. Hughes, 1960; Lattimore, 1962a, 178–86
5. Allan, 1965, 288
6. Silberman, 1959, 560; Davies, 1966; Barth, 1962, 341; Helaissi, 1959, 533
7. Lattimore, 1962b, 185–6; Leeuw, 1965, 186
8. Johnson, 1969, 16, 156–68; Ruthenberg, 1971, 252; Clarke, 1955 and 1959; Barth, 1959, 1–11; Patai, 1951; Bacon, 1954; Krader, 1955
9. Deshler, 1965, 153–4
10. Krader, 1959, 508; Ruthenberg, 1971, 225, 258–9
11. Dyson-Hudson and Dyson-Hudson, 1969, 79–80; Deshler, 1965, 154, 158; Clarke, 1955, 159; 1959, 99
12. Nicolaisen, 1954, 87–8
13. Bacon, 1954, 46; Krader 1959, 505; English, 1967
14. Warren, 1967, 184; Allan, 1965, 319; Raswan, 1930, 494; Lewis, 1955; Sweet, 1965, 138
15. Barth, 1959, 2, 8–9
16. Carter 1967; Stenning, 1957
17. Krader, 1955, 316; Capot-Rey, 1964, 475
18. Johnson, 1969, 9–10
19. Krader, 1968; Isaac, 1970, 4, 46; Forde, 1950, 397
20. Ryder, 1966, 10
21. Phillips, 1965, 18
22. Isaac, 1970, 93–4; Phillips, 1965, 18; Herre, 1963, 246
23. Phillips, 1965, 46
24. Gumilev, 1966a, 40
25. Wissman, 1956, 292; Phillips, 1965, 78
26. Lattimore, 1951, 55
27. Phillips, 1969, 22; Lattimore, 1951, 61
28. Cahen, 1968, 1–2; Menges, 1968, 17–18
29. Smith, 1959, 79–86; Parker, 1968, 51, 58, 73, 80, 81, 87, 95, 104, 160–1
30. McNeill, 1964, 4–5, 9, 120
31. Mikesell, 1955, 242
32. Bacon, 1954, 48; Awad, 1954, 242
33. Murdock, 1959, 126; Despois, 1961, 228
34. Holt, Lambton and Lewis, 1970, 444

35. Despois, 1961, 229; Murdock, 1959, 392; Murphey, 1951, 122–3
36. Murdock, 1959, 392
37. Murphey, 1951; Despois, 1945, 355; 1961, 230–1; Murdock, 1959, 405; Graham, 1967, 102
38. Planhol, 1959, 525–7; Lewis, 1955, 48
39. Seddon, 1968; Simoons, 1971
40. Stenning, 1959, 20; Murdock, 1959, 413–17
41. Murdock, 1959, 170, 314–50; Ehret, 1967; Lewis, I. M., 1966
42. Parker, 1968, 161; McNeill, 1964
43. Parker, 1968, 161
44. Tregear, 1970, 102
45. Tregear, 1970, 54; Cressey, 1955, 289; Tuan, 1970, 172–5
46. Berque, 1959, 482, 491; Despois, 1961, 234
47. Lewis, 1955, 48–55
48. Tursunbayev and Potapov, 1959, 514
49. Awad, 1962, 325–6
50. Albano, 1956, 57–60
51. Hughes, 1960; Jackson, 1962b, 79; Tregear, 1970, 94–5
52. Lattimore, 1962b, 178–86
53. Allan, 1965; Dunbar, 1970
54. Ruthenberg, 1971, 258–9; Dresch, 1966

Chapter 8

1. Whittlesey, 1936
2. Fryer, 1965, 100
3. Birot and Dresch, 1953, 110; Siegfried, 1948, 108
4. Houston, 1964, 140
5. Amiran, 1964, 104
6. Blok, 1966, 4; Martinez-Allier, 1971, 22; Franklin, 1969, 124
7. Yates, 1960, 207; O.E.C.D., 1969a, 20
8. Kish, 1954; Davies, 1941, 158; Matley, 1968, 235; Clarke, 1955, 159
9. O.E.E.C., 1951, 24; Newbigin, 1930, 54; Arnon, 1963; Clarke, 1955
10. Houston, 1964, 431
11. Bull, 1936, 148; Hofmeister, 1971, 16; Pinchemel, 1969, 287; Thompson, 1970, 426
12. F.A.O., 1969b, 5, 12
13. Blache, 1950, 125; F.A.O., 1968a, 5, 8, 9, 18, 115, 146, 166; Amiran, 1964, 111; Pepelasis and Thompson, 1960, 150; Arnon, 1963, 129
14. Dovring, 1959 and 1965; Zelinsky, 1963; Grigg, 1971; F.A.O., 1956, 16–17; 1968b, 21–4
15. O.E.C.D., 1969a, 81–2, 238
16. Shaw, 1963; Naylon, 1959; O.E.C.D., 1969a, 8, 18, 48, 51–2, 82, 238; Duckham and Masefield, 1970, 278; Thompson, 1970, 131; Houston, 1964, 440; Clough, 1964, 163; Amiran, 1964, 109; Franklin, 1969, 124–30; I.A.A.E., 1969, 427–8; Pepelasis and Thompson, 1960, 157; Hofmeister, 1971, 16; Martinez-Allier, 1971, 15, 22
17. F.A.O., 1968b
18. Newbigin, 1929; Mathews, 1924
19. Smole, 1963, 31
20. Aguirre, 1961
21. *U.S. Census of Agriculture, 1964*, vol. 1, pt 48
22. F.A.O., 1968b, 213; Impey, 1962; Griffin, 1955
23. James, 1969, 557; Cole, 1965, 402
24. *U.S. Census of Agriculture, 1964*, vol. 1, pt 48
25. Griffin and Chatham, 1958, 195; Meigs, 1941; Zierer, 1956, 156; Hartman, 1964, 173–9
26. James, 1969, 558; Aguirre, 1961, 49–50; Luebke, 1936, 372; Smole, 1963, 110
27. Cole, 1966, 197
28. Douglas, 1959; Cole, 1954; Cole, 1966, 205–13, 216

29. Spurling, 1963; Smith, 1970
30. McBride, 1936; Jefferies, 1971
31. Baker, 1930, 179, 290, 292
32. *U.S. Census of Agriculture, 1964,* vol. 1, pt 48
33. Meigs, 1964, 17–22
34. Newberry, 1937–8
35. White, 1961; Vicens Vives, 1969, 39–49
36. Michell, 1953, 249–50; Rostovtzeff, 1959, vol. 1, 92–3; Casson, 1954
37. Dunbabin, 1948, 214; Rostovtzeff, 1957, vol. 1, 18; Smith, 1967, 75
38. Semple, 1931, 386; White, 1970*b*
39. Bourne, 1960, 50–1
40. Lennie, 1936; White, 1970*b*, 246–61; Contenau, 1954, 43–8
41. Glick, 1970; Isaac, 1959
42. Reifenberg, 1955, 51, 91; Glick, 1970, 188–9; White, 1963*a*; Vita-Finzi, 1961
43. Warmington, 1928, 211, 217; Adams, 1962*c*, 115–18; Whyte, 1961, 96; Rostovtzeff, 1959, 1166; Heichelheim, 1959, 129
44. Parain, 1966, 132; Matley, 1968; Smith, 1967, 247–8; White, 1970*b*, 276–7, 306
45. White, 1967, 126–30; Stevens, 1966, 94–5, 98–9, 102; Fussell, 1967, 18–22; Aitken, 1956; Smith, 1967, 80; White, 1963*b*
46. Stevens, 1966, 116–22; Jones, A.H.M., 1959
47. Latouche, 1967, 18–28
48. Slicher van Bath, 1963; Ostrogorsky, 1966, 205, 206, 214, 216
49. Vicens Vives, 1969, 88
50. Jones, 1966, 343–4; Lopez, 1943, 14
51. Clark, C., 1967, 64; Russell, 1969, 5, 7, 19, 21–2, 22–3
52. Slicher van Bath, 1963, 59
53. Parain, 1966, 132; King, 1971, 171; Dozier, 1957, 490–1; Jones, P., 1966, 364–6
54. Smith, 1966, 439; Klein, 1920; Vicens Vives, 1969, 111, 250, 252–7
55. Jones, 1966, 380–3, 392
56. Kish, 1954, 302–4; Braudel, 1966, 88–9
57. Gabrieli, 1968, 190–1
58. Glick, 1970; Parain, 1966, 147–8
59. Miskimin, 1969, 68
60. Webber and Batchelor, 1943, vol. 1, 4, 6, 11–16; Candolle, 1904, 184, 215; Isaac, 1959; Smith, 1967, 150
61. Parry, 1966, 160; Candolle, 1904, 159; Houston, 1959, 175; East, 1950, 167, 191; Masefield, 1966, 290; Birot and Dresch, 1953, 97, 103; Smith, 1967, 524
62. Candolle, 1904, 10; Houston, 1964, 118; Jones, 1966, 370; Smith, 1966, 440–1
63. Parain, 1966, 165, 179
64. Vicens Vives, 1969, 108–125
65. East, 1950, 167
66. Planhol, 1970, 459
67. Planhol, 1970, 459–60; Cahen, 1970, 519
68. Clark, C., 1967, 67; Jones, 1966, 344
69. Parain, 1966, 148; Smith, 1967, 252; Latouche, 1967, 287
70. Dowd, 1961, 146–56; Jones, 1966, 353–76; Cipolla, 1949
71. Parry, 1966, 155–60
72. Smith, 1967, 416–26; Cipolla, 1952, 178
73. Vicens Vives, 1969; Dovring, 1965, 635; Pinchemel, 1969, 265
74. Sanchez-Albornoz, 1970, 160; Dovring, 1965, 607–14
75. Mikesell, 1969, 24–25; Cipolla, 1965, 579; Macdonald, 1963, 65–9
76. Lamour, 1961, 229
77. F.A.O., 1968*a*, 25
78. Willis, 1971, 120
79. Houston, 1964; Wagstaff, 1965, 276; Basile, 1941, 114, 117; Zangheri, 1969, 25; Lutz, 1962, 10–11; Sbarounis, 1959, 13; Enggass, 1968

80. Aitken, 1945, 60; Arbos, 1923; Kish, 1954, 304; Vicens Vives, 1969, 517
81. Walker, 1967, 42–6; Monkhouse, 1965, 366; Monbeig, 1934, 303
82. Braudel and Spooner, 1966
83. Houston, 1964, 594
84. Agnew, 1946; Galtier, 1960; Lamour, 1961; Graves, 1965; Thompson, 1970, 429
85. Blanchard and Blanchard, 1929; Monbeig, 1934, 301; Vicens Vives, 1969, 649-52; Drain, 1961, 387
86. Branas, 1956, 144; Siegfried, 1948, 119; Isnard, 1949
87. Franklin, 1969, 134; Walker, 1967; Coppa, 1970, 750; Tirone, 1970
88. Houston, 1964, 558
89. Vicens Vives, 1969, 652
90. Monbeig, 1934, 301
91. Despois, 1961, 233; Houston, 1964, 675; Poncet, 1951
92. Wagstaff, 1965, 276
93. Bonnet, 1950, 206; Wiss, 1970; Walker, 1967, 46
94. Jones, 1963, 247
95. Mendel, 1969, 110
96. Monbeig, 1934, 301–3; Houston, 1959; Halpern, 1934, 150–5; Vicens Vives, 1969, 653
97. Ahlmann, 1925, 310–12; Basile, 1941, 110–12
98. Duckham and Masefield, 1970; Dobby, 1936, 229
99. Mendel, 1969; Amiran, 1964, 103
100. Stewart, 1964, 85, 94–5; Gadille, 1957, 144, 153, 154
101. Mendel, 1969, 110; Hirst and Panaretos, 1958
102. Bull, 1963
103. Caroús, 1971; Saez, 1971; Cani, 1970
104. Walker, 1967, 196; Monkhouse, 1965, 366–7, 399, 423, 444; Way, 1966, 133, 228, 239; Robertson, 1938, 573–4
105. Willis, 1971, 131
106. O.E.C.D., 1966, 8; Gottmann, 1943, 191–2
107. Robertson, 1935; Houston, 1952; Dobby, 1936; Bethemont, 1962
108. Prentice, 1957, 164; Merriam, 1926, 91
109. Naylon, 1967, 179
110. Chaine, 1959, 326; Houston, 1950
111. Gibson, 1966, 113
112. Parry, 1963, 283
113. Haring, 1947, 253–4; West and Augelli, 1966, 281
114. Martinez-Allier, 1971, 54–61
115. Parry, 1966, 100–86; Rowe, 1957, 180; Lockhart, 1968, 11; Gibson, 1966, 55, 143, 152
116. Jefferies, 1971, 222
117. Frank, 1969, 47, 59–62, 70–5, 85
118. Zierer, 1956, 111–15, 118
119. Bennett, 1939, 159–60; Zierer, 1956, 185
120. Goodan and Shatto, 1948, 141; Baker, 1930, 187; Coulter, 1929, 88–9
121. Zierer, 1956, 161; Smith and Phillips, 1942, 645
122. Paterson, 1970, 49–50; Zierer, 1956, 150
123. Hartman, 1964, 227–9
124. Zierer, 1956, 152
125. Zierer, 1956, 342
126. Hartman, 1964, 218; Baker, 1930, 181; Haystead and Fite, 1955, 253, 264; Griffin and Chatham, 1958; Colby, 1924, 50
127. Hartman, 1964, 225–6
128. Haystead and Fite, 1955, 259

Chapter 9

1. Whittlesey, 1936

2. Yates, 1960, 19
3. Dovring, 1959; Grigg, 1971
4. Dovring, 1960, 132
5. Grigg, 1966*a*
6. Jones and Darkenwald, 1954, 266
7. I.A.A.E., 1969, 122, 128, 172
8. Mayhew, 1970; Clout, 1968; Lambert, 1961; 1963; Perry, 1969
9. Yates, 1960, 106, 111
10. Jonasson, 1925, 282; Clout, 1971, 10
11. Weaver, 1954*a, b*; Weaver, Hoag and Fenton, 1956
12. Hoag, 1962
13. Shaw, 1942*a*
14. Dewhurst, Coppock and Yates, 1961, 482
15. Yates, 1940, 31; Duckham and Masefield, 1970, 227
16. *Dutch Agriculture,* 1959, 70
17. Dexter, 1967; Anon, 1961
18. F.A.O., 1968*b*, 37–8
19. Dovring, 1965, 639, 668; Renborg, 1969; M.A.F.F., 1970; Astor and Rowntree, 1940
20. Fussell, 1967, 39
21. Duby, 1968, 22
22. Blum, 1971, 157; Latouche, 1967, 30–2
23. Parain, 1966, 136
24. Manning, 1964, 57–8, 64; Wilson, 1962
25. Applebaum, 1958
26. Darby, 1956, 183
27. Bolin, 1966, 634, 649
28. Aubin, 1966, 449
29. Stevens, 1966, 108; Applebaum, 1958, 70
30. Latouche, 1967, 40–1; Smith, 1967; Lambert, 1971, 34
31. Smith, 1967, 80
32. Koebner, 1966, 28–61
33. Latouche, 1967, 33; Slicher van Bath, 1963, 54–7; Bloch, 1966*b*, 50
34. Duby, 1968, 18
35. Parain, 1966, 142–3
36. Slicher van Bath, 1963, 64
37. Slicher van Bath, 1963, 61–2; Thirsk, 1964; Blum, 1971; Ault, 1965; Duby, 1968, 93–4; Postan, 1966, 572; Bolin, 1966, 647; Parain, 1966, 140; Slicher van Bath, 1963, 60
38. Pounds, 1967; Latouche, 1967, 77
39. Bloch, 1966*a*, 264–5
40. Bloch, 1966*a*, 235–6
41. Bloch, 1966*a*, 264–5
42. Bolin, 1966, 652; Duby, 1968, 37–9, 193
43. Bloch, 1966*a*, 238
44. Postan, 1966, 583, 605; Duby, 1968, 232–7
45. Latouche, 1967, 273, 290–2; Ganshof and Verhulst, 1966, 312–15, 322–4, 327–9; Duby, 1968, 281–304, 332
46. Lopez, 1971, 16–17; Duby, 1968, 25, 130; Latouche, 1967, 245–52
47. Smith, 1967, 167; Postan, 1966, 563; Duby, 1968, 119–24
48. Koebner, 1966, 62–84; Ganshof and Verhulst, 1966, 291–4
49. Latouche, 1967, 59; Duby, 1968, 81; Bloch, 1966*b*, 14
50. Smith, 1967, 174
51. Smith, 1967, 161, 164–81
52. Genicot, 1966, 661
53. Genicot, 1966, 663; Ganshof and Verhulst, 1966, 296–7; Slicher van Bath, 1963, 132
54. Duby, 1968, 102, 110; Parain, 1966, 125–6, 153; Bloch, 1966*b*, 25
55. Slicher van Bath, 1963, 170–1; Latouche, 1967, 294–5

56. Postan, 1966, 582; Latouche, 1967, 294–5
57. Postan, 1966, 558–9; Parain, 1966, 179; Duby, 1968, 295; Pounds, 1969–70, 225–47
58. Postan, 1966, 587; Genicot, 1966; Parain, 1966, 126; Slicher van Bath, 1963, 88–134
59. Maddalena, 1970, 23–33; Du Boulay, 1965; Bloch, 1966b, 149
60. Duby, 1968, 126, 130, 134, 137, 153–5; Slicher van Bath, 1963, 16; Bloch, 1966b, 22
61. Pounds and Roome, 1971, 123, 128
62. Bairoch, 1969, 35
63. Aubin, 1966, 480; Parain, 1966, 169
64. Bloch, 1966b, 23; East, 1950, 106–7
65. Slicher van Bath, 1963, 143–4, 176–9; Genicot, 1966, 717–18; Parain, 1966, 141; Smith, 1967, 520; Slicher van Bath, 1963, 241–3; 1966, 24–32; 1969
66. Fussell, 1969
67. Kerridge, 1967; Chambers and Mingay, 1966; Riches, 1967
68. Chambers and Mingay, 1966; Grigg, 1966b; Bourde, 1953
69. Chambers and Mingay, 1966, 77
70. Yates, 1940, 53–5; Dahl, 1961; Thorpe, 1951
71. Bloch, 1966b, 209, 233; Maddalena, 1970, 26; Blum, 1971; Soboul, 1956, 83
72. Dovring, 1965, 622, 628–9; Dovring, 1960, 51–2; Wright, 1964, 6
73. Clapham. 1951, 43; Warriner, 1964, 10–17; Lefebvre, 1966; Wright, 1964, 3
74. Slicher van Bath, 1963, 142, 213–17, 283; Mingay, 1956
75. Clapham, 1951, 7–9; Grigg, 1966b, 150
76. Bennett, 1935; Crouzet, 1967, 153
77. Bairoch, 1969, 42; Slicher van Bath, 1963, 221
78. Dovring, 1965, 638, 645; Grigg, 1966b, 192; Jones, 1964; Collins, 1969; Hunt, 1967
79. I.A.A.E., 1969, 32, 47, 104; Yates, 1940, 57, 283, 368; Clapham, 1951, 208; Kindleberger, 1964, 215; Dovring, 1960, 73
80. Franklin, 1969, 26
81. Yates, 1960, 160; Collins, 1969
82. Franklin, 1969, 87; Eyre, 1957; Sutton, 1971; Darby, 1964; Phillips and Clout, 1970; Mead, 1953, 82; 1958, 104; Dovring, 1965, 618; Fullerton, 1954; Lambert, 1971, 254; Williams, 1970b; Darby, 1940; Grigg, 1966b
83. Clapham, 1951, 208; Warriner, 1964, 74
84. Yates, 1940, 518; Coppock, 1959
85. Bull, 1962; Dovring, 1965, 622
86. I.A.A.E., 1969, 470; Jones, 1962, 111; Orwin and Whetham, 1964, 344; Coppock, 1971, 19–20
87. Yates, 1960, 198; Beaumont and Higgs, 1958, 1, 2; Dovring, 1965, 654–60; Thompson, 1968
88. Dovring, 1965, 663
89. Warriner, 1964, 63
90. Wright, 1964, 10
91. Yates, 1940, 53
92. Dovring, 1969, 184
93. Kindleberger, 1964, 212; Clapham, 1951, 177
94. Postan, 1967, 177
95. *Dutch Agriculture*, 1959, 23; F.A.O., 1969a, 479–80; I.A.A.E., 1969, 95
96. Tracy, 1964
97. Yates, 1940, 10; Coppock, 1971, 11–12
98. Tracy, 1964, 26–7; Yates, 1940, 394
99. Fletcher, 1961; Orwin and Whetham, 1964, 240–89; Stearns, 1932; Coppock, 1959
100. Gerschenkron, 1966; Wright, 1964, 17
101. Bloch, 1966b, 2–4; Clapham, 1951, 24; Yates, 1940, 30–1; Dovring, 1965, 636
102. Clapham, 1951, 51; Poggi, 1930
103. Bergman, 1967, 390; Shaw, 1942a, 287–8
104. Dovring, 1965, 634
105. Dovring, 1965, 638

106. F.A.O., 1969*a*
107. Slicher van Bath, 1963, 295; Clapham, 1951, 176, 220; F.A.O., 1969; Tracy, 1964, 34; Hart, 1956, 260–74
108. Clapham, 1951, 174, 220; Tracy, 1964, 102, 110; M.A.F.F., 1968, 122; F.A.O., 1969*a*
109. Haystead and Fite, 1955, 143; Akin, 1968, 173
110. Paterson, 1970, 164; Laut, 1968*b*, 272; Fryer, 1965, 105; Baker, 1927*b*, 447; Shaw, 1936, 370; Jones and Darkenwald, 1954, 268
111. Duckham and Masefield, 1970, 143
112. Alexander, 1963, 140; U.S. Bureau of the Census, 1964, 650–9
113. Akin, 1968, 73–8; Weaver, 1954*a*, *b*; Alexander, 1944; Hoag, 1962, 2, 6; Grotewald, 1955, 14; Gibson, 1948, 249
114. Brown, 1948, 51; Carr-Saunders, 1936
115. Bidwell and Falconer, 1925, 33, 97–8; Gates, 1960, 169; Bogue, 1963*a*, 21
116. Scofield, 1938, 657
117. Paterson, 1970; Carrier, 1968, 204
118. Zelinsky, 1962
119. Shannon, 1961, 26
120. U.S. Department of Agriculture, *Yearbook 1922* (1923), 1009; 1009; F.A.O., 1968*b*
121. Bidwell and Falconer, 1925, 232, 241–2
122. Bidwell and Falconer, 1925, 168, 281, 300–1; Shannon, 1961, 132, 136; Leighty, Warburton, Stine and Baker, 1922, 178
123. Higbee, 1958, 232–49; Spencer and Horvath, 1963
124. Leighty, Warburton, Stine and Baker, 1922, 222; Higbee, 1958, 234
125. Carrier, 1968, 270; McManis, 1964, 1; Bogue, 1959, 14
126. Bogue, 1959, 48, 68; 1963*b*, 10
127. Carrier, 1968, 399; Bogue, 1959, 52, 59, 69, 116, 147; 1963*b*, 17
128. Shannon, 1961, 137
129. U.S. Department of Agriculture, 1922, 509; U.S. Bureau of the Census, 1964, 649
130. U.S. Department of Agriculture, 1922, 509; Large, 1960, 113–14; U.S. Bureau of the Census, 1964, 644

Chapter 10

1. Coppock, 1971, 152; Higbee, 1958, 263; Silvey, 1967, 17; Yates, 1940, 354; Yli-Jokipii, 1970, 1; Butterwick and Rolfe, 1968, 110
2. F.A.O., 1969*c*, 12
3. Ellert, 1962, 8; Cumberland and Whitelaw, 1970, 103; Jones and Darkenwald, 1954, 125; Bask, 1963, 426; Butterwick and Rolfe, 1968, 115; Bewley, 1970, 38; Alexander, 1963, 125; Coppock, 1971, 153; Bunting, 1968, 160; Lewthwaite, 1971, 81
4. Boal and McAodha, 1961, 174; Highsmith and Northam, 1968, 177; Coppock, 1971, 162; Jones and Darkenwald, 1954, 297, 305; Alexander, 1963, 129
5. Jaatinen and Mead, 1957, 35; Bateman, 1969, 217; Bollman and Ward, 1958, 78; Butterwick and Rolfe, 1968, 110–11
6. Yates, 1940, 263; Gregor, 1963
7. Durand, 1949, 141
8. F.A.O., 1969*d*, 90–5
9. White, 1970*a*, 69, 277, 315; Brothwell and Brothwell, 1969, 50–2; Zeuner, 1963, 218, 224; Cranstone, 1969; Parain, 1966, 177
10. Wheatley, 1965*a*; Simoons, 1971, 431–7; Murdock, 1959, 19; Bose, 1942, vol. 1, 67; Zeuner, 1963, 236, 248; Simoons, 1954; Sauer, 1952, 87; Gourou, 1948, 231; Tregear, 1965, 131; Clark, J.G.D., 1952, 126
11. Hecksher, 1954, 22–3; Parain, 1966, 171, 178; Bolin, 1966, 649–50
12. Bull, 1956, 28–9
13. Trow-Smith, 1957, 32
14. Gates, 1960, 227; Fussell, 1966*b*, 327

15. Jensen, 1937, 59; Jones, 1962
16. Fussell, 1966*b*, 327; Simpson, 1959, 98; Schlebecker, 1967, 22; Jenkins, 1970, 31
17. Barnes, 1958, 179–80; McQueen, 1961, 94; Whetham, 1964; Backe, 1943, 223
18. Cheke, 1959, 6–13; Schlebecker, 1967, 6–7
19. Schlebecker, 1967, 23; Cumberland and Whitelaw, 1970, 39; Burnett, 1965, 113; Yates, 1940, 123
20. Shannon, 1961, 257; Schlebecker, 1967, 25
21. Gates, 1960, 240
22. Yates, 1940, 120; Jensen, 1937, 393; M.A.F.F., 1968, 122–3; Buchanan, 1935, 4–7, 23; Larson, *et al.*, 1923, 315
23. Jensen, 1937, 395; F.A.O., 1968*b*, 395; Yates, 1940, 120–1; Commonwealth Secretariat, 1972, 15
24. Bateman, 1968; 1969; Tyler, 1956; Trow-Smith, 1957, 177–9
25. Schlebecker, 1967, 30; Simpson, 1957, 149–56; Edwards, 1949
26. Sears, 1962, 193, 200; Burnett, 1965, 107; Johnston, 1965, 158; Curry, 1962, 174; Jaatinen and Mead, 1957, 33; *Dutch Agriculture*, 1959, 70
27. Trow-Smith, 1957, 167–75
28. Burnett, 1965, 108; Ernle, 1968, 388; Johnston, 1965, 39; Bunting, 1968, 160; Simpson, 1958; Coppock, 1971, 156
29. *Dutch Agriculture*, 1959, 55, 62; Johnston, 1965, 157
30. Whetham, 1970, 317–22; F.A.O., 1968*b*, 489; Bateman, 1968; 1969; Schlebecker, 1967, 40 1969; Schlebecker, 1967, 40
31. Durand, 1964, 11
32. Durand, 1964, 13–14; Chisholm, 1962, 89–92
33. Kohn, 1943; Hatcher, 1944; Durand, 1951; Durand, 1949, 2–4
34. Durand, 1952, 265; 1967, 30
35. Larson, *et al.* 1923, 317; Baker, 1928, 56
36. Larson *et al.*, 1923, 295–316
37. Shannon, 1961, 257; Schlebecker, 1967, 26; Durand, 1952, 272, 276; 1955, 300–2; 1964, 18; Larson *et al.*, 1923, 295–316
38. Durand, 1952, 279–80; Lewthwaite, 1964, 98
39. Yates, 1940, 351; Stern, 1960, 61
40. Orwin and Whetham, 1964, 148–9, 358–9; Barnes, 1955; 1958
41. Thorpe, 1951
42. Jensen, 1937, 210, 220, 232, 247, 316
43. Stern, 1960, 60–1; Bunting, 1968
44. Cumberland and Whitelaw, 1970, 43; Cumberland, 1968, 222–38; Bewley, 1970; Lewthwaite, 1971; Buchanan, 1935

Chapter 11

1. Zimmerman. 1951, 374–97
2. Jones, W. O., 1968; Gregor, 1965; Courtenay, 1965; 1970; Higman, 1969
3. Steward, 1959, 8
4. Church, 1969, 430
5. Buchanan, 1938, 159; Ruthenberg, 1971, 209
6. Gregor, 1965, 225; Courtenay, 1970, 86; Ruthenberg, 1971, 205
7. Pelzer, 1953, 324; Waibel, 1942, 310
8. Buchanan, 1938, 160–3; Courtenay, 1965, 53
9. Thompson, 1935; 1941; 1959; 1960
10. Gregor, 1965; Courtenay, 1970, 89
11. Wickizer, 1960
12. Wickizer, 1960; Fryer, 1965, 85–6; Ruthenberg, 1971, 190–201, 244–7
13. Wagley, 1960, 7
14. Deerr, 1949, vol. 1, 100–2, 116
15. Hammond, 1966, 128–9

16. Paget, 1956; Galloway, 1964
17. Brown, 1948, 31, 59
18. Ragatz, 1928, 37–79; Parry and Sherlock, 1966, 117–58
19. Ratekin, 1954; Haring, 1947, 219
20. Curtin, 1969, 46, 87–9, 268
21. Hammond, 1966, 53
22. Brown, 1948, 59, 131; Robert, 1967, 18
23. Gallman, 1970; Prunty, 1955
24. Galloway, 1968; Diégues, 1959, 104–7; Furtado, 1963, 6–34, 45, 48
25. West and Augelli, 1966, 82–99; Parry and Sherlock, 1966, 117–58
26. Hammond, 1966, 123–30, 182; *U.S. Census of Agriculture,* 1964, vol. 2, 751, 765; Baker, 1927c, 84–5; Hart, 1967, 25; Prunty, 1955, 459–69
27. Graham, 1968, 161; James, 1932, 238–44; 1969, 761–2, 781–9
28. Sanchez, 1964, 126–35; Crist, 1946, 494; Ortiz, 1947; Dyer, 1956; 1967; James, 1969, 238, 244–6; Mintz, 1953; 1958–9
29. Preston, 1965
30. Stephens, 1944; Rogers, 1966–7; Glade, 1969, 296
31. Gray, 1933, vol. 1, 674–81, 689; Hammond, 1966, 27; Moore, 1956
32. Gray, 1933, vol. 2, 700
33. Agelasto *et al.,* 1922, 348
34. U.S. Bureau of the Census, 1960, 301
35. Hart, 1967, 21, 24–6; Fulmer, 1950, 116
36. Parry and Sherlock, 1966, 144, 172; West and Augelli, 1966, 88, 103; Courtenay, 1965, 35–6; Furtado, 1963, 123; Stein, 1953
37. Graham, 1968, 71, 161; James, 1932, 225–44; 1969, 755–6, 787, 791; Rowe, 1963, 27–53; Dambaugh, 1959; Stein, 1953; Dozier, 1956; Butland, 1955
38. Monbeig, 1952, 255–72; James, 1938; 1969, 734
39. Haring, 1947, 219; Ratekin, 1954, 1–19; West and Augelli, 1966, 282
40. Haring, 1947, 253; Parry, 1966, 54, 103, 228, 240, 242, 268; Steward, 1959, 9
41. Diégues, 1959, 104–7; Furtado, 1963, 6–34, 45, 48, 62, 65, 69, 72, 73, 75, 99; Galloway, 1968; Boxer, 1957, 17–21, 34, 140, 143; 1962, 4, 11, 14, 150
42. Parry and Sherlock, 1966, 56–8, 63–158; West and Augelli, 1966, 82–99; Galloway, 1964; Rodway, 1912, 39, 47, 61–2, 250–6; Deerr, 1949, vol. 1, 208; Sanchez, 1964, 9–27; Hoy, 1962; Ragatz, 1928, 37–79; Paget, 1956; Thomas, 1968
43. Parry, 1966, 278–88; Gibson, 1966, 169; Crist, 1946, 493–5; Sanchez, 1964, 31–42, 71–9, 133–79; Parry and Sherlock, 1966, 45–8; Curtin, 1969, 234; Ortiz, 1947; Dyer, 1956; 1967; James, 1969, 238, 244–6
44. McFarlane, 1964, 38–55; West and Augelli, 1966, 384
45. Shaw, 1942b; Simmonds, 1966, 317–26; West and Augelli, 1966, 398; Jones and Morrison, 1952, 5–10
46. Stouse, 1967; Jones and Morrison, 1952, 5–10; West and Augelli, 1966, 398
47. Preston, 1965, 77–90; Parsons, 1957; Arthur, Houck and Beckford, 1968
48. Porter, 1847, 528; Schlote, 1952, 156
49. Porter, 1847, 28, 516; Simkin, 1968, 294, 302, 305, 307, 308; Parkinson, 1948, 163
50. Fisher, 1968
51. Caldwell, 1964, 73–4; Allen and Donnithorne, 1957, 23, 78–80; Geertz, 1963, 53
52. Geertz, 1963, 54–60
53. Geertz, 1963, 83–8; Allen and Donnithorne, 1957, 67–70, 89–92
54. Geertz, 1963, 104; Broek, 1940, 194; Allen and Donnithorne, 1957, 31, 59–104
55. Caldwell, 1964, 88
56. Geertz, 1963, 61, 113–14; Allen and Donnithorne, 1957, 140; Khan, 1961, 47–55; Fisher, 1968; Caldwell, 1964; Fryer, 1970, 305–33; Reksohadiprodjo, 1964
57. Mackie, 1961
58. Jackson, 1967
59. Allen and Donnithorne, 1957, 109, 111
60. Ooi Jin-bee, 1963, 201–6

61. Fisher, 1964*a,* 612; Keong, 1967, 43–6; Ho., 1967, 189
62. Jackson, 1967; Ooi Jin-bee, 1963, 196, 254–5; Gray, 1963
63. Chaudhuri, 1966; 1971, 2, 26, 31–4; Anstey, 1952, 115, 279–88; Greenberg, 1951, 3
64. Harler, 1964, 132; Griffiths, 1967, 125, 143
65. Rasmussen, 1960; Subramaniyam, 1954, 93
66. McCune, 1949; Forrest, 1967, 29, 41, 94, 288; Folke, 1966
67. Forrest, 1967, 288
68. Lim, 1968; Subramaniyam, 1954, 100; Harler, 1964, 139
69. Bovill, 1966
70. Fage, 1962, 48
71. Hellen, 1969, 338
72. Wrigley, 1959, 15, 21–2, 25, 31; Hellen, 1969, 330–9; Morgan and Pugh, 1969, 497–501
73. Udo, 1965; 1967
74. Fuggles-Couchman, 1964, 22
75. Church, 1957; Newbury, 1971, 91–2; Waibel, 1943
76. Dickson, 1969, 145; Oyenuga, 1967, 71, 76; Morgan, 1959*a,* 53; Prothero, 1955, 22; Morgan, 1955, 174–5
77. Buchanan and Pugh, 1955, 152–4; Pim, 1940, 48, 60, 97; Church, 1969
78. Prothero, 1957; Church, 1957; Morgan and Pugh, 1969, 364–5
79. Erneholm, 1948, 52–9, 85–96
80. Hill, 1960, 9–12; 1963, 1, 11, 15–17, 170–2; Hunter, 1961, 161–72; 1963, 61–9
81. Morgan and Pugh, 1969, 416–500, 629–30, 700; O'Connor, 1966, 72–80; Berry, 1971, 59; Van Dongen, 1961, 320–8; Pim, 1940

Chapter 12

1. Strickon, 1965, 230; Whittlesey, 1936, 216
2. Highsmith and Northam, 1968, 150; Cumberland, 1944, 205
3. Heathcote, 1969*b,* 320–1
4. Ruthenberg, 1971, 271
5. Logan, 1961*a,* 284–5; Becker, 1969, 44
6. Jones and Darkenwald, 1965, 127, 131; Alexander, 1963, 111; Curry, 1963, 100
7. Bank of London and South America, 1969, 27
8. F.A.O., 1968*b,* 303
9. Bishko, 1952; Tinker, 1962, 191
10. Street, 1962; Sanchez, 1964, 31–42
11. James, 1950, 345; Boxer, 1962, 239–42
12. Morrisey, 1951
13. Crist, 1944, 589–92; Boxer, 1962, 226–32
14. Fitzgibbon, 1953, 253; Ferrer, 1967, 46–9
15. James, 1950, 49, 64–6; Jones, 1930, 17–21
16. Brand, 1961; West and Augelli, 1966, 286–91; Tinker, 1962, 190–2; Morrisey, 1951, 115–21; Denhardt, 1951, 145–8; Chevalier, 1963, 96–8
17. Faulk, 1965; Nostrand, 1970
18. Baker, 1931, 149
19. Shannon, 1961, 200; Webb, 1931, 189, 211, 216; Lupton, 1966–7; Mackintosh, 1934, 115–16; MacEwan, 1952, 118–33
20. Mather, 1950, 81–2
21. Heathcote, 1969*b,* 318; Osgood, 1929, 184
22. Osgood, 1929, 222
23. Shannon, 1961, 203
24. Osgood, 1929, 225
25. Dale, 1960, 98–109; Webb, 1931, 254, 298, 334, 336
26. Dale, 1960, 54, 101, 147–50; Webb, 1931, 23
27. Doerr and Morris, 1960, 82
28. Logan, 1961*a,* 279–81

29. Henderson, 1954; Logan, 1961a, 284–5
30. Jordan, 1969; Dunbar, 1961; Henlein, 1961
31. Brand, 1961
32. Kollmorgen, 1969
33. Ferrer, 1967, 46
34. Jones, 1928, 25; Scobie, 1967, 55
35. Fearns, 1960, 416; James, 1969, 640, 674; Hore, 1957, 199–200; Nyhus, 1940, 5
36. Jones, 1928, 25
37. Jones, 1928, 25
38. James, 1969, 645
39. Winsberg, 1970; Fitzgibbon, 1953; Jones, 1928, 160–3
40. Talbot, 1961, 299–307; Cole, J.P., 1965, 101–12, 238–9; Agnew, 1959, 224–30; Pollock and Agnew, 1963, 57–67
41. Talbot, 1961, 304, 308
42. Talbot, 1961, 308–13, 315, 324–9; McGuire, 1959, 124–31
43. Shann, 1948, 78
44. Marshall, 1966
45. Powell, 1968
46. Jay, 1957, 37; Roberts, 1924, 155–63; Perry, 1969
47. Shann, 1948, 86, 122–3; Allen, 1959, 38–41
48. Roberts, 1924, 169; Laut, 1968b, 411; Shann, 1948, 120–3, 130–1
49. Laut, 1968b, 114
50. Williams, 1967, 13, 67, 73; Davis, 1954, 479; Laut, 1968b, 65; Shann, 1948, 380; Roberts, 1924, 178
51. Roberts, 1924, 181, 190, 223, 233; Heathcote, 1965b, 1, 5, 6
52. Wadham, 1961, 346–8; Butlin, 1962, 292–3
53. McDonald, 1968, 382; Wadham, 1961, 354; Bank of New South Wales, 1965
54. Cumberland and Whitelaw, 1970, 30, 34, 40, 67
55. Cumberland and Whitelaw, 1970, 67; Duncan, 1962, 171–5; Buchanan, 1935, 4–5, 43–6
56. Cumberland and Hargreaves, 1955, 100; Hargreaves, 1965, 145, 151; Stephens, 1965, 55–62; Curry, 1963, 100
57. Costin, 1964, 60; Relph, 1958, 136–8; Cumberland and Whitelaw, 1970, 70–7; Miller, 1960, 131; Cumberland, 1944; Fielding, 1963

Chapter 13

1. Highsmith and Northam, 1968, 127; Alexander, 1963, 169, 175; Zimmerman, 1951, 204
2. Stern, 1960; Westerman, 1969, 23–4
3. Haystead and Fite, 1955, 187; Highsmith and Northam, 1968, 130; James, 1969, 649
4. Collins and Dibb, 1967, 97; Dunlop, 1970, 157
5. Fryer, 1965, 96
6. Highsmith and Northam, 1968, 131; Kemmerer and Jones, 1959, 421
7. Kollmorgen and Jenks, 1958a, b; Williams, 1970a
8. Fryer, 1965, 97; Dunlop, 1970, 161
9. Ward, 1946
10. Baker, 1925, 18
11. Mackintosh, 1934, 55; Shann, 1948, 292; Scobie, 1967, 90
12. Alexander, 1963, 178
13. Parker, 1968, 95
14. James, 1969, 630–3
15. Cumberland, 1968, 92–3; C.S.I.R.O., 1966, 21, 72–3
16. Hayter, 1939, 189–202
17. Primack, 1962
18. Wadham, Wilson and Wood, 1967, 56–61
19. Scobie, 1967, 32–3, 46; James, 1969, 640–1, 643, 645, 647–50
20. Roberts, 1924, 223, 233, 238–40; Kemmerer and Jones, 1959, 284–7; MacEwan, 1952, 52, 71–2; Murchie, 1936, 86

21. Haystead and Fite, 1955, 187
22. Treadgold, 1957, 172, 213; Lyaschenko, 1949, 318, 345–6; Lorimer, 1946, 6, 15; Parker, 1968, 160
23. Treadgold, 1957, 178
24. Gates, 1960, 272–90; Shannon, 1961, 126–37; Higgins, 1958
25. Shannon, 1961, 129
26. Dunsdorf, 1956, 102–3, 148–56, 189, 194, 199; Andrews, 1966; Shann, 1948, 49, 219, 222
27. Shannon, 1961, 144; Calvert, 1956, 19; Kemmerer and Jones, 1959, 141–2
28. Fite, 1966, 134
29. Mackintosh, 1934, 79; Fite, 1966, 52
30. Shannon, 1961, 157–8
31. Shann, 1948, 346, 395; Hargreaves, 1948
32. Richards, 1968, 426; Cleary, 1965, 101, 104
33. Lorimer, 1946, 10
34. Allen, 1940, 231; McNeill, 1964, 195–200; Blum, 1961, 341; Parker, 1968, 158–61, 233, 238, 240; Lyaschenko, 1949, 310, 318, 345, 346
35. Falkus, 1966, 418
36. Ames, 1947, 57–74; Treadgold, 1957, 74
37. Blum, 1961, 340
38. Parker, 1968, 250; Stern, 1960; Falkus, 1966, 418
39. Treadgold, 1957, 31, 33, 69, 72, 74, 90, 100–1, 131, 169, 178–9, 207, 212, 215
40. Jackson, 1956; 1962a; Cleary, 1965
41. Fite, 1966, 50, 173
42. Fite, 1966, 75–93, 153–5, 171–4; Meinig, 1968
43. Fite, 1966, 47, 51, 132
44. Kraenzel, 1955, 309; Calvert, 1956, 19
45. Baker, 1927a, 1928, 1933; Bailey, 1958, 150
46. Kelly, 1971; Weir, 1968, 141, 146, 149–51; Bicha, 1964; MacEwan, 1952, 96
47. Mackintosh, 1934, 1–26; Watts, 1960; 1968; Richards, 1968; Jones, L. R., 1928
48. Easterbrook and Aitken, 1956, 430–2, 435–8, 482–4, 487–8, 490–1; Mackintosh, 1934, 55–6
49. Dunlop, 1970, 156–68; Richards, 1968; Johnson, 1948
50. Scobie, 1967, 9–13; James, 1950, 305
51. Scobie, 1967, 72–87; James, 1950, 309–17, 321, 326
52. Jefferson, 1926, 52; James, 1950, 305, 309, 316–17, 322
53. Cole, 1965, 379–80, 396; Ferrer, 1967, 136
54. James, 1969, 645–54; Winsberg, 1970, 191–2
55. Shann, 1948, 196; Meinig, 1962
56. Williams, 1967, 7; Andrews, 1966, 21; Dunsdorf, 1956, 148
57. Dunsdorf, 1956, 114, 117, 127–8; Shann, 1948, 393
58. Millington, 1957; Wadham, 1961, 353–62; McLennan, 1963; Andrews, 1936, 110; Donald, 1967, 70

BIBLIOGRAPHY

Aartsen, J. P. van (1954), 'Geographic aspects of rice growing', *Tijdschrift voor Economische en Sociale Geografie*, **45**, 57–65

Aberg, F. A. (1957), 'The early plough in Europe', *Gwerin*, **1**, 171–81

Adams, J. and Hancock, N. (1970), 'Land and economy in traditional Vietnam', *Journal of South East Asian Studies*, **1**, 90–8

Adams, R. M. (1962a), 'Factors influencing the rise of civilisation in the alluvium: Mesopotamia', in C. H. Kraeling and R. M. Adams (eds.), *City Invincible: a symposium on urbanisation and cultural development in the ancient Near East*, Chicago, 26–9

(1962b), 'Early civilisations; subsistence and environment', in C. H. Kraeling and R. M. Adams (eds.), *City Invincible: a symposium on urbanisation and cultural development in the ancient Near East*, Chicago, 274–83

(1962c), 'Agriculture and urban life in early south west Iran', *Science*, **136**, 109–22

Adhya, G. L. (1966), *Early Indian economics*

Agelasto, A. M., Doyle, C. B., Meloy, G. S. and Stine, O. C. (1922), 'The cotton situation', United States Department of Agriculture, *Yearbook 1921*, Washington, D.C., 323–406

Agnew, S. (1946), 'The vine in Bas Languedoc', *Geographical Review*, **36**, 67–79

(1959), 'South African farming and the pioneer legacy', in R. Miller and J. Wreford Watson (eds.), *Geographical essays in memory of Alan G. Ogilvie*, 221–46

Agrawal, D. P. (1964), 'Harappa culture; new evidence for a shorter chronology', *Science*, **143**, 950–2

Aguirre, R. (1961), 'Chilean agriculture', *World Crops*, **13**, 47–50

Ahlmann, H. W. (1925), 'Etudes de géographie humaine sur l'Italie sub-tropicale', *Geografiska Annaler*, **7**, 257–322

Ahmad, N. (1956), 'Pattern of rural settlement in East Pakistan', *Geographical Review*, **46**, 388–98

(1958), *An economic geography of Pakistan*

(1961), 'The rural population of Bihar', *Geographical Review*, **51**, 253–76

(1968), *An economic geography of East Pakistan*

Aitken, R. (1945), 'Routes of transhumance on the Spanish Meseta', *Geographical Journal*, **106**, 59–69

(1956), 'Virgil's plough', *Journal of Roman Studies*, **46**, 97–106

Akin, W. E. (1968), *The North Central United States*, New York

Albano, H. K. (1956), 'Livestock organization in the formerly nomadic areas of the Soviet Union', *Yearbook of the Association of Pacific Coast Geographers*, **18**, 57–62

Alexander, J. W. (1944), 'Freight rates as a geographic factor in Illinois', *Economic Geography*, **20**, 25–30

(1963), *Economic geography*

Allan, W. (1965), *The African husbandman*

Allchin, B. and Allchin, F. R. (1968), *The birth of Indian civilization: India and Pakistan before 500 B.C.*

Allchin, F. R. (1969), 'Early cultivated plants in India and Pakistan', in P. J. Ucko and G. W. Dimbleby (eds.), *The domestication and exploitation of plants and animals*, 323–30

Allen, G. C. and Donnithorne, A. (1957), *Western enterprise in Indonesia and Malaya*

Allen, H. C. (1959), *Bush and backwoods: a comparison of the frontier in Australia and the United States*, East Lansing, Michigan

Allen, P. G. (1947), 'Indians of Southeastern Colombia', *Geographical Review*, **37**, 567–82

Allen, W. E. D. (1940), *The Ukraine*

Allison, K. J. (1957), 'The sheep–corn husbandry of Norfolk in the sixteenth and seventeenth centuries', *Agricultural History Review*, **5**, 12–30

Amerine, M. A. (1969), 'An introduction to the pre-repeal history of grapes and wine in California', *Agricultural History*, **43**, 259–68

Ames, D. (1939), *Economic annuals and human cultures*, Botanical Museum, Harvard

Ames, E. (1947), 'A century of Russian railroad construction: 1837–1936', *American Slavonic and East European Review*, **6**, 57–74

Amiran, D. H. K. (1964), 'Land use in Israel', in U.N.E.S.C.O., *Land use in semi-arid Mediterranean climates*, Arid Zone Research, No. 26, Paris, 101–12

Anderson, E. (1952), *Plants, man and life*, Boston, Mass.

Anderson, R. H. (1936), 'Grain drills through 39 centuries', *Agricultural History*, **10**, 157–205

Andrews, J. (1936), 'The present situation in the wheat-growing industry in south eastern Australia', *Economic Geography*, **12**, 109–35

   (1966), 'The emergence of the wheat belt in south eastern Australia to 1930', in J. Andrews (ed.), *Frontiers and men*, 5–24

Andrus, J. R. (1957), *Burmese economic life*, Stanford, Calif.

Anon, (1961), 'Productivity measurement in agriculture', *Economic Trends*, **91**, ii–v

Anstey, V. (1952), *The economic development of India*

Applebaum, S. (1958), 'Agriculture in Roman Britain', *Agricultural History Review*, **6**, 66–86

Arbos, P. (1923), 'The geography of pastoral life', *Geographical Review*, **13**, 559–75

Arkell, A. J. and Ucko, P. J. (1965), 'Review of pre-dynastic development in the Nile valley', *Current Anthropology*, **6**, 145–66

Arnon, I. (1963), 'The transition from primitive to intensive agriculture in a Mediterranean environment', *World Crops*, **15**, 126–34

Arthur, H. B., Houck, J. P. and Beckford, G. L. (1968), *Tropical agribusiness structures and adjustments – bananas*, Boston, Mass.

Asakawa, K. (1929), 'Agriculture in Japanese history; a general survey', *Economic History Review*, **2**, 81–92

Astor, Viscount and Rowntree, S. B. (1940), *Mixed farming and muddled thinking*

Aubin, H. (1966), 'Medieval agrarian society in its prime: The lands east of the Elbe and German colonization eastwards', in M. M. Postan (ed.), *The Cambridge economic history of Europe*, vol. 1, *The agrarian life of the Middle Ages* (2nd edn), 449–86

Ault, W. O. (1965), 'Open-field husbandry and the village community', *Transactions of the American Philosophical Society*, **55**, 5–102

Awad, M. (1954), 'The assimilation of nomads in Egypt', *Geographical Review*, **44**, 240–52

   (1962), 'Nomadism in the Arab lands of the Middle East', in U.N.E.S.C.O., *The problems of the arid zone*, Arid Zone Research, No. 18, Paris, 325–39

Backe, H. (1943), *Um die Nahrungsfreiheit Europas*, Leipzig

Bacon, E. (1954), 'Types of nomadic pastoralism in Central and South west Asia', *Southwestern Journal of Anthropology*, **10**, 44–68

Bailey, W. R. (1958), 'Land and problems in the wheat regions', in *Land: the yearbook of agriculture, 1958*, U.S. Department of Agriculture, Washington, D.C., 150–60

Bairoch, P. (1969), 'Agriculture and the industrial revolution', *The Fontana economic history of Europe*, vol. 3, section 8, 5–74

Baker, H. G. (1964), *Plants and civilisation*

Baker, O. E. (1925), 'Geography and wheat production', *Economic Geography*, **1**, 15–52

   (1927a), 'Agricultural regions of North America: part 3', *Economic Geography*, **3**, 327–39

   (1927b), 'Agricultural regions of North America: part 4, The Corn Belt', *Economic Geography*, **3**, 447–65

   (1927c), 'Agricultural regions of North America: part 2, The South', *Economic Geography*, **3**, 50–86

   (1928), 'Agricultural regions of North America: part 6', *Economic Geography*, **4**, 399–434

   (1930), 'Agricultural regions of North America: part 8', *Economic Geography*, **6**, 166–90, 278–308

Bibliography

(1931), 'Agricultural regions of North America: part 9', *Economic Geography*, **7**, 109–53 and 325–78

(1932), 'Agricultural regions of North America: part 10', *Economic Geography*, **8**, 325–78

(1933), 'Agricultural regions of North America, part 11', *Economic Geography*, **9**, 167–98

Ball, C. R. (1930), 'A history of American wheat improvement', *Agricultural History*, **4**, 48–71

Ballas, D. J. (1965), 'Some notes on agriculture in Han China', *Professional Geographer*, **17**, 13–14

(1968), 'An introduction to the historical geography of Han China', *Professional Geographer*, **20**, 155–62

Bank of London and South America (1969), 'Argentina and the beef trade', *Bank of London and South America Review*, **3**, 271–82

Bank of New South Wales (1965), 'Trends in the distribution of Australia's sheep population', *Bank of New South Wales Review*, **55**, 7–11

Barnard, M. F. (1962), *A history of Australia*

Barnes, F. A. (1955), 'Dairying in Anglesey', *Transactions and Papers of the Institute of British Geographers*, **21**, 137–56

(1958), 'The evolution of the salient patterns of milk production and distribution in England and Wales', *Transactions and Papers of the Institute of British Geographers*, **25**, 167–95

(1965), 'The geographical typology of agriculture: report of a discussion', in E. S. Simpson (ed.), *Agricultural geography, I.G.U. Symposium*, Department of Geography Research Paper No. 3, University of Liverpool, 59–74

Barrau, J. (1958), 'Subsistence agriculture in Melanesia', *Bernice P. Bishop Museum Bulletin*, No. 219, Honolulu

(1960), 'Plant introduction in the tropical Pacific', *Pacific Viewpoint*, **1**, 1–10

(1961), 'Introduction', in J. Barrau (ed.), *Plants and the migrations of Pacific peoples: a symposium*, Tenth Pacific Science Congress, Honolulu, 1–6

Barth, F. (1959), 'The land use pattern of migratory tribes of South Persia', *Norsk Geografisk Tidsskrift*, **17**, 1–11

(1962), 'Nomadism in the mountain and plateau areas of South West Asia', in U.N.E.S.C.O., *The problems of the arid zone*, Arid Zone Research, No. 18, Paris, 341–55

Bartlett, H. H. (1956), 'Fire, primitive agriculture and grazing in the tropics', in W. L. Thomas (ed.), *Man's role in changing the face of the earth*, 692–720

Barton, T. F. (1960), 'Growing rice in Thailand', *Journal of Geography*, **59**, 153–64

(1963), 'Rainfall and rice in Thailand', *Journal of Geography*, **62**, 414–18

Basile, D. G. (1941), 'Agricultural Sicily', *Economic Geography*, **17**, 109–120

Bask, E. (1963), 'Farming in Finland', *World Crops*, **15**, 424–7

Bateman, F. (1968), 'Improvement in American dairy farming, 1850–1910: a quantitative analysis', *Journal of Economic History*, **28**, 253–73

(1969), 'Labour inputs and productivity in American dairy agriculture, 1850–1910', *Journal of Economic History*, **29**, 206–29

Baumgartel, E. (1965), *Predynastic Egypt*, Cambridge

Beardsley, R. K. (1955), 'Japan before history: a survey of the archaeological record', *Far Eastern Quarterly*, **14**, 317–46

Beaumont, T. O. and Higgs, J. W. Y. (1958), 'Agriculture: farm implements', in C. Singer, E. J. Holmyard, A. R. Hall and T. I. Williams (eds.), *A history of technology*, vol. 4

Becker, B. B. (1969), 'Changing land use patterns in Brazil: the spread of cattle raising in São Paulo State', *Revista Geográfica*, **71**, 35–44

Bell, G. D. H. (1968), 'Plant breeding for crop improvement in Britain: methods, achievements and objectives', *Proceedings of the Royal Society*, (Series B) **171**, 145–73

Belshaw, D. G. and Jackson, B. G. (1966), 'Type-of-farm areas: the application of sampling methods', *Transactions of the Institute of British Geographers*, **38**, 89–93

Bennett, D. C. (1961), 'The basic food crops of Java and Madura', *Economic Geography*, **37**, 75–87

Bennett, M. K. (1935), 'British wheat yields per acre for seven centuries', *Economic History*, **3**, 12–29

(1939), 'Climate and agriculture in California', *Economic Geography*, **15**, 153–64

Bergman, M. (1967), 'The potato blight in the Netherlands and its social consequences, 1845–47', *International Review of Social History*, **12**, 390–431

Bergmann, J. F. (1969), 'The distribution of cacao cultivation in pre-Columbian America', *Annals of the Association of American Geographers*, **59**, 85–96

Berque, J. (1959), 'Nomads and nomadism in the Arid Zone; introduction', *International Social Science Journal*, **11**, 481–98

Berry, L. (1971), *Tanzania in maps*

Bethemont, J. (1962), 'Le riz et la mise en valeur de la Camargue', *Revue de géographie de Lyon*, **37**, 153–206

Bewley, J. K. (1970), 'A survey of changes in production, manufacturing and marketing in the New Zealand dairy industry, 1947–48 to 1967–68', *New Zealand Geographer*, **26**, 36–49

Beyer, H. O. (1953), 'The origin and history of the Philippine rice terraces', *Proceedings of the Eighth Pacific Science Congress*, **1**, 387–98

Bhatia, S. S. (1965), 'Patterns of crop concentration and diversification in India', *Economic Geography*, **41**, 39–56

Bicha, K. D. (1964), 'The American farmer and the Canadian West, 1896–1914: a revised view', *Agricultural History*, **38**, 43–6

Bidwell, P. W. and Falconer, J. I. (1925), *History of agriculture in the northern United States, 1620–1860*, Washington, D.C.

Birch, J. W. (1954), 'Observations on the delimitation of farming-type regions, with special reference to the Isle of Man', *Transactions and Papers of the Institute of British Geographers*, **20**, 141–58

(1960), 'A note on the sample-farm survey and its use as a basis for generalizing mapping', *Economic Geography*, **36**, 254–9

Birot, P. and Dresch, J. (1953), *La Méditerranée et le Moyen-Orient*, vol. 1, *La Méditerranée Occidentale*, Paris

Bishko, C. J. (1952), 'The peninsular background of Latin American cattle ranching', *Hispanic American Historical Review*, **32**, 491–515

Bishop, C. W. (1923), 'The historical geography of early Japan', *Geographical Review*, **13**, 40–63

(1936), 'Origin and early diffusion of the traction-plough', *Antiquity*, **10**, 261–81

Bisschop, J. H. R. (1936), 'Parent stock and derived types of African cattle', *South African Journal of Science*, **33**, 852–70

Blache, P. V. de la (1950), *Principles of human geography*

Blanchard, W. O. and Blanchard, E. R. (1929), 'The grape industry of Spain and Portugal', *Economic Geography*, **5**, 183–93

Blaut, J. M. (1959), 'Micro-geographic sampling: a quantitative approach to regional agricultural geography', *Economic Geography*, **35**, 79–88

Bloch, M. (1966a), 'The rise of dependent cultivation and seignorial institutions', in M. M. Postan (ed.), *The Cambridge economic history of Europe*, vol. 1, *The agrarian life of the Middle Ages* (2nd edn), 235–89

(1966b), *French rural history*

Blok, A. (1966), 'Land reform in a West Sicilian latifondo village', *Anthropological Quarterly*, **39**, 1–16

Blum, J. (1961), *Landlord and peasant in Russia from the ninth to the nineteenth century*, Princeton, N.J.

(1971), 'The European village as a community; origins and functions', *Agricultural History*, **45**, 157–78

Blyn, G. (1966), *Agricultural trends in India, 1891–1947: output, availability and productivity*, Philadelphia

Boal, F. W. and McAodha, B. S. (1961), 'The milk industry of Northern Ireland', *Economic Geography*, **37**, 170–80

Boeke, J. H. (1954), *Economics and economic policy of dual societies*, New York

Bogue, A. G. (1963a), 'Farming in the Prairie Peninsula, 1830–1890', *Journal of Economic History*, **23**, 3–29

(1963b) *From Prairie to Corn Belt*, Chicago

Bogue, M. B. (1959), 'Patterns from the sod', *Collections of the Illinois State Historical Library*,

Bibliography

34, Land Series, vol. 1

Bolin, S. (1966), 'Medieval agrarian society in its prime: Scandinavia', in M. M. Postan (ed.), *The Cambridge economic history of Europe*, vol. 1, *The agrarian life of the Middle Ages* (2nd edn), 633–59

Bollman, F. H. and Ward, A. B. (1958), 'The changing distribution of Australian dairy cattle', *Quarterly Review of Agricultural Economics*, **11**, 75–84

Bonnet, P. (1950), 'The olive industry of France and French North Africa', *World Crops*, **2**, 205–8

Borgstrom, G. (1967), 'Food and agriculture in the nineteenth century', in M. Kranzberg and C. W. Pursell (eds.), *Technology in western civilisation*, 408–24

Bose, A. (1942), *Social and rural economy of Northern India c. 600 B.C. to 200 A.D.*, 2 volumes, Calcutta

Boserup, E. (1965), *The conditions of agricultural growth: the economics of agrarian change under population pressure*

Bourde, A. J. (1953), *The influence of England on the French agronomes, 1750–1789*

Bourne, F. A. (1960), 'The Roman alimentary program and Italian agriculture', *Proceedings and Transactions of the American Philological Association*, **91**, 47–75

Bovill, E. (1966), *The golden trade of the Moors*

Bowling, G. A. (1942), 'The introduction of cattle into colonial North America', *Journal of Dairy Science*, **25**, 129–54

Boxer, C. R. (1957), *The Dutch in Brazil, 1624–54*

(1962), *The golden age of Brazil, 1695–1750*

Braddell, Dato Sir Roland, (1956), 'Malayadvipa: a study in early Indianisation', *Journal of Tropical Geography*, **9**, 1–20

Braidwood, R. J. (1970), 'Prehistory into history in the Near East', in I. V. Olsson (ed.), *Radiocarbon variations and absolute chronology*, New York, 81–90

Braidwood, R. J. and Howe, B. (1962), 'South western Asia beyond the lands of the Mediterranean littoral', in R. J. Braidwood and G. Willey (eds.), *Courses towards urban life*, Viking Fund Publications, No. 32, 134–42

Branas, J. (1956), 'Progress in the French wine-growing industry', *World Crops*, **8**, 143–5

Brand, D. (1961), 'The early history of the range cattle industry in Northern Mexico', *Agricultural History*, **35**, 132–9

Braudel, F. P. (1966), *La Méditerranée et le monde Méditerranéen à l'époque de Philippe II*, Paris, 2 volumes

Braudel, F. P. and Spooner, F. (1966), 'Prices in Europe from 1450 to 1750', in E. E. Rich and C. H. Wilson (eds.), *The Cambridge economic history of Europe*, vol. 4, *The economy of expanding Europe in the sixteenth and seventeenth centuries*, 378–486

Brayer, H. O. (1949), 'The influence of British capital on the Western range-cattle industry', *Journal of Economic History*, **9**, 85–98

Brémaud, O. and Pagot, J. (1962), 'Grazing lands, nomadism and transhumance in the Sahel', in U.N.E.S.C.O., *The problems of the arid zone*, Arid Zone Research, No. 18, Paris, 311–24

Broek, J. O. M. (1932), 'The Santa Clara Valley, California: a study in landscape changes', *Geographische en Geologische Mededeelingen*, No. 4, Utrecht

(1940), 'The economic development of the outer provinces of the Netherlands Indies', *Geographical Review*, **30**, 187–200

Brothwell, D. and Brothwell, P. (1969), *Food in antiquity*

Brown, R. H. (1948), *Historical geography of the United States*

Bruchey, S. (1967), *Cotton and the growth of the American economy 1790–1860*, New York

Brunger, E. (1955), 'Dairying and urban development in New York state, 1850–1900', *Agricultural History*, **29**, 169–73

Buchanan, D. H. (1966), *The development of capitalistic enterprise in India*

Buchanan, K. M. (1970), *The transformation of the Chinese earth*

Buchanan, K. M. and Pugh, J. C. (1955), *Land and people in Nigeria*

Buchanan, R. O. (1935), 'The pastoral industries of New Zealand', *Institute of British Geographers*, No. 2, 1–99

(1938), 'A note on labour requirements in plantation agriculture', *Geography*, **23**, 158–64

Buck, J. L. (1964), *Land utilization in China*

Büdel, J. (1966), 'Deltas – a basis of culture and civilisation', *Scientific problems of the humid tropical zone deltas and their implications: Proceedings of the Dacca Symposium, 1964,* Paris, (U.N.E.S.C.O)

Bull, G. B. G. (1956), 'Thomas Milne's land utilization map of the London area in 1800', *Geographical Journal,* 122, 25–30

(1962), 'The Netherlands delta plan', *Geography,* 47, 87–9

Bull, M. R. (1963), 'Agriculture on the Maltese Islands', *World Crops,* 15, 470–1

Bull, W. E. (1936), 'The olive industry of Spain', *Economic Geography,* 12, 136–54

Bunting, B. T. (1968), 'The present re-organisation of agriculture in Denmark', *Geography,* 53, 157–62

Burkhill, I. H. (1935), *A dictionary of the economy and products of the Malay peninsula*

(1951), 'The rise and decline of the Greater Yam in the service of man', *Advancement of Science,* 7, 443–8

(1962), 'Habits of man and the origins of the cultivated plants of the Old World', in P. L. Wagner and M. W. Mikesell (eds.), *Readings in cultural geography,* 248–81

Burnett, J. (1965), 'The impact of dairying on the landscape of lowland Taranaki', in R. F. Watters (ed.), *Land and society in New Zealand,* Wellington, 101–19

Bushnell, G. (1961), 'Radio carbon dates and New World chronology', *Antiquity,* 35, 285–91

Butland, G. J. (1955), 'The colonization of northern Parana', *Geography,* 40, 126–8

Butlin, N. G. (1962), 'Distribution of sheep population: preliminary statistical picture, 1860–1957', in A. Barnard (ed.), *The simple fleece,* Melbourne, 292–6

Butterwick, M. and Rolfe, E. N. (1968), *Food, farming and the Common Market*

Butzer, K. W. (1964), *Environment and archaeology: an introduction to Pleistocene geography*

Cahen, C. (1968), *Pre-ottoman Turkey*

(1970), 'Economy, society, institutions', in P. D. Holt, A. K. S. Lambton and B. Lewis (eds.), *The Cambridge history of Islam,* vol. 2, *The further Islamic lands, Islamic society and civilisation,* 511–38

Caldwell, J. A. M. (1964), 'Indonesian exports and production from the decline of the Culture system to the First World War', in C. D. Cowan (ed.), *The economic development of Southeast Asia,* 72–101

Callaghan, A. R. and Millington, A. J. (1956), *The wheat industry in Australia,* Sydney

Calvert, W. L. (1956), 'The technological revolution in agriculture, 1910–1955', *Agricultural History,* 30, 18–27

Candolle, A. de (1904), *The origin of cultivated plants,* New York

Cani, Y. (1970), 'La floriculture sanrémoise', *Méditerranée,* 1, 51–82

Capot-Rey, R. (1962), 'The present state of nomadism in the Sahara', in U.N.E.S.C.O., *The problems of the arid zone,* Arid Zone Research, No. 18, Paris, 301–10

(1964), 'Problems of nomadism in the Sahara', *International Labour Review,* 90, 472–502

Carneiro, R. (1960), 'Slash and burn agriculture: a closer look at its implications for settlement patterns', in A. F. C. Wallace (ed.), *Men and cultures,* Philadelphia, 227–34

Caroús, J. (1971), 'Ancontecimientos historicos y cientificos importantes en el desarollo de la floricultura mediterranea', *Options Méditerranéennes,* 10, 18–26

Carr-Saunders, A. (1936), *World population: past growth and future trends*

Carrier, E. H. (1932), *Water and grass, a study in the pastoral economy of Southern Europe*

Carrier, L. H. (1968), *The beginnings of agriculture in America*

Carter, G. F. (1950), 'Plant evidence for early contacts with America', *Southwestern Journal of Anthropology,* 6, 161–82

Carter, J. (1967), 'The Fulani in Bamenda', *Journal of Tropical Geography,* 25, 1–7

Cary, M. (1949), *The geographic background of Greek and Roman history*

Caskel, W. (1954), 'The Bedouinization of Arabia', in G. E. von Grunebaum, *Studies in Islamic cultural history,* American Anthropological Association, Memoir No. 76, 36–46

Casson, L. (1954), 'The grain trade of the Hellenistic world', *Transactions and Proceedings of the American Philological Association,* 85, 168–87

Catling, H. W. (1957), *Cyprus in the Neolithic and Bronze Age periods*

Chaîne, G. (1959), 'Problèmes agricoles sur les bords septentrionaux du bassin Méditerranéen', *Annales de Géographie,* 68, 318–32

313

Bibliography

Chambers, J. D. and Mingay, G. E. (1966), *The agricultural revolution 1780–1880*

Chang, Chih-yi (1949), 'Land utilization and settlement possibilities in Sinkiang', *Geographical Review*, **39**, 57–75

Chang, J. (1968), 'The agricultural potential of the humid tropics', *Geographical Review*, **58**, 333–61

Chang, K. (1959), 'Chinese prehistory in Pacific perspective', *Harvard Journal of Asian Studies*, **22**, 100–49

  (1962), 'China', in R. J. Braidwood and G. Willey (eds.), *Courses towards urban life*, Viking Fund Publications, No. 32, 179–87

  (1963), *The archaeology of Ancient China*

  (1965), 'Relative chronologies of China to the end of Chou', in R. W. Ehrich (ed.), *Chronologies in Old World Archaeology*, 508–16

  (1968*a*), 'Archaeology of Ancient China', *Science*, **162**, 519–25

  (1968*b*), *Archaeology of Ancient China*, New Haven, Conn.

  (1970), 'The beginnings of agriculture in the Far East', *Antiquity*, **44**, 175–89

Chang, K. and Stuiver, M. (1966), 'Recent advances in the prehistoric archaeology of Formosa', *Proceedings of the National Academy of Science*, **55**, 1539–43

Ch'ao-Ting Chi (1936), *Key economic areas in Chinese history*

Chatterjee, A. B. (1963), 'The Hooghly river and its west bank: a study in historical geography', *Geographical Review of India*, **25**, 164–82

Chatterjee, D. (1951), 'Note on the origin and distribution of wild and cultivated rices', *Indian Journal of Genetics and Plant Breeding*, **11**, 18–22

Chaudhuri, K. N. (1966), 'India's foreign trade and the cessation of the East India Company's Trading Activities, 1828–40' *Economic History Review*, **19**, 345–63

  (1971), *The economic development of India under the East India Company, 1814–1858*

Cheesman, E. E. (1944), 'Notes on the nomenclature, classification and possible relationship of cacao populations', *Tropical Agriculture*, **21**, 144–59

Cheke, V. (1959), *The story of cheese-making in Britain*

Cheng, S. (1968), *The rice industry of Burma 1852–1940*, Kuala Lumpur

Chêng, T. (1960), *Archaeology in China: Shang China*

  (1963), *Archaeology in China: Chou China*

  (1966), *New light on prehistoric China*

Chevalier, F. (1963), 'The North Mexican hacienda; eighteenth and nineteenth centuries', in A. R. Lewis and T. F. McGann (eds.), *The New World looks at its history*, Austin, Texas, 95–107

Chisholm, M. (1962), *Rural settlement and land use*

Chittick, N. (1965), 'The Indian origins of some African cultivated plants and African cattle', *Uganda Journal*, **12**, 68–71

Chowdhury, K. A. and Buth, G. M. (1970), '4500 year old seeds suggest that true cotton is indigenous to Nubia', *Nature*, **227**, 85–7

Christian, J. L. (1941), 'Anglo-French rivalry in South east Asia; its historical geography and diplomatic climate', *Geographical Review*, **31**, 272–82

Ch'uan Han-sheng (1956), 'Production and distribution of rice in southern Sung', in E-Tu Zen Sun and John de Francis (eds.), *Chinese social history: translations of selected studies*, American Council of Learned Societies, Washington, D.C., 222–8

Church, R. J. H. (1957), *West Africa: a study of the environment and man's use of it*

  (1969), 'The Firestone rubber plantations in Liberia', *Geography*, **54**, 430–8

Cipolla, C. M. (1949), 'Revisions in economic history: the trends in Italian economic history in the later Middle Ages', *Economic History Review*, **2**, 181–4

  (1952), 'The decline of Italy: the case of a fully matured economy', *Economic History Review*, **5**, 178–87

  (1965), 'Four centuries of Italian demographic development', in D. V. Glass and D. E. C. Eversley (eds.), *Population in history*, 570–87

Citarella, A. O. (1968), 'Patterns in medieval trade: the commerce of Amalfi before the Crusades', *Journal of Economic History*, **28**, 531–55

Clapham, J. H. (1951), *The economic development of France and Germany, 1815–1914*

Clark, A. H. (1949), *The invasion of New Zealand by people, plants and animals*

314

Clark, C. (1967), *Population growth and land use*

Clark, C. and Haswell, M. (1970), *The economics of subsistence agriculture*

Clark, C. M. H. (1962), *A history of Australia*, vol. 1

Clark, H. (1957), 'The origin and early history of the cultivated barleys', *Agricultural History Review*, **15**, 1–18

Clark, J. D. (1962a), 'The spread of food production in sub-Saharan Africa', *Journal of African History*, **3**, 221–8

(1962b), 'Africa south of the Sahara', in R. J. Braidwood and G. Willey (eds.), *Courses towards urban life*, Viking Fund Publications, No. 32, 1–28

(1967), 'The problem of Neolithic culture in sub-Saharan Africa', in W. W. Bishop and J. D. Clark, (eds.), *Background to evolution in Africa*, 602–18

(1970), *The prehistory of Africa*

Clark, J. G. D. (1952), *Prehistoric Europe: the economic basis*

(1961), *World prehistory, an outline* (1st edn)

(1969), *World prehistory, a new outline* (2nd edn)

Clarke, J. I. (1955), 'Summer nomadism in Tunisia', *Economic Geography*, **31**, 157–67

(1959), 'Studies of semi-nomadism in North Africa', *Economic Geography*, **35**, 95–108

Clarke, W. C. (1966), 'From extensive to intensive cultivation: a succession from New Guinea', *Ethnology*, **5**, 352–5

Cleary, J. W. (1965), 'The Virgin lands', *Survey*, **56**, 95–105

Clough, S. B. (1959), *The economic development of western civilisation*

(1964), *The economic history of modern Italy*

Clout, H. D. (1968), 'Planned and unplanned changes in French farm structures', *Geography*, **53**, 311–15

(1971), *Studies in contemporary Europe; agriculture*

Cochrane, G. R. (1963), 'Commercial viticulture in south Australia', *New Zealand Geographer*, **19**, 60–82

Coe, M. D. (1964), 'The chinampas of Mexico', *Scientific American*, **211**, 90–8

Coedès, G. (1964), 'Some problems in the ancient history of the hinduized states of south-east Asia', *Journal of South East Asian History*, **5**, 1–14

(1966), *The making of south east Asia*

Colby, C. C. (1924), 'The California Raisin industry; *Annals of the Association of American Geographers*, **14**, 49–108

Cole, J. P. (1965), *Latin America: an economic and social geography*

Cole, M. M. (1954), 'The growth and development of the South African citrus industry', *Geography*, **39**, 102–13

(1961), *South Africa* (1st edn.)

(1966), *South Africa* (2nd edn.)

Collier, D. (1960), 'The development of civilisation on the coast of Peru', in Pan-American Union, *Irrigation civilisations; a comparative study*, Social Science Monographs, Washington, D.C., 19–27

Collins, E. J. T. (1968), 'Harvest technology and labour supply in Britain, 1790–1870', *Economic History Review*, **22**, 453–70

(1969), 'Labour supply and demand in European agriculture, 1800–1880', in E. L. Jones and S. J. Woolf (eds.), *Agrarian change and economic development*, 61–94

Collins, F. M. and Dibb, P. (1967), 'Wheat production in the Soviet Union and the five year plan', *Quarterly Review of Agricultural Economics*, **20**, 95–104

Collins, J. L. (1951), 'Antiquity of the pineapple in America', *Southwestern Journal of Anthropology*, **7**, 145–55

Commonwealth Scientific and Industrial Research Organisation (1966), *The Australian environment*

Commonwealth Secretariat (1972), *Dairy produce: a review*

Conklin, H. A. (1961), 'The study of shifting cultivation', *Current Anthropology*, **2**, 27–61

Contenau, G. (1954), *Everyday life in Babylon and Assyria*

Cook, O. F. (1921), 'Milpa agriculture, a primitive tropical system', *Annual Report of the Smithsonian Institute for 1919*, 307–26

Bibliography

Coppa, F. J. (1970), 'The Italian tariff and the conflict between agriculture and industry: the commercial policy of liberal Italy, 1860–1922', *Journal of Economic History*, **30**, 742–69

Coppock, J. T. (1959), 'The changing arable in England and Wales, 1870–1956', *Tijdschrift voor Economische en Sociale Geografie*, **50**, 121–30

    (1964), 'Crop, livestock and enterprise combinations in England and Wales', *Economic Geography*, **40**, 65–81

    (1971), *An agricultural geography of Great Britain*

Costin, A. B. (1964), 'Mountain land problems: South Island impressions and Australian comparisons', *New Zealand Geographer*, **20**, 60–73

Cotter, M. G. (1968), 'Towards a social history of the Vietnamese southwards movement', *Journal of South East Asian History*, **9**, 12–24

Coulter, J. W. (1929), 'A critical situation in two one-crop wheat farming districts in California', *Economic Geography*, **5**, 87–98

Coursey, D. G. (1965), 'The role of yams in West African food economics', *World Crops*, **17**, 74–82

    (1968), *Yams*

Courtenay, P. P. (1965), *Plantation agriculture*

    (1970), 'An approach to the definition of the plantation', *Geographia Polonica*, **19**, 81–90

Cranstone, B. A. L. (1969), 'Animal husbandry: the evidence from ethnography', in P. J. Ucko and G. W. Dimbleby (eds.), *The domestication and exploitation of plants and animals*. 247–63

Cressey, G. B. (1934), 'The agricultural regions of Asia; part 6, China', *Economic Geography*, **10**, 109–42

    (1955), *Land of the 500 million*

Crist, R. E. (1944), 'Cultural crosscurrents in the valley of the Rio São Francisco'. *Geographical Review*, **34**, 587–612

    (1946), 'History of the coffee industry in Cuba', *Geographical Review*, **36**, 493–5

Crouzet, F. (1967), 'England and France in the eighteenth century: a comparative analysis of two economic growths', in R. M. Hartwell (ed.), *The origins of the industrial revolution*, 139–74

Cumberland, K. B. (1944), 'High country "run": the geography of extensive pastoralism in New Zealand', *Economic Geography*, **20**, 204–20

    (1968), *South west Pacific*

Cumberland, K. B. and Hargreaves, R. P. (1955), 'Middle Island ascendant: New Zealand in 1881', *New Zealand Geographer*, **11**, 95–118

Cumberland, K. B. and Whitelaw, J. S. (1970), *The world's landscapes: New Zealand*

Curry, L. (1962), 'The climatic resources of intensive grassland farming: the Waikato, New Zealand', *Geographical Review*, **52**, 174–94

    (1963), 'Regional variation in the seasonal programming of livestock farms in New Zealand', *Economic Geography*, **39**, 95–118

Curtin, P. D. (1969), *The Atlantic slave trade; a census*

Curwen, E. C. and Hatt, G. (1961), *Plough and pasture: the early history of farming*, New York

Cutler, H. C. (1968), 'Origins of agriculture in the Americas', *Latin American Research Review*, **3**, 3–21

Dahl, S. (1961), 'Strip fields and enclosure in Sweden', *Scandinavian Economic History Review*, **9**, 56–67

Dale, E. E. (1960), *The range cattle industry*

Dale, I. R. (1955), 'The Indian origin of some African plants and African cattle', *Uganda Journal*, **19**, 68–72

Dales, G. F. (1966), 'The decline of the Harappans', *Scientific American*, **214**, 92–101

Dambaugh, L. N. (1959), *The coffee frontier in Brazil*, Gainesville, Florida

Daniel, G. and Evans, J. D. (1967), *The west Mediterranean*

Darby, H. C. (1940), *The draining of the Fens*

    (1956), 'The clearing of the woodland in Europe', in W. L. Thomas (ed.), *Man's role in changing the face of the earth*, 183–216

    (1964), 'The draining of the English clay lands', *Geographische Zeitschrift*, **52**, 190–201

Darlington, C. D. (1963), *Chromosome botany and the origins of cultivated plants*

Datta, J. M. (1962), 'Population of India about 320 B.C.', *Man in India*, **42**, 277–91

Davies, D. H. (1934), 'Present status of settlement in Hokkaido', *Geographical Review*, **24**, 386–99

Davies, E. (1941), 'Patterns of transhumance in Europe', *Geography*, **26**, 155–68

Davies, H. R. J. (1966), 'Nomadism in the Sudan: aspects of the problem and suggested lines for its solution', *Tijdschrift voor Economische en Sociale Geografie*, **57**, 193–202

Davies, O. (1968), 'The origins of agriculture in west Africa', *Current Anthropology*, **9**, 479–80

Davis, C. M. (1954), 'Merino sheep on the Australian Riverina', *Geographical Review*, **44**, 475–94

Davis, K. (1951), *The population of India and Pakistan*, Princeton, N.J.

(1960), 'The origin and growth of urbanisation in the world', in H. M. Mayer and C. F. Kohn (eds.), *Readings in urban geography*, 59–68

Deerr, N. (1949), *The history of sugar*, 2 volumes

Dempster, P. (1967), *Japan advances: a geographical study*

Denhardt, R. M. (1951), 'The horse in New Spain and the Borderlands', *Agricultural History*, **25**, 145–50

Deshler, W. W. (1965), 'Native cattle keeping in eastern Africa', in A. Leeds and A. P. Vayda (eds.), *Man, culture, and animals*, American Association for the Advancement of Science, No. 78, Washington, D.C., 153–68

Despois, J. (1945), 'Types of native life in Tripolitania', *Geographical Review*, **35**, 352–67

(1961), 'Development of land use in northern Africa', in L. D. Stamp (ed.), U.N.E.S.C.O., *A history of land use in arid regions*, Arid Zone Research, No. 17, Paris, 219–37

Dewhurst, J. F., Coppock, J. O. and Yates, P. L. (1961), *Europe's needs and resources; trends and prospects*

Dexter, K. (1967), 'Productivity in agriculture', in J. Ashton and S. J. Rogers (eds.), *Economic change and agriculture*, 67–83

Dickson, K. B. (1969), *A historical geography of Ghana*

Diégues, M. Jr (1959), 'Land tenure and use in the Brazilian plantation system' in Pan-American Union, *Plantation systems of the New World*, Washington, D.C., 104–25

Dion, H. G. (1950), *Agriculture in the Altiplano of Bolivia*, F.A.O., Rome

Dion, R. (1959), *Histoire de la vigne et du vin en France des origines au 19e siècle*, Paris

Dobby, E. H. G. (1936), 'The Ebro delta', *Geographical Journal*, **88**, 455–69

(1950), *South East Asia*

(1955), 'The changing significance of padi-growing in south-east Asia', *Journal of Tropical Geography*, **6**, 81–8

(1962), *Monsoon Asia*

Doerr, A. H. and Morris, J. W. (1960), 'The Oklahoma Panhandle – a cross section of the Southern High Plains', *Economic Geography*, **36**, 70–88

Dogget, H. (1965), 'The development of the cultivated sorghums', in J. B. Hutchinson (ed.), *Crop plant evolution*, 50–66

Donald, C. M. (1967), 'Innovation in agriculture', in D. B. Williams (ed.), *Agriculture in the Australian economy*, Sydney, 58–73

Donath, E. J. (1957), 'Location of wheat growing in Australia', *World Crops*, **9**, 166–7

Douglas, W. S. (1959), 'The deciduous fruit industry of the Cape', *Tydskrif vir Aardrykskunide*, **1**, 13–22

Dovring, F. (1959), 'The share of agriculture in a growing population', *Monthly Bulletin of Agricultural Economics and Statistics*, **8**, 1–11

(1960), *Land and labour in Europe, 1900–1950*, The Hague

(1965), 'The transformation of European agriculture', in H. J. Habakkuk and M. M. Postan (eds.), *The Cambridge economic history of Europe*, vol. 6, *The industrial revolutions and after*, part 2, 603–72

(1969), 'Eighteenth century changes in European agriculture: a comment', *Agricultural History*, **43**, 181–6

Dowd, D. F. (1961), 'The economic expansion of Lombardy, 1300–1500', *Journal of Economic History*, **21**, 143–60

Dozier, C. L. (1956), 'Northern Parana, Brazil: an example of organised regional development', *Geographical Review*, **46**, 318–33

Bibliography

(1957), 'Establishing a framework for development in Sardinia: the Campidano', *Geographical Review*, **47**, 490–506

Drain, M. (1961), 'Situation actuelle du vignoble de Xérès', *Annales de Géographie*, **70**, 378–97

Dresch, J. (1966), 'Utilisation and human geography of the deserts', *Transactions of the Institute of British Geographers*, **40**, 1–10

Du Boulay, F. R. (1965), 'Who were farming the English Demesnes at the end of the Middle Ages?', *Economic History Review*, **17**, 443–55

Duby, G. (1968), *Rural economy and country life in the Medieval West*

Duckham, A. N. (1959), 'The current agricultural revolution', *Geography*, **44**, 71–8

Duckham, A. N. and Masefield, G. B. (1970), *Farming systems of the world*

Dumond, D. E. (1961), 'Swidden agriculture and the rise of Maya civilisation', *Southwestern Journal of Anthropology*, **17**, 301–16

(1965), 'Population growth and cultural change', *Southwestern Journal of Anthropology*, **21**, 302–24

Dumont, R. (1957), *Types of rural economy*

Dunbabin, T. J. (1948), *The western Greeks*

Dunbar, G. S. (1961), 'Colonial Carolina cow-pens', *Agricultural History*, **35**, 125–30

(1970), 'African Ranches Ltd, 1914–31; an ill-fated stockraising enterprise in Northern Nigeria', *Annals of the Association of American Geographers*, **60**, 102–21

Duncan, J. S. (1962), 'The land for the people: land settlement and rural population movements, 1886–1906', in M. McCaskill (ed.), *Land and livelihood*, Christchurch, 170–90

Dunlop, J. S. (1970), 'Changes in the Canadian wheat belt, 1931–69', *Geography*, **55**, 156–68

Dunsdorf, E. (1956), *The Australian wheat growing industry 1788–1948*, Melbourne

Duprée, L. (1964), 'Prehistoric archeological surveys and excavations in Afghanistan, 1959–60 and 1961–63', *Science*, **146**, 638–40

Durand, J. D. (1960), 'The population statistics of China, A.D. 2–1953', *Population Studies*, **13**, 209–56

Durand, L. Jr (1949), 'The American dairy regions', *Journal of Geography*, **48**, 1–20

(1951) 'The lower peninsula of Michigan and the western Michigan dairy region', *Economic Geography*, **27**, 163–83

(1952), 'The migration of cheese manufacturing in the United States', *Annals of the Association of American Geographers*, **42**, 263–82

(1955), 'The American Centralizer Belt', *Economic Geography*, **31**, 301–20

(1964), 'The major milksheds of the North eastern Quarter of the United States', *Economic Geography*, **40**, 9–33

(1967), 'The historical and economic geography of dairying in the North Country of New York State', *Geographical Review*, **57**, 24–47

Dutch Agriculture, (1959), The Hague

Dwyer, D. J. (1964), 'Irrigation and land problems in the Central plain of Luzon: comment on a sample study', *Geography*, **49**, 236–46

Dyer, D. R. (1956), 'Sugar regions of Cuba', *Economic Geography*, **32**, 177–84

(1967), 'Cuban sugar regions', *Revista Geográfica*, **67**, 21–30

Dyson-Hudson, R. and Dyson-Hudson, N. (1969), 'Subsistence herding in Uganda', *Scientific American*, **220**, 76–89

East, W. G. (1950), *An historical geography of Europe*

Easterbrook, W. T. and Aitken, H. J. (1956), *Canadian economic history*, Toronto

Edwards, E. E. (1948), 'The settlement of grasslands', in *Grass: the yearbook of agriculture 1948*, United States Department of Agriculture, Washington, D.C., 18–19

(1949), 'Europe's contribution to the American dairy industry', *Journal of Economic History*, **9**, 72–84

Ehret, C. (1967), 'Cattle keeping and milking in eastern and southern African history; the linguistic evidence', *Journal of African History*, **8**, 1–17

Ellert, H. (1962), *The dairy industry of Denmark*, Arhus

Enggass, P. M. (1968), 'Land reclamation and resettlement in the Guadalquivir Delta – Las Marismas', *Economic Geography*, **44**, 125–43

English, P. E. (1967), 'Urbanites, peasants and nomads; the Middle Eastern ecological trinity',

Journal of Geography, **66,** 54–9

Epstein, H. (1955), 'Domestication features in animals as functions of human society', *Agricultural History,* **29,** 137–46

Erneholm, I. (1948), *Cacao production of South America; historical development and present distribution,* Gothenburg

Ernle, Lord, (1968), *English farming, past and present*

Evans, E. E. (1956), 'The ecology of peasant life in western Europe', in W. L. Thomas (ed.), *Man's role in changing the face of the earth,* 217–39

(1970), 'Introduction', in A. Gailey and A. Fenton (eds.), *The spade in northern and Atlantic Europe,* 1–9

Eyre, S. R. (1957), 'The upward limit of enclosure on the East Moor of North Derbyshire', *Transactions of the Institute of British Geographers,* **23,** 61–74

Fage, J. D. (1962), *An introduction to the history of West Africa*

Fage, J. D. (1969), *A history of West Africa*

Falkus, M. (1966), 'Russia and the international wheat trade', *Economica,* **33,** 416–29

Farmer, B. H. (1957), *Pioneer peasant colonization in Ceylon*

(1960), 'On not controlling subdivision in paddy lands', *Transactions of the Institute of British Geographers,* **28,** 225–35

Faucher, D. (1949), *Géographie agraire: types et cultures,* Paris

Faulk, O. B. (1965), 'Ranching in Spanish Texas', *Hispanic American Historical Review,* **45,** 257–66

Fay, C. R. (1936), 'Plantation agriculture', *Economic Journal,* **46,** 622–3

Fazle, Karim Khan, (1960), 'Agricultural origins in East Pakistan and adjoining areas', *Oriental Geographer,* **4,** 47–56

Fearns, H. S. (1960), *Britain and Argentina in the nineteenth century*

Ferrer, A. (1967), *The Argentine economy,* Berkeley, Calif.

Fielding, G. J. (1963), 'Sheep farming in New Zealand – a review', *New Zealand Geographer,* **19,** 160–9

Finch, V. C., Trewartha, G. T., Robinson, A. H. and Hammond, E. H. (1957), *Elements of geography physical and cultural*

Finley, M. I. (1965), 'Technical innovation and economic progress in the Ancient World', *Economic History Review,* **18,** 29–45

Fisher, C. A. (1954), 'The role of Korea in the Far East', *Geographical Journal,* **120,** 282–98

(1964a), *South-east Asia; a social, economic and political geography*

(1964b), 'Some comments on population growth in South-East Asia with special reference to the period since 1830', in C. D. Cowan (ed.), *The economic development of South-East Asia,* 48–72

(1968), 'Social and economic consequences of Western commercial agriculture in South East Asia', in *Land use and resources: studies in applied geography,* Institute of British Geographers, Special Publication No. 1, 147–54

Fite, G. C. (1966), *The farmer's frontier, 1865–1900,* New York

Fitzgibbon, R. H. (1953), 'Uruguay's agricultural problems', *Economic Geography,* **29,** 251–62

Flannery, K. V. (1965), 'The ecology of early food production in Mesopotamia', *Science,* **147,** 1247–56

Fletcher, T. W. (1961), 'The great depression of English agriculture, 1873–1896', *Economic History Review,* **13,** 417–32

Folke, S. (1966), 'Evolution of plantations, migration and population growth in Nilgiris and Coorg (South India)', *Geografisk Tiddskrift,* **65,** 198–239

F.A.O. (1956), *Production yearbook,* vol. 10

(1957), 'Shifting cultivation', *Tropical agriculture,* **34,** 159–64

(1962), *Production yearbook,* vol. 16

(1966), *Rice: grain of life,* World Food Problems, vol. 6, Rome

(1968a), *Horticulture in the Mediterranean area: outlook for production and trade,* Commodity Bulletin Series, vol. 42, Rome

(1968b), *Production yearbook,* vol. 22

(1969a), *Production yearbook,* vol. 23

Bibliography

(1969b), *The world wine and vine products economy: a study of trends and problems*, Commodity Bulletin Series, vol. 43, Rome

(1969c), *The world dairy economy in figures*, F.A.O. Commodity Reference Series, vol. 5, Rome

(1969d), *Trade yearbook*, vol. 23

Forbes, R. J. (1955), *Studies in ancient technology*, 2 volumes

Forde, C. D. (1933), 'The North Arabian Badawin', *Geography*, **18**, 205–19

(1950), *Habitat, economy and society*

Forrest, D. M. (1967), *A hundred years of Ceylon tea, 1867–1967*

Forster, R. (1970), 'Obstacles to agricultural growth in eighteenth century France', *American Historical Review*, **75**, 1600–15

Foster, G. M. (1960), *Culture and conquest*, Viking Publications in Anthropology, No. 27

Fox, J. W. and Cumberland, K. B. (1962), *Western Samoa: land, life and agriculture in tropical Polynesia*

Frank, A. G. (1969), *Capitalism and underdevelopment in Latin America*

Frankel, F. R. (1971), *India's Green Revolution: political costs of economic growth*, Princeton University Press

Frankel, O. H. (1954), 'Invasion and evolution of plants in Australia and New Zealand', *Caryologia*, **6**, (supplement), 600–19

Franklin, S. H. (1969), *The European peasantry: the final phase*

French, M. (1966), *European breeds of cattle*, F.A.O. Agricultural Studies No. 67, vol. 1, Rome

Freyre, G. (1956), *The masters and the slaves*, New York

Frumkin, G. (1970), *Archaeology in Soviet Central Asia*, Leiden

Fryer, D. W. (1965), *World economic development*

(1970), *Emerging South East Asia*

Fuggles-Couchman, N. R. (1964), *Agricultural change in Tanganyika 1945–60*, Stanford Food Research Institute

Fullerton, B. (1954), 'The northern margin of grain production in Sweden in the 20th century', *Transactions of the Institute of British Geographers*, **20**, 181–91

Fulmer, J. L. (1950), *Agricultural progress in the Cotton Belt since 1920*, Chapel Hill

Furnivall, J. S. (1948), *Colonial policy and practice: a comparative study of Burma and the Netherlands Indies*

Furtado, C. (1963), *The economic growth of Brazil*

Fussell, G. E. (1952), *The farmer's tools 1500–1900*

(1958), 'Growth of food production', in C. Singer, E. J. Holmyard, A. R. Hall and T. I. Williams (eds.), *A history of technology*, vol. 5, 1–25

(1960), 'The Hainault scythe in England', *Man*, **60**, 105–8

(1965), *Farming techniques from prehistoric to modern times*

(1966a), 'Ploughs and ploughing before 1800', *Agricultural History*, **40**, 177–86

(1966b), *The English dairy farmer 1500–1900*

(1967), 'Farming systems of the classical era', *Technology and culture*, **8**, 16–44

(1969), 'The classical tradition in west European farming – the fourteenth and fifteenth centuries', *Agricultural History Review*, **17**, 1–8

Gabrieli, F. (1968), *Muhammad and the conquests of Islam*

Gadille, J. (1957), 'L'agriculture européenne au Maroc; étude humaine et économique, *Annales de Géographie*, **66**, 144–58

Gallman, R. E. (1970), 'Self-sufficiency in the cotton economy of the Antebellum South', *Agricultural History*, **54**, 5–23

Galloway, J. H. (1964), 'The sugar industry in Barbados during the seventeenth century', *Journal of Tropical Geography*, **19**, 35–41

(1968), 'The sugar industry of Pernambuco during the nineteenth century', *Annals of the Association of American Geographers*, **58**, 285–303

Galtier, G. (1960), *Le vignoble du Languedoc méditerranéen et du Roussillon: étude comparative d'un vignoble de masse*, Montpellier, 3 volumes

Ganshof, F. L. and Verhulst, A. (1966), 'Medieval agrarian society in its prime: France, the Low Countries and Western Germany', in M. M. Postan (ed.), *The Cambridge economic history of Europe*, vol. 1, *The agrarian life of the Middle Ages* (2nd edn.), 291–339

Gates, P. W. (1960), *The farmer's age, 1815–1860*

Geddes, A. (1927), *Au pays de Tagore*, Paris

(1941), 'Half a century of population trends in India: a regional study of net change and variability, 1881–1931', *Geographical Journal*, **98**, 228–53

Geertz, C. (1963), *Agricultural involution: the process of ecological change in Indonesia*

Genicot, L. (1966), 'Crisis; from the Middle Ages to modern times', in M. M. Postan (ed.), *The Cambridge economic history of Europe*, vol. 1, *The agrarian life of the Middle Ages* (2nd edn.), 660–741

George, P. (1963), *Précis de géographie rurale*, Paris

Gerschenkron, A. (1966), *Bread and democracy in Germany*

Ghose, R. L. M., Ghatge, M. B. and Subrahmanyan, V. (1960), *Rice in India*, New Delhi

Ghosh, O. K. (1959), 'Some problems of Indian history in the light of geography', *Geographical Review of India*, **21**, 43–50

Gibson, C. (1966), *The Spanish in America*

Gibson, L. E. (1948), 'Characteristics of a regional margin of the corn and dairy belts', *Annals of the Association of American Geographers*, **38**, 244–70

Ginsburg, N. (1958), *The pattern of Asia*

Glade, W. P. (1969), *The Latin American economies*

Gleave, M. B. and White, H. P. (1969), 'Population density and agricultural systems in West Africa', in M. F. Thomas and G. W. Whittington (eds.), *Environment and land use in Africa*, 273–300

Glick, T. F. (1970), *Irrigation and society in medieval Valencia*, Cambridge, Mass.

Goodan, D. and Shatto, T. C. (1948), 'Changing land use in Ygnacio Valley, California', *Economic Geography*, **24**, 135–48

Goor, G. A. W. van de (1966), 'Agriculture with special reference to rice cultivation in humid tropical deltas', in U.N.E.S.C.O., *Scientific problems of the humid tropical zone deltas and their implications*, Paris, 305–16

Gorman, C. (1969), 'Hoabinhian: a pebble tool complex with early plant associations in south east Asia', *Science*, **163**, 671–3

(1971), 'The Hoabinhian and after: subsistence patterns in south east Asia during the late Pleistocene and early recent periods', *World Archeology*, **2**, 300–20

Gottmann, J. (1943), 'Economic problems of French North Africa', *Geographical Review*, **33**, 175–96

Gourou, P. (1948), 'Notes on China's unused uplands', *Pacific Affairs*, **21**, 227–38

(1952), *The tropical world* (1st edn.)

(1965), *Les paysans du Delta-Tonkinois*, Paris (Reprint)

(1966), *The tropical world* (4th edn.)

Graham, A. M. S. (1967), 'Northeast Africa', in B. W. Hodder and D. R. Harris (eds.), *Africa in transition*, 97–162

Graham, R. (1968), *Britain and the onset of modernisation in Brazil, 1850–1914*

Gras, N. S. B. (1925), *A history of agriculture in Europe and America*

Graumann, H. O. and Hein, M. A. (1962), 'Crops for our grasslands', in *After a hundred years: yearbook of agriculture 1962*, U.S. Department of Agriculture, Washington, D.C., 133–6

Graves, N. J. (1965), 'Une Californie française: the Languedoc and lower Rhône irrigation project', *Geography*, **50**, 71–3

Gray, B. S. (1963), 'The potential of oil-palm in Malaya', *Journal of Tropical Geography*, **17**, 127–32

Gray, L. C. (1933), *History of agriculture in the Southern United States to 1860*, Washington, D.C. (2 volumes)

Greenberg, M. (1951), *British trade and the opening of China, 1800–1842*

Greenfield, K. R, (1934), *Economics and liberalism in the Risorgimento – a study of nationalism in Lombardy, 1814–1848*, Baltimore

Greenway, P. J. (1944), 'Origins of some East African food plants', *East African Agricultural Journal*, **10**, 34–9, 115–19, 177–80, 251–6, and **11**, 56–63

Gregor, H. F. (1963), 'Industrialised drylot dairying: an overview', *Economic Geography*, **39**,

Bibliography

299–318

(1965), 'The changing plantation', *Annals of the Association of American Geographers*, **55**, 221–38

Griffin, P. F. (1955), 'The olive industry of California', *Journal of Geography*, **54**, 429–40

Griffin, P. F. and Chatham, R. L. (1958), 'Urban impact on agriculture in Santa Clara County, California', *Annals of the Association of American Geographers*, **48**, 195–208

Griffiths, Sir Percival, (1967), *History of the Indian tea industry*

Grigg, D. B. (1965) 'The logic of regional systems', *Annals of the Association of American Geographers*, **55**, 465–91

(1966a), 'The geography of farm-size: a preliminary survey', *Economic Geography*, **42**, 204–35

(1966b), *The agricultural revolution in South Lincolnshire*

(1967), 'Regions, models and classes', in R. J. Chorley and P. Haggett (eds.), *Models in geography*, 461–510

(1969a), 'Degrees of concentration; a note on world population concentration', *Geography*, **54**, 325–9

(1969b), 'The agricultural regions of the world: review and reflections', *Economic Geography*, **45**, 95–132

(1970), *The harsh lands*

(1971), 'Trends in the world's agricultural population', *Geography*, **56**, 320–5

(1973), 'The Rural Revolution', *Geographical Magazine*, **45**, 734–9

Grist, D. H. (1953), *Rice* (1st edn.)

(1959), *Rice* (2nd edn.)

Grotewald, A. (1955), 'Regional changes in corn production in the United States from 1909 to 1949', *Department of Geography Research Paper*, No. 40, University of Chicago

Grove, A. T. (1951), 'Soil erosion and population problems in South east Nigeria', *Geographical Journal*, **117**, 291–306

Gulliver, P. H. (1955), *The family herds*

Gumilev, L. N. (1966a), 'Heterochronism in the moisture supply of Eurasia in antiquity', *Soviet Geography*, **7**, 34–45

(1966b), 'Khazaria and the Terek', *Soviet Geography*, **7**, 14–27

Guthrie, M. (1962), 'Some developments in the prehistory of the Bantu languages', *Journal of African History*, **3**, 273–82

Gwynne, M. D. (1967), 'The possible origin of the dwarf cattle of Socotra', *Geographical Journal*, **133**, 39–42

Habib, I. M. (1965), *The agrarian structure of Mughal India, 1566–1707*, Bombay

(1969a), 'An examination of Wittfogel's theory of Oriental Despotism', in K. S. Lal (ed.), *Studies in asian history: Proceedings of the Asian History Congress, 1961*, 378–92

(1969b), 'Potentialities of capitalistic development in the economy of Mughal India', *Journal of Economic History*, **25**, 32–78

Hagerty, M. (1940), 'Comments on writings concerning Chinese sorghums', *Harvard Journal of Asiatic Studies*, **5**, 234–60

Hall, A. R. (1963), *The London Capital Market and Australia 1870–1914*, Canberra

Hall, D. G. E. (1968), *A history of South-east Asia*

Hall, R. B. (1962), 'A map of "Buraku" settlements in Japan', *Papers of the Michigan Academy of Science, Arts and Letters*, **47**, 521–7

Halpern, E. (1934), 'La Huerta de Valence', *Annales de Géographie*, **43**, 146–62

Hamdan, G. (1961), 'The evolution of irrigation agriculture in Egypt', in L. D. Stamp (ed.), U.N.E.S.C.O., *A history of land use in arid regions*, Arid Zone Research, No. 17, Paris, 119–42

Hammond, M. B. (1966), *The cotton industry, an essay in American economic history*

Han-Sheng Ch'uan, (1956), 'Production and distribution of rice in southern Sung', in E-Tu Zen Sum and John De Francis, *Chinese social history; translations of selected studies*, American Council of Learned Societies, Washington, D.C.

Haney, E. B. (1968), *The nature of shifting cultivation in Latin America*, Madison, Wis.

Hargreaves, M. W. M. (1948), 'Dry farming alias scientific farming', *Agricultural History*, **22**, 39–55

Hargreaves, R. P. (1965), 'Farm fences in pioneer New Zealand', *New Zealand Geographer*, **21**, 144–55

Haring, C. H. (1947), *The Spanish Empire in America*

Harlan, J. R. and Zohary, D. (1966), 'Distribution of wild wheats and barley', *Science*, **153**, 1074–80

Harler, C. R. (1964), *The culture and marketing of tea*

Harris, D. R. (1961), 'The distribution and ancestry of the domestic goat', *Proceedings of the Linnaean Society*, **173**, 79–91

(1969a), 'Agricultural systems, ecosystems and the origins of agriculture', in P. J. Ucko and G. W. Dimbleby (eds.), *The domestication and exploitation of plants and animals*, 3–16

(1969b), 'The ecology of agricultural systems', in R. U. Cooke and J. H. Johnson (eds.), *Trends in geography*, 133–42

Hart, J. F. (1956), 'The changing distribution of sheep in Britain', *Economic Geography*, **32**, 260–74

(1967), *The South-eastern United States*

Hartley, C. W. S. (1967), *The oil-palm*

Hartley, W. (1963), 'The development of forage crops', *Span*, 6

Hartley, W. and Williams, R. J. (1956), 'Centres of distribution of cultivated pasture grasses and their significance for plant introduction', *Seventh International Grassland Conference, Palmerstone North, New Zealand*, Paper No, 17

Hartman, D. N. (1964), *California and man*

Hatcher, H. (1944), 'Dairying in the South', *Economic Geography*, **20**, 54–64

Havinden, M. A. (1970), 'The history of crop cultivation in West Africa: a bibliographic guide', *Economic History Review*, **23**, 532–55

Hawkes, J. G. (1967), 'The history of the potato', *Journal of the Royal Horticultural Society*, **92**, 207–24, 249–62, 288–302

Hawkes, J. and Woolley, Sir Leonard (1963), *Prehistory and the beginnings of civilisation*

Haystead, L. and Fite, G. C. (1955), *The agricultural regions of the United States*

Hayter, E. W. (1939), 'Barbed-wire; a prairie invention', *Agricultural History*, **13**, 189–207

Heathcote, R. L. (1965a), 'Changes in pastoral land tenure and ownership', *Australian Geographical Studies*, **3**, 1–16

(1965b), *Back of Bourke*

(1969a), 'Drought in Australia: a problem of perception', *Geographical Review*, **59**, 175–94

(1969b), 'The pastoral ethic', in W. G. McGinnies and B. J. Goldman (eds.), *Arid lands in perspective*, 313–24

Hecksher, G. F. (1954), *An economic history of Sweden*

Heichelheim, F. M. (1959), *Roman Syria*, in T. Frank (ed.), *An economic survey of ancient Rome*, vol. 4

Helaissi, A. S. (1959), 'The Bedouins and tribal life in Saudi Arabia', *International Journal of Social Science*, **11**, 532–49

Helbaek, H. (1959), 'Domestication of food plants in the Old World', *Science*, **130**, 365–72

Helburn, N. (1957), 'The bases for a classification of world agriculture', *The Professional Geographer*, **9**, 2–7

Hellen, J. A. (1969), 'Colonial administrative policies and agricultural patterns in tropical Africa', in M. F. Thomas and G. W. Whittington (eds.), *Environment and land use in Africa*, 321–54

Henderson, D. A. (1954), 'Corn-belt feeding in Eastern Colorado's irrigated valleys', *Economic Geography*, **30**, 364–72

Hendry, G. W. (1923), 'The history of alfalfa', *Journal of the American Society of Agronomy*, **15**, 171–6

Henlein, P. C. (1961), 'Early cattle ranges of the Ohio Valley', *Agricultural History*, **35**, 150–4

Herre, W. (1963), 'The science and history of domestic animals', in D. Brothwell and E. Higgs (eds.), *Science in archeology*, 241–7

Hester, J. J. (1968), 'Origins of African agriculture; comment', *Current Anthropology*, **9**, 497–8

Heyerdahl, T. (1964), 'Plant evidence for contacts with America before Columbus', *Antiquity*, **38**, 120–33

Higbee, E. (1958), *American agriculture*

Bibliography

Higgins, F. H. (1958), 'John M. Horner and the development of the combine harvester', *Agricultural History*, **32**, 14–24
Higgs, E. S. and Jarman, M. R. (1969), 'The origins of agriculture: a reconsideration', *Antiquity*, **43**, 30–40
Highsmith, R. M., Jr and Northam, R. M. (1968), *World economic activities: a geographic analysis*
Higman, B. W. (1969), 'Plantations and typological problems in geography; a review article', *Australian Geographer*, **11**, 192–203
Hill, P. (1960), 'The migration of Southern Ghanaian cocoa farmers', *Bulletin of the Ghana Geographical Association*, **5**, 9–19
(1963), *The migrant cocoa-farmers of Southern Ghana: a study in rural capitalism*
(1970), *Studies in rural capitalism in West Africa*
Hill, R. D. (1966), 'Dry rice cultivation in peninsular Malaya', *Oriental Geographer*, **10**, 10–14
(1970), 'Peasant rice cultivation systems with some Malaysian examples', *Geographia Polonica*, **19**, 91–9
Hirst, H. and Panaretos, A. (1958), 'The citrus industry in Cyprus', *World Crops*, **10**, 180–2
Ho, P. (1955), 'The introduction of American food plants into China', *American Anthropologist*, **57**, 191–201
(1956), 'Early-ripening rice in Chinese history', *Economic History Review*, **9**, 200–18
(1959), *Studies in the population of China, 1368–1953*, Harvard East Asian Studies No. 4
(1969), 'The loess and the origin of Chinese agriculture', *American Historical Review*, **75**, 1–36
Ho, R. (1965), 'Land settlement projects in Malaya: an assessment of the role of the federal land development authority', *Journal of Tropical Geography*, **20**, 1–15
(1967), 'Rubber production by peasants of the Terachi valley, Malaya', *Transactions and Papers of the Institute of British Geographers*, **41**, 187–201
(1968), 'A major clearing in the jungle; on J. E. Spencer's "Shifting cultivation in Southeastern Asia"', *Pacific Viewpoint*, **9**, 173–89
Hoag, L. P. (1962), 'Location determinants for cash-grain farming in the Corn Belt', *Professional Geographer*, **14**, 1–7
Hofmeister, B. (1971), 'Types of agriculture with predominant olive-growing in Spain', *Geoforum*, **5**, 15–30
Hole, F. (1966), 'Investigating the origins of Mesopotamian civilisation', *Science*, **153**, 605–11
Hole, F. and Flannery, K. V. (1957), 'The prehistory of southwest Iran; a preliminary report', *Proceedings of the Prehistoric Society*, **33**, 147–206
Holt, P. M., Lambton, A. K. S. and Lewis B. (eds.) (1970), *The Cambridge history of Islam*, vol. 1, *The central Islamic lands*
Holt, P. M., Lambton, A. K. S. and Lewis, B. (eds.) (1970), *The Cambridge history of Islam*, vol. 2, *The further Islamic lands, Islamic society and civilisation*
Hopkins, L. C. (1935), 'The cas-chron *v.* the Lei-ssu', *Journal of the Royal Asiatic Society*, **101**, 707–16
Hore, T. E. (1957), 'The sheep and wool industry of Argentina', *Quarterly Review of Agricultural Economics*, **10**, 196–204
Hornell, J. (1934), 'Indonesian influence on East African culture', *Journal of the Royal Anthropological Institute*, **64**, 305–22
Hourani, G. F. (1951), *Arab seafaring in the Indian Ocean in ancient and early medieval times*, Princeton, N.J.
Houston, J. M. (1950), 'Irrigation as a solution to agrarian problems in modern Spain', *Geographical Journal*, **116**, 55–63
(1952), 'Social geography of rice cultivation in Spain', in G. Kuriyan (ed.), *Indian Geographical Society Jubilee Souvenir and N. Subrahmanyam Memorial Volume*, 36–40
(1959), 'Land use and society in the plain of Valencia', in R. Miller and J. W. Watson (eds.), *Geographical essays in memory of Alan G. Ogilvie*, 166–94
(1964), *The West Mediterranean world; an introduction to its regional landscapes*
Howells, W. W. (1960), 'The distribution of man', *Scientific American*, **203**, 113–27
Hoy, D. R. (1962), 'Changing agricultural land use in Guadeloupe', *Annals of the Association of American Geographers*, **52**, 441–54

Hsiang-Lin, L. (1967), 'The southward expansion of Chinese civilisation and the advancement of learning in Kwantung province', in F. S. Drake (ed.), *Symposium on historical, archaeological and linguistic studies on Southern China, South-east Asia and the Hong Kong Region*, Hong Kong, 139–52

Hsieh, Chiao-Min (1964), *Taiwan-ilha Formosa: a geography in perspective*

Hughes, R. (1960), *The Chinese communes*

Hugot, H. J. (1968), 'The origins of agriculture in Africa: the Sahara', *Current Anthropology*, **9**, 483–8

Huke, R. E. (1963), *Shadows on the land*, Manilla

Hung, F. (1958), 'Notes on the historical geography of Taiwan', *The Oriental Geographer*, **2**, 47–60

Hungerford, T. A. G. (1954), 'The Australian sugar industry', *Tijdschrift voor Economische en Sociale Geographie*, **45**, 138–42

Hunt, E. H. (1967), 'Labour productivity in English agriculture', *Economic History Review*, **20**, 280–92

Hunter, J. M. (1961), 'Akotuakrom: a case study of a devastated cocoa village in Ghana', *Transactions and Papers of the Institute of British Geographers*, **29**, 161–86

(1963), 'Cocoa migration and patterns of land ownership in the Densu valley near Suhum, Ghana', *Transactions and Papers of the Institute of British Geographers*, **33**, 61–87

Hutchinson, J. B. (1962), 'The history and relationships of the world's cottons', *Endeavour*, **21**, 5–15

Hutchinson, J. B., Silow, R. A. and Stephens, S. G. (1947), *The evolution of Gossypium and the differentiation of the cultivated cottons*

Impey, L. H. (1962), 'The olive industry in South Africa', *South African Geographical Journal*, **44**, 34–49

Ingram, J. C. (1964), 'Thailand's rice trade and the allocation of resources', in C. D. Cowan (ed.), *The economic development of South East Asia*, 102–26

Inskeep, R. R. (1969), 'The archaeological background', in M. Wilson and L. Thompson (eds.), *The Oxford history of South Africa*, vol. 1, 1–39

International Association of Agricultural Economists (1969), *World atlas of agriculture*, vol. 1, *Europe, U.S.S.R., Asia Minor*, Instituto Geografico De Agostini, Novara

Isaac, E. (1959), 'Influence of religion on the spread of citrus', *Science*, **129**, 179–80

(1970), *Geography of domestication*

Islam, M. A. (1965), 'Crop combination regions in East Pakistan', *Oriental Geographer*, **9**, 1–16

Isnard, H. (1949), 'Vigne et colonisation en Algérie', *Annales de Géographie*, **58**, 212–19

(1959), 'Agriculture européenne et agriculture indigéne en Algérie', *Cahiers d'Outre-Mer*, **12**, 147–59

Jaatinen, S. and Mead, W. R. (1957), 'The intensification of Finnish farming', *Economic Geography*, **33**, 31–40

Jack, H. W. (1957), 'Rice', *World Crops*, **9**, 485–9

Jackson, J. C. (1967), 'Oil-palm; Malaya's post-independence boom crop', *Geography*, **52**, 319–21

(1968), *Planters and speculators: Chinese and European agricultural enterprise in Malaya, 1786–1921*, Kuala Lumpur

(1969), 'Towards an understanding of plantation agriculture', *Area*, **4**, 36–41

Jackson, W. A. D. (1956), 'The virgin and idle lands of Western Siberia and Northern Kazakhstan; a geographical appraisal', *Geographical Review*, **46**, 1–19

(1962a), 'The virgin and idle lands program reappraised', *Annals of the Association of American Geographers*, **53**, 69–79

(1962b), *The Russo-Chinese borderlands*

Jacobsen, T. and Adams, R. N. (1958), 'Salt and silt in Mesopotamian agriculture', *Science*, **128**, 1251–8

James, P. E. (1932), 'The coffee lands of south east Brazil', *Geographical Review*, **22**, 225–44

(1938), 'Changing patterns of population in São Paulo state', *Geographical Review*, **28**, 353–62

(1950), *Latin America* (1st edn.)

(1953), 'Trends in Brazilian agricultural development', *Geographical Review*, **43**, 301–28

(1969), *Latin America* (4th edn.)

Bibliography

Jay, L. J. (1957), 'Pioneer settlement on the Darling Downs', *Scottish Geographical Magazine*, **73**, 35–49

Jefferies, A. (1971), 'Agrarian reform in Chile', *Geography*, **56**, 221–30

Jefferson, M. (1926), *Peopling the Argentine Pampas*, American Geographical Society Research Series, No. 16, New York

Jeffreys, M. D. W. (1963a), 'How ancient is West African maize?' *Africa*, **33**, 115–31

(1963b), 'The banana in the Americas', *Journal d'Agriculture tropicale et de Botanique appliqué*, **10**, 196–203

Jenkins, A. (1970), *Drinka pinta: the story of milk and the industry that serves it*

Jenkins, J. A. (1948), 'The origin of the cultivated tomato', *Economic Botany*, **2**, 379–92

Jenks, H. L. (1963), *The migration of British capital to 1875*

Jensen, E. (1937), *Danish agriculture: its economic development*, Copenhagen

Johnson, C. W. (1948), 'The relative decline of wheat in the Prairie Provinces of Canada', *Economic Geography*, **24**, 209–16

Johnson, D. L. (1969), 'The nature of nomadism; a comparative study of pastoral migrations in southwestern Asia and northern Africa', *Department of Geography, University of Chicago, Research Paper* No. 118

Johnson, K. (1971), 'Iowa dairying at the turn of the century: the new agriculture and progressivism', *Agricultural History*, **45**, 95–110

Johnston, B. F. (1958), *Staple food economies of West Africa*, Stanford, Calif.

(1964), 'Changes in agricultural productivity', in M. J. Herskovits and M. Harwitz (eds.), *Economic transition in Africa*, 151–78

Johnston, W. B. (1953), 'Land, people and progress in the Cook islands', *Economic Geography*, **29**, 107–15

(1965), 'New Zealand agriculture: the new frontier', *Erdkunde*, **19**, 155–61

Jonasson, O. (1925), 'Agricultural regions of Europe', *Economic Geography*, **1**, 277–314

(1926), 'Agricultural regions of Europe', *Economic Geography*, **2**, 19–48

Jones, A. H. M. (1959), 'Over-taxation and the decline of the Roman Empire', *Antiquity*, **33**, 39–43

Jones, C. F. (1928), 'Agricultural regions of South America', *Economic Geography*, **4**, 1–30, 155–87, 267–95

(1929), 'Agricultural regions of South America', *Economic Geography*, **5**, 101–41, 277–308, 390–422

(1930), 'Agricultural regions of South America', *Economic Geography*, **6**, 1–37

Jones, C. F. and Darkenwald, G. G. (1954), *Economic Geography* (1st edn.), New York

(1965), *Economic Geography* (3rd edn.), New York

Jones, C. F. and Morrison, P. C. (1952), 'Evolution of the banana industry of Costa Rica', *Economic Geography*, **28**, 1–19

Jones, D. R. W. (1963), 'Apple production in the Lebanon: a study of agricultural development in an underdeveloped area', *Economic Geography*, **39**, 245–57

Jones, E. L. (1962), 'The changing basis of English agricultural prosperity', *Agricultural History Review*, **10**, 102–19

(1964), 'The agricultural labour market in England, 1793–1872', *Economic History Review*, **17**, 322–38

Jones, L. R. (1928), 'Some physical controls in the economic development of the prairie provinces', *Geography*, **14**, 284–302

Jones, P. (1966), 'Medieval agrarian society in its prime: Italy', in M. M. Postan (ed.), *The Cambridge economic history of Europe*, vol. 1. *The agrarian life of the Middle Ages* (2nd edn.), 340–431

Jones, W. D. and Whittlesey, D. S. (1932), 'Nomadic herding regions', *Economic Geography*, **8**, 378–85

Jones, W. O. (1957), 'Manioc: an example of innovation in African economies', *Economic Development and Cultural Change*, **5**, 100–10

(1959), *Manioc in Africa*, Stanford, Calif.

(1968), 'Plantations', *International Encyclopedia of the Social Sciences*, **12**, 154–9

Jordan, T. (1969), 'The origin of Anglo-American cattle ranching in Texas: a documentation of diffusion from the lower South', *Economic Geography*, **45**, 63–83

Joshi, N. R., McLaughlin, E. and Phillips, R. W. (1957), *Types and breeds of African cattle*, F.A.O. Agricultural Studies, No. 37, Rome

Joshi, N. R. and Phillips, R. W. (1953), *Zebu cattle of India and Pakistan*, F.A.O. Agricultural Studies, No. 19, Rome

Kakiuchi, G. (1964), 'Wet rice in north-east Japan', *Journal of Geography*, **63**, 155–61

Kay, D. E. and Smith, E. H. G. (1960), 'A review of the market and world trade in bananas', *Tropical Science*, **2**, 154–61

Kay, G. (1970), *Rhodesia: a human geography*

Kayser, B. (1969), *L'agriculture et la société rurale des régions tropicales*, Paris

Kelly, K. (1965), 'Land use regions in the Central and Northern portions of the Inca Empire', *Annals of the Association of American Geographers*, **55**, 327–38

Kelly, K. (1971), 'Wheat farming in Simcoe County in the mid-nineteenth century', *Canadian Geographer*, **15**, 95–112

Kemmerer, D. L. and Jones, C. C. (1959), *American economic history*

Kemmler, G. (1962), 'Paddy manuring in Japan', *World Crops*, **14**, 176–80

Kenwood, A. G. and Lougheed, A. L. (1971), *The growth of the international economy, 1820–1960*

Kenyon, K. (1969), 'The origins of the Neolithic', *Advancement of Science*, **26**, 144–60

Keong, V. P. (1967), 'The rubber small-holding industry in Selangor, 1895–1920', *Journal of Tropical Geography*, **24**, 43–9

Kerridge, E. (1967), *The agricultural revolution*

Khan, M. Halim (1961), 'The rise and decline of cash crops in Java', *Indonesian Geographical Journal*, 47–55

Kihara, H. (1959), 'Considerations on the origin of cultivated rice', *Seiken Zihô*, Report of the Kihara Institute for Biological Research, Yokohama, Japan, No. 10, 68–79

Kikuchi, T. (1959), 'Geographical function of the reclamation settlements during the period of the Shogunate, 1603–1867', *Proceedings of the I.G.U. Regional Conference in Japan, 1957*, Tokyo

Kindleberger, C. P. (1964), *Economic growth in France and Britain, 1851–1950*

King, F. H. (1911), *Farmers of forty centuries*, Madison, Wis.

King, R. (1971), 'Development problems in a Mediterranean environment', *Tijdschrift voor Economische en Sociale Geografie*, **62**, 171–9

Kirk, W. (1947–9), 'Some factors in the historical geography of Burma', *Journal of the Manchester Geographical Society*, **54**, 16–26

Kirkbride, D. (1968), 'Beidha; early Neolithic village life south of the Dead Sea', *Antiquity*, **42**, 263–74

Kish, G. (1954), 'Transhumance in Southern Italy', *Papers of the Michigan Academy of Science, Arts and Letters*, **39**, 301–8

Klages, K. W. H. (1942), *Ecological crop geography*, New York

Klein, J. (1920), *The Mesta*

Koebner, R. (1966), 'The settlement and colonization of Europe', in M. M. Postan (ed.), *The Cambridge economic history of Europe*, vol. 1, *The agrarian life of the Middle Ages* (2nd edn.), 1–91

Kohlmeyer, F. W. and Herum, F. L. (1961), 'Science and engineering in agriculture: a historical perspective', *Technology and Culture*, **1**, 368–80

Kohn, C. F. (1943), 'Development of dairy farming in Mississippi', *Economic Geography*, **19**, 188–95

Kollmorgen, W. M. (1969), 'The woodsman's assault on the domain of the cattleman', *Annals of the Association of American Geographers*, **59**, 215–39

Kollmorgen, W. M. and Jenks, G. F. (1958a), 'Suitcase farming in Sully County, South Dakota', *Annals of the Association of American Geographers*, **48**, 27–40

(1958b), 'Sidewalk farming in Toole County, Montana, and Traill County, North Dakota', *Annals of the Association of American Geographers*, **48**, 208–31

Kostrowicki, J. (1964), 'Geographical typology of agriculture, principles and methods', *Geographia Polonica*, **1**, 111–46

(1966), 'Principles, basic notions and criteria of agricultural typology', *I.G.U. Commission for*

Bibliography

Agricultural Typology, Warsaw (mimeographed)

(1968), 'Agricultural typology. Agricultural regionalization, agricultural development', *Geographia Polonica*, **14**, 265–74

(1970), 'Some methods of determining land use and agricultural "orientations" as used in Polish land utilization and typological studies', *Geographia Polonica*, **18**, 93–120

Kostrowicki, J. and Helburn, N. (1967), *Agricultural typology, principles and methods: preliminary conclusions*, Boulder, Colorado (mimeographed)

Kovda, V. A. (1961), 'Land use development in the arid regions of the Russian plain, the Caucasus and Central Asia', in L. D. Stamp (ed.), U.N.E.S.C.O., *A history of land use in arid regions*, Arid Zone Research, No. 17, Paris, 175–218

Krader, L. (1955), 'Ecology of Central Asian pastoralism', *Southwestern Journal of Anthropology*, **11**, 301–26

(1959), 'The ecology of nomadic pastoralism', *International Social Science Journal*, **11**, 499–510

(1968), 'Pastoralism', *International Encyclopedia of the Social Sciences*, **11**, 453–61

Kraenzel, C. F. (1955), *The Great Plains in transition*

Kroef, J. M. van der (1951), 'The Hinduization of Indonesia reconsidered', *Journal of Asian Studies*, **11**, 17–30

Kuriyan, G. (1945), 'Rice in India', *Indian Geographical Journal*, **20**, 25–36, 76–84, 110–26

Ladurie, E. Le Roy (1966), *Les paysans de Languedoc*, Paris, 2 volumes

Laessøe, J. (1953), 'Reflections on modern and ancient oriental waterworks', *Journal of Cuneiform Studies*, **7**, 5–26

Lambert, A. (1961), 'Farm consolidation and improvement in the Netherlands', *Economic Geography*, **37**, 115–23

(1963), 'Farm consolidation in Western Europe', *Geography*, **48**, 31–48

(1971), *The making of the Dutch landscape; an historical geography of the Netherlands*

Lambrick, H. T. (1964), *Sind: a general introduction*, Hyderabad

Lamour, P. (1961), 'Land and water development in southern France', in H. Jarrett (ed.), *Comparisons in resource management*

Lampard, E. E. (1963), *The rise of the dairy industry in Wisconsin*, Madison, Wis.

Lanning, E. P. (1965), 'Early man in Peru', *Scientific American*, **213**, 68–76

(1967), *Peru before the Incas*

Lao Kan (1956), 'Population and geography in the two Han dynasties', in E-Tu Zen Sun and John de Francis (eds.), *Chinese social history: translations of selected studies*, Washington, D.C. 83–102

Large, D. C. (1960), 'Hybrid corn plantings in the United States', *Geography*, **45**, 113–14

Larson, C. W., Juve, C. A., Stine, O. C., Wight, A. E., Pistor, A. J. and Langworthy, C. F. (1923), 'The dairy industry', in U.S. Department of Agriculture, *Yearbook 1922*, Washington, D.C., 281–394

Lathrap, D. W. (1965), 'Origins of central Andean civilisation; new evidence', *Science*, **148**, 796–8

(1970), *The upper Amazon*

Latouche, R. (1967), *The birth of western economy: economic aspects of the Dark Ages*

Lattimore, O. (1951), *Inner Asian frontiers of China*

(1962a) *Nomads and commissars*, New York

(1962b), *Studies in frontier history: collected papers, 1928–1958*

Laufer, B. (1929), 'The American plant migration', *Scientific Monthly*, **28**

Laut, P. (1968a), *Agricultural geography; systems, subsistence and plantation agriculture*, Sydney

(1968b), *Agricultural geography: mid-latitude commercial agriculture*, Sydney

Lee, M. (1921), *The economic history of China*, Studies in History, Economics and Public Law, Columbia University, No. 1

Leeuw, P. N. de, (1965), 'The role of savanna in nomadic pastoralism: some observations from western Bornu, Nigeria', *Netherlands Journal of Agricultural Science*, **13**, 178–89

Lefebvre, G. (1966), 'The place of the revolution in the agrarian history of France', in D. K. Warner, (ed.), *Agrarian conditions in modern European history*, 79–94

Leighty, C. E., Warburton, C. W., Stine, O. C. and Baker, O. E. (1922), 'The corn crop', in U.S. Department of Agriculture, *Yearbook 1921*, Washington, D.C., 161–226

Lemmer, G. F. (1947), 'The spread of improved cattle through the eastern U.S. to 1850', *Agricultural History*, **21**, 79–93

Lennie, A. B. (1936), 'Agriculture in Mesopotamia in ancient and modern times', *Scottish Geographical Magazine*, **52**, 33–46

Lévy, J. (1967), *The economic life of the ancient world*

Lewis, A. R. (1958), 'The closing of the medieval frontier', *Speculum*, **33**, 475–83

Lewis, I. M. (1966), 'Introduction' in I. M. Lewis (ed.), *Islam in tropical Africa*, 4–96

Lewis, N. (1955), 'The frontier of settlement in Syria, 1800–1950', *International Affairs*, **31**, 48–60

Lewis, O. (1949), 'Plow culture and hoe culture – a study in contrasts', *Rural Sociology*, **14**, 116–27

Lewis, R. A. (1966), 'Early irrigation in West Turkestan', *Annals of the Association of American Geographers*, **56**, 467–91

Lewthwaite, G. R. (1964), 'Wisconsin cheese and farm types: a locational hypothesis', *Economic Geography*, **40**, 95–112

(1971), 'Commonwealth and Common Market: the dilemma of the New Zealand dairy industry', *Geographical Review*, **61**, 72–101

Lien-Sheng, Y. (1945–7), 'Notes on the economic history of the Chin dynasty', *Harvard Journal of Asiatic Studies*, **9**, 107–85

Lim, Y. (1968), 'Impact of the tea industry on the growth of the Ceylonese economy', *Social and Economic Studies*, **17**, 453–67

Linnard, W. (1970), 'Terms and techniques in shifting cultivation in Russia', *Tools and Tillage*, **1**, 192–7

Lisitsina, G. N. (1969), 'The earliest irrigation in Turkmenia', *Antiquity*, **43**, 279–88

Lockhart, J. (1968), *Spanish Peru 1532–1560, a colonial society*

Logan, R. F. (1961a), 'Post-Columban developments in the arid regions of the United States of America', in L. D. Stamp (ed.), U.N.E.S.C.O., *A history of land use in arid regions*, Arid Zone Research, No. 17, Paris, 277–97

(1961b), 'Land utilization in southern Africa: part 11, South West Africa', in L. D. Stamp (ed.), U.N.E.S.C.O., *A history of land use in arid regions*, Arid Zone Research, No. 17, Paris, 331–8

Long, W. Harwood (1963), 'The development of mechanization in English agriculture', *Agricultural History Review*, **11**, 15–26

Lopez, R. S. (1943), 'Mohammed and Charlemagne: a revision', *Speculum*, **18**, 14–38

(1971), *The commercial revolution of the Middle Ages, 1050–1350*, Englewood Cliffs, N.J.

Lorimer, F. (1946), *The population of the Soviet Union: history and prospects*, Geneva, League of Nations

Luce, G. H. (1940), 'The economic life of the early Burman', *Journal of the Burma Research Society*, **30**, 283–8

(1965), 'Rice and religion: a study of old Mon-Khmer evolution and culture', *Journal of the Siam Society*, **53**, 139–52

Luckwill, L. C. (1943), 'The evolution of the cultivated tomato', *Journal of the Royal Horticultural Society*, **68**, 19–25

Luebke, B. H. (1936), 'A geographical interpretation of "El Vergel", a *fundo* of the Central Valley of Chile', *Scottish Geographical Magazine*, **52**, 361–75

Lupton, A. A. (1966–7), 'Cattle ranching in Alberta, 1874–1910; its evolution and migration', *Albertan Geographer*, **3**, 48–58

Lutz, V. (1962), *Italy: a study in economic development*

Luzzatto, G. (1961), *An economic history of Italy from the fall of the Roman Empire to the beginning of the sixteenth century*

Lyaschenko, P. (1949), *History of the national economy of Russia to the 1917 Revolution*, New York

Lyddeker, R. (1912), *The sheep and its cousins*

McBride, G. M. (1936), *Chile, land and society*, American Geographical Society, Research Series, No. 19

McCune, S. (1949), 'Sequence of plantation agriculture in Ceylon', *Economic Geography*, **35**, 226–35

Bibliography

McCune, S. (1957), *Korea's heritage: a regional and social geography*, Tokyo

McDonald, G. T. (1968), 'Recent pasture development of the northern Tablelands of New South Wales', *Australian Geographer*, **10**, 382–91

Macdonald, J. S. (1963), 'Agricultural organisation, migration and labour militancy in rural Italy', *Economic History Review*, **16**, 61–9

MacEwan, G. (1952), *Between the Red and the Rockies*, Toronto

McFarlane, D. (1964), 'The future of the banana industry in the West Indies', *Social and Economic Studies*, **13**, 38–93

McGuire, K. (1959), 'Developments in the South African sheep and wool industry', *Quarterly Review of Agricultural Economics*, **12**, 124–32

Mackie, J. A. C. (1961), 'Indonesia's government estates and their masters', *Pacific Affairs*, **34**, 337–60

Mackintosh, W. A. (1934), *Prairie settlement; the geographical setting*, Toronto

McLennan, L. W. (1963), 'Recent wheat acreage changes in Australian states and likely future movements', *Quarterly Review of Agricultural Economics*, **16**, 136–44

McManis, D. R. (1964), 'The initial evaluation and utilization of the Illinois Prairies, 1815–1840', *Department of Geography, Research Paper* 94, *University of Chicago*

McMaster, D. N. (1962), 'Speculations on the coming of the banana to Uganda', *Journal of Tropical Geography*, **16**, 57–69

McNeill, W. H. (1964), *Europe's steppe frontier, 1500–1800*

(1965), *The rise of the West*

MacNeish, R. S. (1964), 'Ancient Mesoamerican civilisation', *Science*, **143**, 531–45

(1965), 'The origins of American agriculture', *Antiquity*, **39**, 87–94

McPhee, A. (1926), *The economic revolution in West Africa*

McQueen, J. D. W. (1961), 'Milk surpluses in Scotland', *Scottish Geographical Magazine*, **77**, 93–105

Maddalena, A. de (1970), 'Rural Europe 1500–1750', in *The Fontana economic history of Europe*, vol. 2, section 4, 5–112

Maity, S. K. (1957), *The economic life of Northern India in the Gupta Period*, Calcutta

Majumdar, R. C. (1955), *Ancient Indian colonisation in South east Asia*, Baroda

Malcolm, D. W. (1953), *Sukumuland: a land and its people*

Malefakis, E. E. (1970), *Agrarian reform and peasant revolution in Spain*, New Haven, Conn.

Malenbaum, W. (1953), *The world wheat economy, 1885–1939*, Harvard Economic Studies, No. 92

Malin, J. C. (1944), *Winter wheat in the Golden Belt of Kansas*, Kansas

Manning, W. H. (1964), 'The plough in Roman Britain', *Journal of Roman Studies*, **54**, 54–65

Marschner, F. J. (1959), *Land use and its patterns in the United States*, U.S. Department of Agriculture, Agricultural Handbook No. 153

Marshall, A. (1966), 'The "environment" and Australian wool production: one hundred and fifty years', in J. Andrews (ed.), *Frontiers and men*, 120–37

Martinez-Allier, J. (1971), *Labourers and landowners in Southern Spain*

Masefield, G. B. (1950), *A short history of agriculture in the British colonies*

(1962), *Agricultural change in Uganda, 1945–1960*

(1967), 'Crops and livestock', in E. E. Rich and C. H. Wilson (eds.), *The Cambridge economic history of Europe*, vol. 4, *The economy of expanding Europe in the sixteenth and seventeenth centuries*, 276–307

Mason, I. L. (1963), 'On the hump of the zebu', in A. E. Mourant and F. E. Zeuner (eds.), *Men and cattle; proceedings of Symposium on Domestication*, Royal Anthropological Institute, Occasional Paper No. 18, 17–19

Masson, V. M. (1961), 'The earliest farmers in Turkmenia', *Antiquity*, **35**, 203–7

Mather, E. (1950), 'The production and marketing of Wyoming beef cattle', *Economic Geography*, **26**, 81–93

Mather, E. and Hart, J. F. (1954), 'Agriculture in the Deep South and the Border States', *Tijdschrift voor Economische en Sociale Geographie*, **45**, 161–6

Mathews, H. A. (1924), 'A comparison between the Mediterranean climates of Eurasia and the Americas', *Scottish Geographical Magazine*, **40**, 150–9

Matley, I. M. (1968), 'Transhumance in Bosnia and Herzegovina', *Geographical Review*, **58**, 231–61

Matsuo, T. (1959), *Rice culture in Japan*, Tokyo

Mayhew, A. (1970), 'Structural reform and the future of West German agriculture', *Geographical Review*, **60**, 54–68

Mead, W. R. (1953), *Farming in Finland*

　(1958), *An economic geography of the Scandinavian States and Finland*

Meigs, P. (1941), 'Current trends in Californian orchards and vineyards', *Economic Geography*, **20**, 275–86

　(1964), 'Classification and occurrence of Mediterranean-type dry climates', in U.N.E.S.C.O., *Land use in semi-arid Mediterranean climates*, Arid Zone Research, No. 26, Paris, 17–21

Meinig, D. W. (1959), 'Colonization of wheat lands; some Australian comparisons', *Australian Geographer*, **7**, 145–56

　(1962), *On the margins of the good earth; the South Australian wheat frontier, 1869–1884*

　(1968), *The Great Colombia Plain: a historical geography, 1810–1910*

Mellaart, J. (1964), 'A neolithic city in Turkey', *Scientific American*, **210**, 94–104

　(1967), *The earliest western settlements*, Cambridge

Mendel, K. (1969), 'Citrus production in Israel', *World Crops*, **21**, 110–14

Menges, K. H. (1968), *The Turkic languages and peoples*, Wisbaden

Merriam, G. P. (1926), 'The regional geography of Anatolia', *Economic Geography*, **2**, 86–107

Merrill, E. D. (1940), 'Man's influence on the vegetation of Polynesia , with special reference to introduced species', *Proceedings of the Sixth Pacific Science Congress*, **4**, 629–39

Michell, H. (1953), 'Land tenure in ancient Greece', *Canadian Journal of Economic and Political Science*, **19**, 245–53

Mighell, R. L. and Black, J. D. (1951), *Interregional competition in agriculture with special reference to dairy farming in the Lake States and New England*

Mikesell, M. W. (1955), 'Notes on the dispersal of the dromedary', *Southwestern Journal of Anthropology*, **11**, 231–45

　(1961), *Northern Morocco, a cultural geography*, University of California Publications in Geography, No. 14

　(1969), 'The deforestation of Mount Lebanon', *Geographical Review*, **59**, 1–28

Miller, N. R. (1960), 'Sheep in New Zealand', *Quarterly Review of Agricultural Economics*, **13**, 127–35

Millington, A. J. (1957), 'Ley farming in the Australian wheat belt', *World Crops*, **9**, 98–102

Mingay, G. E. (1956), 'The agricultural depression, 1730–1750', *Economic History Review*, **8**, 323–38

Ministry of Agriculture, Fisheries and Food (1968), *A century of agricultural statistics*, H.M.S.O.

　(1970), *Modern farming and the soil*, H.M.S.O.

Mintz, S. (1953), 'The culture history of a Puerto Rican sugar-cane plantation, 1876–1949', *Hispanic American Historical Review*, **33**, 224–51

　(1958–9), 'Labour and sugar in Puerto Rico and Jamaica, 1800–1850', *Comparative Studies in Society and History*, **1**, 273–83

Miracle, M. P. (1964), *Traditional agricultural methods in the Congo Basin*, Food Research Institute, Stanford

　(1965), 'The introduction and spread of maize in Africa', *Journal of African History*, **6**, 39–55

　(1966), *Maize in tropical Africa*

Miskimin, H. A. (1969), *The economy of early Renaissance Europe, 1300–1460*

Monbeig, P. (1934), 'Quelques aspects de l'économie espagnole', *Annales de Géographie*, **43**, 299–306

　(1952), *Pionniers et planteurs de São Paulo*, Paris

Monkhouse, F. J. (1965), *A regional geography of western Europe*

Monod, T. and Toupet, C. (1961), 'Land use in the Sahara–Sahel region', in L. D. Stamp (ed.), U.N.E.S.C.O., *A history of land use in arid regions*, Arid Zone Research, No. 17, Paris, 239–53

Montelius, S. (1953), 'The burning of forest land for the cultivation of crops', *Geografiska Annaler*, **35**, 41–54

Bibliography

Moodie, D. W. and Kay, B. (1969), 'The northern limit of Indian agriculture in North America', *Geographical Review*, **59**, 513–29

Moore, J. H. (1956), 'Cotton breeding in the Old South', *Agricultural History*, **30**, 95–104

Moreland, W. H. (1920), *The agrarian system of Moslem India*

Morgan, W. B. (1955), 'The Nigerian oil palm industry', *Scottish Geographical Magazine*, **71**, 174–7

(1959*a*), 'The influence of European contacts on the landscape of Southern Nigeria', *Geographical Journal*, **125**, 48–64

(1959*b*), 'Agriculture in Southern Nigeria', *Economic Geography*, **35**, 138–50

(1969), 'Peasant agriculture in tropical Africa', in M. F. Thomas and G. W. Whittington (eds.), *Environment and land use in Africa*, 241–72

Morgan, W. B. and Pugh, J. C. (1969), *West Africa*

Morris, T. N. (1958), 'Management and preservation of food', in C. Singer, E. J. Holmyard, A. R. Hall and T. I. Williams (eds.), *A history of technology*, vol. 5, 26–52

Morrisey, R. J. (1951), 'The Northward expansion of cattle ranching in New Spain, 1550–1600', *Agricultural History*, **25**, 115–21

(1957), 'Colonial agriculture in New Spain', *Agricultural History*, **31**, 24–9

Mortimore, M. J. and Wilson, J. (1965), *Land and people in the Kano close-settled zone*, Ahmadu Bello University, Department of Geography, Occasional Paper No. 1

Mountjoy, A. B. (1957), 'Vegetable oils and oilseeds: aspects of production and use', *Geography*, **42**, 37–49

Murchie, R. W. (1936), *Agricultural progress on the Prairie frontier*, Toronto

Murdock, G. P. (1959), *Africa; its peoples and their culture history*

(1960), 'Staple subsistence crops of Africa', *Geographical Review*, **50**, 523–40

Murphey, R. (1951), 'The decline of North Africa', *Annals of the Association of American Geographers*, **41**, 116–32

(1956), 'The ruin of ancient Ceylon', *Journal of Asian Studies*, **16**, 181–200

Murray, J. (1970), *The first European agriculture: a study of the osteological and botanical evidence until 2000 B.C.*

Narr, K. J. (1956), 'Early food producing populations', in W. L. Thomas (ed.), *Man's role in changing the face of the earth*, 134–51

Naval Intelligence Division (1943), *Indo-China*, Geographical Handbook Series, B.R. 510

Naylon, J. (1959), 'Land consolidation in Spain', *Annals of the Association of American Geographers*, **49**, 361–73

(1967), 'Irrigation and internal colonization in Spain', *Geographical Journal*, **133**, 178–81

Needham, J. (1954), *Science and civilisation in China*, vol. 1

Newberry, P. E. (1937–8), 'On some African species of the genus *Olea* and the original home of the cultivated olive-tree', *Proceedings of the Linnean Society*, **150**, 3–16

Newbigin, M. (1929), 'The Mediterranean climatic type: its world distribution and the human response', *South African Geographical Journal*, **12**, 14–22

Newbigin, M. I. (1930), *The Mediterranean lands*

Newbury, C. W. (1971), 'Prices and profitability in early nineteenth century West African trade', in C. Meillassoux (ed.), *The development of indigenous trade and markets in West Africa*, 91–106

Nicolaisen, S. (1954), 'Some aspects of the problem of nomadic cattle breeding among the Tuareg of the Central Sahara', *Geografisk Tidsskrift*, **53**, 62–105

Niel, R. van (1964), 'The function of land rent under the cultivation system in Java', *Journal of Asian Studies*, **23**, 357–75

Nishiyama, I. (1961), 'The origin of the sweet potato', in J. Barrau (ed.), *Plants and the migration of Pacific peoples: a symposium*, Tenth Pacific Science Congress, Honolulu, 119–28

North, D. C. (1958), 'Ocean freight rates and economic development, 1750–1913', *Journal of Economic History*, **18**, 537–47

Nostrand, R. L. (1970), 'The Hispanic American borderland: definition of an American culture region', *Annals of the Association of American Geographers*, **60**, 638–61

Nye, P. H. and Greenland, D. J. (1960), *The soil under shifting cultivation*, Technical Communication No. 51, Commonwealth Bureau of Soils, Harpenden

Nyhus, P. O. (1940), 'The Argentine pastures and the cattle grazing industry', *Foreign Agriculture,* **4,** 3–30

O'Connor, A. M. (1966), *An economic geography of East Africa*

Ogot, B. A. (1968), 'The role of the pastoralist and the agriculturalist in African history', in T. O. Ranger (ed.), *Emerging themes in African history,* Nairobi, 125–33

Oliver, R. (1966), 'The problem of the Bantu expansion' *Journal of African history,* **8,** 361–76

Ooi Jin-bee (1963), *Land, people and economy in Malaya*

O.E.C.D. (1966), *Production of fruit and vegetables in O.E.C.D. member countries; present situation and 1970 prospects: 1. Portugal. 2. Italy. 3. Netherlands, Switzerland. 4. France, Belgium, Luxembourg. 5. Turkey, Yugoslavia. 6. U.S., Canada*

(1969a) *Agricultural development in Southern Europe,* Paris

(1969b), *The development of the production of beef and veal: Mediterranean countries of O.E.C.D.,* Paris

O.E.E.C. (1951), *Pasture and fodder development,* Paris

Ortiz, F. (1947), *Cuban counterpoint: tobacco and sugar,* New York

Orwin, C. S. and Whetham, E. H. (1964), *History of British Agriculture, 1846–1914*

Osgood, E. S. (1929), *The day of the cattlemen*

Ostrogorsky, G. (1966), 'Agrarian conditions in the Byzantine Empire in the Middle Ages', in M. M. Postan (ed.), *The Cambridge economic history of Europe,* vol. 1, *The agrarian life of the Middle Ages* (2nd edn.), 205–34

Oyenuga, V. A. (1967), *Agriculture in Nigeria,* Rome

Paget, E. (1956), 'Land use and settlement in Jamaica', in R. W. Steel and C. A. Fisher (eds.), *Geographical essays on tropical lands,* 181–224

Palerm, A. (1967), 'Agricultural systems and food patterns', in M. Nash (ed.), *Social anthropology, handbook of Middle American Indians,* vol. 6, Austin, Texas, 26–52

Parain, C. (1966), 'The evolution of agricultural technique' in M. M. Postan (ed.), *The Cambridge economic history of Europe,* vol. 1, *The agrarian life of the Middle Ages* (2nd edn.), 125–79

Parker, W. H. (1968), *An historical geography of Russia*

Parkinson, C. N. (1948), *The trade winds*

Parry, J. H. (1963), *The age of reconnaissance*

(1966), *The Spanish seaborne Empire*

(1967), 'Transport and trade routes', in E. E. Rich and C. H. Wilson (eds.), *The Cambridge economic history of Europe,* vol. 4, *The economy of expanding Europe in the sixteenth and seventeenth centuries,* 155–219

Parry, J. H. and Sherlock, P. M. (1966), *A short history of the West Indies*

Parsons, J. J. (1949), 'Antioqueña colonisation in Western Columbia', *Ibero-Americana,* 32

(1957), 'Bananas in Ecuador', *Economic Geography,* **33,** 201–16

Patai, R. (1951), 'Nomadism: Middle Eastern and Central Asia', *Southwestern Journal of Anthropology,* **7,** 401–14

Paterson, J. H. (1970), *North America: a geography of Canada and the United States*

Paullin, C. O. (1932) *Atlas of the historical geography of the United States,* New York

Payne, S. (1969), 'The origins of sheep and goats – a reconsideration in the light of the fossil evidence', *Proceedings of the Prehistoric Society,* **34,** 368–84

Payne, W. J. A. (1964), 'The origin of domestic cattle in Africa', *Empire Journal of Experimental Agriculture,* **32,** 97–113

Peet, J. R. (1969), 'The spatial expansion of commercial agriculture in the nineteenth century: a Von Thunen interpretation', *Economic Geography,* **45,** 283–301

(1970–1), 'Von Thunen theory and the dynamics of agricultural expansion', *Explorations in Economic History,* **8,** 181–202

Pelzer, K. J. (1945), *Pioneer settlements in the Asiatic tropics,* American Geographical Society Special Publication, No. 29, New York

(1953), 'Geography and the tropics', in G. Taylor (ed.), *Geography in the twentieth century,* 311–44

(1958), 'Land utilization in the humid tropics: agriculture', *Proceedings Ninth Pacific Science Congress, 1957,* Bangkok, vol. 20, 124–43

Pendleton, R. L. (1962), *Thailand: aspects of landscape and life,* American Geographical Society, New York

Bibliography

Pepelasis, A. A. and Thompson, K. (1960), 'Agriculture in a restrictive environment: the case of Greece', *Economic Geography*, **36**, 145–57

Perkins, D. Jr (1964), 'Prehistoric fauna from Shanidar, Iraq', *Science*, **144**, 1565–6

Perkins, D. H. (1969), *Agricultural development in China, 1368–1968*

Perrot, J. (1962), 'Palestine–Syria–Cilicia', in R. J. Braidwood and G. Willey (eds.), *Courses towards urban life*, Viking Fund Publications, No. 32, 147–64

Perry, P. J. (1969), 'The structural revolution in French agriculture: the rôle of "sociétés d'Aménagement foncier et d'Etablissment rural"', *La Revue de Géographie de Montreal*, **23**, 137–51

Peterson, G. E. (1967), 'The discovery and development of 2, 4-D', *Agricultural History*, **41**, 243–53

Phillips, A. D. M. and Clout, H. D. (1970), 'Underdraining in France during the second half of the nineteenth century', *Transactions of the Institute of British Geographers*, **51**, 71–94

Phillips, E. D. (1965), *The royal hordes*
(1969), *The Mongols*

Phillips, R. W. (1961), 'World distribution of the main types of cattle', *Journal of Heredity*, **52**, 207–13

Piggot, S. (1950), *Prehistoric India*

Pim, Sir Alan (1940), *The financial and economic history of the African tropical territories*
(1946), *Colonial agricultural production*

Pinchemel, P. (1969), *France: a geographical survey*

Pitt-Rivers, J. (1963), *Mediterranean countrymen: essays in the social anthropology of the Mediterranean*, Paris

Planhol, X. de (1959), 'Geography, politics and nomadism in Anatolia', *International Social Science Journal*, **11**, 525–31
(1970), 'The geographical setting', in P. M. Holt, A. K. S. Lambton and B. Lewis (eds.), *The Cambridge history of Islam*, vol. 2, *The further Islamic lands, Islamic society and civilisation*, 443–68

Poggi, E. M. (1930), 'The German sugar-beet industry', *Economic Geography*, **6**, 81–93

Polharnus, L. (1962), *Rubber: botany, cultivation and utilization*

Pollock, N. C. and Agnew, S. (1963), *A historical geography of South Africa*

Poncet, J. (1951), 'Problèmes actuels des campagnes Tunisiennes', *Annales de Géographie*, **60**, 255–69

Poole, D. M. (1951), 'The Spanish conquest of Mexico: some geographical aspects', *Geographical Journal*, **117**, 27–40

Porter, G. R. (1847), *The progress of the nation*

Postan, M. M. (1966), 'Medieval agrarian society in its prime: England', in M. M. Postan (ed.), *The Cambridge economic history of Europe*, vol. 1, *The agrarian life of the Middle Ages* (2nd edn.), 548–632
(1967), *An economic history of Western Europe, 1945–1964*

Pounds, N. J. G. (1967), 'North west Europe in the ninth century: its geography in the light of the polyptyques', *Annals of the Association of American Geographers*, **57**, 439–61
(1969–70), 'Overpopulation in Northwest Europe in the thirteenth century', *Journal of Social History*, **3**, 225–47

Pounds, N. J. G. and Roome, C. C. (1971), 'Population density in fifteenth century France and the low countries', *Annals of the Association of American Geographers*, **61**, 116–30

Powell, J. M. (1968), 'A pioneer sheep station: the Clyde Company in Western Victoria, 1836–1840', *Australian Geographical Studies*, **6**, 59–66

Prentice, A. (1957), 'The commercial crops of North Greece', *World Crops*, **9**, 163–5

Preston, D. A. (1965), 'Changes in the economic geography of banana production in Ecuador', *Transactions of the Institute of British Geographers*, **37**, 77–100

Primack, M. L. (1962), 'Land clearing under nineteenth century techniques; some preliminary calculations', *Journal of Economic History*, **22**, 484–97

Primmer, G. H. (1939), 'United States soy bean industry', *Economic Geography*, **15**, 205–21

Pritchard, E. H. (1963), 'Thoughts on the historical development of the population of China', *Journal of Asian Studies*, **23**, 3–20

Prothero, R. M. (1955), 'Recent developments in Nigerian export crop production', *Geography,* **40,** 18–27

(1957), 'Land use at Soba, Zaria province', *Economic Geography,* **33,** 73–86

Prunty, M. (1955), 'The renaissance of the Southern plantation', *Geographical Review,* **45,** 459–91

Purseglove, J. W. (1963), 'Some problems of the origin and distribution of tropical crops', *Genetica Agraria,* **17,** 104–27

(1968), *Tropical crops: dicotyledons* (2 volumes)

Ragatz, L. J. (1928), *The fall of the planter class in the British Caribbean, 1763–1833*

Raikes, R. L. (1965), 'The Mohenjo-daro floods', *Antiquity,* **39,** 196–203

Ramiah, K. and Ghose, R. L. M. (1951), 'Origin and distribution of cultivated plants of South Asia; rice', *Indian Journal of Genetics and Plant Breeding,* **2,** 7–13

Randhawa, M. S. (1962), *Agriculture and animal husbandry in India,* New Delhi

Rasmussen, T. F. (1960), 'Population and land utilization in the Assam Valley', *Journal of Tropical Geography,* **14,** 51–76

Rasmussen, W. D. (1962), 'The impact of technological change on American agriculture, 1862–1962', *Journal of Economic History,* **22,** 578–91

(1967), 'Scientific agriculture', in M. Kranzberg and C. W. Pursell (eds.), *Technology in western civilisation,* Madison, Wis., vol. 2, 338–43

Raswan, C. R. (1930), 'Tribal areas and migration lines of the North Arabian Bedouins', *Geographical Review,* **20,** 494–502

Ratekin, M. (1954), 'The early sugar industry in Española', *Hispanic American Historical Review,* **34,** 1–19

Reed, C. A. (1969), 'The pattern of animal domestication in the prehistoric Near East', in P. J. Ucko and G. Dimbleby (eds.), *The domestication and exploitation of plants and animals,* 361–80

Reifenberg, A. (1955), *The struggle between the desert and the sown,* Jerusalem

Reksohadiprodjo, I. (1964), 'Ups and downs of the sugar-cane industry in Indonesia', *Indonesian Journal of Geography,* **4,** 61–3

Reksohadiprodjo, I. and Soedarsono, B. (1961), 'Double cropping in wet-rice cultivation in relation to soil and climate', *Madjalal Geografi Indonesia* **3,** 4–6

Relph, D. H. (1958), 'A century of human influence on High Country vegetation' *New Zealand Geographer,* **14,** 131–46

Renborg, U. (1969), 'Tendencies towards concentration and specialisation in agriculture', in U. Papi and C. Nunn (eds.), *Economic problems of agriculture in industrial societies,* 209–33

Rich, E. E. (1967), 'Colonial settlement and its labour problems', in E. E. Rich and C. H. Wilson (eds.), *The Cambridge economic history of Europe,* vol. 4, *The economy of expanding Europe in the sixteenth and seventeenth centuries,* 308–77

Richards, J. H. (1968), 'The Prairie region', in J. Warkentin (ed.), *Canada: a geographical perspective,* 396–437

Riches, N. (1967), *The agricultural revolution in Norfolk*

Rippy, J. F. (1959), *British investments in Latin America,* Minneapolis

Robequain, C. (1944), *The economic development of French Indo-China*

(1954), *Malaya, Indonesia, Borneo and the Philippines*

Robert, J. C. (1967), *The story of tobacco in America,* Chapel Hill, N.C.

Roberts, S. H. (1924), *History of land settlement in Australia, 1788–1920,* Melbourne

Robertson, C. J. (1935), 'Italian rice production in its regional setting', *Geography,* **20,** 13–27

(1938), 'Agricultural regions of the North Italian Plain', *Geographical Review,* **28,** 573–96

(1956), 'The expansion of the arable area', *Scottish Geographical Magazine,* **72,** 1–20

Rodden, R. J. (1965), 'An early Neolithic village in Greece', *Scientific American,* **212,** 89–92

Rodrigues, J. H. (1962), 'The influence of Africa on Brazil and of Brazil on Africa', *Journal of African History,* **3,** 49–67

Rodway, J. (1912), *Guiana, British, Dutch and French*

Rogers, E. J. (1966–7), 'Monoproductive traits in Brazil's economic past', *The Americas,* **23,** 130–41

Rostovtzeff, M. (1957), *The social and economic history of the Roman Empire,* 2 volumes

(1959), *The social and economic history of the Hellenistic world,* 2 volumes

335

Bibliography

Rouse, I. (1962), 'The intermediate area: Amazonia and the Caribbean area', in R. J. Braidwood and G. Willey (eds.), *Courses towards urban life*, Viking Fund Publications, No. 32, 37–49

(1964), 'The prehistory of the West Indies', *Science*, **144**, 499–513

Rowe, J. H. (1957), 'The Incas under Spanish colonial institutions', *Hispanic American Historical Review*, **37**, 155–99

Rowe, J. W. F. (1963), *The world's coffee*

Russell, E. J. (1966), *A history of agricultural science in Great Britain, 1620–1954*

Russell, J. C. (1969), 'Population in Europe, 500–1500', in C. M. Cipolla (ed.), *The Fontana economic history of modern Europe*, vol. 1, section 1, 15–59

Ruthenberg, H. (1971), *Farming systems in the tropics*

Rutherford, J. (1966), 'Double-cropping of wet padi in Penang, Malaya', *Geographical Review*, **56**, 239–55

Ruttan, V. W., Soothipan, A. and Venegas, E. C. (1966), 'Changes in rice growing in the Philippines and Thailand', *World Crops*, **18**, 18–33

Ryder, M. L. (1966), 'The exploitation of animals by man', *Advancement of Science*, **23**, 9–18

Sach, F. (1968), 'Proposal for the classification of pre-industrial tilling implements', *Tools and Tillage*, **1**, 3–27

Saez, A. G. (1971), 'Possibilidades de la floriculture Española', *Options Méditerranéennes*, **10**, 32–3

Salaman, R. N. (1949), *The history and social influence of the potato*

(1950), 'The influence of food plants on social structure', *Advancement of Science*, **7**, 200–11

Sanchez, R. G. (1964), *Sugar and society in the Caribbean*, New Haven, Conn.

Sanchez-Albornoz, N. (1970), 'La modernisation démographique de l'Espagne: le cycle vital annuel 1863–1960', in P. Duprez (ed.), *Population and economics*, Winnipeg, 159–69

Sankalia, H. D. (1962), 'India', in R. J. Braidwood and G. Willey (eds.), *Courses towards urban life*, Viking Fund Publications, No. 32, 68–79

Saraswati, S. K. (1937), 'Forgotten cities of Bengal', *Calcutta Geographical Review*, **1**, 13–24

Sato, T. (1968), 'Problems in field crop production', *Asian Survey*, **8**, 829–35

Sauer, C. (1952), *Agricultural origins and dispersals*, American Geographical Society, New York

Sbarounis, A. J. (1959), *Economic development of Greece*, Athens

Schacke, E. (1951), 'The Danish Heath Society', *Scottish Geographical Magazine*, **67**, 45–54

Schlebecker, J. T. (1960), 'The world metropolis and the history of American agriculture', *Journal of Economic History*, **20**, 187–208

(1967), *A history of American dairying*, Chicago

Schlippe, P. de (1956), *Shifting cultivation in Africa; the Zande system of agriculture*

Schlote, W. (1952), *British overseas trade from 1700 to the 1930s*

Schmidt, L. B. (1925a), 'The rise of the corn kingdom' in L. B. Schmidt and E. D. Ross (eds.), *Readings in the economic history of American agriculture*, New York, 381–9

(1925b), 'The westward movement of wheat', in L. B. Schmidt and E. D. Ross (eds.), *Readings in the economic history of American agriculture*, New York, 370–80

Schwaritz, F. (1966), *The origin of cultivated plants*

Schwartzberg, J. E. (1963), 'Agricultural labour in India; a regional analysis with particular reference to population growth', *Economic Development and Cultural Change*, **16**, 337–52

Schwarz, H. (1967), *Statistical handbook of the U.S.S.R.*

Scobie, J. R. (1967), *Revolution on the Pampas; a social history of Argentine wheat, 1860–1910*, Latin American Monographs No. 1, Institute of Latin American Studies, University of Texas

Scofield, E. (1938), 'The origin of settlement patterns in rural New England', *Geographical Review*, **28**, 652–63

Scott, J. G. (1921), *Burma: a handbook of practical information*

Sears, P. D. (1962), 'Regional differences in grassland farming practice: New Zealand conditions and some overseas comparisons', in M. McCaskill (ed.), *Land and livelihood: geographical essays in honour of George Jobberns*, Christchurch, 191–202

Seddon, D. (1968), 'The origins and development of agriculture in East and Southern Africa', *Current Anthropology*, **9**, 489–94

Segal, H. H. and Simon, M. (1961), 'British foreign capital issues 1865–1894', *Journal of Economic History*, **21**, 566–81

Semple, E. C. (1931), *The geography of the Mediterranean region in relation to its ancient history*
Shann, E. (1948), *An economic history of Australia*
Shannon, F. A. (1961), *The farmer's last frontier: agriculture 1860–1897*, New York
Sharp, A. (1961), 'Interpreting eastern Polynesian prehistory', *Journal of the Polynesian Society*, **70**, 349–52
Shaw, D. J. (1963), 'The problem of land fragmentation in the Mediterranean area: a case study', *Geographical Review*, **53**, 40–51
Shaw, E. B. (1936), 'Swine production in the Corn Belt of the United States', *Economic Geography*, **12**, 359–72
 (1938), 'Swine industry of China', *Economic Geography*, **14**, 381–97
 (1942*a*), 'Potato-fed swine in Germany', *Economic Geography*, **18**, 287–97
 (1942*b*), 'Recent changes in the banana production of Middle America', *Annals of the Association of American Geographers*, **32**, 371–83
Sheridan, R. B. (1963), 'Temperate and tropical: aspects of European penetration into tropical regions', *Caribbean Studies*, **3**, 3–21
Shutler, R. (1961), 'Peopling of the Pacific in the light of radio carbon dating', *Asian Perspectives*, **5**, 207–12
Siegfried, A. (1948), *The Mediterranean*
Silberman, L. (1959), 'Somali nomads', *International Social Science Journal*, **11**, 559–71
Silvey, D. R. (1967), 'Milk and milk products in the Common Market', *Agriculture*, **74**, 17–20
Simkin, C. G. F. (1968), *The traditional trade of Asia*
Simmonds, N. W. (1960), 'The growth of post-war West Indies banana trades', *Tropical Agriculture*, **37**, 79–85
 (1966), *Bananas*
Simon, M. (1968), 'The pattern of new British portfolio foreign investment, 1865–1914', in A. R. Hall (ed.), *The export of capital from Britain 1870–1914*, 15–44
Simoons, F. J. (1954), 'The non-milking area of Africa', *Anthropos*, **49**, 58–66
 (1971), 'The antiquity of dairying in Asia and Africa', *Geographical Review*, **61**, 431–9
Simpson, E. S. (1957), 'The Cheshire grass-dairying region', *Transactions and Papers of the Institute of British Geographers*, **23**, 141–62
Simpson, E. S. (1958), 'The cattle population of England and Wales: its breed structure and distribution', *Geographical Studies*, **5**, 45–60
 (1959), 'Milk production in England and Wales; a study in the influence of collective marketing', *Geographical Review*, **49**, 95–111
Slater, W. (1961), 'The revolution in agriculture', *The Advancement of Science*, **18**, 249–56
Slicher van Bath, B. H. (1963), *The agrarian history of western Europe, A.D. 500–1850*
 (1966), 'The rise of intensive husbandry in the Low Countries', in C. K. Warner (ed.), *Agrarian conditions in modern European history*, 24–41
 (1969), 'Eighteenth century agriculture in the continent of Europe: evolution or revolution?', *Agricultural History*, **43**, 169–79
Smalley, I. J. (1968), 'The loess deposits and neolithic culture of northern China', *Man*, **3**, 224–41
Smith, C. T. (1967), *A historical geography of Europe*
Smith, C. W. (1963), 'Cattle-breeds; a study in progressive hybridization', in A. E. Mourant and F. E. Zeuner (eds.), *Men and cattle: proceedings of a symposium on domestication*, Royal Anthropological Institute
Smith, D. L. (1970), 'Viticulture in the Barossa region: prospects and costs', *Australian Geographical Studies*, **8**, 101–120
Smith, J. Russell and Phillips, J. O. (1942), *North America*
Smith, R. E. F. (1959), *The origins of farming in Russia*, Paris
Smith, R. S. (1966), 'Medieval agrarian society in its prime: Spain' in M. M. Postan (ed.), *The Cambridge economic history of Europe*, vol. 1, *The agrarian life of the Middle Ages* (2nd edn.), 432–48
Smith, T. C. (1959), *The agrarian origins of modern Japan*, Stanford, Calif.
Smole, W. J. (1963), 'Owner-cultivatorship in Middle Chile', *University of Chicago, Department of Geography, Research Paper* No. 89
Soboul, A. (1956), 'The French rural community', *Past and Present*, **10**, 78–95

Bibliography

Soen, S. K. (1968), *Prospects for agricultural development in Indonesia with special reference to Java,* Wageningen

Solheim, W. G. (1967), 'Southeast Asia and the West', *Science,* **157,** 896–902

Soma, M. (1959), 'The cultivation of mitsumata on shifting fields in Shikoku', *Proceedings I.G.U. Regional Conference in Japan 1957,* Tokyo, 470–7

Spate, O. H. K. (1956), *India and Pakistan: a general and regional geography*

Spate, O. H. K. and Learmonth, A. (1967), *India and Pakistan: a general and regional geography*

Spence, C. C. (1960), *God speed the plow; the coming of steam cultivation to Great Britain,* Urbana

Spencer, J. E. (1963), 'The migration of rice from mainland southeast Asia into Indonesia', in J. Barrau (ed.), *Plants and the migrations of Pacific peoples: a symposium,* Tenth Pacific Science Congress, Honolulu, 1961, 83–90

(1964), 'The development and spread of agricultural terracing in China', in S. G. Davis (ed.), *Land use problems in Hong Kong,* Hong Kong, 105–10

(1966), 'Shifting cultivation in Southeastern Asia', *University of California Publications in Geography,* No. 19

Spencer, J. E. and Hale, G. A. (1961), 'The origin, nature and distribution of agricultural terracing', *Pacific Viewpoint,* **2,** 1–40

Spencer, J. E. and Horvath, R. J. (1963), 'How does an agricultural region originate?', *Annals of the Association of American Geographers,* **53,** 74–92

Spurling, M. (1963), 'The citrus industry in South Australia', *World Crops,* **15,** 20–7

Stamp, L. D. (1962), 'Climatic limitations to development in the tropics', *Proceedings of the Nutrition Society,* **21,** 84–90

Stearns, R. P. (1932), 'Agricultural adaptation in England, 1875–1900', *Agricultural History,* **6,** 84–154

Stein, B. (1967), 'Integration of the agrarian society of South India' in R. E. Trykenberg (ed.), *Land control and social structure in Indian history*

Stein, S. J. (1953), 'The passing of the coffee plantation in the Paraiba valley', *Hispanic American Historical Review,* **33,** 331–64

Stenning, D. J. (1957), 'Transhumance, migratory drift and migration: patterns of pastoral Fulani nomadism', *The Journal of the Royal Anthropological Institute,* **87,** 57–73

(1959), *Savannah nomads*

Stephens, P. R. (1965), 'The age of the great sheepruns' in R. F. Watters (ed.), *Land and society in New Zealand,* 50–65

Stephens, S. G. (1944), 'Cotton growing in the West Indies during the eighteenth and nineteenth centuries', *Tropical agriculture,* **21,** 2

Stern, R. M. (1960), 'A century of food exports', *Kyklos,* **13,** 44–64

Sternstein, L. (1966), 'The distribution of Thai centres at mid-nineteenth century', *Journal of South East Asian History,* **7,** 66–72

Stevens, C. E. (1966), 'Agriculture and rural life in the later Roman empire', in M. M. Postan (ed.), *The Cambridge Economic History of Europe,* vol. 1. *The agrarian life of the Middle Ages* (2nd edn.), 92–124

Steward, J. H. (1959), 'Perspectives on plantations', in Pan-American Union, *Plantation systems of the New World,* Social Science Monographs, 7, Washington, D.C.

Steward, J. H. and Farion, L. C. (1959), *Native peoples of South America*

Stewart, C. F. (1964), *The economy of Morocco, 1912–1962,* Harvard Middle Eastern Monographs, No. 12

Stewart, J. A. (1921), 'Kyaukse irrigation: a sidelight on Burmese history', *Journal of the Burma Research Society,* **11,** 1–4

Stewart, O. C. (1956), 'Fire as the first great force employed by man', in W. L. Thomas (ed.), *Man's role in changing the face of the earth,* 115–33

Stouse, P. A. D., Jr (1967), 'Effective agricultural development of former banana lands: the west coast of Costa Rica', *Revista Geografica,* **66,** 153–62

Street, J. M. (1962), 'Feral animals in Hispaniola', *Geographical Review,* **52,** 400–6

Strickon, A. (1965), 'The Euro-American ranching complex', in A. Leeds and A. P. Vayda (eds.), *Man, culture and animals,* American Association for the Advancement of Science, Publication No. 78, 229–58

Subramaniyam, N. (1954), 'Tea industry in Ceylon', *Indian Geographical Journal*, **29**, 89–105

Sutton, K. (1971), 'The reduction of wasteland in the Sologne: nineteenth century French regional improvement', *Transactions of the Institute of British Geographers*, **52**, 129–44

Swan, M. (1957), *British Guiana*

Sweet, L. E. (1965), 'Camel pastoralism in North Arabia and the minimal camping unit', in A. Leeds and A. P. Vayda (eds.), *Man, culture and animals*, American Association for the Advancement of Science Publication No. 78, 129–52

Sweet, L. E. and O'Leary, T. J. (1969), *Circum-Mediterranean peasantry: introductory bibliographies*

Sweetser, J. (1962), 'Rural settlement patterns of Hokkaido', *Journal of Geography*, **61**, 352–60

Symons, L. (1967), *Agricultural geography*

Taeuber, I. B. (1958), *The population of Japan*, Princeton, N.J.

Talbot, W. J. (1961), 'Land utilization in the arid regions of southern Africa; part 1, South Africa', in L. D. Stamp (ed.), U.N.E.S.C.O., *A history of land use in arid regions*, Arid Zone Research, No. 17, Paris, 299–331

Tanioka, T. (1959), 'Le jôri dans le Japon ancien', *Annales*, **14**, 625–39

Terra, G. J. A. (1954), 'Mixed-garden horticulture in Java', *Malayan Journal of Tropical Geography*, **4**, 33–43

   (1958), 'Farm systems in south east Asia', *Netherlands Journal of Agricultural Science*, **6**, 157–82

Teulières, R. (1966), 'L'évolution récente de la riziculture au Vietnam du Sud', *Les Cahiers D'Outre-Mer*, **19**, 382–98

Thirsk, J. (1964), 'The common fields', *Past and Present*, **29**, 3–25

Thomas, R. P. (1968), 'The sugar colonies of the Old Empire: profit or loss for Great Britain?', *Economic History Review*, **21**, 30–45

Thompson, E. T. (1935), 'Population expansion and the plantation system', *American Journal of Sociology*, **41**, 314–26

   (1941), 'The climatic theory of the plantation', *Agricultural History*, **15**, 49–59

   (1959), 'The plantation as a social system', in *Plantation systems of the New World*, Washington, D.C., Social Science Monographs, No. 8, Pan-American Union, 26–41

   (1960), 'The plantation cycle and problems of typology', in V. Rubin (ed.), *Caribbean Studies: a symposium*, Seattle, 29–33

Thompson, F. M. L. (1968), 'The second agricultural revolution, 1815–1880', *Economic History Review*, **21**, 62–77

Thompson, I. B. (1970), *Modern France; a social and economic geography*

Thorpe, H. (1951), 'The influence of enclosure on the form and pattern of rural settlement in Denmark', *Transactions and Papers of the Institute of British Geographers*, **17**, 111–30

Tinker, E. L. (1962), 'Horsemen of the Americas', *Hispanic American Historical Review*, **42**, 191–8

Tirone, L. (1970), 'La vigne dans l'exploitation agricole en Italie', *Méditerranée*, **1**, 339–63

Tosti, J. A. and Voertman, R. F. (1964), 'Some environmental factors in the development of the tropics', *Economic Geography*, **40**, 189–205

Tracy, M. (1964), *Agriculture in Western Europe: crisis and adaptation since 1880*

Treadgold, D. W. (1957), *The great Siberian migration*, Princeton, N.J.

Tregear, T. R. (1965), *A geography of China*

   (1970), *An economic geography of China*

Trewartha, G. T. (1938), 'Ratio maps of China's farms and crops', *Geographical Review*, **28**, 102–11

   (1945), *Japan: a physical, cultural and regional geography*, Madison, Wis.

   (1965), *Japan: a geography*

   (1969), *A geography of population: world patterns*, New York

Trewartha, G. T. and Gosal, G. (1957), 'The regionalism of population change in India', *Cold Springs Harbor Symposia in Quantitative Biology*, **12**, 71–81

Trewartha, G. T. and Yang, S. J. (1948), 'Notes on rice growing in China', *Annals of the Association of American Geographers*, **38**, 277–81

Bibliography

Trewartha, G. T. and Zelinsky, W. (1955), 'Population distribution and change in Korea, 1925–49', *Geographical Review*, **45**, 1–26
Trow-Smith, R. (1951), *History of British livestock husbandry, 1700–1900*
   (1957), *History of British livestock husbandry to 1700*
Tuan, Yi-Fu (1970), *The world's landscapes: China*
Turner, F. J. (1920), *The frontier in American history*
Tursunbayev, A. and Potapov, A. (1959), 'Some aspects of the socio-economic and cultural development of nomads in the U.S.S.R.', *International Social Science Journal*, **11**, 511–24
Tyler, C. (1956), 'The development of feeding standards for livestock', *Agricultural History Review*, **4**, 97–107
Ucko, P. J. and Dimbleby, G. W. (1969), *The domestication and exploitation of plants and animals*
Udo, R. K. (1965), 'Sixty years of plantation agriculture in Southern Nigeria, 1902–1962', *Economic Geography*, **41**, 356–68
   (1967), 'British policy and the development of export crops in Nigeria', *Nigerian Journal of Economic and Social Studies*, **9**, 299–314
United Nations (1958), *Demographic yearbook*
   (1970), *Demographic yearbook*
   (1971), *Demographic yearbook*
U.N.E.S.C.O. (1958), *Japan, its land, people and culture*, Tokyo
U.S. Bureau of the Census (1960), *Historical statistics of the United States, colonial times to 1957*, Washington, D.C.
   (1964), *Statistical abstract of the United States, 1964*, Washington, D.C.
U.S. Department of Agriculture (1922), *Yearbook 1921*, Washington, D.C.
   (1923), *Yearbook 1922*, Washington, D.C.
Urquhart, M. C. and Buckley, K. A. H. (1965), *Historical statistics of Canada*
Van Dongen, I. S. (1961), 'Coffee trade, coffee regions and coffee ports in Angola', *Economic Geography*, **37**, 320–46
Van Roy, E. (1967), 'The Malthusian squeeze on Thailand's rice economy', *Asian Survey*, **7**, 469–81
Van Royen, W. (1954), *The agricultural resources of the world*, New York
Van Zeist, W. (1969), 'Reflections on prehistoric environments in the Near East', in P. J. Ucko and G. W. Dimbleby (eds.), *The domestication and exploitation of plants and animals*, 35–46
Varjo, U. (1965), 'The Finnish farm as seen from the viewpoint of geographical typology of agriculture', *Fennia*, **92**, 1–18
Vavilov, N. I. (1949–50), 'The origin, variation, immunity and breeding of cultivated plants', *Chronica Botanica*, **13**, 1–366
Vicens, J. Vives (1969), *The economic history of Spain*
Vilar, P. (1958), 'Agricultural progress and the economic background in eighteenth century Catalonia', *Economic History Review*, **11**, 113–20
Vince, S. W. (1952), 'Reflections on the structure and distribution of rural population in England and Wales', *Transactions and Papers of the Institute of British Geographers*, **18**, 53–76
Vita-Finzi, C. (1961), 'Roman dams in Tripolitania', *Antiquity*, **35**, 14–20
Vlieland, C. A. (1934), 'The population of the Malay peninsula; a study in human migration', *Geographical Review*, **24**, 61–78
Volker, A. (1966), 'The delta area of the Irrawaddy river in Burma', *Scientific problems of the humid tropical zone deltas and their implications*, Proceedings of the Dacca Symposium, 1964, Paris, U.N.E.S.C.O., 373–9
Wadham, Sir Samuel (1961), 'The problem of arid Australia', in L. D. Stamp (ed.), U.N.E.S.C.O., *A history of land use in arid regions*, Arid Zone Research, No. 17, Paris, 339–62
Wadham, Sir Samuel, Wilson, R. K. and Wood, J. (1967), *Land utilization in Australia*
Wagley, C. (1960), 'A culture sphere', in V. Rubin (ed.) *Caribbean studies: a symposium*, Seattle, 3–13
Wagstaff, J. M. (1965), 'An outline of the agriculture in the Máni region of southern Greece', *Tijdschrift van het K. Nederlandsch aardnjkskundig genootschap*, **82**, 270–80
Waibel, L. (1942), 'The climatic theory of the plantation: a critique', *Geographical Review*, **32**, 307–10

(1943), 'The political significance of tropical vegetable fats for the industrial countries of Europe', *Annals of the Association of American Geographers*, **33**, 118–28

(1950), 'European colonization in Southern Brazil', *Geographical Review*, **40**, 529–47

Waley, A. (1948), 'Note on iron and the plough in Early China', *Bulletin of the School of Oriental and African Studies*, **12**, 803–4

Walker, D. S. (1967), *A geography of Italy*

Ward, R. E. (1946), 'Northern Great Plains as a producer of wheat', *Economic Geography*, **22**, 231–44

Ward, R. G. (1965), *Land use and population in Fiji: a geographical study*

Warmington, E. H. (1928), *The commerce between the Roman Empire and India*

Warren, A. (1967), 'East Africa', in B. W. Hodder and D. R. Harris (eds.), *Africa in transition*, 163–220

Warriner, D. (1964), *Economics of peasant farming*

Watters, R. F. (1960), 'The nature of shifting cultivation: a review of recent research', *Pacific Viewpoint*, **1**, 59–99

Watters, R. F. (1971), *Shifting cultivation in Latin America*, F.A.O. Forestry Development Paper No. 17, Rome

Watts, F. B. (1960), 'The natural vegetation of the Southern Great Plains of Canada', *Geographical Bulletin*, **14**, 25–43

(1968) 'Climate, vegetation, soil', in J. Warkentin (ed.), *Canada: a geographical interpretation*, 78–111

Way, R. (1966), *A geography of Spain and Portugal*

Weaver, J. C. (1954a), 'Changing pattern of cropland use in the Middle West', *Economic Geography*, **30**, 1–47

(1954b), 'Crop-combination regions for 1919 and 1929 in the Middle West', *Geographical Review*, **44**, 560–72

Weaver, J. C., Hoag, L. P. and Fenton, B. L. (1956), 'Livestock units and combination regions in the Middle West', *Economic Geography*, **32**, 237–59

Webb, W. P. (1931), *The Great Plains*

Webber, H. J. (1943), 'History and development of the citrus industry', in H. J. Webber and L. D. Batchelor (eds.), *The citrus industry: botany and breeding*, vol. 1, Berkeley, Calif., 2–27

Webber, H. J. and Batchelor, L. D. (1943), *The citrus industry: botany and breeding*, Berkeley, Calif., 2 volumes

Weigend, G. G. (1954), 'The basis and significance of viticulture in south west France', *Annals of the Association of American Geographers*, **44**, 75–101

Weir, T. R. (1968), 'The people', in J. Warkentin (ed.), *Canada: a geographical interpretation*, 137–76

Wellman, F. L. (1961), *Coffee: cultivation and utilization*

Wernstedt, F. L. and Spencer, J. E. (1967), *The Philippine island world; a physical, cultural and regional geography*, Berkeley, Calif.

West, R. C. (1957), *The Pacific lowlands of Colombia*, Social Science Series, No. 8, Baton Rouge, La.

West, R. C. and Augelli, J. P. (1966), *Middle America: its lands and people*

Westerman, P. (1969), 'Changes in the world wheat situation and the 1967 International Grains Arrangements', *Quarterly Review of Agricultural Economics*, **22**, 20–34

Westermann, W. L. (1919), 'The development of the irrigation system of Egypt', *Classical Philology*, **14**, 158–64

Wheatley, P. (1961), *The golden Kheronese*, Kuala Lumpur

(1965a), 'A note on the extension of milking practices into south-east Asia during the first millenium A.D.', *Anthropos*, **60**, 577–90

(1965b), 'Agricultural terracing: discursive scholia on recent papers on agricultural terracing and on related matters pertaining to Northern Indo-China and neighbouring areas', *Pacific Viewpoint*, **6**, 123–44

Wheeler, Sir Mortimer (1968), *The Indus civilisation* (3rd edn)

Whetham, E. H. (1964), 'The London milk trade, 1860–1900', *Economic History Review*, **17**, 369–80

Bibliography

(1970), 'The mechanisation of British farming, 1910–1945', *Journal of Agricultural Economics*, **21**, 317–33

White, K. D. (1963*a*), 'Roman agriculture in North Africa', *Nigerian Geographical Journal*, **6**, 39–49

(1963*b*), 'Wheat-farming in Roman times', *Antiquity*, **37**, 207–12

(1965), 'The productivity of labour in Roman agriculture', *Antiquity*, **39**, 102–7

(1967), *Agricultural implements of the Roman world*

(1970*a*), *Roman farming*

(1970*b*), 'Fallowing crop rotation, and crop yields in Roman times', *Agricultural History*, **44**, 281–90

White, L. (1940), 'Technology and invention in the Middle Ages', *Speculum*, **15**, 141–59

(1962), *Medieval technology and social change*

White, M. E. (1961), 'Greek colonisation', *Journal of Economic History*, **21**, 443–54

Whitehouse, R. D. (1968), 'The early Neolithic of Southern Italy', *Antiquity*, **42**, 188–93

Whittlesey, D. (1936), 'Major agricultural regions of the earth', *Annals of the Association of American Geographers*, **26**, 199–240

(1937), 'Fixation of shifting cultivation', *Economic Geography*, **13**, 139–54

Whyte, R. O. (1961), 'Evolution of land use in south western Asia', in L. D. Stamp (ed.), *A history of land use in arid regions*, U.N.E.S.C.O., Paris, 57–118

Wickizer, V. D. (1958), 'Plantation crops in tropical agriculture', *Tropical Agriculture*, **35**, 171–87

(1960), 'The smallholder in tropical export crop production', *Food Research Institute Studies*, **1**, 49–99

Wickizer, V. D. and Bennett, M. K. (1941), *The rice economy of South East Asia*, Stanford, Calif.

Wiens, H. J. (1954), *China's march towards the tropics*, Hamden, Conn.

Wikkramatileke, W. (1957), 'Whither chena? The problem of an alternative to shifting cultivation in the dry zone of Ceylon', *Geographical Studies*, **4**, 81–9

Willet, F. (1962), 'The introduction of maize into Africa', *Africa*, **32**, 1–13

Willey, G. R. (1960), 'New world prehistory', *Science*, **131**, 73–86

(1966), *An Introduction to American archeology*, vol. 1, *North and Middle America*, New York

Willey, G. R., Ekholm, G. F. and Millon, R. F. (1964), 'The patterns of farming life and civilisation', in R. C. West (ed.), *Natural environment and early cultures*, vol. 1, *Handbook of Middle American Indians*, Austin, Texas, 446–500

Williams, D. B. (1967), *Agriculture in the Australian economy*, Sydney

Williams, M. (1970*a*), 'Town-farming in the mallee lands of South Australia and Victoria', *Australian Geographical Studies*, **8**, 173–91

(1970*b*), 'The enclosure and reclamation of waste land in England and Wales in the eighteenth and nineteenth centuries', *Transactions of the Institute of British Geographers*, **51**, 55–70

Williamson, C. and Payne, W. J. A. (1965), *An introduction to animal husbandry in the tropics*

Willis, F. R. (1971), *Italy chooses Europe*, New York

Wills, J. B. (1962), 'The general pattern of land use', in J. B. Wills (ed.), *Agriculture and land use in Ghana*, 201–13

Wilson, D. M. (1962), 'Anglo-Saxon rural economy', *Agricultural History Review*, **10**, 65–79

Wilson, J. A. (1951), *The burden of Egypt*, Chicago

Wilson, M. (1969*a*), 'The hunters and herders', in M. Wilson and L. Thompson (eds.), *The Oxford history of South Africa*, vol. 1, 40–74

(1969*b*), 'The Sotho, Venda and Tsonga', in M. Wilson and L. Thompson (eds.), *The Oxford history of South Africa*, vol. 1, 131–82

Winsberg, M. D. (1970), 'The introduction and diffusion of the Aberdeen Angus in Argentina', *Geography*, **55**, 187–95

Wiss, C. B. L. (1970), 'Olive oil in Italy', *World Crops*, **22**, 116

Wissman, H. von (1956), 'On the role of nature and man in changing the face of the dry belt of Asia', in W. L. Thomas (ed.), *Man's role in changing the face of the earth*, 203–303

Woodruff, W. (1966), *Impact of western man*

Wright, G. (1964), *Rural revolution in France*, Stanford, Calif.

Wright, H. E. (1968), 'Natural environment of early food production north of Mesopotamia', *Science*, **161**, 334–9

Wrigley, C. C. (1957), 'Buganda: an outline economic history', *Economic History Review*, **10**, 69–80

(1959), 'Crops and wealth in Uganda, a short agrarian history', *East African Studies*, **12**, 1–84

(1960), 'Speculations on the economic prehistory of Africa', *Journal of African History*, **1**, 189–203

Wylie, L. (1964), *Village in the Vaucluse*

Yang, L. (1945–6), 'Notes on the economic history of the Chin dynasty', *Harvard Journal of Asiatic Studies*, **9**, 107–85

Yates, P. L. (1940), *Food production in western Europe*

(1960), *Food, land and manpower in western Europe*

Yawata, I. (1961), 'Rice cultivation of the ancient Mariana islanders', in J. Barrau (ed.), *Plants and the migration of Pacific peoples: a symposium*, Tenth Pacific Science Congress, Honolulu, 91–2

Yli-Jokipii, P. (1970), 'Regional changes in the Finnish dairy industry, 1910–1967', *Fennia*, **100**, 5–65

Youngson, A. J. (1965), 'The opening up of new territories', in H. J. Habakkuk and M. M. Postan (eds.), *The Cambridge economic history of Europe*, vol. 6, *The industrial revolutions and after*, part 1, 139–211

Zangheri, R. (1969), 'The historical relationship between agricultural and economic development in Italy', in E. L. Jones and S. J. Woolf (eds.), *Agrarian change and economic development: the historical problems*, 23–40

Zelinsky, W. (1962), 'Changes in the geographic pattern of rural population in the United States, 1790–1960', *Geographical Review*, **52**, 492–524

(1963), 'Rural population dynamics as an index to social and economic development: a geographic overview', *Sociological Quarterly*, **4**, 99–121

Zeuner, F. E. (1963), *A history of domesticated animals*

Zierer, C. M. (1956), *California and the South West*, New York

Zimmerman, C. C. (1937), 'Some phases of land utilization in Siam', *Geographical Review*, **27**, 378–93

Zimmerman, E. W. (1951), *World resources and industries*

Zohary, D. (1969), 'The progenitors of wheat and barley in relation to domestication and agricultural dispersal in the Old World', in P. J. Ucko and G. W. Dimbleby (eds.), *The domestication and exploitation of plants and animals*, 47–66

INDEX

Bakewell, Robert, 201
Bali, 81
Balkans, 16, 30, 40, 116
Baltic Sea, 15
Baluchistan, 16
Bamboo, 9
Bananas, 9, 22, 28, 29, 31, 36, 211, 212, 213, 214, 218; in Africa, 67, 236; in Americas, 229–30; refrigeration of, 49, 63
Bangkok, 102
Bangla Desh, 79
Bantu, 5, 66–7, 119
Barbados, 216
Barbarian invasions, 135–6
Barbecho, 69
Barbed-wire, 247, 262
Barley, 11, 14, 15, 16, 17, 18, 20, 21, 22, 26, 28, 35, 155
Barschina, 266
Bas-Languedoc, 127
Bassac river, 102, 105
Bathurst plains, 251
Bay of Plenty, 209
Beans, 20, 21, 22
Bedouin, 118, 120, 121
Beef, 242, 248; chilled, 49, 249
Beja, 119
Belgium, 33
Bengal, 60, 95, 234–5; Greater, 97–8; sheep, 251
Beozar goat, 42
Berbers, 118, 119
Bering Straits, 20
Berlin, 195
Bihar, 79, 95
Biharis, 231, 235
Bison, 246
Blache, V. de la, 127
Black Death, 136, 162, 164
Black Sea, 117
Blaxland, Gregory, 251
Bligh, Captain, 37
Blue Mountains, 251
Boar, wild, 43
Boers, 131, 250–1
Bogor, 35
Bolero jacket, 244
Boll weevil, 223
'Bonanza' wheat farms, 275
Bondage, 207
Bordeaux mixture, 54
Borden, Gail, 198
Boro people, 60
Bos brachyceros, 40
Bos indicus, 40
Bos primigenius, 16, 40

Bos taurus, 40
Bosch, J. Van den, 232
Boserup, Ester, 73
Boston, Mass., 37, 195, 229
Botanical gardens, 35
Bougainville, 37, 39
Boundary riders, 252
Bow, 117
Bowring, Sir John, 102, 104
Brabant, 165
Bradford, 253
Brahmaputra, 235
Brandenburg, 163
Branding, 244
Brantas valley, 99
Brassica, 31
Brazil, 29, 32, 35–6; Germans in, 70; plantations, 216; ranching in, 244–5; rubber in, 37; zebu cattle, 41
Breadfruit, 9, 63
Breadwheat, 15
Breaking plough, 183, 262
Brie, 193
British Isles, 15, 188
Broadcasting, 19, 51, 52
Brown Swiss cattle, 40, 41
Buck, J. L., 89
Bucket-lifts, 93
Buckwheat, 176
Buddekin river, 251
Buenos Aires, 48, 244, 278
Buffalo, water, 41–2, 82, 105
Bull, John, 264
Bull-fighting, 244
Burma, 33; wet-rice in, 101–4
Bus, in Sahara, 120
Bushmanoid people, 66
Butter, 187, 192, 193, 196, 202, 207, 208; exports, 198, 203; factories, 196
Butter-fat content, 201–2
Byzantine Empire, 135

Caatinga, 70
Cabral, 29
Cacao, 32; *see also* Cocoa
Caingin system, 108
Calicut, 29
California, 36; fruit in, 130, 148; sheep in, 129; wheat in, 268
Cambodia, 102
Camel, 113, 115; Bactrian, 115, 116
Cameroons, 65, 114
Campbell, H., 265
Campinas, 226
Canada, wheat in, 276–8
Canadas, 141

345

Canadian Pacific Railway, 276
Canale Royale, 142
Canals, irrigation, 14, 21
Canary Islands, 36–7, 227, 236
Candles, 236, 250
Canning: of fruit, 130; of meat, 241
Canterbury Plains, 241, 253
Canton, 29
Cape Colony, merino in, 43
Capetown, 250
Cape of Good Hope, 29, 33
Capital: British in overseas, 49–50; in Cuba, 218; in dairying, 109; Indian in Burma, 103; in ranching, 243, 246; in tea industry, 235
Caribbean, 10, 38
Carolingian period, 161
Carrying capacity, 243
Carthage, 43, 133
Caspian Sea, 11, 15, 42
Cassava, *see* Manioc
Caste, 96
Castillo, 37
Catherine II, 263
Cattle, 11, 15, 17, 18, 20, 21, 22, 172; Chilean exports, 149; dairy, 193, 201–2, 241–50; densities, 177; domestication of, 40–2; *see also* Livestock, *and various breeds*
Cauvery delta, 95
Central Plain, of Thailand, 105
Centralo, 218
Cerd, 15
Cereals, 9, 17; domestication of, 11–19
Ceylon: chena, 60; coffee, 35; irrigation, 95; tea, 234–5; *see also* Sri Lanka
Chaco, 241
Champa, 86
Chang Chien, 28
Chaparreros, 245
Charlemagne, 163
Check-rower, 181
Cheese, 187, 192, 193, 196; exports, 198, 202, 203, 206, 208; factories, 196–7
Chekiang, 86
Chena 60
Ch'engtu plains, 84
Chernozem soils, 260
Chesapeake Bay, 216
Cheshire, 193
Chestnut soils, 260
Chettyars, 103
Chiang Kan river, 86
Chiapis, 37
Chicago, 246
Chichimec, 245
Chile, 36; crops in, 129; livestock in, 131
Chillies, 21

China, 18, 19, 26, 28, 29; cattle in, 41; Great Wall of, 117, 120; nomads in, 117, 120–2; North, 11, 17, 22; pigs in, 44; rice in, 83–9; South, 9, 10, 22, 24, 79; tea in, 234–5
Chinampas, 70
Chinese, 17, 18; in Malaya, 233–4; milk vetch, 82
Cincinnati, 183
Cistercians, 163
Citron, 26, 134
Citrus, 26, 36; Arabs and, 137; in California, 150–1; in Classical times, 134, 145–6; in Mediterranean, 127; in North America, 38
Civil War, American, 102
Clay soils, 52
Climate: and crop distribution, 24; and grass, 205; *see also* Drought, Rainfall
Clover, 165, 201, 281
Club wheat, 16
Coa, 20, 51, 58, 69
Cochin-China, 105
Cocoa, 29; in Asia, 35; in Americas, 37; in Ghana, 235–40
Coconuts, 9, 22, 28, 39, 63
Coedès, G., 101
Coffea arabica, 33, 233
Coffea canephora, 33
Coffea liberica, 33
Coffea robusta, 33, 233
Coffee: in Africa, 33, 236, 238, 240; in Americas, 37; in Brazil, 226–7; in Ceylon, 235; overproduction of, 226, 232; rust, 232
Coloni, enserfment of, 135
Colonial governments, and shifting cultivation, 64
Coloño, 258
Columbia, 70
Columbus, Christopher, 5, 20, 28, 29, 35, 36, 41, 244
Comanche, 245
Combine-harvester, 54–5, 149, 173, 264
Commercial crops and livestock, 152
Commercialisation of agriculture, 79, 153
Communal land tenure, 58–9, 94
Concentrates, 177
Congo, Belgian, 237; Free State, 237
Coniferous forest, 15
Consolidation, 166
Convertible husbandry, 165
Convict labour, 251
Co-operative dairies, 209
Cordoba, 127
Corn Belt, 178–86; soils of, 184; westward movement of, 184–5, 200, 247
Corn-binder, 181
Corn Laws, repeal of, 259

Inland Sea, 89
Inquilinos in Chile, 132, 149
International Geographical Union, 3
Intertillage, 9, 58
Inter-tropical front, 114
Iran, 11, 112, 114, 116, 117
Iraq, 11, 117
Ireland, 24, 30
Iron, diffusion of in Africa, 68
Irrawaddy delta, 79, 102, 103
Irrigation, 13, 14, 15, 19, 20, 22, 26, 28, 30; Arab, 137; early Indian, 95, 98; in Mediterranean, 125, 127, 135, 137, 138, 141, 147; in Mekong delta, 105; in Roman times, 135; and wet-rice cultivation, 26, 80, 86, 94
Irtysh river, 117
Islam, 26; in Indonesia, 108
Italians, in Argentina, 263
Italy, 30, 138–9, 143, 145
Ivory Coast, 32, 65, 238

Jamaica, 36, 37, 219, 229
Japan, 10, 24; shifting cultivation in, 62; wet-rice cultivation in, 89–93
Japanese: Formosa, 94–5; Korea, 93
Java, 34–5, 79, 80; plantation crops in, 232–3; wet-rice in, 98–100
Jaxartes river, 26
Jerez de la Frontera, 143
Jersey cattle, 40, 201, 202
Jews, 26
Jezirah, 121, 188
Joint-stock companies, 214
Jordan valley, buffalo in, 42
Jôri system of land tenure, 89
Judean hills, 132, 135
Junkers, 167; and protection, 174
Jute, 24, 26, 98, 211, 230
Jutland, 207

Kaffir potato, 66
Kalahari, 251
Kano, 239
Kansas, 38
Kanto plains, 89
Karachi, 133
Karoo, 241, 250, 251
Katanga, 66
Kazak nomads, 120
Kazakhstan, 121, 265
Kedah, 107
Kedjawen, 99
Kelantan delta, 107
Kempenland, 169

Kentucky, 183
Kenya, 32–3, 122, 237
Kerala, 79, 96
Keynes, J. M. Lord, 3
Khirgiz, 114
Khoikhoi, 66
Kholkoz, 121, 267
Khorat plateau, 105
Khmer, 102
Kinki plains, 89
Knives, reaping, 11, 15
Koch, 195
Kochi, 92
Kopet Dagh, 15, 133
Korea: shifting cultivation in, 62; wet-rice cultivation in, 94
Krishna river, 17, 98
Krobo, 238
Kuban, 120, 260
Kuznetz, 116
Kwantung, 79, 95
Kyautse plains, 101
Kyushu, 89

Labour: costs, 158, 213–14, 264, 276; in dairying, 189, 202; and double cropping, 80; in European agriculture, 153–4, 157; forced, 232, 235; and mechanisation, 172–3; in Mediterranean regions, 127, 141; productivity, 54; in ranching, 243; seasonal, 130, 215; in sheep farming, 254; in U.S.A., 180–1; in wet-rice cultivation, 75, 82, 87
Labourers, landless, 79; in medieval Europe, 162, 167; in India, 96
Ladang, 107
Lake George, 251
Lake Titicaca, 10
Lancashire textile industry, 219
Land Act, 1872 (Canada), 276
Landolphia, 239
Languedoc, 142–3, 146
Lasso, 245
Land tenure, 3, 242; in Chile, 132; in medieval Europe, 161–2; of shifting cultivators, 58–9; see also Communal land tenure; Hacienda; Latifundia; Peonage; Share-croppers
Landlords, absentee, 138
Latifundia, 128; in classical times, 134, 135
Latin America, 2, 5, 24, 26, 30; shifting cultivation in, 69
Latosols, 58
Laval, 196
Lavradores, 217
Lawes, John, 54
Leaching, 77
Leaseholders, 164

Migration, 5; Annamite, 93; Bantu, 66–7; to Brazil, 218; Chinese, 45–7; European, 24, 45–7; to Malaya, 107; from Mediterranean, 139–40; to towns, 168–9; to Siberia, 266

Milk: breeds, 201; condensed, 187, 198; cooling, 195; dried, 187; fluid consumption of, 192, 195; manufacture of, 192; New Zealand, 208–9; output of, 190–1; production of, 187–8; quality of, 195; and railways, 194; amongst Romans, 134; seasonal output of, 190–1; in U.S.A., 204–6; urban demand for, 194–5; in Western Europe, 207–8; yields, 158, 193–4, 199–202

Milking, 11; in Africa, 192; of buffaloes, 42; early history of, 192–3; amongst Indians and Chinese, 83; machines, 189–90, 202; in South East Asia, 41

Millet (*Panicum miliaceum*), 16, 17

Millets, 22, 28, 31

Milpa, 7

Minneapolis, 203

Mir, 267

Missionaries and viticulture in the Americas, 36, 148

Mistral, 145

Mixed farming, 3, 4, 13; in agricultural depression, 174–5; arable, 169–70; in Corn Belt, 183–5; crops, 155–6, 175–6; distribution of, 152; and enclosure, 166–7; in Europe, 152–78; and farm size, 154; importance of livestock in, 155, 157, 158, 178; and industrialisation, 168, 171–3; and labour force, 193–4, 168–9, 170, 180–1; medieval changes in, 162–5; and open fields, 160–1; origins of, 158; productivity of, 158; in U.S.A., 178–86

Mixed gardens, 22, 81

Mohair, 250

Mohammed, 28

Mohenjodaro, 17

Moluccas, 29

Mombasa, 28

Mon, 101

Mongol Empire, 118; Mongol invasions of China, 86

Mongolia, 112, 115, 117; Inner, 120; Outer, 122

Mongols, 28, 114, 117, 120

Monsoon, 75

Montevideo, 245

Moors, 243–4

Moradores, 217

Morgan, W. B., 65

Morocco, 26; cities in, 146, 147

Mortality rates, 45, 68, 94, 139, 168

Moselle, 162, 165

Motor car industry and rubber, 37, 48

Mozambique, 66; Portuguese in, 237

Mughal Empire, 95, 96

Mulberry tree, 18, 22

Mullens, 263

Multiple-cropping, 80

Murdock, G. P., 19

Murge Basse, 143

Murrumbidgee river, 251

Mutton, 242, 249

Napoleonic Code, 167

Narmada, 17

Navdatoli, 17

Navigation Laws, 228

N'dama cattle, 40

Negdel, 122

Neolithic, Chinese, 17–18

Netherlands, 157, 163, 201, 202, 207

New England, 30; maize and wheat in early, 38, 179

New Guinea, 74

New Leicester, 201

New Orleans, 229

New Plantation System, 231

New South Wales, 251

New York, 194

New York State, 194, 196, 206

New Zealand, 10, 29; cheese factories in, 196; dairying in, 188, 196, 208–9; plant introduction in, 39; sheep in, 253–4

Nicaragua, 70, 229

Nienhuys, Jacob, 232

Niger river, 19

Nigeria: nomads in, 113, 122; plantation crops in, 237, 239

Night-soil, 52, 165

Nile river, 11, 13, 14, 15, 21

Nilgiri Hills, 235

Nilo-Hamitic herders, 114, 119

Nilotes, 119

Nineteen Counties of N.S.W., 252

Nitrogen, 77; and legumes, 165, 201

Noble blade, 265, 276

'Noble' sugar-cane, 37

Nomadism: horizontal, 113; vertical, 113

Norfolk four course, 158, 175

Noria, 52, 135, 137

North Dakota, 38

North Sea, 15

Nutritional density, 79, 95, 96, 98, 99, 105, 107; in wet-rice regions, 109–11

Nyasaland, 32, 33, 237

Oats, 16, 21, 35

Tungu-speaking, 117
Turkestan, 15, 21, 26, 28, 112, 116
Turkey, 11, 14
Turkey, the, 20
Turkic-speaking, 117
Turks, 114; and spread of maize, 30
Turnips, 31, 165
Two-field system, 52, 136, 159
Typology, agricultural, 2–5

Ubaiad culture, 11
Uganda, 33, 237
Ukraine, 15, 260
Ulluco, 10
Underemployment, 140; in China, 87
Unilever, 237
United Fruit Company, 219, 229
United States: ranching in, 241; wheat growing in, 267–76
Upland cotton, 33; origin of, 37
Ural (sheep), 42
Ural river, 116
Urbanisation, 11, 47, 68, 128, 168, 169, 194
Uruguay, 241, 242, 244, 248–50

Valencia, 28, 146; oranges, 145
Valorisation, 226
Vavilov, N., 19, 24
Vegeculture, 9, 10, 19, 20–1, 22, 63, 109
Vegetable oils, 11, 32; nineteenth-century demand for, 48, 231, 250
Vegetables, 15, 127, 134; in Mediterranean, 127, 141, 146–7; *see also* Horticulture
Venetians, 227
Venezuela, ranching in, 245
Vermouth wine, 143
Vetch, 11, 16, 20
Victoria, 251, 281
Vienna, 163
Vietnam, 33, 93–4; *see also* Cochin China; Mekong delta; Tonkin delta
Vikings, and manor, 161
Villages, early farming, 11
Villeins, 162
Vilmorin, Pierre Philippe de, 31
Vine, 11, 36; *see also* Grape-vine; Viticulture
Virgin Lands 'scheme', 120, 257, 267
Virgina, 38
Visigoths, 135
Viticulture: in Americas, 36; in California, 151; in medieval Europe, 164; in Mediterranean, 127, 130, 142–3, 144, 147; *see also* Grape-vine; Wine
Volcanic soils, 99
Volga river, 117, 267

Wabash river, 183
Waikato, 209
Wakefield, Edward, 253, 281
War-chariots, 116
Water-mills, 172
Water-wheel, 15
Weeds: and domestication, 16, 19; in fallow, 125; in swiddens, 58
Wei Ho, 17, 84
Wells, 18
West African Shorthorn, 40
West Indies, 29, 33; bananas in, 37, 218–19, 229–30; coffee in, 35, 226; slaves in, 216, 218; sugar-cane in, 36–7, 217, 218, 227–9
Wet-rice cultivation, 3, 18, 19, 22, 32, 35, 63, 72, 75–111; in China, 84–5; and climate, 75; distribution of, 75; early history of, 84ff; and farm size, 77–8; in Guiana, 35; in India, 95–8; and irrigation, 80; in Japan, 89–93; in Java, 98–100; in Korea, 94; and labour supply, 79; in Malaya, 107–8; methods of, 77; multiple-cropping in, 80–1; origins of, 83–4; and population densities, 79; in South East Asia, 100–7; in Vietnam, 93–4
Wheat, 11, 14, 15, 16, 17, 18, 20, 21, 22, 24, 26, 35; in Argentina, 249, 278; in Australia, 241, 253, 257, 281–3; in California, 149; in Canada, 276, 278–81; and climate, 262; exports of, 259; and mechanisation, 264; in Mediterranean regions, 125, 129, 130, 140; new varieties of, 265; and railways, 260; in ranching regions, 241–2; in Russia, 260, 265–7; in United States, 269, 267–76; yields of, 257
Whitney, Eli, 50, 219
Whittlesey, Derwent, 2, 3, 4, 152
Wine: Chilean, 130; Mediterranean, 138, 142, 143, 144; and religion, 164; Spanish American, 36
Winnipeg, 277
Wisconsin, 196; cheese, 206
Woad, 165
Wool, 163, 249, 250–4; in Europe, 176; and freight rates, 48; in medieval Spain, 136; merino, 43; and nomads, 113; *see also* Sheep

Yam, the greater, 22, 28, 32, 36
Yamato culture, 89
Yams, 9, 10, 22, 31–2, 36, 67–8
Yangshao culture, 17
Yangtse river, 5, 18, 84, 86, 87
Yates, P. Lamartine, 152
Yayoi culture, 89

357

Yemen, 33

Yields, 13, 14, 19, 53, 55, 275, 281; in Corn Belt, 178; in Mediterranean, 125; in Middle Ages, 162; of rice, 77, 82–3, 99, 103, 105, 108, 111; in shifting cultivation, 72; of tea, 235; of tree crops, 211–13; in Western Europe, 173, 177; of wheat, 125, 158, 257

Yunnan, 33, 102

Zagros mountains, 11; nomads in, 112

Zambesi river, 66

Zapotes, 20

Zebu cattle, 17, 22; in Americas, 42; in Asia, 82; origin of, 40

Zeeland, 165

Zhob valley, 16

Zuider Zee, 171